ODYSSEY SERIES IN LITERATURE

ROBERT SHAFER, *General Editor*

PARADISE LOST

W.Dolle. *sculpsit.*

Ioannis Miltoni Effigies
Ætat 63. 1671.

JOHN MILTON

PARADISE LOST

Edited by MERRITT Y. HUGHES
Professor of English, University of Wisconsin

THE ODYSSEY PRESS, INC.

New York

CONTENTS

Ronald Coleman

vii

CHRONOLOGY

1608, Dec. 9.   Birth in Bread Street, Cheapside, London.

1620.   Attendance at St. Paul's School begun.

1625, Feb. 12.   Matriculation at Christ's College, Cambridge.

1632, July 3.   Graduation to the degree of M. A.

1632–1638.   Residence at his father's home in Horton, Berkshire, engaged in a wide course of systematic study.

1634, Sept. 29.   First performance of *Comus.*

1638, April–1639, July.   Visits to Paris, Florence, Rome, Naples, Venice and Geneva.

1640–1647.   Residence in London, mainly in Aldersgate Street: schoolmastering, marriage and pamphleteering.

1641, May.   *Of Reformation in England,* Milton's first step into politico-ecclesiastical controversy, published.

1642, Whitsuntide.   Marriage with Mary Powell, separation following after about one month and reunion in 1645. Of this marriage were born Milton's three daughters, Anne, Mary and Deborah, and one son who died in infancy. Mary Powell died in 1652.

1643, Aug. 1.   *Doctrine and Discipline of Divorce* first published.

1644, June.   *Of Education* published.

1644, Nov.   *Areopagitica* published.

1645.   Publication of *Tetrachordon, Colasterion* and the collected edition of the minor poems. Beginning of research for the *History of Britain* and *De Doctrina Christiana.*

1649, Feb.   *Tenure of Kings and Magistrates* published.

March.   Appointment as Secretary for Foreign Tongues to the Council of State.

Oct.   *Eikonoklastes,* published.

1651, March.   *Defensio pro Populo Anglicano,* the "First Defence" of the English for the execution of Charles in reply to their indictment by the Dutch scholar, Salmasius, in *Defensio Regia pro Carolo I.*

Total blindness.

1654. *Defensio Secunda,* the "Second Defence," in answer this time to an anonymous tract called *Regii Sanguinis Clamor,* "The Cry of the King's Blood."

1655. Relief from a large part of the duties of the Latin secretaryship. Beginning of the actual writing of the *History of Britain* and probably of "The Christian Doctrine."

1656, Nov. Marriage with Katherine Woodcock, who died in February, 1658.

1660. Withdrawal from public life after the publication of *A Ready and Easy Way to establish a Free Commonwealth.* Establishment, shortly after the Restoration of Charles II, in a house in Artillery Walk, Bunhill Fields, London.

1663, Feb. Marriage with Elizabeth Minshull, who survived until 1727.

1667. First edition of *Paradise Lost.*

1671. First editions of *Paradise Regained* and *Samson Agonistes.*

1674, Nov. 8. Death.

INTRODUCTION

1. For a man who was the acknowledged literary champion of a revolution which overturned both a monarchy and an established church after a violent civil war, and who was also the most outspoken critic of the revolutionists within their own party, Milton has suffered amazingly little from gossip. He has profited much down the years from calumny, as he did while he was alive; and if he could enjoy his fame today, he would be most confident of its endurance because men still find it interesting to calumniate him. Perhaps the most direct way to try to solve the riddle of his personality is to notice the three points of attack upon him which calumny in the twentieth century has chosen; his pride, his bad sportsmanship in controversy, and his attitude to women. Because every century makes up its own myths about the personalities which interest it in the past, we cannot hope to solve the riddle; but we can at least make an effort to escape from some of the illusions which beset us.

2. Milton's pride was reported very gently by the gossip that he left behind him. Two of his early biographers—and one of them Anthony Wood, a rather grudging admirer—report the "gait, erect and manly, bespeaking courage and undauntedness," and the habit of wearing a sword all his life, even after his total blindness, without the shadow of a suspicion that in these traits an anxious sense of personal inferiority was trying to defend itself. He was "a spare man," says the meatiest of the early biographers, John Aubrey, who was quite undisturbed by the moderate height which we know from Milton's own words was a little galling to him. Aubrey thought that "his harmonical and ingenious soul did lodge in a beautiful and well-proportioned body." Wood tells us that at Cambridge Milton was "esteemed to be a virtuous and sober

person, yet not to be ignorant of his own parts"; but he adds his testimony to the general opinion that by the time he left the University Milton had a talent for friendship with men of the world. No better proof could be asked than the fact that King James's former ambassador to Venice, Sir Henry Wotton, "delighted in his company," but there is even more striking evidence in the habit which his nephew, Edward Phillips, reports of him a little later, when, returned from his Italian year and living a life of "hard study and spare diet" with his pupils in the house in Aldersgate Street in London, "once in three weeks or a month, he would drop into the society of some young sparks of his acquaintance, . . two gentlemen of Gray's Inn, the beaux of those times, . . [and] would so far make bold with his body, as now and then to keep a gawdy-day." Affability is one of his qualities upon which his biographers agree. It was the quality which fitted him for a diplomatic career; and appreciation of that side of his nature, together with admiration for his scholarship, and the desire to enlist in the cause of the Commonwealth the skilful controversialist who had just issued *The Tenure of Kings and Magistrates,* must have played some part in his appointment as Latin Secretary. He had the reputation of being a hard-working diplomatic correspondent, and he was undoubtedly an able one. In such a position as his, then as now, survival is proof of success. In the rhetoric and formality of the Latin letters which have been preserved, it is not easy for us, even when they are turned into English, to realize the extraordinary tact that inspired them, the genuine courtesy, the perception of the weak points in an opponent's position, and the art of outmanoeuvering the enemy by excusing him for having taken an untenable position. Milton must have been a born diplomat, for only a very genial and shrewd man could have made so many acquaintances as he did during his short visits in Florence, Rome, and Naples, and kept so many of them as correspondents afterwards. The story of his courage in professing his Protestant principles in Rome when the English Jesuits were said to be plotting against his safety may be exaggerated by his nephew, Phillips; but it is marvellous that the man who was about to plunge into a pamphleteering career in which he was to make many an attack upon the Roman faith and hierarchy should have entered as a matter of course upon cordial relations with Lucas Holstein, the librarian of the Vatican. Certainly Milton was not sailing under false colours in Rome. To suspect that is as absurd as it would be to suppose, if there is truth in the story that Charles II secretly invited him to become his Latin secretary, that the offer was secured by any deception about Milton's political record or principles. The fact seems to be simply that Milton had more than a common share of the conviction of the high Renaissance, of which he is in many ways a better representative than of his own times, that friendship is a virtue and an art. Urbanity is a word that surprises us here and there in some of his most asperous tracts; yet he valued that forgotten Aristotelian virtue and possessed it.

3. Against facts like these it seems rash to suggest that Milton's character was morbidly proud and distorted by a craving for fame to compensate for physical weakness or to satisfy an individualistic passion born of Calvinist theology and Machiavellian ethics. Both charges have been laid against him, and the first has been based—in a series of studies some of which were dated by their German author from the front, where he was a soldier in active service at the time—on the theory that a syphilitic strain explains the weak eyes which he inherited from his mother, and which he ruined by hard study from his twelfth year. The medical evidence for this theory has been finally disposed of by Miss Gertrude Brown's volume, *Milton's Blindness,* but the broader aspects of the charge against Milton remain. The evidence for them is collected from his own confessions, like the ardently personal passage on fame in *Lycidas,* where the young poet breathlessly argues with himself that a youth spent entirely in study must bring true glory somehow, if not in an immortal reputation then in the eye of all-judging Jove. It is collected from Milton's confession to his friend, Charles Diodati, that his

object in the grand course of study which he pursued after leaving Cambridge was, in a word, immortality, and from that much more astonishing confession which he made to the whole English public in the preface to the second book of his *Reason of Church Government Urged against Prelaty* in 1642. That confession is long, but it must be quoted in considerable part, for its evidence about Milton's nature and also for its evidence about the gestation of *Paradise Lost*. Milton is complaining at the cursed spite which obliges him to interrupt his studies to compose the pamphlet in hand, and he says:

I should not choose this manner of writing, wherein knowing myself inferior to myself, led by the genial power of nature to another task, I have the use, as I may account it, but of my left hand. And though I shall be foolish in saying more to this purpose, yet, since it will be such folly, as wisest men go about to commit, having only confessed and so committed, I may trust with more reason, because with more folly, to have courteous pardon. For although a poet, soaring in the high region of his fancies, with his garland and singing robes about him, might, without apology, speak more of himself than I mean to do; yet for me sitting here below in the cool element of prose, a mortal thing among many readers of no empyreal conceit, to venture and divulge unusual things of myself, I shall petition to the gentler sort, it may not be envy to me. I must say, therefore, that after I had for my first years, by the ceaseless diligence and care of my father, (whom God recompense!) been exercised to the tongues, and some sciences, as my age would suffer, by sundry masters and teachers, both at home and at the schools, it was found that whether aught was imposed me by them that had the overlooking, or betaken to of mine own choice in English, or other tongue, prosing or versing, but chiefly this latter, the style by certain vital signs it had, was likely to live. . . . I began thus far to assent . . . to divers of my friends . . . and not less to an inward prompting which now grew daily upon me, that by labor and intent study, (which I take to be my portion in this life,) joined with the strong propensity of nature, I might perhaps leave something to aftertimes, as they should not willingly let it die. . . .

Time serves not now, and perhaps I might seem too profuse to give any certain account of what the mind at home, in the spacious circuits of her musing, hath liberty to propose to herself, though of highest hope and hardest attempting; whether that epic form ·whereof the two poems of Homer, and those other two of Virgil and Tasso, are a diffuse, and the book a brief model: or whether the rules of Aristotle herein are strictly to be kept, or nature to be followed, which in them that know art, and use judgment, is no transgression, but an enriching of art: and lastly, what king or knight, before the conquest, might be chosen in whom to lay the pattern of a Christian hero. . . . These abilities, wheresoever they be found, are the inspired gift of God, rarely bestowed, but yet to some (though most abuse) in every nation; and are of power, beside the office of a pulpit, to imbreed and cherish in a great people the seeds of virtue and public civility, to allay the perturbations of the mind, and set the affections in right tune; to celebrate in glorious and lofty hymns the throne and equipage of God's almightiness, and what he works, and what he suffers to be wrought with high providence in his church.

4. Obviously, the man who wrote these words felt that he had exceptional claims both upon the public and upon destiny. When he at last knew that he was in a fair way to make good every word in this passage and spoke of himself in the exordium to the ninth book of *Paradise Lost* as "long choosing and beginning late," his temper had not changed. It is not a sufficient reply to Professor Liljegren, who charges him with a megalomaniac individualism, to point to the fulfilment of his hopes of himself in the poems which he wrote, in the main, after his pamphleteering days ended at the age of fifty-two. The question at issue is the nature of those poems themselves as expressions of Milton's nature. Professor Liljegren (in *Studies in Milton*) pointed out that he always thought of himself as standing on the rostrum from which he pretended to be addressing the English Parliament and indeed the whole nation in *Areopagitica;* that he regarded himself as rebel and prophet asserting himself against a stupid world. And so the idea that the real hero of *Paradise Lost* is Satan, to which the poet Blake gave its most attractive form, is revived in the charge that the real hero and indeed "the only dramatic person" in the poem "is Satan, the proud genius,

conscious of immense superiority, gnashing his teeth at the shadow of a challenge, waging war against a Lord" of whose intelligence he entertains confident doubts. Professor Lilje-gren seems to me right in insisting that the spirit of Milton's prose is still awake in his epic. Indeed, the vital connexion of his prose with all his poetry cannot be overestimated, and it is the clarification of that matter which seems to me to con-stitute the chief value of the two most valuable, general studies of his life which have appeared since 1900; Mr. E. M. W. Til-yard's *Milton* and M. Denis Saurat's *Milton, Man and Thinker*. Neither of these writers, however, accepts the view that Satan is Milton's hero. Rejection of that view implies a denial in the prose of very much more than the crass individualism which we usually associate with Machiavellism and are inclined to associate with Calvinism. It implies that in his controversial writing Milton transcended that subtler form of individualism which was more characteristic of the seventeenth century than it was of the sixteenth, and which goes usually by the name of Stoicism, or Neo-Stoicism. Mr. T. S. Eliot speaks of it as "the refuge of the individual in an indifferent or hostile world too big for him" and as "the reverse of Christian humility."

5. By dipping into Milton's prose it is easy to find evidence of what seems an amazing "reverse of Christian humility" scattered throughout the controversial pamphlets. To begin with, there is the disconcerting paradox that his republicanism, which seemed "surly" to a Tory like Dr. Johnson, is com-bined with a fiercely aristocratic contempt of the mob. We are prepared to find that his republicanism should be a form of Platonic political idealism. In these times of Fascism and Communism most of us are still close enough to the liberal tradition that we inherit from Milton to understand his faith in a philosophical senate of "best and wisest men," which the drafters of the American Constitution were confident might be assembled by a pyramid of selective elections such as Milton contrived in his *Ready and Easy Way to establish a Free Com-monwealth*. But we are not prepared to find his treatment

of social and intellectual inferiors quite so merciless as it is.
We wince when we find him baiting an opponent—anonymous, it is true, and probably venal, but not contemptible
merely because he had got a smattering of law rather late in
life and climbed out of a serving man's position—as "an un-
buttoned fellow," moiling at a trestle in a garret to bring
"forth his cullionly paraphrase of St. Paul, whom he brings in
discoursing such idle stuff to the maids and widows, as his
own servile inurbanity forbears not to put into the apostle's
mouth, 'of the soul's conversing'; and this he presumes to do,
being a bayard, who never had the soul to know what conversing means, but as his provender and the familiarity of the
kitchen schooled his conceptions."   It is worth while to quote
this fragment because, incidentally, it throws a keen shaft of
light upon Milton's passion for urbanity and also upon his devotion to St. Paul, with whose epistles some parts of *Paradise
Lost* are most intimately involved.   The facts about Milton's
attitude toward his inferiors are far from complete, however,
when we have cited his treatment of his enemy in *Colasterion.*
The last fact in that exhibit is John Toland's statement that
not only did "his learned and great friends in London" follow his body to St. Giles Church, but that it was followed also
by "a friendly concourse of the vulgar."

6. Still more disconcerting to modern taste is Milton's treatment of his great Continental opponent, Salmasius, who
voiced the horror of monarchists and moderate men outside
of England at the execution of Charles I in January, 1649, by
publishing his *Defence of Royalty on behalf of Charles I* in
the following October.   The invective against Salmasius ought
not to shock us, especially if we know something about the
pamphlets exchanged between Thomas Nashe and his enemies
in Elizabeth's times, or have read Aretino.   That was a part
of the game of controversy in those days, and Milton has the
moral advantage of having played that game disinterestedly,
as the champion of a cause in which he ardently believed.
The ugly aspect of his quarrel with Salmasius is his joy in his
victory.   We suffer as we read his dedication of his *Second*

Defence of the English People to Queen Christina of Sweden and find him boasting, as his nephew Phillips says that he did, that by his *First Defence* Salmasius, who "had till then been chief minister and superintendent" in her court, "dwindled in esteem to that degree, that he at last vouchsafed to speak to the meanest servant." This seems like Achilles' insult to the body of Hector. In the pleasure of "our little English David," as one of his admirers called him in that connexion, because he had triumphed over the Dutch Goliath at the court of Queen Christina, we are inclined to see nothing except personal and national vanity. We are not content to accept the evidence of his reputation with men of the party opposed to him, like Sir Robert Howard, and of the French ambassador to the court of Charles II, to say nothing of the nameless "foreign scholars" who are said to have annoyed him by their frequent visits to the house in Bunhill Fields where he finished *Paradise Lost* and wrote *Paradise Regained* and *Samson Agonistes.* Contemporary opinion evidently held that he had fought fairly and deserved his honours. We today are not altogether ready to admit that. Professor Liljegren has tried desperately to show that in at least one case Milton's controversial tactics were unethical, even by the code of his own age. That instance is in his *Eikonoklastes,* the attempt to demolish the picture of King Charles which was drawn in the collection of papers and records published by the Royalists in February, 1649, under the title *Eikon Basilike,* "The Royal Image." In the second edition of that "pathetical" book, which the revolutionaries must have known to be really dangerous, there appeared a prayer which Charles was said to have used on the eve of execution, a prayer which, because it does not mention God, Milton could call "pagan," and which he was able to show came word for word out of "that vain amatorious romance," Sir Philip Sidney's *Arcadia.* Professor Liljegren has produced elaborate evidence to show that this prayer was interpolated in the second edition of *Eikon Basilike* for the express purpose of exploitation in Milton's reply and that the initiative for the imposture was Milton's. This case against him has been broken down by M. Saurat and I think that the charge may be dismissed. The episode, however, serves to throw light upon one of the strands which connects Milton's prose with *Paradise Lost*. If the stress laid upon the King's use of a pagan prayer had not seemed exaggerated by modern standards, suspicion never would have fastened upon that feature of *Eikonoklastes*. The real key to Milton's excitement and prolixity about the prayer is his passion for informal and original worship and his hatred of all ritual. To that feeling we owe the prayer of Adam and Eve in Book IV (724–35) and others like it. They are not the objects for which we read the poem now, although they were one of the objects for which Joseph Addison read it. Even today they are interesting and moving, once their relation to Milton's character and to his great underlying sense of human freedom in *Paradise Lost* has been grasped.

7. Although Milton be cleared of the charge against him, we may still doubt the integrity of the reasoning in his work. The question for us is one of Milton's attitude toward authority, the authority of the Bible and of tradition generally and the authority of his own mind. In his times, we know, men believed in Authority. We have his own words in the treatise *On Christian Doctrine* (which he wrote seemingly with great deliberation and partly at least for his private satisfaction, although he does address the whole Christian Church in the way that in *Areopagitica* he addresses the Lords and Commons of England) in a most absolute statement: "I enrol myself among the number of those who acknowledge the word of God alone as the rule of faith." No one today would think of condemning Milton because he did not live up to that profession. Most of us may be inclined to condemn him for making it at all, and to find the penetration of his mind by passages from all parts of the Bible our greatest obstacle in reading him. In the notes to this edition I have tried to indicate how Milton's historical sense, as well as the panorama of world history which he paints in Books XI and XII, was shaped in many details by the Bible. I have tried also in the

notes to give the reader the key to Milton's sense that the prophecies and Psalms in the Old Testament were integrated with the doctrine of Christ in the New Testament as "one perfect man" who recovered by his life and death the moral perfection which Adam lost. This conception of Christ, with its unorthodox indifference to his death as a sacrifice in which men can share sacramentally, indicates, of course, that Milton read his Bible independently. Christ, with "a charming pipe," he tells us in *The Doctrine and Discipline of Divorce,* "sounded and proclaimed liberty." The liberty brought by Christ, he urged, amounted to the cancellation of whatever in the Mosaic law might seem to interfere with his own humane conception of marriage. Yet his strongest support for that conception was really found in the Old Testament, as he very well understood, and he pleaded for the prestige of both Testaments and for the right to interpret them liberally. His appeal was to "men with a diffuse and various knowledge of divine and human things." To that enlightened and sympathetic jury he was always appealing, and most of all in the *Christian Doctrine,* where he wished to defend a heterodox conception of God which permitted him to regard Christ as divine only in a derivative way. On that conception depends much in *Paradise Lost;* the creation of the universe by the Son of God, working somewhat as Plato in the *Timaeus* imagined his Demiurge as working; the conception of the universe as shaped out of unformed matter instead of being created in orthodox fashion out of absolutely nothing by God himself; and the conception of Christ finally redeeming mankind by a kind of repetition of his original creative process, establishing a limited cosmos of righteousness among men as he once carved the universal cosmos out of a vast, surrounding ocean of chaos.

8. These ideas, together with the related principle that all created things have freedom of will and complete moral responsibility for their acts, were the seeds from which *Paradise Lost* developed. To read the poem with pleasure we must know something about them—enough at least to understand

that they were not the results of merely fantastic or wishful thinking. To understand them completely in terms of all their sources in the Bible, the Apocrypha, the various rabbinical traditions, the Fathers of the Church the Greek and Latin classics, and the transformations of those sources by the writers of the centuries immediately preceding Milton is, of course, impossible. A modern reader finds it hardest, perhaps, to have complete poetic faith in Milton's way of imagining the creation. All accounts of the origin of the world, even those advanced in the twentieth century, he knows are myths, however scientifically they may be disguised; but he also knows that a true poet is always imbued with the science of his time and cannot keep his poetic sanity if he ignores it.

9. There is no difficulty in sympathizing with Milton's rationalization of the story of the creation in Genesis. In that we know that he was following the example of the "best thinkers" of his time. Genesis tells the story of creation as having happened in seven days, but Milton explains in the *Christian Doctrine* that it was really an instantaneous act. The story, then, is an allegory, but it is an allegory which has the support of reason and also of ancient tradition coming down by pagan as well as Jewish channels. Ovid's account of the creation seemed to Milton's contemporary, Ralph Cudworth, to corroborate the myth in Genesis. In what seems to us today the essentially playful interpretation of the classical creation myths in the first book of the *Metamorphoses* Cudworth saw a universe emerging from chaos "by the *Providence* and *Command* of *One Unmade Deity,* which was also that that furnish'd all the several Parts of the World with respective Animals." And Cudworth went on to quote from Sandys' translation of Ovid:

> Before that Sea and Earth and Heaven was fram'd,
> One face had Nature which they Chaos nam'd.
> No Titan yet the World with Light adorns,
> Nor waxing Phoebe fills her wained Horns;
> Nor hung the self-poiz'd Earth in thin Air plac'd.

That last line from Ovid left its stamp on *Paradise Lost* (VII, 242), when Milton imagined the whole universe of stars and planets (which is what he means there by "Earth") as conglobing or being moulded out of the surrounding Chaos. The image is possible, no matter whether we conceive of the universe as Aristotle and Ptolemy did, with the earth at the centre of everything, or as Copernicus had begun to teach men to think of it in the revolutionary book which he published in 1543. And behind it are the poetic imagination of Ovid, to whom Milton paid a spiritual reverence which had some scientific tinge, and the greater authority of Job, where Milton read that God "stretcheth out the north over empty space, and hangeth the earth upon nothing."

10. The strange thing, then, is that Milton should have imagined the cosmos where his poem unfolds its action as "Ptolemaic." So it is usually called, but the fact is that it was really Miltonic, with more resemblances to the ideal universe which Aristotle bequeathed to posterity than it had to the Copernican universe. Its outlines are not quite easy to grasp when the poem is read for the first time, but they really correspond to the outline of the action itself. From Hell, which is far below Heaven in this stupendous image where reality seems to be bounded by the floor of hell spreading infinitely beneath and the floor of heaven with a landscape like that of earth spreading as widely far above, Satan sets out to find the newly created universe which lies somewhere between them. And he finds it after swimming through the sea of Chaos for distances whose description suggests gulfs like those measured by the light-years of contemporary astronomy. At first sight, it seems no bigger to him than a star. When he reaches it, he finds that it is a vast, solid sphere with an opening at the top, where a chain of gold (which is later said to be the path of angels) attaches it to the floor of heaven. There he finds the only entrance and inside he discovers the starry heavens that we know, with the planets and the sun far below him, arranged above the earth at the centre of it all

and circling around the earth at a prodigious speed, as the Ptolemaic theory taught.[1]

11. No one can suppose that Milton really imagined the universe as corresponding to Satan's discoveries on his long journey; still less that Milton thought of any reality corresponding to the limbo of fools that he placed just *outside* the opening through the shell of the universe where Satan entered, or to the bridge which Sin and Death built from Hell's mouth to that opening. The interesting thing is that in this solid sphere where the orbs of the seven planets and that of the fixed stars which contains them are as definitely specified as the rest of Milton's universe is vaguely drawn, there should be many suggestions of the new and wider outlook upon the heavens. When, in the eighth book, the angel Raphael explains the celestial motions to Adam he concludes with the surprising statement that it is hard to tell

> Whether the Sun, predominant in heaven,
> Rise on the Earth, or Earth rise on the Sun.

Throughout the whole poem there is, as everyone knows, evidence of fascination with the discoveries of Galileo and with the bold suggestion of Giordano Bruno, which Thomas Digges, the Elizabethan astronomer, had anticipated in 1576; that the stars may be and probably are inhabited, or be the centres of systems of inhabited planets. Milton's conclusion about the whole matter is to make room for both the new and the old systems in his universe, and it is gratifying to find him unafraid in the presence of the new sense of infinite spaces among the stars and beyond them which terrified Pascal.

12. Two more points are worth making in connexion with Milton's astronomy. One is that his notion of the fixed stars as all being equidistant from the earth in their orb, and of a heaven definitely beyond those stars, was almost literally

---

[1]Suggestive designs of Milton's scheme are available in Professor James H. Hanford's *Milton Handbook*, p. 174, and in Thomas N. Orchard's *Milton's Astronomy*, London, 1913.

Copernican. Copernicus himself believed that the fixed stars were all at one distance from the sun in his new, heliocentric universe; and Thomas Digges, who first challenged that idea in England and printed a drawing which represented the stars as scattered broadcast beyond "the Orbe of Saturne," could describe the upper reaches of that infinite spherical altitude as "the very court of cœlestiall angelles devoyd of greiefe and replenished with perfite endlesse joye the habitacle for the elect."

13. In one other strange feature in his cosmos Milton had the support of current speculation nourished by tradition. It was the idea of the spheres or orbs of the planets singing and making music that is always heard in heaven and sometimes on earth. In Book V (160–208), where he gives his imagination freest rein on the subject, he is plainly dealing in allegory, but in allegory which he feels corresponds to metaphysical as well as to moral truth. All earth is but a type of heaven, he tells us, and there seems to be an analogy between the music of the spheres and the songs of the

> Saints, unmix'd, and from the impure
> Far separate, circling the holy Mount[1]

which is God's throne. Milton's contemporaries rationalized the doctrine of the heavenly harmony of the spheres in terms of the "influence" which the stars were thought to shed upon the earth. Of his belief in such "influence" there is evidence in *Paradise Lost* and something like proof in his remark in his *History of Britain* that a year when an eclipse was seen in May was a time of "sore pestilence." *The Divine Weekes* of Du Bartas represented the world before the Fall of Adam as a part of the great heavenly harmony, bound to it by mysterious "sympathies":

> For th'hidden love that nowadays doth hold
> The steel and loadstone, hydrargire[2] and gold,

---

[1] VI, 742–3.

[2] Mercury or quicksilver.

Th'amber and straw; that lodgeth in one shell
Pearlfish and sharpling, and unites so well
Sargons[1] and goats, the sparage[2] and the rush,
Th'elm and the vine, th'olive and myrtle bush,
Is but a spark or shadow of that love
Which at the first in everything did move,
Whenas the earth's muses with harmonious sound
To heaven's sweet music humbly did resound.
But Adam, being chief of all the strings
Of this large lute, o'er retched,[3] quickly brings
All out of tune.[4]

Incidentally, it may be pointed out that this passage is an interesting sidelight on Milton's account (X, 648–713) of the disorder which God deliberately introduced among the stars and in the sun's path, after the Fall. Most of Milton's contemporaries believed that the universe was in a process of decay which had been going on for centuries and which they associated with apparent signs of disorder in the heavens such as the precession of the equinoxes. A part of that celestial confusion was the irregularities of the planets in their orbits which troubled the astronomers so seriously and which they tried to explain by girding the celestial sphere

> With Centric and Eccentric scribbl'd o'er,
> Cycle and Epicycle, orb in orb.[5]

Many thinkers, like the Cambridge Platonist, Henry More, tried to equate the theories of Galileo with the cosmology of Pythagoras. One way of reconciling this whole complex tangle of contemporary astronomical theory with the old Pythagorean idea of the music of the spheres is suggested in the drawing here reproduced from a volume which was famous in Milton's

---

[1]Fish which were supposed to leave the sea to play with goats.

[2]Asparagus.

[3]Over-reached.

[4]Quoted from *The Divine Weeks of Joshua Sylvester,* edited by Theron W. Haight, p. 205.

[5]VIII, 83–4.

youth, Robert Flud's *Utriusque Cosmi Historia,* or "The History of both Worlds." That it played any part in actually shaping Milton's conception of the universe I do not pretend, although M. Saurat has shown that Milton was interested in Flud's book. Its value is its indication of the reasons why a man could be keenly interested all his life in astronomy and yet, like Milton, never cease to think of the compulsion of music to

> keep unsteady Nature to her law,
> And the low World in measured motion draw,
> After the heavenly Tune.[1]

14. Harder than Milton's science for the poetic faith of the modern reader is his metaphysics, and the most striking expression of that metaphysics in his angels and demons. Here there is the complicating influence of theology and of folklore. Milton felt that he had the warrant of the Bible for the fact that a host of angels rebelled against God, were cast out of heaven, then, moved by envy of His creature, Man, invaded the new-created world and tempted him, and later deceived him in the shape of false gods and in other disguises. For those principles he could go to Hooker's *Laws of Ecclesiastical Polity,* where they are stated as axiomatic and a part of the foundation of the whole Christian system. If he turned to the book of his friend, Hugo Grotius, *On The Truth of the Christian Religion,* he found a great section there devoted to proof that the evil spirits were worshipped as gods by the Pagans. What he thought about this matter it is not easy to say, but he certainly held no dogmatic opinions. His whole poem rests upon the assumption that the devils were expelled from heaven before the creation of the universe, yet in the *Christian Doctrine* he questions the point. One Hebrew tradition has it that the devils fell because they were tempted by the beauty of the daughters of men. If it had suited his purpose, we may be sure that Milton would have adopted that legend. It suited his scheme to open his poem with a council of the in-

---

[1]*Arcades,* 70-2.

TRACTATUS I. LIB. III.[1]

Hic autem monochordum mundanum cum suis proportionibus, confo-
nantiis & intervallis exactius compofuimus, cujus motorem extra mundum effe
hoc modo depinximus.

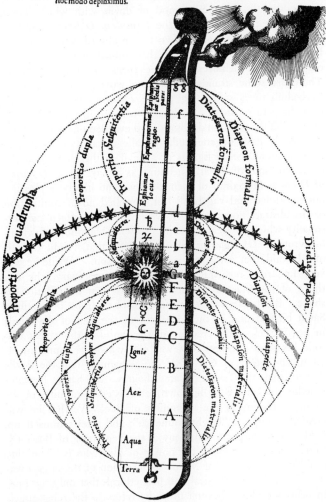

[1] A divine hand plays a cosmic string whose nodes are the planets and
the divisions between the regions of fire, air, water, and earth which were
supposed to lie below the moon.

fernal angels, and he had examples before him for that plan in the slightly ridiculous synod of devils with which Tasso opened the fourth canto of the *Jerusalem Delivered,* and in many a less artistic poem down to the absurd *Apollyonists* of Phineas Fletcher. Of them all, his council of demons is the only one that achieves dramatic form or characterization. There are some strands of tradition woven into his figures. Beëlzebub owes something to the *Faust Book* and Moloch something to records of his bloody worship in the Old Testament. But the two best devils are medieval demons which might very easily have degenerated into allegorical figures. Belial, Milton knew, hardly figures as a devil in the Bible; and the hebraism "sons of Belial," meaning, as he says in the *Doctrine of Divorce,* "the draff of men, to whom no liberty is pleasing but unbridled and vagabond lust," implied no personification of the abstract noun to which we instinctively attach the personality which he created for it. So with Mammon, of whom he wrote in *Of Reformation in England* that, "right truly it may be said, that Antichrist is Mammon's son." While he was very far from regarding the devils as "imaginary," he did think of them as raw material for his own imagination to shape. But he kept close to the track of tradition in handling Satan himself and in the treatment of the Fall of the devils in heaven before the creation of the world. About that episode his most constant idea was one which he found in St. Augustine's *City of God* (XII, xiii); namely, that the devils denied that they were created beings. So Satan hesitates whether to believe in his own self-existence; admits, in his candid soliloquy at the beginning of Book IV, that he was created to enjoy a "bright eminence"; and screws himself up, in the more desperate soliloquy at the beginning of Book IX, to a sophistical doubt of the power of him who is "Almighty styl'd." The essence of Milton's conception of the angels was the idea, half metaphysical and half ethical, that only the pure in heart see God. Several times he refers to the rebel angels as having lost what Dante called, in common with all the Middle Ages, the beatific vision. Hence their ignorance and their presumptuous doubts about their own nature, and hence also their speculation in hell about the freedom of their own wills, and their surmise that the will of God is not free, but subject to Fate.

15. Most modern readers find it easier to accept Milton's devils than they do his angels. If the charge of Sir Walter A. Raleigh that *Paradise Lost* is "a monument to dead ideas" holds true of any of its elements, we feel that it holds of the rôles of the angels, who fight a pitched battle on the plains of Heaven against the devils and their artillery, and who descend to earth to guard Adam and Eve and instruct them, in conversations lasting for over six books, about the creation and destiny of the world. Milton's contemporaries were divided on the question whether supernatural actors should be admitted in "heroic poetry" at all. At the very time when Milton was at work on his epic, Boileau, the great French critic, laid down the principle, in the third chant of his *Art poétique,* that the Christian religion ought not to furnish theological beings for epic poetry and opined rashly that Satan could not have an iota of poetic value. Meanwhile John Dryden could express himself very favourably about the appearance of the supernatural beings of Christian and Platonic tradition in poetry. And Ralph Cudworth, the Cambridge Platonist, was speculating that "there is no Repugnancy at all to Reason, but that there may be as well, *Aerial* and *Etherial,* as there are *Terrestrial Animals;* and that the *Dull and Earthy Stupidity* of men's *Minds,* is the Only thing which makes them, so prone to think, that there is no *Understanding Nature,* Superior to Mankind; but that in the world, all is Dead about Us."[1] Milton was interested in the ideas of the Cambridge Platonists about the spirit world, for he was able to reconcile them with his own belief in the basic goodness of matter and in the material constitution of all created things, angels as well as men included. The Cambridge thinkers, no less than the idyllic stories in Genesis about the angels who were entertained by Adam and by Abraham, helped him to give body to

---

[1]*Intellectual System of the Universe.* London, 1688, p. 835.

his spirits. Hence we have "the sociable angel," Raphael, who brings "real hunger" and "concoctive heat" (V, 437) to the enjoyment of the meal which Eve sets before him, and confesses, blushing, to Adam that,

> Easier than Air with Air, if Spirits embrace,
> Total they mix, Union of Pure with Pure.[1]

16. Three very ancient traditions helped to determine Milton's treatment of his angels. One of them goes back to the belief in Hesiod's *Works and Days* (252–55) that "upon the beauteous earth Zeus has thrice ten thousand spirits, watchers of mortal men, and these keep watch on judgments and deeds of wrong, as they roam, clothed in mist, all over the earth." There is an echo of these lines in Adam's words to Eve:

> Millions of spiritual Creatures walk the Earth
> Unseen, both when we wake, and when we sleep.[2]

The other two traditions stemmed from Jewish and Christian literature. One is related to a verse in Zechariah's Prophecy (iii, 9) which speaks of seven eyes in one stone, a passage which was interpreted as referring to seven supreme angels who are God's eyes or spies upon the earth. The third tradition came down through a famous work, which was attributed to Dionysius the Areopagite, the disciple of St. Paul, and the title of which the dramatist, Thomas Heywood, paraphrased as the title of his *Hierarchie of the Blessed Angels*. "Dionysius" classified the heavenly hierarchy into nine ranks and the names or titles of those nine orders of heavenly nobility are repeated in many a sonorous invocation in *Paradise Lost*. The highest order was the Seraphim (to use the Hebrew plural which Milton usually preferred), and then followed the Cherubim, Thrones, Dominations, Virtues, Powers, Principalities, Archangels, and Angels. The origin

---

[1] VIII, 626–7.
[2] IV, 677–8.

of these meaningless and imposing names is to be sought in
St. Paul's allusions to the spiritual foes of the Christian as
"angels, principalities or powers" (Romans VIII, 38) and in
St. Jude's reference to the angels "which kept not their first
estate (or 'principality,' as the margin in the Authorized Version reads)," and whom God has "reserved in everlasting
chains, under darkness, unto the judgment of the great day."
(Jude, 6.) The fallen angels were supposed to keep the titles
that they had enjoyed in heaven, and Milton found it convenient to use them in hell. It is quite impossible to pin him
down to any of his classifications of his angels in any of these
ranks. Michael, for example, who is captain general of the
whole angelic host in the war with Satan and his forces in
Book VI, is never specifically called a seraph and is usually
mentioned by his medieval title of archangel. Uriel, the angel
of the sun, is once called an angel, and so is Raphael, yet they
both hold seraphic commands as marshals under Michael.

17. The celestial ranks, then, did not interest Milton except
as titles to use when there were solemn invocations to be
made. The names of the angels themselves, however, held a
great fascination for him, and so did their legends. He shared
the interest of his times in the strange tale which the
Apocryphal Book of Tobit has to tell about the sociable
Raphael. In the Old Testament habit of imagining the angels
as the eyes of God he found a significant point of contact with
Neo-Platonic modes of imagining deity as light or vision. He
knew that it had been Plutarch's theory of the daemons or
spirits, inherited by the Greeks from a past older even than
Hesiod, that they were composed of the most refined of all
substances, a kind of celestial fire more rarefied than any
earthly flame. Milton thought of his seraphs as "ardors" or
fervent flames in both a literal and an allegorical sense (e. g.,
in V, 249), and of his devils as degenerating from that fiery
essence and changing their constitution to that of earthly fire
and even of others of the "four elements" of this universe.[1]
His spiritual essences, then, were very much like the light

[1] II, 274-8.

which he apostrophizes at the beginning of Book III as all but identical with God himself.

18. So Milton was a materialist, but his "materialism" has more in common with that of the twentieth century than with that of the nineteenth, for he was inclined to think of matter as a function of energy. Energy, however, if it was of a high order, meant to him the principle of self-control; and his name for that form of energy was Reason. Like St. Augustine, and like the German reformer, Melancthon, and indeed like all the Neo-Platonizing theologians of the Renaissance, he understood the biblical saying that man was made in God's image as referring to man's reason. "The spiritual and rational faculty," he wrote in *The Christian Doctrine,* "contains the corporeal, that is, the sentient and vegetative faculty. For not even divine virtue and efficiency could produce bodies out of nothing, according to the commonly received opinion, unless there had been some bodily power in the substance of God."[1]

19. In all of Milton's prose one of the most valuable passages for the interpretation of *Paradise Lost* is his remark in the First Book of *The Reason of Church Government Urged against Prelaty* that "Lucifer, before Adam, was the first prelate angel; and both he, as is commonly thought, and our forefather Adam, as we all know, for aspiring above their orders, were miserably degraded." Milton was straining the evidence of the Bible in an effort, very characteristic of him, to corroborate his prejudice against episcopacy in the Church of England as by its very nature a proud institution. He alluded quite casually to the analogy between Satan's fall and that of Adam; so we may be sure that the analogy was a part of his habitual thinking. Tradition had long been busy with fancies about the splendour of "Lucifer, the son of the morning" before he fell, as Isaiah's Prophecy (XIV, 12) was interpreted as saying that he had done, although we now know that the prophetic passage referred really to the King of Babylon. It was, of course, pride which Christian tradition said had caused his fall;

[1] *Christian Doctrine,* I, vii.

and his pride was supposed to have been a mixture of arrogance over his high, seraphic rank and envy of God's preëminence, or of the preëminence of his Son, as Milton and the
Dutch poet Vondel (in *Adam in Ballingschap*) held.[1] Traditionally, it was envy of God, or of the divinity which was
denied to them, which caused the Fall of Adam and Eve. So,
in Du Bartas' version of the temptation, Satan pleads:

> Eve, Second honour of this Universe!
> Is't true, I pray, that jealous God, perverse,
> Forbids . . . both you and all your race
> All the fair fruits . . . ? . . .
>
> Sith the suspected vertue of This Tree
> Shall soon disperse the cloud of Idiocy,
> Which dims your eyes; and further, make you seem
> Excelling us, even equal Gods to him.
> O Worlds rare glory! reach thy happy hand,
> Reach, reach, I say.[2]

Milton's Satan, when he seduces his cohorts in heaven to follow him in revolt against God's Son, has persuaded them

> Their Deities to assert: who, while they feel
> Vigour divine within them, can allow
> Omnipotence to none.[3]

When he first approaches Eve, in a dream, it is to persuade
her that the Tree of Knowledge is able to make gods of men:

> And why not Gods of men, since good, the more
> Communicated, more abundant grows . . . ?
> Taste this, and be henceforth among the Gods
> Thyself a Goddess; not to Earth confin'd,
> But sometimes in the Air, as we; sometimes
> Ascend to Heaven, by merit thine, and see
> What life the Gods live there, and such live thou.[4]

---

[1] Compare the notes on V, 603, 689, and 835–57.
[2] *The Divine Weeks,* Haight's edition, p. 192.
[3] VI, 157–9.
[4] V, 71–81.

It is the affectation of godhead that is the essence of man's disobedience, as Milton makes God Himself say;[1] but for reasons which will be considered a little later, modern criticism
has found it attractive to regard sensuality as the essence of
the Fall as Milton understood it. Milton's own conception of
the matter was quite different and very much more interesting, for it involved an attempt to paint Adam in the perfection that he enjoyed before his banishment from Eden. The
painting of Adam's "prelapsarian perfection" was a favourite
intellectual sport of Milton's contemporaries. For example,
there was Joseph Glanvill, whose *The Vanity of Dogmatizing* (1661, revised and republished in 1665) opens with a portrait of "that Creature whose crown it was to be like his
Maker." "What was the portion of Heavens Favorite," Glanvill inquires, "when *Omniscience* itself sat in Councel to furnish him with all those accomplishments which his specifick
capacity could contain? which questionless were as much
above the Hyperbolies that fond Poetry bestowes upon its admired objects, as their flatter'd beauties are really below them.
The most refined glories of subcoelestial excellencies are but
more faint resemblances of these. For all the powers and
faculties of this copy of the Divinity, this meddal of God, were
as perfect as beauty and harmony in Idea. The soul was not
clogged by the inactivity of its masse, as ours; nor hindered in
its actings, by the distemperature of indisposed organs. Passions kept their place, as servants of the higher powers, and
durst not arrogate the Throne, as now: no countermands
came hence, to repeal the decretals of the Regal faculties; that
Batrachomyomachia of one passion against an other, and both
against reason, was yet unborn."[2]

20. This general conception we may be sure that Milton
shared with Glanvill, although he certainly did not follow
Glanvill in his amazing claims about "the circumference of
our *Protoplast's* senses," as extending to the bounds of the

---

[1] III, 203-10.

[2] *The Vanity of Dogmatizing.* Facsimile Text Society edition, pp. 3-4.

created universe itself. Glanvill seriously argued that Adam
understood the Copernican constitution of the heavens because
he saw them and all their movements no less distinctly than
we see the scrap of the world immediately around us. Milton
is sometimes blamed for having accepted the myth of perfection and happiness in Eden too complacently. His admirers,
indeed, found it easy to sentimentalize the scenes in Eden.
Richard Steele reported a tea party where he overheard some
women whisper that Milton made our first parents say "some
of the tenderest things ever heard." Glanvill was really a
greater sentimentalist than these women, greater even than the
designer of a contemporary fan which, according to a report
unearthed by Professor Hanford, displayed Milton's Adam
and Eve in each other's arms in Paradise. One of the greatest dangers in the influence of the myth of Eden is its temptation to idealize the past. The crude optimism of recent evo-
lutionary thought has made it difficult to understand such
retrospective Utopianism as Glanvill's, although it was possible for W. H. Hudson, in *A Hind in Richmond Park,* to surmise from some noble, prehistoric skeletons that the earth
was once walked by a race of pacific, vegetarian giants of immeasurably finer capacities than ours.

21. In contrast with speculation about Adam like Glanvill's,
Milton imagined his Adam a very human sort of person in
Eden. It is not altogether fair to say, as Professor Saurat does,
that he imagined him as a Miltonic sort of person, and that
the real hero of the poem is Milton himself. Milton thought
of him as a representative spirit. He saw him as representative not only of mankind, but of all created consciousnesses as
well. He thought of his predicament as essentially just like
that of Satan before his fall and like that of the good angels
and of the Son of God himself. All of them were images of
God. But Adam in Eden was human, and his temptation was
just the impulse of any conscious creature to escape from its
limitations. The only limitation against which Adam could
revolt in Paradise was ignorance. He was absolute proprietor
of the world and of "the whole animal creation," to which

Milton amazedly remarked that he gave names "with such sudden intelligence."[1]

> His fair large Front and Eye sublime declar'd
> Absolute rule[2]

even over Eve. In power he was already almost divine. So it is against the lust of knowledge that Raphael warns him. On that key the long interview between him and the angel ends in Book VIII, where the warning to Adam to be "lowly wise" and leave the secrets of astronomy to God seems to a modern reader a great disappointment and a blemish on Milton's character. The final discussion of his opinions about what we call scientific curiosity, and what in the Middle Ages was called the lust of knowledge, must be left for the preface to *Paradise Regained* in a later volume of the present series. Milton's position in *Paradise Lost* was a part of his view of Adam's sin as involving pride in the sense of *hybris,* the defiance of divine limitations upon men which he met in Greek tragedy, and especially in the *Prometheus* of Aeschylus. God speaks to Michael of Adam's sin as "excess."[3] The angels themselves are in danger of that sin, as appears from Uriel's strange way of congratulating the disguised Satan when they meet in the sun, as the Fiend passes by with the pretext that he is curious about God's works in the newly created universe. Uriel says:

> Fair Angel, thy desire, which tends to know
> The works of God, thereby to glorify
> The great Work-Master, leads to no excess
> That reaches blame, but rather merits praise
> The more it seems excess.[4]

In the fragment which has been quoted from *The Reason of Church Government* there is as much evidence of a voracious desire of knowledge on Milton's part as there is of his passion for glory; but it is significant that even there he shows

[1] *Christian Doctrine,* I, vii.
[2] IV, 300–1.
[3] XI, 110.
[4] III, 693–7.

a trace of his later impulse to limit his scientific curiosity, as
opposed to his historical and broadly philosophical interest.
At Cambridge Milton had responded to the influence oí
Bacon, but with all its "materialism" *The Advancement of
Learning* held that "the highest link of nature's chain must
needs be tied to the foot of Jupiter's chair."[1]   It is with that
commission that Raphael tells Adam that he has been sent
from heaven; to teach him the dependence of nature on God
and answer his "desire of knowledge within bounds."   And
the angel adds:

> beyond abstain,
> To ask, nor let thine own inventions hope
> Things not reveal'd, which th'invisible King,
> Only Omniscient hath supprest in Night,
> To non communicable in Earth or Heaven.[2]

22. Loss of power is the result of Adam's Fall and the lesson of moderation must be relearned.   He is obliged to master
it as every intelligent man must, by discovering that in history
as well as in his own experience men suffer from their impulse
to overreach themselves.   It is now a matter of limiting the
lust for power as well as that for knowledge.   One of the
first events in the vision of the future which Michael reveals
to Adam is Nimrod's usurpation of power over a society which
Milton imagined in its primitive virtues as resembling the
Commonwealth to which, even as late as 1660, he had still
been so ready to point "the ready and easy way."   From the
whole dismal pageant, relieved at only a few places by the
emergence of a great personality, Michael warns Adam to
learn "true patience" and to be

> equally inur'd
> By moderation either state to bear.[3]

The words seem like a paraphrase of the title of a once famous work by Petrarch, the *Remedies against both Good and*

[1] I, i, 3.
[2] Vii, 120–4.
[3] XI, 362–3.

Evil Fortune, a work in which the contempt of this world taught by Innocent III was faintly humanized by the Aristotelian ideal of temperance, as it was very much more effectively humanized in the ethics of St. Thomas Aquinas. Milton was thinking of an even more humane ideal of moderation or temperance than those of either Petrarch or St. Thomas. It was, I am convinced, an ideal of personality which he had had constantly in mind since he wrote *The Reason of Church Government.* In the context of the long passage which has been quoted from that pamphlet he refers to Torquato Tasso as having looked far and wide in the fields of medieval history and romance, precisely as he did himself, for an epic subject. What Tasso was looking for was a hero possessed of just the qualities of Temperance or Reason which Milton failed to find in the Arthurian legends which he once considered. In one of Tasso's forgotten prose works, the Discourse of *Heroic Virtue and of Charity,* that virtue was identified with the love or charity of St. Paul's Christianity. A famous tract of Giordano Bruno identified heroic virtue with possession of the four "heroic passions" of the Platonists. It was a mixture of such Christian and Hellenic ideals that Milton intended to display as *developing* in Adam after the Fall. That was his conscious purpose in his epic; and he would have appealed to it, if he had been challenged with M. Saurat's charge that he is subconsciously his own hero, or if he had been confronted with the criticism that no poem whose outcome is unfortunate can be properly "heroic," an impertinence which some neo-classic critics threw at *Paradise Lost.*

23. The traditions surrounding the Fall in the Middle Ages had represented Eve's eating of the fruit of the Tree of Knowledge as mere greediness, and gluttony as the "sin" involved. In Milton's time there was a tendency, which had the support of good rabbinical tradition, for making lust or uxoriousness the "sin."[1] Sir Thomas Browne rationalized

---

[1] In *Christian Doctrine,* I, xi, Milton insisted that the Fall included all varieties of sin generally and none in particular. Compare the note on line 16 in Book X.

this tradition, or accepted its current rationalization, by suggesting that "the temptation of the Man by the Woman [might be] the seduction of the higher parts by the inferiour and feminine faculties."[1] In the same way Milton found the story in Genesis allegorized in the boldly free-thinking work of the French lawyer and philosopher, Jean Bodin, whose *Heptoplomeres* was written about 1580 and still enjoyed a reputation such that Milton had difficulty in securing a manuscript copy from a friend on the Continent. Now, a warning against lust plays a rather conspicuous part in Raphael's great dialogue with Adam, and an act of lust consummates the eating of the fruit of the forbidden tree. Theories that Milton was both "over-sexed" and "under-sexed" have been built upon that fact, coupled with the surprisingly frank account of the "kisses pure"[2] which roused the envy of the Fiend in Eden, and with Raphael's admonition to Adam against Eve's "outside":

> fair no doubt, and worthy well
> Thy cherishing, thy honouring, and thy love,
> Not thy subjection: weigh her with thyself;
> Then value.[3]

24. The reply to such theories is the divorce tracts. Milton's marriage was hasty and unfortunate. He may have been duped by Mary Powell's outside when, about Whitsuntide in 1642, he took that journey into the country from which, as his nephew Phillips says drily, "after a month's stay, home he returns a married man, that went forth a bachelor." Separation followed after about a month, and reconciliation after three years. She was hardly more than a child, and there is excellent reason to believe that the marriage, the separation, and the reconciliation were all largely due to her parents. They were Royalists and their treatment of Milton corresponded suspiciously with the vicissitudes of their party's cause

---

[1]*Pseudodoxia Epidemica,* I, i.
[2]IV, 502.
[3]VIII, 568–71.

in the Civil War. *The Doctrine and Discipline of Divorce* appeared on 1 August, 1643. The convictions expressed can hardly have been invented as an outlet for his disappointment, although his chagrin doubtless precipitated the pamphlet. Incompatibility got its first great defence as the proper cause for divorce in that tract and its three successors. Milton's own case against the divorce laws is put in the question: "The soberest and best governed men are least practiced in these affairs; and who knows not that the bashful muteness of a virgin may ofttimes hide all the unliveliness and natural sloth which is really unfit for conversation."[1] He admitted the "disappointment of an impetuous nerve," but his theme was "the ingenuous grievance of a man unreasonably yoked." It was inevitable that a decade of Freudian literary criticism should read a reflection of his first marriage in his treatment of the myth of the Fall, for a dubious tradition reports that the great reconciliation scene which begins, "Forsake me not thus, Adam,"[2] was a recollection of Mary Powell's dramatic appeal to him when they were reunited in 1645. The only unmistakably personal passage in his entire treatment of Adam and Eve, however, seems to me to be Adam's complaint that man

> never shall find out fit Mate, but such
> As some misfortune brings him, or mistake,
> Or whom he wishes most shall seldom gain
> Through her perverseness, but shall see her gain'd
> By a far worse, or if she love, withheld
> By Parents, or his happiest choice too late
> Shall meet, already linkt and Wedlock-bound
> To a fell Adversary.[3]

His previous recrimination against Eve as "that bad woman" is certainly to be read as no less dramatic than the words of Ventidius anent Cleopatra in *All for Love:*

[1] I, iii.
[2] X, 914.
[3] X, 899–906.

> O Women! Women! Women! all the gods
> Have not such pow'r of doing good to Man,
> As you of doing harm.

No one thinks of holding Dryden responsible for these words or reading a jot of autobiography into them. The greater part of Milton's treatment of Eve is no less dramatic. What we have in it is a very original and symbolic treatment of an old rabbinical tradition that Adam yielded to Eve out of a kind of sentimental chivalry. And fused with that tradition is the Renaissance rationalization of the myth in Genesis as an allegory of the surrender of the masculine and reasonable part of man to the feminine and physical part.

25. It was as a drama, perhaps, that Milton for a long time thought of *Paradise Lost* during the years of pamphleteering, when the poem was waiting to be written. In the Cambridge Manuscript we have notes of four schemes for dramas about the Fall, and it is worth observing that they remind us of Greek tragedy as well as of moralities and masques. The first two sketches are mere lists of persons, and the gallery of abstractions presented betrays a scenic and allegorical purpose even more abstract than that which inspired *Comus*. The list for the first drama is worth citing, for among many elements which it explains in *Paradise Lost* is the allegory of Death and Sin, rising like a splendid prehistoric creature in the midst of the less uncouth narratives of Satan's voyages in Books II and X. Michael was the first name in the list, and the rest were Heavenly Love, Chorus of Angels, Lucifer, Adam (with the serpent), Eve, Conscience, Death, Labour, Sicknesse, Discontent, Ignorance with others (Labour and the rest associated with it are marked "mutes"), Faith, Hope, and Charity. In the third sketch it has been observed that Milton, perhaps unconsciously, reproduced some of the great themes of the medieval moralities. Justice and Mercy, two of St. Bernard's Four Daughters of God, debate the destiny of man in the first act. Although the personifications have vanished, there is a clear survival of that motif in God's weighing

of the claims of justice and mercy in heaven in the third book of *Paradise Lost*. The three central acts as Milton planned them were to handle the temptation and the Fall, and the last act was to develop the medieval theme of the Coming of Death. Adam and Eve, driven out of Paradise, are presented by an angel with a company of mutes: Labour, Grief, Hatred, Envy, War, Famine, Pestilence, Sickness, Discontent, Ignorance, Fear, Death. Finally Faith, Hope and Charity comfort *him* and instruct *him*. Here is the substance of Michael's revelation of the murders, the wars and misery of the future to Adam, and here also is the note of qualified hope on which *Paradise Lost* was to end.

26. The fourth sketch shows the influence of Greek tragedy and gives indications of the drift in Milton's thinking toward an appreciation of the epic rather than the dramatic form for the story of the Fall. The scene opens with the angel Gabriel descending and showing that "since this globe was created, his frequency [has been] as much on earth as in heav'n." He explains that his business in Paradise since Lucifer's rebellion is to keep watch, as we find him doing in the fourth book of *Paradise Lost,* and he explains to a chorus of angels what he knows

Of man, as the creation of Eve, with their love, and marriage. After this Lucifer appears after his overthrow, bemoans himself, seeks revenge on man. The Chorus prepare resistance at his first approach. At last, after discourse of enmity on either side, he departs, whereat the Chorus sings of the battle, and victory in heaven against him and his accomplices, as before, after the first act, was sung a hymn of the creation. Man next and Eve having by this time been seduc't by the serpent, appears confusedly cover'd with leaves. Conscience in a shape accuses him, Justice cites him to the place whither Jehova call'd for him. In the meanwhile the chorus entertains the stage, and is informed by some angel the manner of his fall. Adam then and Eve return, accuse one another, but especially Adam lays the blame on his wife, is stubborn in his offence. Justice appears, reasons with him, convinces him. The Angel is sent to banish them out of Paradise, but before causes to pass before his eyes in shapes a mask of all the evils of this life and world. He is humbled, relents, despairs.   At last appears Mercy, comforts him, and brings in *faith, hope* and *charity,* promises the Messiah.

And a note adds that Faith, Hope and Charity move him to repentance by Lucifer's example of impenitence and bring him to submission to his penalty.   The chorus "briefly concludes." In this draft we feel that the elements of Greek tragedy, the chorus and the unity of place especially, make the whole design painfully artificial.   Milton was to transform them into some of the most dramatic elements in his epic.   The chorus becomes Gabriel's guard of angels, led by Ithuriel and Zephon, who surprise Satan whispering into the ear of Eve as she sleeps while he lurks beside her, "squat like a toad." The result is one of the most dramatic and beautiful scenes in the whole poem.   No trace of the unity of place remains. *Paradise Lost* opens with the great debate among the fiends in hell where Milton's characterization is at its best.   It is a question whether Satan, Beëlzebub, or Belial is the most vividly conceived, and the most perfectly projected character.   The best reply to those who say that Satan is the hero of the poem is to observe that none of his speeches, not even the great soliloquies, achieves the perfect effect of the living voice which makes a vital personality of Belial.   It is a paradox of the history of the growth of *Paradise Lost* that it became more dramatic by changing in Milton's imagination from a drama to an epic.   All the great lyric and choric effects which the drama might have contained are probably in the poem as we have it.   Phillips tells us that the great invocation of Satan to the Sun in Book IV was actually written as a part of one of the intended dramas.   Doubtless there are other survivals. The long narratives which would have become intolerable as episodes in a play are vital in their native epic element, and the scenes in hell and the conversation between Raphael and Adam (if not that between Michael and Adam) are more convincing dramatically as parts of a story than they would be in a drama which added to all its other demands upon the reader's credulity the initial acceptance of its supernatural

actors. But the dramatic power of the epic is closed to us
if we read it feeling that Milton lacked the dramatic instinct,
and did not possess the power to project himself into his
characters impersonally which Coleridge said that Shakespeare possessed in a supreme degree, but which he said also
is essential to every great artist.

THE PRESENT EDITION

The basis of the text of *Paradise Lost* in this volume is the
second edition of the poem, which was issued with Milton's
own corrections in 1674, seven years after the appearance of
the first edition. There were no changes of serious importance, but Milton took advantage of the opportunity to increase the original ten books to twelve by dividing the seventh
book into the present seventh and eighth books, and the tenth
into the present eleventh and twelfth. To mark the pauses,
he inserted what are now the first three lines of Book VIII,
and slightly modified the fourth line of this Book and the first
five lines in Book XII. Those two additions are the most
considerable single changes that he made (with one exception),
but the second edition bears evidence everywhere of careful
scrutiny and revision. There can be no doubt of its greater
authority and, except in a very few instances of obvious mistake which are set right by its predecessor, I have followed it
undeviatingly. Without seeking to produce a critical text,
I have tried to be accurate; and, without pretending to deal
systematically with textual questions, in notes which are
crowded with more important interests, I have tried to indicate what some of the most significant of those questions are.

The punctuation, in accordance with the general editorial
policy of the series in which this book appears, has been
somewhat modernized, but as little as is compatible with ready
intelligibility to a twentieth-century reader. Milton's punctuation is a part of the essence of his rhythm and is the mortar
which binds his verse together. It is not the punctuation of
today, but his language is not the language of the twentieth

century nor has it much in common with the medium in which even the most "classical" living poet writes. His sentences accumulate to lengths which are those of classical Latin periods and are built upon a hidden structure of logic which is really Latin. When on a first reading they seem labyrinthine, they prove on a second transit to be symmetrical palaces where the sign-boards of modern pointing would be an impertinence. His use of the colon where we would use a period and his blocking off of the spheres of influence of his master verbs by semicolons are the keys to a comprehension of his style, and an understanding reader soon learns to value them as a part of his spaciousness.

The spelling has been treated on a quite different principle and modernized with virtual completeness. There is no reason for perpetuating the orthographical uncertainty and ineptness of the seventeenth century and still less for preserving the vagaries of Milton's printers. How little they represented his preferences can be seen from his careful correction of the spelling of the few words whose spelling did seem to him to matter. In very many cases ordinary words appear with two or even three variant spellings for which no motive in emphasis or meaning can be found, and in general no violence is done by bringing them all down to the standard of the *New English Dictionary*. In some cases I have kept the form in which Milton wrote the word, even though it has become obsolete, because it seems to me to represent his pronunciation of a vowel. Few poets have been greater or more conscious masters of vowel music than Milton and a modern editor ought to create as few discords as possible. So I have preferred in most cases to keep the initial *i* in words like *imbalm* and *ingender,* although Milton himself was not consistent in his practice. For the same reason I retain the spelling *anough* and its variant, the less recognizable *anow*. Some of Milton's obsolete words were obsolescent in his own time and yet he preferred them. A good example is *fardest,* which he uses consistently, although Shakespeare adopted the modern form, *furthest*. A greater problem is offered by the many cases of words like *magazin* (IV, 816) and *vultur* (III, 431), which I have spelled as Milton did because the modern spelling deforms his pronunciation; but I have added the modern *e* to words like *apostat* (V, 852) because, at least in America, in spite of the final *e,* we do not make a long diphthong of the *a* in the last syllable. Whenever the *N. E. D.* tolerates a Miltonic spelling I have preserved it, preferring his *groveling* (I, 280 and *splendor* (II, 447) to the more usual forms. A few words such as *aery* and *sovran* I print in the forms in which Milton liked to write them, because they were favourite ideograms of his, vocables of special connotation of which their form was a part. *Sovran* he spelled in this way probably because it had associations for him in its partly Italianized form with the studies and the experience in Italy which are woven richly into his work. Geographical names stand just as they do in the second edition of *Paradise Lost.* In an age of tremendous excitement about an opening world, when both the places and the languages behind hundreds of strange names were equally unfamiliar and fabulous, pronunciation itself could not be controlled, to say nothing of spelling. Some of Milton's geographical terms are simply obsolete and others are unknown because the course of trade and empire has not followed the channels which he and his contemporaries thought most promising. We are far more ignorant of ancient geography today than were Milton's contemporaries, for they imaged the eastern Mediterranean countries, central Asia, and north Africa with the aid of Strabo and Herodotus quite as much as they did through contemporary narratives like those in Purchas's *Pilgrimes* and *Pilgrimage* and Sandys's *Relation.* For them the world's geography centred, as it did for Milton, around Palestine and the dubious site of Eden in the Mesopotamian plain or in Armenia. The greatest landmarks outside of the immediate western world for them were the mountains bounding Canaan, the Hermon range on the northeast and Carmel by the Sea on the southwest, with Mount Pisgah overlooking it all and Moses remembered on the summit, as Fuller drew him in his chart of the region.

It is impossible to modernize Milton's obsolete names, like
Rhene and *Danaw* (I, 352), and it would be pedantic and insufferably misleading to tamper with his spelling of the names
of new-found lands like *Quiloa* (XI, 399) and *Petsora* (X, 292),
for which he offered the alternative *Pechora* in his *History of
Moscovia.* The italicization of geographical names may not
be necessary in a modern edition and to some readers it may
be offensive, but, like that of proper names, it is a part of the
distinctive effect of the page in the early editions and to me
it is pleasant.

One peculiarity of Milton's spelling has been generally and
I believe rightly recognized in recent editions of his poems.
It is the practice of scrupulously distinguishing between stressed
and unstressed personal pronouns by spelling *mee, wee, hee,
shee* and *their* when the words are stressed, and when they
are unstressed by spelling *me, we, he, she* and *thir.* Milton
made this distinction carefully all his life and obliged his
printers to make it, although the practice was neither definitely established nor on the increase among his contemporaries. It is worth while to keep this distinction in *Paradise
Lost,* for it is a constant check upon our interpretation of the
rhythm and sometimes even of the sense. For example, in
Book I, 384, the spelling of the pronouns shows that the
repeated word *Altar* should bear greater stress than the contrasted pronouns *Thir* and *his.* The nuance of scansion is
indicated by the form given to the pronominal adjective in
the line,

> Of thir great Sultan waving to direct.[1]

The rhetorical force of many a phrase is pointed up by the
emphatic spelling of a pronoun, as happens in

> These troublesome disguises which wee wear,[2]

or

> Fruitless to mee, though Fruit be here to excess,
> The credit of whose virtue rest with thee.[3]

---

[1] I, 348.
[2] IV, 740.
[3] IX, 648-9.

Mark Pattison's remark that the enjoyment of Milton is a final reward of scholarship was interpreted by a ribald student as meaning that *Paradise Lost* is the happiest hunting ground of the writer of footnotes. So I have found it, but the pleasure has sometimes been dear bought. Above all, I have tried to produce notes that would be instantly intelligible to every reader and would be interesting and complete within the shortest possible compass; but I have tried also to make them genuinely original and authoritative. When I have followed a previous editor in a quotation I have tried to verify it as frequently as possible and the only large class of authorities quoted at second hand is that of voyagers and geographers. In their case I have relied mainly upon Professor Allan H. Gilbert's *A Geographical Dictionary of Milton* and upon previous editors. For the rabbinical material which has been recently explored by Miltonists I have gone to M. Denis Saurat's *Milton, Man and Thinker* (referred to in the notes as Saurat's *Milton*) and to Mr. Harris F. Fletcher's *Milton's Rabbinical Readings* (referred to in the notes as *Rabbinical Readings*). One of the most difficult problems in writing notes which are not intended primarily for scholars but must be scholarly to be of any value is the precise line of exclusion of bibliographical matter and of secondary evidence for points in dispute. Reginald Scot's *Discoverie of Witchcraft* and Bartholomaeus Anglicus' *De proprietatibus rerum,* in the translation by Stephen Batman known as *Batman uppon Bartholome,* are familiar already in Mr. Verity's notes as the sources of many illuminating parallels to Milton's thought. To these and their kind I have ventured, following M. Saurat's lead, to add Robert Flud's *Utriusque Cosmi Historia*. I mention one other Renaissance work which the reader will not find accessible in any English translation. This is the great handbook of mythology by Natale Conti, *Mythologiae, sive explicationis fabularum Libri decem* (Frankfurt, 1596; it is referred to in the notes simply as "Conti"). Here and there Conti seems to me to supply the key to a passage as no other "source" does. For example, Milton has been much praised for bringing together from Diodorus Siculus and other authors just the elements which work the magic of his allusion to the Nyseian isle in Book IV, 275; but the whole background of this passage, including a translation from Diodorus, is to be found in Conti's chapter on Bacchus. To point this out in a note is no more "pedantic" than it is to point to Diodorus as the source, unless pedantry is defined as "exact knowledge." In the literal sense of the word, of course, Milton had no "sources" for his mythology and in the broad sense he had all classical literature and its offspring in the Renaissance. One way of studying his "classical background" is to trace his mythological allusions to possible origins in Greek or Latin literature, as Professor Osgood does in *The Classical Mythology of Milton's English Poems,* but the reader who is interested in Milton's poetic processes will welcome an occasional footnote which is written from the point of view upon the whole problem from which Professor Douglas Bush has written his *Mythology and the Renaissance Tradition.*

One of my greatest difficulties has been the treatment of Milton's relation to the famous translation of *Les Divines Semaines* of the French Calvinist soldier and poet, Du Bartas, which Joshua Sylvester published in 1605. No complete copy of the work has been obtainable and I have been obliged to rely upon *The Divine Weeks of Joshua Sylvester,* edited by T. W. Haight, and upon Professor George C. Taylor's *Milton and Du Bartas,* from which most of my references are taken. Since Lauder's absurd charges of plagiarism in the eighteenth century circumstances have conspired either to exaggerate or to obscure the common elements in the two great cosmic poems. Professor Taylor's book, admirably modest in its claims though it is, appears to me to focus attention too narrowly upon Du Bartas. Only a special study could discuss a tithe of the parallels which he suggests, but in my notes I have tried to recognize Du Bartas's influence upon the form of Milton's eleventh book and upon Milton's language and thought in many other parts of *Paradise Lost.*

In the notes on biblical and classical "parallel passages" I

have tried, not to be exhaustive, but to be complete in the
sense that every unquestionably conscious reminiscence of
the Bible or of a Greek or Latin classic which has been
noticed by preceding editors or which I have remarked myself is mentioned, and mentioned in a way to indicate to the
lay reader *why* Milton was drawn to it. I have avoided all
quotations in foreign languages, using Dryden's translation
of Virgil freely and summarizing or translating the great
majority of Milton's allusions to Greek, Latin and Italian
authors. Foreign titles are translated in almost every case
and abbreviations are avoided, except in the most obvious
cases. The names of the books of the Bible are abbreviated
only in the references enclosed between brackets. In the
text of the notes I have preferred to print them in full, because my students find the standard abbreviations of the names
of the books of the Bible all but incomprehensible. Over
and over, the annotator's task is to make clear just why Milton
fused a biblical with a classical allusion, or to indicate the in-
terplay of his memories of the Bible with his impressions
gleaned from parallel sources like Josephus' *Antiquities of
the Jews* or *Wars of the Jews* (referred to as *Antiquities* and
Wars respectively in the notes), or with his ideas gathered
from patristic tradition or Renaissance Neo-Platonism.

I should like to acknowledge the kindness of my colleagues,
Professors Willard H. Durham and George R. Potter, in criti-
cizing the notes to the first book of *Paradise Lost* with a view
to the needs of their students in the second year survey
course in the University of California, and to express my
thanks to the Librarians at the Leland Stanford University
who allowed me to borrow and keep for an exceptionally long
time the copy of the second edition of *Paradise Lost* from
which the portrait and title page are reproduced in this volume.

A LIST OF THE ABBREVIATIONS USED IN THE BIBLIOGRAPHY AND IN THE NOTES TO *PARADISE LOST*.

Advancement: Sir Francis Bacon's *Advancement of Learning.*

Aen.: Virgil's *Aeneid.*

Anatomy: Robert Burton's *Anatomy of Melancholy.*

Antiquities: Flavius Josephus' *Antiquities of the Jews.*

du Bartas: *The Divine Weekes* of Guillaume de Salluste, sieur du Bartas, translated by Joshua Sylvester, London, 1605. Selections edited by T. W. Haight, Waukesha, Wisconsin, 1908.

C. D.: Milton's *De doctrina christiana,* in the translation of Bishop Sumner as revised in the edition of Milton's *Prose Works* in Bohn's Standard Library.

Conti: Natalis Comitis *Mythologiae.* Frankfurt, 1596.

Diodorus: Diodorus Siculus' *Bibliotheca historica.*

Discoverie: Reginald Scot's *Discoverie of Witchcraft,* edition of 1665.

F. Q.: Edmund Spenser's *Faerie Queene.*

Hakluyt: Richard Hakluyt's *Principall Navigations, Traffiques and Discoveries of the English Nation.* London, 1598–1600.

Hierarchy: Thomas Heywood's *Hierarchy of the blessed Angels. Their Names, orders and Offices. The fall of Lucifer with his Angels.* London, 1634.

Il.: Homer's *Iliad.*

Inf.: Dante's *Inferno.*

J. E. G. P.: *Journal of English and Germanic Philology.*

J. D.: Torquato Tasso's *Jerusalem Delivered.* Quotations are from Edward Fairfax's translation, edited by L'Estrange, Dublin, 1726.

Keightley: *The Poems of John Milton, with notes,* by T. Keightley. London, 1859. 2 Vols.

Masson: *The Poetical Works of John Milton, with Memoir, Introductions, Notes, and an Essay on Milton's Versification.*

Edited by David Masson. London, 1894. 3 Vols. (First published, 1874.)

Met.: Ovid's *Metamorphoses*.

M. L. R.: Modern Language Review.

N. E. D.: New English Dictionary.

Newton: *The Complete Poetical Works of John Milton, with a Life of the Poet and Notes on His Works,* by Thomas Newton. London, 1749–52.

Od.: Homer's *Odyssey*.

O. F.: Ludovico Ariosto's *Orlando Furioso*.

Pilgrimage: Purchas his *Pilgrimage*. 2nd Ed., London, 1617.

Pilgrimes: Purchas his *Pilgrimes*. London, 1625. Reprinted at Glasgow, 1905–7.

P. L.: Paradise Lost.

P. M. L. A.: Publications of the Modern Language Association of America.

P. R.: Paradise Regained.

P. W.: Prose Works of Milton in the *Bohn Standard Library*. So far as possible references to Milton's prose are made by book and chapter.

Relation: A Relation of a Journey begun in An. Dom. 1610. By George Sandys. Edition of 1673.

S. A.: Samson Agonistes.

S. P.: Studies in Philology.

Todd: *The Poetical Works of John Milton.* Edited by H. J. Todd. 4th edition. London, 1842. 4 Vols. (First published, 1801.)

Vanity: Joseph Glanvill's *Vanity of Dogmatizing*. London, 1661. Facsimile Text Society reprint.

Verity: *Milton: Paradise Lost.* Edited by A. W. Verity. Cambridge University Press. 1929. 2 Vols. (First published, 1910.)

Wars: Flavius Josephus' *Wars of the Jews*.

Abbreviations of the books of the Bible are those used in Alexander Cruden's *Complete Concordance to the Holy Scriptures*.

BIBLIOGRAPHY

In this bibliography no attempt is made to mention all the articles which have been laid under contribution in the notes to *Paradise Lost,* but only to indicate some books and essays which are of outstanding importance to readers who are interested in the poem as an expression of Milton's personality and of the tradition which he inherited. I do not necessarily agree with all the criticism represented here, but every item below seems to me to raise an important question about the poem, whether it answers it adequately or not. For more nearly complete information the student should turn to David H. Stevens' *Reference Guide to Milton from 1800 to the Present Day* and to Harris F. Fletcher's *Contributions to a Milton Bibliography, 1800–1930,* or to E. N. S. Thompson's *Topical Bibliography.*

Even a short bibliography of modern criticism and scholarship is likely to discourage and mislead a beginner. The best approach to *Paradise Lost*—at least for hardy spirits—is the most direct. A good approach to Milton himself is through the short, early account of him by his nephew, Edward Phillips, and through other accounts by John Aubrey, Anthony à Wood, and John Toland, all of which have been frequently republished. And no reader should go far into modern criticism without knowing the historic essays of Addison in *The Spectator,* of Dr. Johnson in *The Lives of the English Poets,* of Macaulay in *The Edinburgh Review* in 1825 (constantly reprinted), of Matthew Arnold in the second series of *Essays in Criticism,* and of James Russell Lowell in the second series of *Among My Books.*

Agar, H.—*Milton and Plato.* Princeton University Press. 1931.

Bailey, John C.—*Milton.* London and New York, 1915. "The Home University Library."

Bailey, Margaret L.—*Milton and Jakob Boehme.* A study of

German mysticism in seventeenth century England. New York. 1922.

Baldwin, Edward C.—*Some Extra-Biblical Semitic Influences on Milton's story of the Fall of Man.* J. E. G. P., XXVIII, 366-401.

Belloc, Hilaire—*Milton.* Philadelphia, 1935.

Bridges, Robert—*Milton's Prosody.* Oxford. Revised, 1921.

Buck, Philo M.—*Milton on Liberty.* University Studies. University of Nebraska. XXV, No. 1.

Bundy, Murry W.—*Milton's View of Education in* Paradise Lost. J. E. G. P., XXI, 127-52.

Bush, Douglas—*Mythology and the Renaissance Tradition in English Poetry.* University of Minnesota Press. 1932.

Dodge, R. E. Neil—*Theology in* Paradise Lost. University of Wisconsin Studies in Language and Literature. 1918. No. 2. Pp. 9-21.

Erskine, John—*The Theme of Death in* Paradise Lost. P. M. L. A., XXXII, 573-82.

Fletcher, Harris F.—*Milton's Rabbinical Readings.* Urbana. 1930.

———*Milton's Semitic Studies and Some Manifestations of them in his Poetry.* University of Chicago Press. 1926.

Gilbert, Allan H.—*Milton and Galileo.* S. P., XIX, 152-85.

———*Milton on the Position of Women.* M. L. R., XV, 7-27, 240-64.

———*Milton's Textbook of Astronomy.* P. M. L. A., XXXVIII, 297-307.

———*Milton and the Mysteries.* S. P., XVII, 147-69.

———*Pierre Davity; His Geography and its use by Milton.* Geographical Review, VII, 322-38.

———*A Geographical Dictionary of Milton.* Cornell University Press. 1919.

———*The Outside Shell of Milton's World.* S. P., XX, 444-7.

———*The Problem of Evil in* Paradise Lost. J. E. G. P., XXII, 175-94.

Greenlaw, Edwin—*"A Better Teacher than Aquinas."* S. P.,
   XIV, 196-217.

———*Spenser's Influence in* Paradise Lost. S. P., XVII,
   320-59.

Grierson, H. J. C.—*John Milton.* The Criterion. VIII, 7-26.

Hanford, J. H.—*A Milton Handbook.* New York. Second
   edition, 1933.

———*Milton and the Return to Humanism.* S. P., XVI,
   1826-47.

———*The Dramatic Element in* Paradise Lost. S. P., XIV,
   178-95.

———*The Temptation Motive in Milton.* S. P., XV, 176-94.

Hartwell, Kathleen E.—*Lactantius and Milton.* Harvard University Press. 1929.

Kellett, E. E.—*Reconsiderations.* Literary Essays. Cambridge University Press. 1928. Contains essays on Milton
   and Dante and on Milton's medieval aspect.

Langdon, Ida—*Milton's Theory of Poetry and Fine Art.* Yale
   University Press. 1924.

Larson, Martin A.—*Milton and Servetus;* A study in the
   sources of Milton's theology. P. M. L. A., XLI, 891-934.

———*The Modernity of Milton.* University of Chicago Press.
   1927.

———*Milton's Essential Relation to Puritanism and Stoicism.*
   Philological Quarterly, VI, 201-20.

Liljegren, S. B.—*La Pensée de Milton et Giordano Bruno.*
   Revue de littérature comparée. III, 516-40.

———*Studies in Milton.* Lund. 1918.

Macaulay, Rose—*Milton.* London. 1934.

Masson, David—*The Life of Milton;* Narrated in Connection
   with the Political, Ecclesiastical, and Literary History of
   His Time. Cambridge and London, 1859-94. 7 Vols.

More, Paul Elmer—*The Theme of Paradise Lost.* Shelburne
   Essays, 4th Series.

Nicolson, Marjorie H.—*Milton and Hobbes.* S. P., XXIII.
   405-33.

————*Milton and the Conjectura Cabbalistica.* Philological Quarterly. VI, 1-18.

————*The Spirit-world of Milton and More.* S. P., XXII, 433-52.

————*Milton and the Telescope.* E. L. H., II, 1-32.

Osgood, Charles G.—*The Classical Mythology of Milton's English Poems.* New York. 1900. Revised edition, 1925.

Pattison, Mark—*Milton.* "English Men of Letters Series." London. 1879.

Raleigh, Sir Walter A.—*Milton.* New York and London. 1900.

Ramsay, R. L.—*Morality Themes in Milton's Poetry.* S. P., XV, 123-58.

Raymond, Dora N.—*Oliver's Secretary; John Milton in an era of Revolt.* New York. 1932.

Robbins, F. E.—*The Hexaemeral Literature.* Chicago. 1912.

Saintsbury, George—*Milton and the Grand Style.* In Milton Memorial Lectures. Oxford. 1908.

Saurat, Denis—*Milton; Man and Thinker.* New York. 1924.

Spaeth, S. G.—*Milton's Knowledge of Music.* Its Sources and its Significance in his Works. Weimar. 1913.

Stoll, E. E.—*Milton a Romantic.* R. E. S., VIII, 425-36.

Thompson, E. N. S.—*Milton's Knowledge of Geography.* S. P., XVI, 148-71.

————*Essays on Milton.* Yale University Press. 1914.

Taylor, George C.—*Milton's Use of Du Bartas.* Harvard University Press. 1934.

Thaler, Alwin—*The Shakespearian Element in Milton.* P. M. L. A., XL, 645-91.

Tillyard, E. M. W.—*Milton.* New York. 1930.

Warren, W. F.—*The Universe as Pictured in Milton's Paradise Lost.* New York. 1915.

Woodhull, Maria—*The Epic of Paradise Lost.* New York. 1909.

Wright, B. A.—*Milton's First Marriage.* M. L. R., XXVI, 383-400, and XXVII, 6-23.

Paradiſe Loſt.

A
POEM
IN
TWELVE BOOKS.

The Author
JOHN MILTON.

𝔗𝔥𝔢 𝔖𝔢𝔠𝔬𝔫𝔡 𝔈𝔡𝔦𝔱𝔦𝔬𝔫
Reviſed and Augmented by the
ſame Author.

LONDON,
Printed by *S. Simmons* next door to the
Golden Lion in *Alderſgate-ſtreet,* 1674.

IN
PARADISUM AMISSAM

SUMMI POETÆ

JOHANNIS MILTONI

Qui legis Amissam Paradisum, grandia magni
  Carmina Miltoni, quid nisi cuncta legis?
Res cunctas, & cunctarum primordia rerum,
  Et fata, & fines continet iste liber.
Intima panduntur magni penetralia mundi,
  Scribitur & toto quicquid in Orbe latet.
Terræque, tractusque maris, cælumque profundum,
  Sulphureumque Erebi flammivomumque specus.
Quæque colunt terras, Pontumque & Tartara cæca,
  Qæque colunt summi lucida regna Poli.
Et quodcunque ullis conclusum est finibus usquam,
  Et sine fine Chaos, & sine fine Deus;
Et sine fine magis, si quid magis est sine fine,
  In Christo erga homines conciliatus amor.
Hæc qui speraret quis crederet esse futurum?
  Et tamen hæc hodie terra Britanna *legit.*
O quantos in bella Duces! quæ protulit arma!
  Quæ canit, et quanta prælia dira tuba.
Cælestes acies! atque in certamine Cælum!
  Et quæ Cælestes pugna deceret agros!
Quantus in ætheriis tollit se Lucifer *armis!*
  Atique ipso graditur vix Michaële *minor!*
Quantis, & quam funestis concurritur iris
  Dum ferus hic stellas protegit, ille rapit!
Dum vulsos Montes ceu Tela reciproca torquent,
  Et non mortali desuper igne pluunt:
Stat dubius cui se parti concedat Olympus,
  Et metuit pugnæ non superesse suæ.

At simul in cœlis Messiæ insignia fulgent,
   Et currus animes, armaque digna Deo,
Horrendumque rotæ strident, & sæva rotarum
   Erumpunt torvis fulgura luminibus,
Et flammæ vibrant, & vera tonitrua rauco
   Admistis flammis insonuere Polo:
Excidit attonitis mens omnis, & impetus omnis,
   Et cassis dextris irrita Tela cadunt.
Ad pœnas fugiunt, & ceu foret Orcus asylum,
   Infernis certant condere se tenebris.
Cedite Romani *scriptores, cedite* Graii
   Et quos fama recens vel celebravit anus.
Hæc quicunque leget tantum cecinisse putabit
   Mæonidem *ranas,* Virgilium *culices.*

S. B., M. D.

ON
PARADISE LOST

WHEN I beheld the Poet blind, yet bold,
In slender Book his vast Design unfold,
Messiah Crown'd, God's Reconcil'd Decree,
Rebelling Angels, the Forbidden Tree,
Heav'n, Hell, Earth, Chaos, All; the Argument
Held me a while misdoubting his Intent,
That he would ruin (for I saw him strong)
The sacred Truths to Fable and old Song
(So *Sampson* grop'd the Temple's Posts in spite)
The World o'erwhelming to revenge his sight.
   Yet as I read, soon growing less severe,
I lik'd his Project, the success did fear;
Through that wide Field how he his way should find
O'er which lame Faith leads Understanding blind;
Lest he perplex'd the things he would explain,
And what was easy he should render vain.
   Or if a Work so infinite he spann'd,
Jealous I was that some less skilful hand
(Such as disquiet always what is well,
And by ill imitating would excel)

Might hence presume the whole Creation's day
To change in Scenes, and show it in a Play.
   Pardon me, Mighty Poet, nor despise
My causeless, yet not impious, surmise.
But I am now convinc'd, and none will dare
Within thy Labours to pretend a share.
Thou hast not miss'd one thought that could be fit,
And all that was improper dost omit:
So that no room is here for Writers left,
But to detect their Ignorance or Theft.
   That Majesty which through thy Work doth Reign
Draws the Devout, deterring the Profane.
And things divine thou treat'st of in such state
As them preserves, and thee, inviolate.
At once delight and horror on us seize,
Thou sing'st with so much gravity and ease;
And above human flight dost soar aloft
With Plume so strong, so equal, and so soft.
The Bird nam'd from that Paradise you sing
So never flags, but always keeps on Wing.
   Where couldst thou words of such a compass find?
Whence furnish such a vast expense of mind?
Just Heav'n thee like *Tiresias* to requite
Rewards with Prophecy thy loss of sight.
   Well mightst thou scorn thy Readers to allure
With tinkling Rime, of thy own sense secure;
While the *Town-Bayes* writes all the while and spells,
And like a Pack-horse tires without his Bells:
Their Fancies like our Bushy-points appear,
The Poets tag them, we for fashion wear.
I too transported by the Mode offend,
And while I meant to Praise thee must Commend.
Thy Verse created like thy Theme sublime,
In Number, Weight, and Measure, needs not Rime.

A. M.

The Verse

The measure is *English* Heroic Verse without Rime, as
that of *Homer* in *Greek,* and of *Virgil* in *Latin;* Rime being
no necessary Adjunct or true Ornament of Poem or good
Verse, in longer Works especially, but the Invention of a
barbarous Age, to set off wretched matter and lame Metre;
grac't indeed since by the use of some famous modern Poets,
carried away by Custom, but much to thir own vexation,
hindrance, and constraint to express many things otherwise,
and for the most part worse than else they would have exprest
them. Not without cause therefore some both *Italian* and
Spanish Poets of prime note have rejected Rime both in
longer and shorter Works, as have also long since our best
English Tragedies, as a thing of itself, to all judicious ears,
trivial and of no true musical delight; which consists only in
apt Numbers, fit quantity of Syllabies, and the sense variously
drawn out from one Verse into another, not in the jingling
sound of like endings, a fault avoided by the learned Ancients
both in Poetry and all good Oratory. This neglect then of
Rime so little is to be taken for a defect, though it may seem
so perhaps to vulgar Readers, that it rather is to be esteem'd an
example set, the first in *English,* of ancient liberty recover'd
to Heroic Poem from the troublesome and modern bondage of
Riming.

6

PARADISE LOST

BOOK I

THE ARGUMENT

THIS first Book proposes, first in brief, the whole Subject, *Man's disobedience, and the loss thereupon of Paradise wherein he was plac't:* Then touches *the prime cause of his fall, the Serpent, or rather* Satan *in the Serpent; who revolting from God, and drawing to his side many Legions of Angels, was by the command of God driven out of Heaven with all his Crew into the great Deep.* Which action past over, the Poem hastes into the midst of things, presenting *Satan with his Angels now fallen into Hell,* describ'd here, *not in the Centre* (for Heaven and Earth may be suppos'd as yet not made, certainly not yet accurst) *but in a place of utter darkness, fitliest call'd* Chaos: *Here* Satan *with his Angels lying on the burning Lake, thunder-struck and astonisht, after a certain space recovers, as from confusion, calls up him who next in Order and Dignity lay by him; they confer of thir miserable fall.* Satan *awakens all his Legions, who lay till then in the same manner confounded; They rise, thir Numbers, array of Battle, thir chief Leaders nam'd, according to the Idols known afterwards in* Canaan *and the Countries adjoining. To these* Satan *directs his Speech, comforts them with hope yet of regaining Heaven, but tells them lastly of a new World and new kind of Creature to be created, according to an ancient Prophecy or report in Heaven; for that Angels were long before this visible* Creation, was the opinion of many ancient Fathers. *To find out the truth of this Prophecy, and what to determine thereon he refers to a full Council. What his Associates thence attempt.* Pandemonium *the Palace of Satan rises, suddenly built out of the Deep: The infernal Peers there sit in Counsel.*

OF Man's First Disobedience, and the Fruit
Of that Forbidden Tree, whose mortal taste

7

8 Spondee   Trochee

Brought Death into the World, and all our woe,
With loss of *Eden,* till one greater Man
Restore us, and regain the blissful Seat,   5
Sing Heav'nly Muse, that on the secret top
Of *Oreb,* or of *Sinai,* didst inspire
That Shepherd, who first taught the chosen Seed,
In the Beginning how the Heav'ns and Earth
Rose out of *Chaos:* Or if *Sion* Hill   10
Delight thee more, and *Siloa's* Brook that flow'd
Fast by the Oracle of God; I thence
Invoke thy aid to my advent'rous Song,
That with no middle flight intends to soar
Above th' *Aonian* Mount, while it pursues   15
Things unattempted yet in Prose or Rhyme.
And chiefly Thou O Spirit, that dost prefer
Before all Temples th' upright heart and pure,

4. In *Man's Disobedience* Milton saw a finer subject than Achilles' wrath and in the *greater Man,* Christ, a better ideal than Renaissance critics recognized in Ulysses. Like George Chapman, he thought that the word "man" in the first line of the *Odyssey* announced that epic as an ideal human portrait.

6. Milton is not merely following the tradition of the classical poets, who, like Hesiod in the *Theogony,* invoked the nine Muses, inspirers of the arts and daughters of Memory, "dancing about the altar of the mighty son of Cronos," Zeus, their father, on Mt. Helicon. The ninth Muse was Urania, whom later pagan tradition made the mistress of the stars and of the heavenly glory of great men. In the cosmic poems of the Renaissance, such as Du Bartas' *Uranie,* she was related to Solomon's Wisdom, who is "privy to the mysteries of the knowledge of God" and "entering into holy souls, maketh them friends of God, and prophets" (*Wisdom of Solomon,* viii, 4 and vii, 27). Milton calls her the sister of Eternal Wisdom and makes her the source of his creative experience (VII, 9 and 28–30).

7. Milton makes Urania the inspirer of Moses on Mt. Horeb and its spur, Sinai, and later of the Hebrew prophets, when God's "oracle" was the Temple of Mt. Zion, overlooking the stream, Siloam. He opposed Zion to the Aonian mount, Helicon, the haunt of the "siren" Muses of the Greeks, because he thought of his epic as not "to be obtained by the invocation of dame memory and her siren daughters, but by devout prayer to that eternal Spirit who can enrich with all utterance and knowledge, and sends out his seraphim, with the hallowed fire of his altar, to touch and purify the lips of whom he pleases." (*P. W.,* III, 149.)

17. The Spirit is the same which in Genesis (i, 2) "moved upon the face of the waters at creation." In *C. D.* Milton recognized it as "that impulse or voice of God by which the prophets were inspired."

In Milton's verse *spirit* is usually a monosyllable.

Instruct me, for Thou know'st; Thou from the first
Wast present, and with mighty wings outspread   20
Dove-like satst brooding on the vast Abyss
And mad'st it pregnant: What in me is dark
Illumine, what is low raise and support;
That to the highth of this great Argument
I may assert Eternal Providence,   25
And justify the ways of God to men.
   Say first, for Heav'n hides nothing from thy view
Nor the deep Tract of Hell, say first what cause
Mov'd our Grand Parents in that happy State,
Favour'd of Heav'n so highly, to fall off   30
From thir Creator, and transgress his Will
For one restraint, Lords of the World besides?
Who first seduc'd them to that foul revolt?
Th' infernal Serpent; he it was, whose guile
Stirr'd up with Envy and Revenge, deceiv'd   35
The Mother of Mankind, what time his Pride
Had cast him out from Heav'n, with all his Host
Of Rebel Angels, by whose aid aspiring
To set himself in Glory above his Peers,
He trusted to have equall'd the most High,   40
If he oppos'd; and with ambitious aim
Against the Throne and Monarchy of God
Rais'd impious War in Heav'n and Battle proud
With vain attempt. Him the Almighty Power
Hurl'd headlong flaming from th' Ethereal Sky   45

---

34. The allusions to Satan as the Serpent look forward to Milton's
version of the story of Eve's temptation and to his metamorphosis of the
devils into serpents in X, 509–40. The unity of his epic derives much
from his treatment of that story in the light of ideas—Cabbalic, Neo-
Platonic and Christian—which were widespread enough to inspire the
German mystic, Jakob Boehme, to write that the devils "lost their
beauteous form and image and became like serpents, dragons, worms and
evil beasts, when reason was extinguished within them" (*Three Principles,*
IV, 64).

38. The first of the rare lines ending in an unstressed and redundant
syllable. Milton's blank verse is distinguished from that of the Jacobean
dramatists by his avoidance of such redundancy in his otherwise richly
varied iambic pattern.

45. Satan's meteoric fall and adamantine chains bring together biblical
memories which stretch from Isaiah's "How art thou fallen from heaven,

With hideous ruin and combustion down
To bottomless perdition, there to dwell
In Adamantine Chains and penal Fire,
Who durst defy th' Omnipotent to Arms.
Nine times the Space that measures Day and Night   50
To mortal men, he with his horrid crew
Lay vanquisht, rolling in the fiery Gulf
Confounded though immortal: But his doom
Reserv'd him to more wrath; for now the thought
Both of lost happiness and lasting pain   55
Torments him; round he throws his baleful eyes
That witness'd huge affliction and dismay
Mixt with obdúrate pride and steadfast hate:
At once as far as Angels ken he views
The dismal Situation waste and wild,   60
A Dungeon horrible, on all sides round
As one great Furnace flam'd, yet from those flames
No light, but rather darkness visible
Serv'd only to discover sights of woe,
Regions of sorrow, doleful shades, where peace   65
And rest can never dwell, hope never comes
That comes to all; but torture without end

O Lucifer, son of the morning!" (xiv, 12) to St. Jude's picture of "the
angels which kept not their first estate . . . in everlasting chains, under
darkness" (i, 6).

50. In Hesiod's myth, when Zeus hurls the vanquished Titans to hell,
they fall nine days and nights from heaven to earth and for nine more
days and nights to Tartarus. Milton's recollection of that story (*Theogony*, 720 ff.) is the first of many draughts upon classic conceptions to
supplement the scanty suggestions for a physical hell in the Bible. The
vagueness which Macaulay contrasted with the clear etching in Dante's
Inferno matches the "cloudy Tartarus" of Homer and Hesiod, and Milton's restless whirlwinds of tempestuous fire recall Hesiod's dreadful
cyclones.

59. I take *ken* to be a verb, and the meaning to be "as far as angels
know" or "see." *Angels* may have been intended as a possessive case
and *ken* as a noun.

63. Milton's "darkness visible" recalls the infernal "fire without bril-
liance, able to burn in darkness, destitute of light" which St. Basil the
Great described in his *Homily on Psalm* xxxiii.

66. The obvious parallel with "All hope abandon, ye who enter here"
(*Inferno*, III, 9) reminds us of the passion for Dante expressed in the
Apology for Smectymnuus.

Still urges, and a fiery Deluge, fed
With ever-burning Sulphur unconsum'd:
Such place Eternal Justice had prepar'd   70
For those rebellious, here their Prison ordained
In utter darkness, and thir portion set
As far remov'd from God and light of Heav'n
As from the Centre thrice to th' utmost Pole.
O how unlike the place from whence they fell!   75
There the companions of his fall, o'erwhelm'd
With Floods and Whirlwinds of tempestuous fire,
He soon discerns, and welt'ring by his side
One next himself in power, and next in crime,
Long after known in *Palestine,* and nam'd   80
Beëlzebub. To whom th' Arch-Enemy,
And thence in Heav'n call'd Satan, with bold words
Breaking the horrid silence thus began.
    If thou beest he; But O how fall'n! how chang'd
From him, who in the happy Realms of Light   85
Cloth'd with transcendent brightness didst outshine
Myriads though bright: If he whom mutual league,
United thoughts and counsels, equal hope,
And hazard in the Glorious Enterprise,
Join'd with me once, now misery hath join'd   90
In equal ruin: into what Pit thou seest
From what highth fall'n, so much the stronger prov'd
He with his Thunder: and till then who knew

68. *Urges* has its Latin force of "push" or "drive."

72. *Utter,* "outer," not "absolute."

74. *Centre* was regularly used to mean the earth, as in line 686. The
cosmic proportions here vaguely recall the *Aeneid* (VI, 577–9), but
the *utmost pole* is a part of Milton's conception of the created universe
as encased in a shell with its nether pole sunk in Chaos and its upper
pole pointing toward the empyrean heaven.

81. Burton quotes Cornelius Agrippa as making Beëlzebub captain of
the first of the nine orders of demons (*Anatomy,* I, ii, 1, 2). Milton has
the support of Selden's *On the Syrian Gods* for ranking Beëlzebub next
to Satan. Selden explains his ridiculous title, god of flies, as due to the
swarms of insects by means of which the priests at his sacrifices professed
to divine the future. Beëlzebub is Satan's first confidant in his conspiracy
against God (V, 673).

93. Milton's story plunges "into the midst of things," but it immediately begins to orientate the reader by referring to its great events

The force of those dire Arms? yet not for those,
Nor what the Potent Victor in his rage   95
Can else inflict, do I repent or change,
Though chang'd in outward lustre; that fixt mind
And high disdain, from sense of injur'd merit,
That with the mightiest rais'd me to contend,
And to the fierce contention brought along   100
Innumerable force of Spirits arm'd
That durst dislike his reign, and me preferring,
His utmost power with adverse power oppos'd
In dubious Battle on the Plains of Heav'n,
And shook his throne.   What though the field be lost?   105
All is not lost; the unconquerable Will,
And study of revenge, immortal hate,
And courage never to submit or yield:
And what is else not to be overcome?
That Glory never shall his wrath or might   110
Extort from me.   To bow and sue for grace
With suppliant knee, and deify his power
Who from the terror of this Arm so late
Doubted his Empire, that were low indeed,
That were an ignominy and shame beneath   115
This downfall; since by Fate the strength of Gods
And this Empyreal substance cannot fail,
Since through experience of this great event
In Arms not worse, in foresight much advanc't,
We may with more successful hope resolve   120
To wage by force or guile eternal War

past and to come. Here the reference, backward in time, though forward in the narrative, is to the war in heaven which is the theme of
Book VI.

98. Milton contrasts the merit by which Satan is raised to his "bad
eminence" (II, 6) with the merit by which Messiah reigns (VI, 43) and
is "more than birthright Son of God." (III, 309.) The repeated stress
upon Satan's merit invests him with tragic quality.

107. *study* has its Latin force of "ardent quest" or "pursuit."

114. *Doubted,* feared for.

115. *ignominy,* perhaps pronounced "ignomy" in *P. L.* and often
spelled so by Milton's contemporaries.

116. In his reply to Abdiel (V, 860–3) Satan denies that the angels
were created by God and boasts that they will conquer in their own
strength, by "fatal course."

Irreconcilable, to our grand Foe,
Who now triúmphs, and in th' excess of joy
Sole reigning holds the Tyranny of Heav'n.
   So spake th' Apostate Angel, though in pain,   125
Vaunting aloud, but rackt with deep despair:
And him thus answer'd soon his bold Compeer.
   O Prince, O Chief of many Throned Powers,
That led th' imbattl'd Seraphim to War
Under thy conduct, and in dreadful deeds   130
Fearless, endanger'd Heav'n's perpetual King;
And put to proof his high Supremacy,
Whether upheld by strength, or Chance, or Fate,
Too well I see and rue the dire event,
That with sad overthrow and foul defeat   135
Hath lost us Heav'n, and all this mighty Host
In horrible destruction laid thus low,
As far as Gods and Heav'nly Essences
Can perish: for the mind and spirit remains
Invincible, and vigor soon returns,   140
Though all our Glory extinct, and happy state
Here swallow'd up in endless misery.
But what if he our Conqueror, (whom I now
Of force believe Almighty, since no less
Than such could have o'erpow'rd such force as ours)   145
Have left us this our spirit and strength entire
Strongly to suffer and support our pains,
That we may so suffice his vengeful ire,
Or do him mightier service as his thralls
By right of War, whate'er his business be   150
Here in the heart of Hell to work in Fire,

---

129. *Seraphim,* the Hebrew plural of *seraph.*

138. *Essences* is hardly a technical word, but it represents the mysteriously substantial bodies of the spirits which Raphael is to explain to Adam. (V, 404-433, and VIII, 620-9.) Whether they were perishable was a question with Satan's less sanguine followers, Moloch and Belial. (II, 99 and 145-154.)

141. *extinct* and *swallow'd* perhaps represent an absolute construction, but their force is felt by understanding *be* with both of them.

148. Milton makes Beëlzebub state the belief to which he subscribed himself in *C. D.* (I, ix), where he describes the bad angels as "sometimes permitted to wander throughout the whole earth, the air, and heaven itself, to execute the judgments of God."

Or do his Errands in the gloomy Deep;
What can it then avail though yet we feel
Strength undiminisht, or eternal being
To undergo eternal punishment?   155
Whereto with speedy words th' Arch-fiend repli'd.
    Fall'n Cherub, to be weak is miserable
Doing or Suffering: but of this be sure,
To do aught good never will be our task,
But ever to do ill our sole delight,   160
As being the contrary to his high will
Whom we resist. If then his Providence
Out of our evil seek to bring forth good,
Our labour must be to pervert that end,
And out of good still to find means of evil;   165
Which oft-times may succeed, so as perhaps
Shall grieve him, if I fail not, and disturb
His inmost counsels from thir destin'd aim.
But see the angry Victor hath recall'd
His Ministers of vengeance and pursuit   170
Back to the Gates of Heav'n: the Sulphurous Hail
Shot after us in storm, o'erblown hath laid
The fiery Surge, that from the Precipice
Of Heav'n receiv'd us falling, and the Thunder,
Wing'd with red Lightning and impetuous rage,   175
Perhaps hath spent his shafts, and ceases now
To bellow through the vast and boundless Deep.
Let us not slip th' occasion, whether scorn,
Or satiate fury yield it from our Foe.
Seest thou yon dreary Plain, forlorn and wild,   180
The seat of desolation, void of light,
Save what the glimmering of these livid flames
Casts pale and dreadful?   Thither let us tend
From off the tossing of these fiery waves,

---

158. *Doing or Suffering,* whether active or passive. Compare II, 199.

162. The "justification" of the ways of God to men rests upon this
challenge to "his providence" and the reply which events make to it
when Adam finally perceives the

> "Goodness immense!
> That all this good of evil shall produce,
> And evil turn to good," (XII, 469–471)

and hesitates whether to regret his sin or congratulate himself upon it.

There rest, if any rest can harbour there,   185
And reassembling our afflicted Powers,
Consult how we may henceforth most offend
Our Enemy, our own loss how repair,
How overcome this dire Calamity,
What reinforcement we may gain from Hope,   190
If not what resolution from despair.
  Thus Satan talking to his nearest Mate   *Description of*
With Head up-lift above the wave, and Eyes   *Satan*
That sparkling blaz'd, his other Parts besides
Prone on the Flood, extended long and large   195
Lay floating many a rood, in bulk as huge
As whom the Fables name of monstrous size,
Titanian, or *Earth-born,* that warr'd on *Jove,*
Briareos or *Typhon,* whom the Den
By ancient *Tarsus* held, or that Sea-beast   200
Leviathan, which God of all his works
Created hugest that swim th' Ocean stream:
Whale

186. *afflicted* has its Latin force of "stricken" or "cast down." *Powers,* armies.

197. *As whom,* like those described in the fables, as Milton disparagingly calls the myths of the Titans, who are here represented by the Cilician Typhon (not the Egyptian Typhon of *Nat. Ode,* 226), whom the giant Briareos helped Zeus to subdue. Both Titans and Giants were earth-born and were confused in the later accounts of the attack upon the Olympian gods. Milton's interest in the myth as well as his contempt for it may have sprung from his sympathy with the theory, by which Sir Walter Raleigh was influenced in his *History of the World* (I, vi, 8), that the gentile myths were perversions but also corroborations of the Mosaic records.

201. Of all the biblical allusions to the mysterious sea-monster, Leviathan, Milton is likeliest to have been thinking of Isaiah's prophecy that the Lord "shall punish leviathan, the piercing serpent, even leviathan, that crooked serpent; and he shall slay the dragon that is in the sea." (xxvii, 1.) The benighted mariners who mistake the creature for an island are found in the tale of Sindbad the Sailor, in "Rabba bar bar Hana's Legends" in the *Talmud,* and in the *Voyage of St. Brandan.* But the allusion to the Norwegian coast suggests that Milton had in mind an almost contemporary version of the story by Olaus Magnus (*Historia de gentibus septentrionibus,* Rome, 1555). Medieval bestiaries are sometimes mentioned as a part of the background and it is important to note that some of them (*e. g.,* the thirteenth century bestiary in Richard Morris's *An Old English Miscellany,* E. E. T. S., 1872) make the treacherous whale a type of Satan.

Him haply slumb'ring on the *Norway* foam
The Pilot of some small night-founder'd Skiff,
Deeming some Island, oft, as Seamen tell,   205
With fixed Anchor in his scaly rind
Moors by his side under the Lee, while Night
Invests the Sea, and wished Morn delays:
So stretcht out huge in length the Arch-fiend lay
Chain'd on the burning Lake, nor ever thence   210
Had ris'n or heav'd his head, but that the will
And high permission of all-ruling Heaven
Left him at large to his own dark designs,
That with reiterated crimes he might
Heap on himself damnation, while he sought   215
Evil to others, and enrag'd might see
How all his malice serv'd but to bring forth
Infinite goodness, grace and mercy shown
On Man by him seduc't, but on himself
Treble confusion, wrath and vengeance pour'd.   220
Forthwith upright he rears from off the Pool
His mighty Stature; on each hand the flames
Driv'n backward slope their pointing spires, and roll'd
In billows, leave i' th' midst a horrid Vale.
Then with expanded wings he steers his flight   225
Aloft, incumbent on the dusky Air
That felt unusual weight, till on dry Land
He lights, if it were Land that ever burn'd
With solid, as the Lake with liquid fire;
And such appear'd in hue, as when the force   230
Of subterranean wind transports a Hill
Torn from *Pelorus,* or the shatter'd side
Of thund'ring *Ætna,* whose combustible
And fuell'd entrails thence conceiving Fire,

---

230. *as when.* Compare *As whom,* with which Milton introduces the
simile in line 197. His theory here recalls Burton's surmise that the
earth "may be full of wind, or a sulphureous, innate fire, as our
Meteorologists inform us, which, sometimes breaking out, causeth those
horrible Earth-quakes, which are so frequent in these days." (*Anatomy,*
II, ii, 3.)   The allusion to Mt. Aetna and to its northern neighbour, the
promontory Pelorus, may be a reminiscence of Virgil's picture of the
volcano lifting globes of fire, torn from its vitals, to the stars. (*Aen.*
III, 570–7.)

Sublim'd with Mineral fury, aid the Winds,   235
And leave a singed bottom all involv'd
With stench and smoke: Such resting found the sole
Of unblest feet. Him follow'd his next Mate,
Both glorying to have scap't the *Stygian* flood
As Gods, and by thir own recover'd strength,   240
Not by the sufferance of supernal Power.
   Is this the Region, this the Soil, the Clime,
Said then the lost Arch-Angel, this the seat
That we must change for Heav'n, this mournful gloom
For that celestial light? Be it so, since hee   245
Who now is Sovran can dispose and bid
What shall be right: fardest from him is best
Whom reason hath equall'd, force hath made supreme
Above his equals. Farewell happy Fields
Where Joy for ever dwells: Hail horrors, hail   250
Infernal world, and thou profoundest Hell
Receive thy new Possessor: One who brings
A mind not to be chang'd by Place or Time.
The mind is its own place, and in itself
Can make a Heav'n of Hell, a Hell of Heav'n.   255

---

235. *Sublim'd* is a term of alchemy, meaning purified by perfect in-
candescence, and *Mineral fury* has its alchemical connotation of "virtue,"
i. e., power or energy.

239. The river Styx, which flowed around the classical Tartarus, fur-
nishes the name for the lake of liquid fire.

242. *Clime.* The word was not yet "poetical" and kept its geographical connotation. Here it means a region. Originally it meant
any zone bounded by parallels of latitude on one of which the day is
half an hour longer than it is on the other.

246. *Sovran* is the Italianized *sovereign.* Compare I, 753; II, 244; *etc.*

255. Satan's boast is an echo of an idea dear to men of every character in Milton's time. The German mystic, Boehme, held that because
"we are of God's substance, we have heaven and hell in ourselves" (*The
Three-fold Life of Man,* xiv, 72) and Marlowe made Mephistopheles say:

> Hell hath no limits, nor is circumscribed
> In any one self place; for where we are is hell,
> And where hell is, must we ever be.
>   (*Doctor Faustus,* ll. 553–5.)

The doctrine shaded off into the Stoic belief which Montaigne found in
Seneca (*De Consolatione,* xix) and Cicero (*Tusculans,* V, xlvi): "That
the Savour of Goods and Ills depends in large part on the Idea that we
have of them." Compare IV, 20 and 75.

What matter where, if I be still the same,
And what I should be, all but less than hee
Whom Thunder hath made greater?   Here at least
We shall be free; th' Almighty hath not built
Here for his envy, will not drive us hence: 260
Here we may reign secure, and in my choice
To reign is worth ambition though in Hell:
Better to reign in Hell, than serve in Heav'n.
But wherefore let we then our faithful friends,
Th' associates and copartners of our loss   265
Lie thus astonisht on th' oblivious Pool,
And call them not to share with us their part
In this unhappy Mansion, or once more
With rallied Arms to try what may be yet
Regain'd in Heav'n, or what more lost in Hell?   270
    So *Satan* spake, and him *Beëlzebub*
Thus answer'd. Leader of those Armies bright,
Which but th' Omnipotent none could have foiled,
If once they hear that voice, thir liveliest pledge
Of hope in fears and dangers, heard so oft   275
In worst extremes, and on the perilous edge
Of battle when it rag'd, in all assaults
Thir surest signal, they will soon resume
New courage and revive, though now they lie
Groveling and prostrate on yon Lake of Fire,   280
As we erewhile, astounded and amaz'd,
No wonder, fall'n such a pernicious highth.
    He scarce had ceas't when the superior Fiend
Was moving toward the shore; his ponderous shield
Ethereal temper, massy, large and round,   285

---

263. Abdiel's warning to Satan in heaven that his rebellious reign in
hell will be mere bondage (VI, 178–188), is the dramatic foil to this
line. Both passages rest upon a tradition which Phineas Fletcher
epigrammatizes in *The Apollyonists:*

> O let him serve in hell,
> Who scornes in heaven to raigne. (I, 18, 9.)

266. *oblivious,* oblivion-giving.
276. *edge,* front line in the battle.
282. *pernicious* is used with its etymological force of "death-giving."
285. By *ethereal temper* Milton implies the subtle substance of the

Behind him cast; the broad circumference
Hung on his shoulders like the Moon, whose Orb
Through Optic Glass the *Tuscan* Artist views   > Gallileo
At Ev'ning from the top of *Fesole,*
Or in *Valdarno,* to descry new Lands,   290
Rivers or Mountains in her spotty Globe.
His Spear, to equal which the tallest Pine
Hewn on *Norwegian* hills, to be the Mast
Of some great Ammiral, were but a wand,
He walkt with to support uneasy steps   295
Over the burning Marl, not like those steps
On Heaven's Azure, and the torrid Clime
Smote on him sore besides, vaulted with Fire;
Nathless he so endur'd, till on the Beach
Of that inflamed Sea, he stood and call'd   300
His Legions, Angel Forms, who lay intrans't
Thick as Autumnal Leaves that strow the Brooks
In *Vallombrosa,* where th' *Etrurian* shades
High overarch't imbow'r; or scatter'd sedge
Afloat, when with fierce Winds *Orion* arm'd   305
Hath vext the Red-Sea Coast, whose waves o'erthrew
Busiris and his *Memphian* Chivalry,
While with perfidious hatred they pursu'd
The Sojourners of *Goshen,* who beheld
From the safe shore thir floating Carcasses   310

---

moon-broad shield. Compare the notes on II, 139 and 275, III, 716, and VII, 63.

The simile allows him to recall his visit in Florence when Galileo, the "Tuscan artist," was living on the neighbouring heights of Fiesole, overlooking the valley of the Arno, Milton's Valdarno.

290. Perhaps Milton thought of Galileo's most influential book, the *Sidereus Nuncius,* which favoured the Pythagorean view of the moon as a world with Seas appearing dark and continents bright.

294. *Ammiral,* admiral ship. The spelling, archaic in Milton's day, indicates his preference in sound.

303. The lines are haunted with memories of Milton's autumn excursion from Florence to Vallombrosa in 1638, but the vision fuses with recollections of travellers' tales of the wrack of seaweed in the Red Sea when the constellation Orion, rising like a giant with club and sword, brings seasonal storms. That in turn becomes a symbol of the overwhelming in those waters of the Egyptian cavalry of Busiris, whom Milton incorrectly names as the Pharaoh who persecuted the Hebrew "sojourners of Goshen."

And broken Chariot Wheels, so thick bestrown
Abject and lost lay these, covering the Flood,
Under amazement of thir hideous change.
He call'd so loud, that all the hollow Deep
Of Hell resounded.   Princes, Potentates,   315
Warriors, the Flow'r of Heav'n, once yours, now lost,
If such astonishment as this can seize
Eternal spirits; or have ye chos'n this place
After the toil of Battle to repose
Your wearied virtue, for the ease you find   ·   320
To slumber here, as in the Vales of Heav'n?
Or in this abject posture have ye sworn
To adore the Conqueror? who now beholds
Cherub and Seraph rolling in the Flood
With scatter'd Arms and Ensigns, till anon   325
His swift pursuers from Heav'n Gates discern
Th' advantage, and descending tread us down
Thus drooping, or with linked Thunderbolts
Transfix us to the bottom of this Gulf.
Awake, arise, or be for ever fall'n.   330
    They heard, and were abasht, and up they sprung
Upon the wing, as when men wont to watch
On duty, sleeping found by whom they dread,
Rouse and bestir themselves ere well awake.
Nor did they not perceive the evil plight   335
In which they were, or the fierce pains not feel;
Yet to thir General's Voice they soon obey'd
Innumerable.   As when the potent Rod
Of *Amram's* Son in *Egypt's* evil day

---

314. Satan's summons to council and his opening words, as well as
many of his ideas here and in his speeches in Pandæmonium later,
vaguely resemble similar features in the infernal council which Vida, in
his Latin epic on the life of Christ, the *Christiad* (Book I, 167–92),
represented Satan as calling to plot against the Saviour when he is on
his way to Jerusalem before the Crucifixion.   Only fugitive verbal resemblances occur, but it is worth observing that Milton's infernal council
had its counterparts in Tasso's *Jerusalem Delivered* (Book IV; compare
the note on IX, 149) and in many other Renaissance and classical poems,
ranging back to Claudian's *Rape of Proserpina* and *Against Rufinus*.

339.   Amram was Moses' father.   The plague of locusts, described in
Exodus (x, 12–15), covered "the face of the whole earth, so that the
land was darkened."

Wav'd round the Coast, up call'd a pitchy cloud   340
Of *Locusts,* warping on the Eastern Wind,
That o'er the Realm of impious *Pharaoh* hung
Like Night, and darken'd all the Land of *Nile:*
So numberless were those bad Angels seen
Hovering on wing under the Cope of Hell   345
'Twixt upper, nether, and surrounding Fires;
Till, as a signal giv'n, th' uplifted Spear
Of thir great Sultan waving to direct
Thir course, in even balance down they light
On the firm brimstone, and fill all the Plain;   350
A multitude, like which the populous North
Pour'd never from her frozen loins, to pass
Rhene or the *Danaw,* when her barbarous Sons
Came like a Deluge on the South, and spread
Beneath *Gibraltar* to the *Lybian* sands.   355
Forthwith from every Squadron and each Band
The Heads and Leaders thither haste where stood
Thir great Commander; Godlike shapes and forms
Excelling human, Princely Dignities,
And Powers that erst in Heaven sat on Thrones;   360
Though of thir Names in heav'nly Records now
Be no memorial, blotted out and ras'd
By thir Rebellion, from the Books of Life.
Nor had they yet among the Sons of *Eve*
Got them new Names, till wand'ring o'er the Earth,   365
Through God's high sufferance for the trial of man,
By falsities and lies the greatest part
Of Mankind they corrupted to forsake

---

353. *Rhene or the Danaw,* the current seventeenth-century spellings of
"Rhine" and "Danube." The comparison of the devils to the barbarian
hordes which flooded the Roman world carries the panorama from the
Gothic migrations across the Danube to the Vandal raids in north Africa,
Libya.

361. This and the following lines prepare for the catalogue of the
demons under the names of pagan divinities. It is to be a list of
princes, for Milton, like Burton, knew that "Our School-men and other
Divines make nine kinds of bad spirits, as Dionysius hath done of
Angels. In the first rank are those false gods of the Gentiles, which
were adored heretofore in several Idols." (*Anatomy,* I, ii, 1, 2.) Milton thought of the demons as having had angelic names which were
erased from the Book of Life and forgotten when they were banished.

God thir Creator, and th' invisible
Glory of him, that made them, to transform   370
Oft to the Image of a Brute, adorn'd
With gay Religions full of Pomp and Gold,
And Devils to adore for Deities:
Then were they known to men by various Names,
And various Idols through the Heathen World.   375
Say, Muse, thir Names then known, who first, who last,
Rous'd from the slumber, on that fiery Couch,
At thir great Emperor's call, as next in worth
Came singly where he stood on the bare strand,
While the promiscuous crowd stood yet aloof?   380
The chief were those who from the Pit of Hell
Roaming to seek thir prey on earth, durst fix
Thir Seats long after next the Seat of God,
Thir Altars by his Altar, Gods ador'd
Among the Nations round, and durst abide   385
Jehovah thund'ring out of *Sion,* thron'd
Between the Cherubim; yea, often plac'd
Within his Sanctuary itself thir Shrines,
Abominations; and with cursed things
His holy Rites, and solemn Feasts profan'd,   390
And with thir darkness durst affront his light.
First *Moloch,* horrid King besmear'd with blood
Of human sacrifice, and parents' tears,
Though for the noise of Drums and Timbrels loud
Thir children's cries unheard, that past through fire   395
To his grim Idol.   Him the *Ammonite*

---

376. The roll of the demons which begins here may be compared with
Homer's Catalogue of the Greek ships at Troy.   (*Il.,* II.)

387. To understand Milton's mood we must be familiar with such invocations in the Psalms as the appeal to the "Shepherd of Israel, . . .
thou that dwellest between the Cherubim" (lxxx, 1), and also with the
indignant account in II Kings (xvi, 10–18) of the pagan altar built in
Jerusalem by the apostate king, Ahaz.

392. Moloch's almost fixed epithet, "king," is Milton's reminder of
the meaning of the name. The allusion in the *Nat. Ode* (208–210) to
the clang of cymbals when children are sacrificed to the grisly king
parallels George Sandys's statement in *A Relation of a Journey begun in
An. Dom. 1610* that lest "their lamentable shreeks should sad the hearts
of their parents, the Priests of Molech did deafe their eares with the
continual clang of trumpets and timbrels."   (Ed. of 1637, p. 186.)

Worshipt in *Rabba* and her wat'ry Plain,
in *Argob* and in *Basan,* to the stream
Of utmost *Arnon.* Nor content with such
Audacious neighbourhood, the wisest heart   400
Of *Solomon* he led by fraud to build
His Temple right against the Temple of God
On that opprobrious Hill, and made his Grove
The pleasant Valley of *Hinnom, Tophet* thence
And black *Gehenna* call'd, the Type of Hell.   405
Next *Chemos,* th' obscene dread of *Moab's* Sons,
From *Aroar* to *Nebo,* and the wild
Of Southmost *Abarim;* in *Hesebon*
And *Horonaim, Seon's* Realm, beyond

---

397. Rabba, the Ammonite capital, was conquered by David's army. (II Sam. xii, 27.)

398. Argob and Basan were districts lying toward the Moabite border stream, Arnon. The names recalled the triumphs of the Israelites over the gigantic Ammonites. (Deut. iii, 12 ff.) Like Shakespeare, Milton preferred the unaspirated form *Basan* to *Bashan,* the form in the King James Bible. Compare *Hesebon* (408 below) for *Heshbon,* and *Sittim* (413 below) for *Shittim.*

401. Beguiled by his wives, Solomon built "an high place for Chemosh, the abomination of Moab, in the hill that is before Jerusalem, and for Molech, the abomination of Ammon." (I Kings xi, 7.) The allusion is repeated below (442–5).

403. *that opprobrious Hill*—the Mount of Olives. Compare 416 and 443 below, where Milton again recollects that it was called the "mount of offence" (II Kings xxiii, 13), in memory of Solomon's pagan shrines.

404. Jeremiah (xix, 5) describes the Israelites as burning their "sons with fire for burnt offerings unto Baal" in the valley of Hinnom. In Greek the name became Gehenna. The valley, especially the part called Tophet, where the rubbish of Jerusalem accumulated, was placed under a kind of formal curse by the reforming king, Josiah (II Kings xxiii, 10) and so became "a type of hell."

406. Milton rightly identifies Chemos with Baal-Peor, the deity whose worship Moses punished atrociously in Shittim. (Num. xxv.)

407. From Aroar, a town near the Arnon, Milton looks north across Moab to Mt. Nebo, the southern peak of the Abarim range, and east to the Asphaltic Pool, *i. e.,* the Dead Sea, and to the neighbouring height, Eliale.

409. Sihon, king of the Amorites, figures in the Psalms (cxxxv, 11, and cxxxvi, 19) among the greatest of Israel's vanquished foes. The destruction of his city, Heshbon, is sung in a chant of triumph in Numbers (xxi, 25), and (Isaiah xv, 5) prophesied that "in the way of Horonaim

The flow'ry Dale of *Sibma* clad with Vines,   410
And *Eleale* to th' *Asphaltic* Pool.
Peor his other Name, when he entic'd
Israel in *Sittim* on thir march from *Nile*
To do him wanton rites, which cost them woe.
Yet thence his lustful Orgies he enlarg'd   415
Even to that Hill of scandal, by the Grove
Of *Moloch* homicide, lust hard by hate;
Till good *Josiah* drove them thence to Hell.
With these came they, who from the bord'ring flood
Of old *Euphrates* to the Brook that parts   420
Egypt from *Syrian* ground, had general Names
Of *Baalim* and *Ashtaroth,* those male,
These Feminine.   For Spirits when they please
Can either Sex assume, or both; so soft
And uncompounded is thir Essence pure,   425
Not ti'd or manacl'd with joint or limb,
Nor founded on the brittle strength of bones,
Like cumbrous flesh; but in what shape they choose
Dilated or condens't, bright or obscure,
Can execute their aery purposes,   430
And works of love or enmity fulfil.
For those the Race of *Israel* oft forsook
Thir living strength, and unfrequented left
His righteous Altar, bowing lowly down
To bestial Gods; for which thir heads as low   435

they shall raise up a cry of destruction." Every name in Milton's list
connoted the defeat of some gentile deity by Jehovah.

417. See the note on 404 above.

420. The Euphrates bounded Palestine to the east and in David's time
the "brook Besor" (I Sam. xxx, 10) was its Egyptian frontier.

422. *Baalim and Ashtaroth*—plural forms. The local cults of the
supreme Phoenecian deity produced many Baals beside Baal-Peor; *e. g.,*
Baal-zephor, lord of the north or of darkness, and Baal-hermon, lord
of Mt. Hermon. With *Ashtaroth* compare the singular form in 438
below.

423. The power of the devils to metamorphose themselves, so important throughout *P. L.,* was inherited from Christian and Hebrew
theology and folk-lore and got indirect support from Neo-Platonic tradition. The Cambridge Platonist, Henry More, believed that the variety
of the devils' "impurities may dispose them to turn themselves into one
brutish shape rather than another; as envying or admiring . . . the condition and properties of such and such beasts."

Bow'd down in Battle, sunk before the Spear
Of despicable foes. With these in troop
Came *Astoreth*, whom the *Phœnicians* call'd
Astarte, Queen of Heav'n, with crescent Horns;
To whose bright Image nightly by the Moon   440
Sidonian Virgins paid thir Vows and Songs,
In *Sion* also not unsung, where stood
Her Temple on th' offensive Mountain, built
By that uxorious King, whose heart though large,
Beguil'd by fair Idolatresses, fell   445
To Idols foul.   *Thammuz* came next behind,
Whose annual wound in *Lebanon* allur'd
The *Syrian* Damsels to lament his fate
In amorous ditties all a Summer's day,
While smooth *Adonis* from his native Rock   450
Ran purple to the Sea, suppos'd with blood
Of *Thammuz* yearly wounded: the Love-tale
Infected *Sion's* daughters with like heat,
Whose wanton passions in the sacred Porch
Ezekiel saw, when by the Vision led   455
His eye survey'd the dark Idolatries
Of alienated *Judah*.   Next came one
Who mourn'd in earnest, when the Captive Ark
Maim'd his brute Image, head and hands lopt off
In his own Temple, on the grunsel edge,   460

438. *Astarte*, the Phoenecian Venus, appears as "mooned Ashtaroth,
Heaven's queen" in *Nat. Ode* (l. 200), and as the "Assyrian queen" in
Comus (l. 1002).

444. Solomon's uxoriousness led him to build a temple to Ashtaroth
on the Mount of Olives.

446. The myth of Thammuz, the Greek Adonis, in which the coming
of autumn was symbolized by the god's death, led to the ritual mourning which Milton first mentioned in *Nat. Ode* (l. 204):

    In vain the Tyrian Maids their wounded Thamuz mourn.

Ezekiel (viii, 14) was shocked to find the women of Jerusalem sitting,
"weeping for Tammuz."   The river Adonis rises in Lebanon.

458. The grim humour of *in earnest*, in contrast with the superstitious
mourning for Thammuz, recalls Milton's youthful project for dramatiz-
ing the fall of Dagon's statue when the stolen ark of God was stored in
his temple.   Later he was to revert to his purpose in *S. A.*, where
Samson triumphs tragically over Dagon, the "sea-idol."

460. The head and hands of the statue broke on the threshold—
Milton's *grunsel-edge*, and "therefore neither the priests of Dagon, nor

Where he fell flat, and sham'd his Worshippers:
Dagon his Name, Sea Monster, upward Man
And downward Fish: yet had his Temple high
Rear'd in *Azotus,* dreaded through the Coast
Of *Palestine,* in *Gath* and *Ascalon,* 465
And *Accaron* and *Gaza's* frontier bounds.
Him follow'd *Rimmon,* whose delightful Seat
Was fair *Damascus,* on the fertile Banks
Of *Abbana* and *Pharphar,* lucid streams.
He also against the house of God was bold: 470
A Leper once he lost and gain'd a King,
Ahaz his sottish Conqueror, whom he drew
God's Altar to disparage and displace
For one of *Syrian* mode, whereon to burn
His odious off'rings, and adore the Gods 475
Whom he had vanquisht.   After these appear'd
A crew who under Names of old Renown,
Osiris, Isis, Orus and their Train
With monstrous shapes and sorceries abus'd
Fanatic *Egypt* and her Priests, to seek 480
Thir wand'ring Gods disguis'd in brutish forms
Rather than human.   Nor did *Israel* scape
Th' infection when thir borrow'd Gold compos'd
The Calf in *Oreb:* and the Rebel King

---

any that come into Dagon's house, tread on the threshold of Dagon in Ashdod unto this day." (I Sam. v, 5.)

464. *Azotus* was the Greek form of *Ashdod,* the name of a Philistine stronghold. The other four names represent Philistine cities.

468. The reference to the curing of the leprous Syrian general, Naaman, by the water of Jordan (II Kings v) gains interest beside Cudworth's words in his Sermon before the Commons: "The Gospel is not like Abana and Pharphar, those common rivers of Damascus, that could only cleanse the outside; but it is a true Jordan." (p. 31.)

478. In *Nat. Ode* (211–5) the animal gods of Egypt retreat to oblivion.

482. The reference is to Aaron's forging a golden calf (Exod. xxxii, 4), which Milton regarded as an idol of the Egyptian bull god, Apis.

484. The rebel king, Jereboam, who led the Ten Tribes in their secession from the kingdom founded by David, erected two golden calves. Milton shares the resentment of the biblical record against him for the proclamation, "Behold thy gods, O Israel, which brought thee up out of the land of Egypt." (I Kings xii, 28.) In contrast, he recalls the miraculous slaying of the first-born children and cattle, in-

Doubl'd that sin in *Bethel* and in *Dan*,   485
Lik'ning his Maker to the Grazed Ox,
Jehovah, who in one Night when he pass'd
From *Egypt* marching, equall'd with one stroke
Both her first born and all her bleating Gods.
Belial came last, than whom a Spirit more lewd   490
Fell not from Heaven, or more gross to love
Vice for itself: To him no Temple stood
Or Altar smok'd; yet who more oft than hee
In Temples and at Altars, when the Priest
Turns Atheist, as did *Ely's* Sons, who fill'd   495
With lust and violence the house of God.
In Courts and Palaces he also Reigns
And in luxurious Cities, where the noise
Of riot ascends above thir loftiest Tow'rs,
And injury and outrage: And when Night   500
Darkens the Streets, then wander forth the Sons
Of *Belial*, flown with insolence and wine.
Witness the Streets of *Sodom*, and that night
In *Gibeah*, when the hospitable door
Expos'd a Matron to avoid worse rape.   505
These were the prime in order and in might;
The rest were long to tell, though far renown'd,
Th' *Ionian* Gods, of *Javan's* Issue held
Gods, yet confest later than Heav'n and Earth

---

cluding the sacred animals or "bleating gods," on the eve of the flight
of the Israelites. (Exod. xii, 12.)

490. Belial, whose name originally was an abstract noun meaning
"worthlessness," is made prince of the third order of angels, the "vessels
of anger and inventors of all mischief" by Burton. (*Anatomy* I, ii, 1,
2.)

495. The story is told in I Sam. ii, 12–27.

501. *Sons of Belial* was a common Biblical jibe among the Puritans
against Charles II's courtiers and Milton may have intended an indictment of them when he referred to the ugly stories in Genesis xix, 4–11,
and in Judges xix, 22–28.

508. Javan, son of Japhet (Gen. x, 2) was regarded as the ancestor
of the Greeks, or Ionians.

509. Greek tradition made heaven and earth the parents of the first
deities, the Titans; but Milton accepted the euhemeristic theory that all
the ancient divinities were men whom popular superstition had deified.
The devils were supposed to have exploited such superstition to usurp
the worship due to God.

Thir boasted Parents; *Titan* Heav'n's first born   510
With his enormous brood, and birthright seiz'd
By younger *Saturn,* he from mightier *Jove,*
His own and *Rhea's* Son, like measure found;
So *Jove* usurping reign'd: these first in *Crete*
And *Ida* known, thence on the Snowy top   515
Of cold *Olympus* rul'd the middle Air
Thir highest Heav'n; or on the *Delphian* Cliff,
Or in *Dodona,* and through all the bounds
Of *Doric* Land; or who with *Saturn* old
Fled over *Adria* to th' *Hesperian* Fields,   520
And o'er the *Celtic* roam'd the utmost Isles.
All these and more came flocking; but with looks
Downcast and damp, yet such wherein appear'd
Obscure some glimpse of joy, to have found thir chief
Not in despair, to have found themselves not lost   525
In loss itself; which on his count'nance cast
Like doubtful hue: but he his wonted pride
Soon recollecting, with high words, that bore
Semblance of worth, not substance, gently rais'd
Thir fainting courage, and dispell'd thir fears.   530
Then straight commands that at the warlike sound
Of Trumpets loud and Clarions be uprear'd
His mighty Standard; that proud honour claim'd
Azazel as his right, a Cherub tall:

---

512. Saturn supplanted his older brother, Titan, and was in turn supplanted by his son, Zeus, who was identified with Jove.

514. Milton surveys the spread of the cult of the Olympian gods from
Mt. Ida in Crete to the Delphian oracle on Mt. Parnassus and to Dodona
and Olympus in the north. Finally the panorama includes the Dorian
territory, Greece south of the Isthmus of Corinth.

516. Milton shared the common view of the air as divided into three
regions and accepted Burton's theory that the "Spirits, which are Princes
of the Air," cause meteors and all other aerial portents. (*Anatomy* II, ii.
3.)   Hence perhaps the origin of the simile in 537 below.   Compare III,
562.

520. With the spread of Greek culture across the Adriatic the gods of
Hesperia, Italy, and of the *Celtic fields,* France, were identified with
those of Greece.

534. In Book III of *The Cabbalistic Art* of the German humanist,
Reuchlin, Azazel appears as one of four standard bearers commanding
the demons; and in the book *On Magic* (III, xxiv) of the alchemist,
Cornelius Agrippa, he is recognized as lord of the element of earth. Now

Who forthwith from the glittering Staff unfurl'd   535
Th' Imperial Ensign, which full high advanc't
Shone like a Meteor streaming to the Wind
With Gems and Golden lustre rich imblaz'd,
Seraphic arms and Trophies: all the while
Sonorous metal blowing Martial sounds: 540
At which the universal Host upsent
A shout that tore Hell's Concave, and beyond
Frighted the Reign of *Chaos* and old Night.
All in a moment through the gloom were seen
Ten thousand Banners rise into the Air   545
With Orient Colours waving: with them rose
A Forest huge of Spears: and thronging Helms
Appear'd, and serried Shields in thick array
Of depth immeasurable: Anon they move
In perfect *Phalanx* to the *Dorian* mood   550
Of Flutes and soft Recorders; such as rais'd
To highth of noblest temper Heroes old
Arming to Battle, and instead of rage
Deliberate valour breath'd, firm and unmov'd
With dread of death to flight or foul retreat,   555
Nor wanting power to mitigate and swage
With solemn touches, troubl'd thoughts, and chase
Anguish and doubt and fear and sorrow and pain
From mortal or immortal minds. Thus they
Breathing united force with fixed thought   560
Mov'd on in silence to soft Pipes that charm'd
Thir painful steps o'er the burnt soil; and now
Advanc't in view they stand, a horrid Front
Of dreadful length and dazzling Arms, in guise
Of Warriors old with order'd Spear and Shield,   565
Awaiting what command thir mighty Chief
Had to impose: He through the armed Files

---

that the demons are assembled on dry land he perhaps asserts his right to
bear the standard. The name Azazel first appears in Leviticus, xvi, 8.

543. Milton is looking forward to the account of Chaos in II, 890–
1009.

550. In the background is Plato's teaching in the *Republic* (Jowett's
Plato, III, 273–4) that the Dorian mode, in contrast with the Lydian, is
"the only one convenient for war-like and temperate men."

556. *swage*, assuage.

Darts his experienc't eye, and soon traverse
The whole Battalion views, thir order due,
Thir visages and stature as of Gods,   570
Thir number last he sums. And now his heart
Distends with pride, and hard'ning in his strength
Glories: For never since created man,
Met such imbodied force, as nam'd with these
Could merit more than that small infantry   575
Warr'd on by Cranes: though all the Giant brood
Of *Phlegra* with th' Heroic Race were join'd
That fought at *Thebes* and *Ilium,* on each side
Mixt with auxiliar Gods; and what resounds
In Fable or *Romance* of *Uther's* Son   580
Begirt with *British* and *Armoric* Knights;
And all who since, Baptiz'd or Infidel
Jousted in *Aspramont* or *Montalban,*

---

573. *since created man,* since the creation of man.

575. The small infantry are "that pygmean race beyond the Indian mount" 780-1 below). Their tradition, stretching back to Pliny and Aristotle, was confirmed by works like Cunningham's *Cosmographical Glasse* (1559), which affirmed that, "Ther are also Pygmeans (men but a cubite in height) which riding on Goats and Rammes do kepe warre with Cranes." The maps show them in central Asia, east of the western Himalayan range, the "Indian mount." Milton alludes here to Homer's reference to migrating cranes as bearing death to the Pygmies. [*Il*. III, 1-5.]

577. *Phlegra,* the Macedonian promontory where the Giants fought with the Olympian gods. Compare note on 197 above.

578. *Thebes* and *Ilium, i.e.,* Troy, evoke the scenes of Aeschylus' tragedy of *The Seven against Thebes* and of the *Iliad,* in many of whose episodes the gods fight side by side with both Greeks and Trojans.

580. *Uther's son,* King Arthur, surrounded by his followers, both British and Armoric (*i. e.,* of Brittany or Lyones), the charm of whose legend for Milton is again confessed in a context of renunciation, in *P. R.,* II, 360.

583. The jousting of Christians with pagans, baptized with infidels, is a feature of the Italian and French romances and *chansons de geste* through which Milton's memory sweeps.

Aspramont, near Nice, furnished the title for an Italian romance, published in 1516, which recounts Charlemagne's repulse of a Saracen invasion led by the king of Carthage.

Montalban, or Montauban, was the castle of the Rinaldo of Pulci's *Il Morgante Maggiore* and of Boiardo's *Orlando Inammorato.*

Biserta, the Tunisian seaport, is the rendez-vous of a Saracen expedition against France in the *Orlando Inammorato.*

Damasco, or *Marocco,* or *Trebisond,*
Or whom *Biserta* sent from *Afric* shore   585
When *Charlemain* with all his Peerage fell
By *Fontarabbia.* Thus far these beyond
Compare of mortal prowess, yet observ'd
Thir dread commander: he above the rest
In shape and gesture proudly eminent   590
Stood like a Tow'r; his form had yet not lost
All her Original brightness, nor appear'd
Less then Arch Angel ruin'd, and th' excess
Of Glory obscur'd: As when the Sun new ris'n
Looks through the Horizontal misty Air   595
Shorn of his Beams, or from behind the Moon
In dim Eclipse disastrous twilight sheds
On half the Nations, and with fear of change
Perplexes Monarchs. Dark'n'd so, yet shone
Above them all th' Arch Angel: but his face   600
Deep scars of Thunder had intrencht, and care
Sat on his faded cheek, but under Brows
Of dauntless courage, and considerate Pride
Waiting revenge: cruel his eye, but cast
Signs of remorse and passion to behold   605
The fellows of his crime, the followers rather

---

584. In Ariosto's *Orlando Furioso* Damascus is the scene of a tournament between Christian and pagan champions (canto XVII). One of
his champions is a king of Morocco.
   In Trebizond, the Byzantine city on the south shore of the Black Sea
which was captured by the Turks in 1461, Milton perhaps alludes to the
most popular version of its saga, *Il Colloandro Fedele* (called *Il Colloandro sconosciuto* in the first edition—Part I at Bracciano, 1640, and
Part II at Bologna, 1641) of Giovanni Ambrogio Marini. The vogue of
Marini's fabulous champions is attested by countless editions in Italy and
by M. de Scudéry's French translation and La Calprenède's plagiarism in
Cléopâtre.

   587. *Fontarabbia,* though forty miles from Roncesvalles, the real scene
of the battle, refers to the death of Roland and the massacre of Charlemagne's rear-guard by the Saracens.

   598. Tradition says that it was on account of a fancied threat to Charles
II in the "fear of change" which perplexes monarchs that Tomkyns, the
licenser of the press, wished to forbid the appearance of *P. L.* In reality
Milton left it "to the astrologer to be dismayed at the portentous blaze
of comets, and impressions in the air, as foretelling . . . changes to states."
(*Of Reformation,* II. *P. W.* II, 400.)

   603. *considerate,* founded upon deliberate thought.

(Far other once beheld in bliss) condemn'd
For ever now to have thir lot in pain,
Millions of Spirits for his fault amerc't
Of Heav'n, and from Eternal Splendors flung   610
For his revolt, yet faithful how they stood,
Thir Glory wither'd. As when Heaven's Fire
Hath scath'd the Forest Oaks, or Mountain Pines,
With singed top thir stately growth though bare
Stands on the blasted Heath. He now prepar'd   615
To speak; whereat thir doubl'd Ranks they bend
From wing to wing, and half enclose him round
With all his Peers: attention held them mute.
Thrice he assay'd, and thrice in spite of scorn,
Tears such as Angels weep, burst forth: at last   620
Words interwove with sighs found out thir way.
   O Myriads of immortal Spirits, O Powers
Matchless, but with th' Almighty, and that strife
Was not inglorious, though th' event was dire,
As this place testifies, and this dire change   625
Hateful to utter: but what power of mind
Foreseeing or presaging, from the Depth
Of knowledge past or present, could have fear'd,
How such united force of Gods, how such
As stood like these, could ever know repulse?   630
For who can yet believe, though after loss,
That all these puissant Legions, whose exile
Hath emptied Heav'n, shall fail to re-ascend
Self-rais'd, and repossess thir native seat?
For mee, be witness all the Host of Heav'n,   635
If counsels different, or danger shunn'd
By mee, have lost our hopes. But he who reigns
Monarch in Heav'n, till then as one secure
Sat on his Throne, upheld by old repute,
Consent or custom, and his Regal State   640
Put forth at full, but still his strength conceal'd,
Which tempted our attempt, and wrought our fall.
Henceforth his might we know, and know our own

---

609. *amerc't,* a legal term meaning "to fine" or "punish."

642. *tempted our attempt.* Such plays upon words of like form and
contrasting force Milton makes into a kind of grim punning. The figure
is called paranomasia. Compare the note on IX, 648.

So as not either to provoke, or dread
New war, provok't; our better part remains   645
To work in close design, by fraud or guile
What force effected not: that he no less
At length from us may find, who overcomes
By force, hath overcome but half his foe.
Space may produce new Worlds; whereof so rife   650
There went a fame in Heav'n that he ere long
Intended to create, and therein plant
A generation, whom his choice regard
Should favour equal to the Sons of Heaven:
Thither, if but to pry, shall be perhaps   655
Our first eruption, thither or elsewhere:
For this Infernal Pit shall never hold
Celestial Spirits in Bondage, nor th' Abyss
Long under darkness cover. But these thoughts
Full Counsel must mature: Peace is despair'd,   660
For who can think Submission? War then, War
Open or understood, must be resolv'd.
    He spake: and to confirm his words, out-flew
Millions of flaming swords, drawn from the thighs
Of mighty Cherubim; the sudden blaze   665
Far round illumin'd hell: highly they rag'd
Against the Highest, and fierce with grasped Arms
Clash'd on thir sounding shields the din of war,
Hurling defiance toward the Vault of Heav'n.
    There stood a Hill not far whose grisly top   670
Belch'd fire and rolling smoke; the rest entire
Shone with a glossy scurf, undoubted sign
That in his womb was hid metallic Ore,
The work of Sulphur. Thither wing'd with speed
A numerous Brígad hasten'd. As when bands   675

---

646. *close,* secret.

651. *fame,* rumour. Compare II, 345–353, and 830–835, and X, 481.
Traditions disagree as to whether Satan's revolt occurred before or after
the creation of the world. Milton preferred the former view, for it permitted Satan's quest of the new universe through Chaos.

674. The passage rests upon the alchemical doctrine that "of Sulphur
and Mercury all Bodyes minerall are made." (*Pater Sapientiae,* cited by
N. E. D. under *sulphur.*)

675. *Brigad*—Milton's spelling corresponds with his pronunciation of
brigade.

Of Píoners with Spade and Pickax arm'd
Forerun the Royal Camp, to trench a Field,
Or cast a Rampart.   *Mammon* led them on,
Mammon, the least erected Spirit that fell
From heav'n, for ev'n in heav'n his looks and thoughts   68o
Were always downward bent, admiring more
The riches of Heav'n's pavement, trodd'n Gold,
Than aught divine or holy else enjoy'd
In vision beatific: by him first
Men also, and by his suggestion taught,   685
Ransack'd the Centre, and with impious hands
Rifl'd the bowels of thir mother Earth
For Treasures better hid.   Soon had his crew
Op'n'd into the Hill a spacious wound
And digg'd out ribs of Gold.   Let none admire   690
That riches grow in Hell; that soil may best
Deserve the precious bane.   And here let those
Who boast in mortal things, and wond'ring tell
Of *Babel,* and the works of *Memphian* Kings,
Learn how thir greatest Monuments of Fame,   695

------

678. Mammon's command of the artisan angels corresponds with the tradition that he was prince of the ninth and lowest order of demons, "those tempters in several kinds." (*Anatomy,* I, ii, 1, 2.) *Mammon* i: an Aramaic word meaning riches which enters the Bible first in Matthew vi, 24, and was misunderstood in the Middle Ages as the name of a devil.

684. The promise that the pure in heart shall see God (Matt. v, 8) was the basis of the medieval conception of the beatific vision which found its best expression in Dante's vision of heaven in the *Paradiso.*

686. Milton travels here in a way already worn when Chaucer translated Boethius in *The Former Age:*

> But cursed was the tyme, I dar wel seye,
> That men first dide hir swety bysinesse
> To grobbe up metal, lurkinge in derknesse,
> And in the riveres first gemmes soghte.

In *Comus* (732–5) the enchanter demurs.

692. *bane,* evil, curse. Milton is fond of the figure of speech, oxymoron, which paradoxically combines verbs or nouns with adverbs or adjectives that contrast with them, as *precious* does with *bane.*

694. Babel was the first city built in the kingdom of Nimrod (Genesis x, 10), where the famous tower rose. *Memphian* was a regular equivalent for *Egyptian,* but here there is a reminder of the great temples of Memphis.

And Strength and Art are easily outdone
By Spirits reprobate, and in an hour
What in an age they with incessant toil
And hands innumerable scarce perform.
Nigh on the Plain in many cells prepar'd,   700
That underneath had veins of liquid fire
Sluic'd from the Lake, a second multitude
With wondrous Art founded the massy Ore,
Severing each kind, and scumm'd the Bullion dross:
A third as soon had form'd within the ground   705
A various mould, and from the boiling cells
By strange conveyance fill'd each hollow nook,
As in an Organ from one blast of wind
To many a row of Pipes the sound-board breathes.
Anon out of the earth a Fabric huge   710
Rose like an Exhalation, with the sound
Of Dulcet Symphonies and voices sweet,
Built like a Temple, where *Pilasters* round
Were set, and Doric pillars overlaid
With Golden Architrave; nor did there want   715
Cornice or Frieze, with bossy Sculptures grav'n,
The Roof was fretted Gold. Not *Babylon,*
Nor great *Alcairo* such magnificence
Equall'd in all thir glories, to inshrine
Belus or *Serapis* thir Gods, or seat   720
Thir Kings, when *Egypt* with *Assyria* strove
In wealth and luxury. Th' ascending pile
Stood fixt her stately highth, and straight the doors
Op'ning thir brazen folds discover wide

---

709. *sound-board* is a technical name for the surface which deflects
the air from an organ's bellows to its pipes. The comparison of the
instrument to the founding devices of the angels anticipates the dulcet
symphony to which Pandæmonium, like Troy and Camelot, was built.

713. The architectural terms suggest a taste for the decorative use of
isolated structural elements—pillars, arches, and walls relieved with
pilasters, friezes and cornices—like that in baroque landscape painting.

717. *Babylon,* although it was the capital of Assyria's sister kingdom,
Babylonia, is represented as rivalling Egyptian Cairo, the city near the
site of ancient Memphis.

720. *Belus* is a variant of *Baal,* the Babylonian deity, and Serapis was
the name given to Osiris as lord of the underworld and patron of the
Nile's fertility.

Within, her ample spaces, o'er the smooth   725
And level pavement: from the arched roof
Pendant by subtle Magic many a row
Of Starry Lamps and blazing Cressets fed
With *Naphtha* and *Asphaltus* yielded light
As from a sky. The hasty multitude   730
Admiring enter'd, and the work some praise
And some the Architect: his hand was known
In Heav'n by many a Tow'red structure high,
Where Scepter'd Angels held thir residence,
And sat as Princes, whom the supreme King   735
Exalted to such power, and gave to rule,
Each in his Hierarchy, the Orders bright.
Nor was his name unheard or unador'd
In ancient *Greece;* and in *Ausonian* land
Men call'd him *Mulciber;* and how he fell   740
From Heav'n, they fabl'd, thrown by angry *Jove*
Sheer o'er the Crystal Battlements: from Morn
To Noon he fell, from Noon to dewy Eve,
A Summer's day; and with the setting Sun
Dropt from the Zenith like a falling Star,   745
On *Lemnos* th' *Ægæan* Isle: thus they relate,
Erring; for he with this rebellious rout
Fell long before; nor aught avail'd him now
To have built in Heav'n high Tow'rs; nor did he scape
By all his Engines, but was headlong sent   750
With his industrious crew to build in hell.
Meanwhile the winged Heralds by command

---

728. *Cressets,* iron baskets or pots, may be thought of as burning broken fragments of the bitumen, or asphalt, from which naphtha was distilled.

739. *Ausonian land.* Ausonia was the ancient Greek name for Italy.

740. *Mulciber,* meaning "founder of metals," is a less familiar Latin name than "Vulcan" for the Greek god Hephaestus, whom Zeus tossed out of heaven. In the *Iliad* (I, 588–595) Hephaestus himself tells the story comically and makes his mother, Hera, laugh. Milton quite changed the spirit of the Homeric tale, although he translated some of its phrases almost literally. His imagination was caught by the picture of the falling god over the Aegean Sea, dropping down upon the island of Lemnos, for in every myth of a pagan deity ejected from heaven he saw a travesty of the truth of the Hebrew myth which was the centre of his epic.

Of Sovran power, with awful Ceremony
And Trumpets' sound throughout the Host proclaim
A solemn Council forthwith to be held   755
At *Pandæmonium,* the high Capital
Of Satan and his Peers: thir summons call'd
From every Band and squared Regiment
By place or choice the worthiest; they anon
With hunderds and with thousands trooping came   760
Attended: all access was throng'd, the Gates
And Porches wide, but chief the spacious Hall
(Though like a cover'd field, where Champions bold
Wont ride in arm'd, and at the Soldan's chair
Defi'd the best of *Paynim* chivalry   765
To mortal combat or career with Lance)
Thick swarm'd, both on the ground and in the air,
Brusht with the hiss of rustling wings. As Bees
In spring time, when the Sun with *Taurus* rides,
Pour forth thir populous youth about the Hive   770
In clusters; they among fresh dews and flowers
Fly to and fro, or on the smoothed Plank,
The suburb of thir Straw-built Citadel,
New rubb'd with Balm, expatiate and confer
Thir State affairs. So thick the aery crowd   775
Swarm'd and were strait'n'd; till the Signal giv'n,
Behold a wonder! they but now who seem'd
In bigness to surpass Earth's Giant Sons
Now less than smallest Dwarfs, in narrow room
Throng numberless, like that Pigmean Race   780

---

756. Pandæmonium. Milton coined the word from the Greek πᾶν, "all," and δαίμων, "a spirit" or "deity."

764. *wont,* "was wont" or "accustomed."

765. Another allusion, like that in 581–7 above, to the tournaments between Christians and paynims, *i. e.,* pagans, as the Crusaders called the Saracens.

769. *Taurus,* the sign of the Bull, the second in the Zodiac, which the sun enters in April.

774. *expatiate:* walk abroad. To men familiar with Virgil's account of bees as the only animals possessing cities and laws. (*Georg.* IV) the simile gained a strange effect because it must have recalled epic comparisons (*Il.* II, 87–90, and *Aen.* I, 430–6) of crowds to bees, and may also have recalled Spenser's simile of bees for importunate tempters.

780. See note on l. 575.

Beyond the *Indian* Mount, or Faery Elves,
Whose midnight Revels, by a Forest side
Or Fountain some belated Peasant sees,
Or dreams he sees, while over-head the Moon
Sits Arbitress, and nearer to the Earth   785
Wheels her pale course, they on thir mirth and dance
Intent, with jocund Music charm his ear;
At once with joy and fear his heart rebounds.
Thus incorporeal Spirits to smallest forms
Reduc'd thir shapes immense, and were at large,   790
Though without number still amidst the Hall
Of that infernal Court. But far within
And in thir own dimensions like themselves
The great Seraphic Lords and Cherubim
In close recess and secret conclave sat   795
A thousand Demi-Gods on golden seats,
Frequent and full. After short silence then
And summons read, the great consult began.

The End of the First Book.

---

781. Comparison with *A Midsummer Night's Dream,* Act II, Scene i,
is usual, but the essence of the lines is Miltonic, like the sound of "airy
tongues . . . On sands and shores and desert wildernesses" in *Comus*
(208–9). The magic is partly wrought by a clear reminiscence of Virgil's
picture of Aeneas in the Elysian Fields, seeing or thinking that he sees
Dido, like the fugitive moon among thick clouds. (*Aen.* VI, 450–5.)

795. *close recess,* a secret meeting place. *conclave* seems to have its
original force of "an inner chamber."

797. *Frequent* has its Latin force of "crowded."

BOOK II

THE ARGUMENT

The Consultation begun, Satan *debates whether another Battle be to be hazarded for the recovery of Heaven: some advise it, others dissuade: A third proposal is preferr'd, mention'd before by* Satan, *to search the truth of that Prophecy or Tradition in Heaven concerning another world, and another kind of creature equal or not much inferior to themselves, about this time to be created: Thir doubt who shall be sent on this difficult search:* Satan *thir chief undertakes alone the voyage, is honour'd and applauded. The Council thus ended, the rest betake them several ways and to several employments, as thir inclinations lead them, to entertain the time till* Satan *return. He passes on his Journey to Hell Gates, finds them shut, and who sat there to guard them, by whom at length they are op'n'd, and discover to him the great Gulf between Hell and Heaven; with what difficulty he passes through, directed by* Chaos, *the Power of that place, to the sight of this new World which he sought.*

HIGH on a Throne of Royal State, which far
Outshone the wealth of *Ormus* and of *Ind,*
Or where the gorgeous East with richest hand
Show'rs on her Kings *Barbaric* Pearl and Gold,
Satan exalted sat, by merit rais'd   5
To that bad eminence; and from despair
Thus high uplifted beyond hope, aspires
Beyond thus high, insatiate to pursue
Vain War with Heav'n, and by success untaught

2. In 1622 the English helped the fleet of the Persian Shah to retake Ormus from the Portuguese. Situated on an island at the mouth of the Persian Gulf, it figures in seventeenth-century geographies as a fabulously wealthy emporium at the gateway to Ind (India).

5. Compare the note on I, 98, and the recurrent stress on Satan's merit below (II, 21).

9. *success,* consequence, in this case, unfortunate.

His proud imaginations thus display'd.   10
    Powers and Dominions, Deities of Heav'n,
For since no deep within her gulf can hold
Immortal vigor, though opprest and fall'n,
I give not Heav'n for lost.   From this descent
Celestial virtues rising, will appear   15
More glorious and more dread than from no fall,
And trust themselves to fear no second fate:
Mee though just right, and the fixt Laws of Heav'n
Did first create your Leader, next, free choice,
With what besides, in Counsel or in Fight,   20
Hath been achiev'd of merit, yet this loss
Thus far at least recover'd, hath much more
Establisht in a safe unenvied Throne
Yielded with full consent.   The happier state
In Heav'n, which follows dignity, might draw   25
Envy from each inferior; but who here
Will envy whom the highest place exposes
Foremost to stand against the Thunderer's aim
Your bulwark, and condemns to greatest share
Of endless pain? where there is then no good   30
For which to strive, no strife can grow up there
From Faction; for none sure will claim in Hell
Precedence, none, whose portion is so small
Of present pain, that with ambitious mind

---

11. For the names of the ranks in the infernal hierarchy see §16 of
the Introduction, and for the background of the demonic council see §14.

15. *virtues,* a rank in the hierarchy of hell.

24. In heaven greater happiness is possessed by the angels of greater
merit.

25. *Dignity* has its Latin force of "worth."

28. *Thunderer* is the first of several of the awe-inspiring titles of
Jove, common in Roman poetry, of which Satan takes advantage to
represent God as a tyrant.   Compare Belial's reference to "his red right
hand" (II, 174), a reminiscence of Horace's picture of Jove threatening
to destroy Rome (*Odes* I, ii), and Moloch's proposal to counter the
Tyrant's lightning with black fire and infernal thunder (II, 66–7).

32. Like Bacon, Milton shared the belief of the times that "when fac-
tions are carried too high and too violently, it is a sign of weakness in
princes" (*Essays,* LI).   He hedged Satan with a kingly divinity above
challenge by any faction among the infernal deities.

Will covet more. With this advantage then   35
To union, and firm Faith, and firm accord,
More than can be in Heav'n, we now return
To claim our just inheritance of old,
Surer to prosper than prosperity
Could have assur'd us; and by what best way,   4c
Whether of open War or covert guile,
We now debate; who can advise, may speak.
    He ceas'd, and next him *Moloch,* Scepter'd King
Stood up, the strongest and the fiercest Spirit
That fought in Heav'n; now fiercer by despair: 45
His trust was with th' Eternal to be deem'd
Equal in strength, and rather than be less
Car'd not to be at all; with that care lost
Went all his fear: of God, or Hell, or worse
He reck'd not, and these words thereafter spake. 50
    My sentence is for open War: Of Wiles,
More unexpert, I boast not: them let those
Contrive who need, or when they need, not now.
For while they sit contriving, shall the rest,
Millions that stand in Arms, and longing wait   55
The Signal to ascend, sit ling'ring here
Heav'n's fugitives, and for thir dwelling place
Accept this dark opprobrious Den of shame,
The Prison of his Tyranny who Reigns
By our delay? no, let us rather choose   60
Arm'd with Hell flames and fury all at once
O'er Heav'n's high Tow'rs to force resistless way,
Turning our Tortures into horrid Arms
Against the Torturer; when to meet the noise
Of his Almighty Engine he shall hear   65
Infernal Thunder, and for Lightning see
Black fire and horror shot with equal rage
Among his Angels; and his Throne itself

---

43. Moloch, the "furious king" (VI, 357, compare note on I, 392),
is "sceptr'd" as Homer often describes his kings when they sit in council
(*e.g., Il.* II, 86 and *Od.* II, 231).

51. *sentence,* like many of Milton's words of Latin origin, has its
etymological force of "decision" or "opinion." Compare II, 291.

52. *unexpert* has its Latin force of "inexperienced."

Mixt with *Tartarean* Sulphur, and strange fire,
His own invented Torments. But perhaps   70
The way seems difficult and steep to scale
With upright wing against a higher foe.
Let such bethink them, if the sleepy drench
Of that forgetful Lake benumb not still,
That in our proper motion we ascend   75
Up to our native seat: descent and fall
To us is adverse. Who but felt of late
When the fierce Foe hung on our brok'n Rear
Insulting, and pursu'd us through the Deep,
With what compulsion and laborious flight   80
We sunk thus low? Th' ascent is easy then;
Th' event is fear'd; should we again provoke
Our stronger, some worse way his wrath may find
To our destruction: if there be in Hell
Fear to be worse destroy'd: what can be worse   85
Than to dwell here, driv'n out from bliss, condemn'd
In this abhorred deep to utter woe;
Where pain of unextinguishable fire
Must exercise us without hope of end
The Vassals of his anger, when the Scourge   90
Inexorably, and the torturing hour
Calls us to Penance?   More destroy'd than thus
We should be quite abolisht and expire.
What fear we then? what doubt we to incense
His utmost ire? which to the highth enrag'd,   95
Will either quite consume us, and reduce

---

69. Milton constantly thinks of hell interchangeably in terms of the Tartarus of the Greeks and of the Inferno of Christian tradition. Compare the note on I, 239.

74. The *forgetful lake,* like the "oblivious pool" of I, 266, is a reminiscence of the river Lethe, whose waters Greek tradition said must be drunk by the spirits of the dead. The "drench" made them forget their previous life. Moloch's contempt for his companions' forgetfulness of their heavenly glory suggests the reference of the ghost in *Hamlet* (I, v, 32–4), to the "dulness" of

> "the fat weed
> That rots itself in ease on Lethe wharf."

89. *exercise* has its Latin force of "torment."

90. *Vassals* has its late Latin meaning of "servant" or "slave," rather than its feudal connotation of "fief-holder."

To nothing this essential, happier far
Than miserable to have eternal being:
Or if our substance be indeed Divine,
And cannot cease to be, we are at worst   100
On this side nothing; and by proof we feel
Our power sufficient to disturb his Heav'n,
And with perpetual inroads to Alarm,
Though inaccessible, his fatal Throne:
Which if not Victory is yet Revenge.   105
     He ended frowning, and his look denounc'd
Desperate revenge, and Battle dangerous
To less than Gods. On th' other side up rose
Belial, in act more graceful and humane;
A fairer person lost not Heav'n; he seem'd   110
For dignity compos'd and high exploit:
But all was false and hollow; though his Tongue
Dropt Manna, and could make the worse appear
The better reason, to perplex and dash
Maturest Counsels: for his thoughts were low;   115
To vice industrious, but to Nobler deeds
Timorous and slothful: yet he pleas'd the ear,
And with persuasive accent thus began.
     I should be much for open War, O Peers,
As not behind in hate; if what was urg'd   120
Main reason to persuade immediate War,
Did not dissuade me most, and seem to cast
Ominous conjecture on the whole success:

---

97. *essential:* Milton often uses adjectives as nouns. Moloch questions whether, in spite of what has happened, the physical essence or
substance of the devils is really subject to gravity or to death. Compare I, 138.

104. Compare Beëlzebub's proposal (I, 133) of a trial whether God's
supremacy is sustained by strength, chance or fate, and Satan's implica-
tion (I, 166) that fate controls God. Moloch does not admit that even
a second victory over the devils would prove God omnipotent.

109. Compare the note at Belial's first appearance (I, 490). His
speech following—one of Milton's finest dramatic characterizations—has
little in tradition to justify it. Belial was often vaguely confused with
Satan or, as in the Faust *Book of Marvels,* regarded as Satan's vice-gerent
in hell. Scot's account (*Discoverie of Witchcraft,* xv, 2) faintly points
Milton's way with Belial, who "taketh the form of a beautifull angel,
he speaketh faire."

When he who most excels in fact of Arms,
In what he counsels and in what excels   125
Mistrustful, grounds his courage on despair
And utter dissolution, as the scope
Of all his aim, after some dire revenge.
First, what Revenge? the Tow'rs of Heav'n are fill'd
With Armed watch, that render all access   130
Impregnable; oft on the bordering Deep
Encamp thir Legions, or with obscure wing
Scout far and wide into the Realm of night,
Scorning surprise. Or could we break our way
By force, and at our heels all Hell should rise   135
With blackest Insurrection, to confound
Heav'n's purest Light, yet our great Enemy
All incorruptible would on his Throne
Sit unpolluted, and the Ethereal mould
Incapable of stain would soon expel   140
Her mischief, and purge off the baser fire
Victorious. Thus repuls'd, our final hope
Is flat despair; we must exasperate
Th' Almighty Victor to spend all his rage,
And that must end us, that must be our cure,   145
To be no more; sad cure; for who would lose,
Though full of pain, this intellectual being,
Those thoughts that wander through Eternity,
To perish rather, swallow'd up and lost
In the wide womb of uncreated night,   150
Devoid of sense and motion? and who knows,

---

124. *fact of Arms,* deeds of arms.

139. Milton imagined the heavenly *mould,* or substance, biblically, remembering that "The Lord thy God is a consuming fire" (Deut. iv, 24),
and "his angels, spirits, his ministers, a flaming fire" (Ps. civ, 4). The
distinction between celestial and "baser," earthly fire was an accepted
belief. Renaissance handbooks of classical mythology allegorized it, as
Spenser did, by making Vesta the symbol

            "of the fire aetheriall,
        Vulcan, of this, with us so usuall." (*F. Q., VII, vii,* 26.)

The conception of a purer substance expelling a baser recurs in the
account of Adam's banishment from Eden (XI, 48–53).

151. Like Burton, Milton was impressed by the arguments of "Cardan,
Martianus, . . . the Platonists and some Rabbins, Porphyrius and Plutarch" that the demons were mortal, but he seems to have felt that

Let this be good, whether our angry Foe
Can give it, or will ever? how he can
Is doubtful; that he never will is sure.
Will he, so wise, let loose at once his ire,   155
Belike through impotence, or unaware,
To give his Enemies thir wish, and end
Them in his anger, whom his anger saves
To punish endless? wherefore cease we then?
Say they who counsel War, we are decreed,   160
Reserv'd and destin'd to Eternal woe;
Whatever doing, what can we suffer more,
What can we suffer worse? is this then worst,
Thus sitting, thus consulting, thus in Arms?
What when we fled amain, pursu'd and strook   165
With Heav'n's afflicting Thunder, and besought
The Deep to shelter us? this Hell then seem'd
A refuge from those wounds: or when we lay
Chain'd on the burning Lake? that sure was worse.
What if the breath that kindl'd those grim fires   170
Awak'd should blow them into sevenfold rage
And plunge us in the flames? or from above
Should intermitted vengeance arm again
His red right hand to plague us? what if all
Her stores were op'n'd, and this Firmament   175
Of Hell should spout her Cataracts of Fire,
Impendent horrors, threat'ning hideous fall
One day upon our heads; while we perhaps
Designing or exhorting glorious war,
Caught in a fiery Tempest shall be hurl'd   180
Each on his rock transfixt, the sport and prey

---

such "paradoxes of their . . . mortality" were inconsistent with Christian
faith (*Anatomy*, I, ii, 1, 2).

174. See note on II, 28.

181. Comparison is possible with Claudio's description of the harried
soul after death (*Measure for Measure*, III, i, 120–5) and with Lear's
"sulfurous and thought-executing fires" (III, ii, 4). Perhaps Milton
recollected Aeschylus' Prometheus protesting,

> ". . . what ignominy of causeless wrongs
> I suffer from the gods, myself a god.
> See what piercing pains shall goad me
> Through long ages myriad-numbered!"
> (Blackie's translation. Everyman. P. 185.)

Of racking whirlwinds, or for ever sunk
Under yon boiling Ocean, wrapt in Chains;
There to converse with everlasting groans,
Unrespited, unpitied, unrepriev'd,   185
Ages of hopeless end; this would be worse.
War therefore, open or conceal'd, alike
My voice dissuades; for what can force or guile
With him, or who deceive his mind, whose eye
Views all things at one view? he from heav'n's highth   190
All these our motions vain, sees and derides;
Not more Almighty to resist our might
Than wise to frustrate all our plots and wiles.
Shall we then live thus vile, the race of Heav'n
Thus trampl'd, thus expell'd to suffer here   195
Chains and these Torments? better these than worse
By my advice; since fate inevitable
Subdues us, and Omnipotent Decree
The Victor's will. To suffer, as to do,
Our strength is equal, nor the Law unjust   200
That so ordains: this was at first resolv'd,
If we were wise, against so great a foe
Contending, and so doubtful what might fall.
I laugh, when those who at the Spear are bold
And vent'rous, if that fail them, shrink and fear   205
What yet they know must follow, to endure
Exile, or ignominy, or bonds, or pain,
The sentence of thir Conqueror: This is now
Our doom; which if we can sustain and bear,
Our Supreme Foe in time may much remit   210
His anger, and perhaps thus far remov'd
Not mind us not offending, satisfi'd
With what is punish't; whence these raging fires
Will slack'n, if his breath stir not thir flames.
Our purer essence then will overcome   215

---

191. Belial acknowledges the vaunt of the Psalmist (ii, 4), "He that sitteth in the heavens shall laugh; the Lord shall have them in derision."

199. The oldest instance of the proverbial opposition of heroic deeds to heroic endurance is in Æschylus' *Choephorœ*, 312. Compare I, 158.

215. See the note on I, 138.

Thir noxious vapour, or enur'd not feel,
Or chang'd at length, and to the place conform'd
In temper and in nature, will receive
Familiar the fierce heat, and void of pain;
This horror will grow mild, this darkness light,   220
Besides what hope the never-ending flight
Of future days may bring, what chance, what change
Worth waiting, since our present lot appears
For happy though but ill, for ill not worst,
If we procure not to ourselves more woe.   225
    Thus *Belial* with words cloth'd in reason's garb
Counsell'd ignoble ease, and peaceful sloth,
Not peace: and after him thus *Mammon* spake.
    Either to disinthrone the King of Heav'n
We war, if war be best, or to regain   230
Our own right lost: him to unthrone we then
May hope, when everlasting Fate shall yield
To fickle Chance, and *Chaos* judge the strife:
The former vain to hope argues as vain
The latter: for what place can be for us   235
Within Heav'n's bound, unless Heav'n's Lord supreme
We overpower? Suppose he should relent
And publish Grace to all, on promise made
Of new Subjection; with what eyes could we
Stand in his presence humble, and receive   240
Strict Laws impos'd, to celebrate his Throne
With warbl'd Hymns, and to his Godhead sing
Forc't Halleluiahs; while he Lordly sits

---

216. *enur'd*, accustomed, used to.

218. *temper*, equivalent to modern "temperament," was a physiological
term for the balance of humours in the body which determined the
physical and psychological character of an individual.

224. *For happy*, from the point of view of happiness.

228. See the note on I, 678. Tradition made Mammon captain of the
ninth and lowest order of demons, "those tempters in several kinds."
(Burton, *Anatomy*, I, ii, 1, 2.)

232. See the Introduction, §14.

243. *Halleluiah* transliterates the Hebrew phrase, "Praise ye Jah," *i.e.*,
Jehovah. Bishop Sanderson said (*Sermons*, I, p. 115) that the whole
Book of Psalms could be summed up in the words *hosannah* and *hal-
leluiah*.

Our envied Sovran, and his Altar breathes
Ambrosial Odours and Ambrosial Flowers,   245
Our servile offerings. This must be our task
In Heav'n, this our delight; how wearisome
Eternity so spent in worship paid
To whom we hate. Let us not then pursue
By force impossible, by leave obtain'd   250
Unácceptable, though in Heav'n, our state
Of splendid vassalage, but rather seek
Our own good from ourselves, and from our own
Live to ourselves, though in this vast recess,
Free, and to none accountable, preferring   255
Hard liberty before the easy yoke
Of servile Pomp. Our greatness will appear
Then most conspicuous, when great things of small,
Useful of hurtful, prosperous of adverse
We can create, and in what place soe'er   260
Thrive under evil, and work ease out of pain
Through labour and endurance. This deep world
Of darkness do we dread? How oft amidst
Thick clouds and dark doth Heav'n's all-ruling Sire
Choose to reside, his Glory unobscur'd,   265
And with the Majesty of darkness round
Covers his Throne; from whence deep thunders roar
Must'ring thir rage, and Heav'n resembles Hell?
As he our darkness, cannot we his Light
Imitate when we please? This Desert soil   270
Wants not her hidden lustre, Gems and Gold;
Nor want we skill or art, from whence to raise

---

245. Ambrosia was the name both of the food of the Olympian gods
and of the perfumed wine poured out to them in libations.

249. *pursue,* try to obtain. Its object, *state,* is modified by the two
incomplete relative clauses, "(what is) by force impossible" and "(what
is, if) by leave obtained, unacceptable."

264. At the dedication of the temple in Jerusalem "the house was
filled with a cloud . . . for the glory of the Lord filled the house of
God. Then said Solomon, the Lord hath said that he would dwell in
the thick darkness." (II Chron. v, 13–vi, 1.) Compare Psalms xviii,
11–13: "He made darkness his secret place; his pavilion round about
him were dark waters and thick clouds of the skies. At the brightness
that was before him his thick clouds passed . . . The Lord also thun-
dered in the heavens."

Magnificence; and what can Heav'n show more?
Our torments also may in length of time
Become our Elements, these piercing Fires   275
As soft as now severe, our temper chang'd
Into their temper; which must needs remove
The sensible of pain. All things invite
To peaceful Counsels, and the settl'd State
Of order, how in safety best we may   280
Compose our present evils, with regard
Of what we are and where, dismissing quite
All thoughts of War; ye have what I advise.

   He scarce had finisht, when such murmur fill'd
Th' Assembly, as when hollow Rocks retain   285
The sound of blust'ring winds, which all night long
Had rous'd the Sea, now with hoarse cadence lull
Sea-faring men o'erwatcht, whose Bark by chance
Or Pinnace anchors in a craggy Bay
After the Tempest: Such applause was heard   290
As *Mammon* ended, and his Sentence pleas'd,
Advising peace: for such another Field
They dreaded worse than Hell: so much the fear
Of Thunder and the Sword of *Michaël*
Wrought still within them; and no less desire   295
To found this nether Empire, which might rise
By policy, and long process of time,

---

273. *Magnificence* meant for Milton "the virtue concerned with wealth" (*Nicomachean Ethics,* IV, ii) which Aristotle described as expressing itself in splendid buildings. Pandæmonium itself (I, 710) is proof of Mammon's words.

275. Universally received tradition assigned to the devils the four elements, fire, air, water and earth. Fiery Spirits or Devils, Aerial Spirits or Devils, Water-devils and Terrestrial devils is Burton's classification. (*Anatomy,* I, ii, 1, 2.) So in *Il Penseroso* (93–4) Milton mentions the "Dæmons" found
           "In fire, air, flood, or underground."
Mammon anticipates the degradation of the celestial essence of the demons which was supposed to have taken place as their "temper" changed to that of the terrestrial elements. In arguing that thus they will be delivered from the *sensible* (*i.e.,* sensation) of pain he echoes Belial.

288. *o'er-watch'd,* worn out with watching.

294. An anticipation of Michael's rôle as marshal of the heavenly host in Book VI.

297. *policy,* statesmanship.

In emulation opposite to Heav'n.
Which when *Beëlzebub* perceiv'd, than whom,
Satan except, none higher sat, with grave   300
Aspect he rose, and in his rising seem'd
A Pillar of State; deep on his Front engraven
Deliberation sat and public care;
And Princely counsel in his face yet shone,
Majestic though in ruin: sage he stood   305
With *Atlantean* shoulders fit to bear
The weight of mightiest Monarchies; his look
Drew audience and attention still as Night
Or Summer's Noon-tide air, while thus he spake.

  Thrones and imperial Powers, off-spring of heav'n,   310
Ethereal Virtues; or these Titles now
Must we renounce, and changing style be call'd
Princes of Hell? for so the popular vote
Inclines, here to continue, and build up here
A growing Empire; doubtless; while we dream,   315
And know not that the King of Heav'n hath doom'd
This place our dungeon, not our safe retreat
Beyond his Potent arm, to live exempt
From Heav'n's high jurisdiction, in new League
Banded against his Throne, but to remain   320
In strictest bondage, though thus far remov'd,
Under th' inevitable curb, reserv'd
His captive multitude: For he, be sure,
In highth or depth, still first and last will Reign

---

302. *Front* has its Latin force of "forehead."

306. The myth of the Titan, Atlas, who supported the sky, was often
applied to "pillars of state." So Spenser described England as supported
by Lord Burleigh,

> "As the wide compasse of the firmament
>   On Atlas mighty shoulders is upstayd."
>   (Sonnets Dedicatory to *The Faerie Queene*.)

312. *style*, the formal title of a king or nobleman.

315. *doubtless,* standing between semicolons, is a flash of sarcasm between the irony of Beëlzebub's opening words and the earnest of his
argument.

324. The words repeatedly attributed to God in the *Apocalypse,* "I am
Alpha and Omega, the beginning and the end, the first and the last"
(Rev. i, 2, xxi, 6 and xxii, 13) inspire Beëlzebub's despair, as they do
the triumph of the angels later (V, 165).

Sole King, and of his Kingdom lose no part   325
By our revolt, but over Hell extend
His Empire, and with Iron Sceptre rule
Us here, as with his Golden those in Heav'n.
What sit we then projecting peace and War?
War hath determin'd us, and foil'd with loss   330
Irreparable; terms of peace yet none
Voutsaf't or sought; for what peace will be giv'n
To us enslav'd, but custody severe,
And stripes, and arbitrary punishment
Inflicted? and what peace can we return,   335
But to our power hostility and hate,
Untam'd reluctance, and revenge though slow,
Yet ever plotting how the Conqueror least
May reap his conquest, and may least rejoice
In doing what we most in suffering feel?   340
Nor will occasion want, nor shall we need
With dangerous expedition to invade
Heav'n, whose high walls fear no assault or Siege,
Or ambush from the Deep. What if we find
Some easier enterprise? There is a place   345
(If ancient and prophetic fame in Heav'n
Err not) another World, the happy seat
Of some new Race call'd *Man,* about this time
To be created like to us, though less
In power and excellence, but favour'd more   350
Of him who rules above; so was his will
Pronounc'd among the Gods, and by an Oath,

---

327. The iron sceptre is a reminiscence of the Lord's promise to his
"Son," "Thou shalt break them with a rod of iron." (Ps. ii, 9.) Iron
was traditionally a symbol of enmity and gold of friendship, a symbolism
which recurs in Abdiel's warning to Satan (V, 886-8).

336. *to our power,* to the limit of our power.

346. Compare I, 651, where Satan anticipates Beëlzebub's argument
from the *fame,* or rumour, of the intended creation of man.

348. Milton was familiar with Origen's doctrine (which St. Thomas
condemned, *Summa Theologica,* I, 961, a. 3) that God created the world
only after the revolt of the angels.

352. Several times in the Old Testament God is represented as taking
an oath, and "because he could swear by no greater, he sware by himself." (Heb., vi, 13. Compare Gen. xxii, 16.) The shaking of
heaven's circumference is an epic convention. So Zeus shakes Olympus

That shook Heav'n's whole circumference, confirm'd.
Thither let us bend all our thoughts, to learn
What creatures there inhabit, of what mould,   355
Or substance, how endu'd, and what thir Power,
And where thir weakness, how attempted best,
By force or subtlety: Though Heav'n be shut,
And Heav'n's high Arbitrator sit secure
In his own strength, this place may lie expos'd   360
The utmost border of his Kingdom, left
To their defence who hold it: here perhaps
Some advantageous act may be achiev'd
By sudden onset, either with Hell fire
To waste his whole Creation, or possess   365
All as our own, and drive as we were driven,
The puny habitants, or if not drive,
Seduce them to our Party, that thir God
May prove thir foe, and with repenting hand
Abolish his own works. This would surpass   370
Common revenge, and interrupt his joy
In our Confusion, and our Joy upraise
In his disturbance; when his darling Sons
Hurl'd headlong to partake with us, shall curse
Thir frail Original, and faded bliss,   375
Faded so soon. Advise if this be worth
Attempting, or to sit in darkness here
Hatching vain Empires. Thus *Beëlzebub*
Pleaded his devilish Counsel, first devis'd
By *Satan,* and in part propos'd: for whence,   380
But from the Author of all ill could Spring
So deep a malice, to confound the race
Of mankind in one root, and Earth with Hell
To mingle and involve, done all to spite
The great Creator? But thir spite still serves   385
His glory to augment. The bold design

---

when he confirms a promise to Thetis with a vow (*Il.* I, 530) and
similarly Jove, when he makes a promise to Cybele (*Aen.* IX, 106).

356. *endu'd,* invested or gifted (with qualities of mind).

375. *Original* seems not to mean "original state," as it does in IX, 150,
but to refer to Adam.

380. Compare I, 650–8.

Pleas'd highly those infernal States, and joy
Sparkl'd in all thir eyes; with full assent
They vote: whereat his speech he thus renews.
  Well have ye judg'd, well ended long debate,   390
Synod of Gods, and like to what ye are,
Great things resolv'd, which from the lowest deep
Will once more lift us up, in spite of Fate,
Nearer our ancient Seat; perhaps in view
Of those bright confines, whence with neighbouring Arms 395
And opportune excursion we may chance
Re-enter Heav'n; or else in some mild Zone
Dwell not unvisited of Heav'n's fair Light
Secure, and at the bright'ning Orient beam
Purge off this gloom; the soft delicious Air,   400
To heal the scar of these corrosive Fires
Shall breathe her balm. But first whom shall we send
In search of this new world, whom shall we find
Sufficient? who shall tempt with wand'ring feet
The dark unbottom'd infinite Abyss   405
And through the palpable obscure find out
His uncouth way, or spread his aery flight
Upborne with indefatigable wings
Over the vast abrupt, ere he arrive
The happy Isle; what strength, what art can then   410

---

387. *States,* used, perhaps, with vague reference to the ranks of the
infernal hierarchy, was a political term meaning the three estates, lords,
clergy, and commons, which composed the parliaments of England and
France.

391. *Synod* means any kind of assembly, but commonly an ecclesiastical
one.

394. *Seat* has its Latin force of "established home." Compare 347
above.

405. *Abyss,* Chaos, for whose description Milton is now preparing, as
he later prepares for the discovery of the light beyond Chaos.

406. *palpable obscure* seems to be a reminiscence of the "darkness
which may be felt" which God sent to plague the Egyptians. (Exod. x,
21.)

407. *uncouth,* unknown. Compare 827 below.

409. *abrupt* has its Latin force of "a breach"; it is the gap between
hell and heaven.

410. *Isle,* the created universe is like an island in the sea of Chaos,
a "voyage" across which Satan is meditating.

Suffice, or what evasion bear him safe
Through the strict Senteries and Stations thick
Of Angels watching round?   Here he had need
All circumspection, and we now no less
Choice in our suffrage; for on whom we send,   415
The weight of all and our last hope relies.

    This said, he sat; and expectation held
His look suspense, awaiting who appear'd
To second, or oppose, or undertake
The perilous attempt; but all sat mute,   420
Pondering the danger with deep thoughts; and each
In other's count'nance read his own dismay
Astonisht: none among the choice and prime
Of those Heav'n-warring Champions could be found
So hardy as to proffer or accept   425
Alone the dreadful voyage; till at last
Satan, whom now transcendent glory rais'd
Above his fellows, with Monarchal pride
Conscious of highest worth, unmov'd thus spake.

    O Progeny of Heav'n, Empyreal Thrones,   430
With reason hath deep silence and demur
Seiz'd us, though undismay'd: long is the way
And hard, that out of Hell leads up to light;
Our prison strong, this huge convex of Fire,
Outrageous to devour, immures us round   435
Ninefold, and gates of burning Adamant
Barr'd over us prohibit all egress.
These past, if any pass, the void profound
Of unessential Night receives him next

---

412. *Senteries*, rather than *sentries*, is metrically necessary. The form
was current in the seventeenth century.

415. *suffrage*, vote to select the emissary in whose choice circumspection is no less necessary than it will be for him in his expedition.

432. Milton remembered the Sibyl's warning to Aeneas that the descent to the infernal regions is easy, but the return difficult (*Aen.* VI,
126-9) and perhaps also Virgil's warning to Dante, as they prepared to
ascend from the centre of the earth toward Purgatory, that the way was
hard. (*Inf.* XXXIV, 95.)

434. *convex*, a sphere. So the sphere of the universe is called in III,
419. When the point of view is definitely from within Milton sometimes uses the term *concave*, as in 635 below.

439. *unessential*, without being or substance, shares the sinister conno-

Wide gaping, and with utter loss of being   440
Threatens him, plung'd in that abortive gulf.
If thence he scape into whatever world,
Or unknown Region, what remains him less
Than unknown dangers and as hard escape.
But I should ill become this Throne, O Peers,   445
And this Imperial Sov'ranty, adorn'd
With splendor, arm'd with power, if aught propos'd
And judg'd of public moment, in the shape
Of difficulty or danger could deter
Me from attempting.   Wherefore do I assume   450
These Royalties, and not refuse to Reign,
Refusing to accept as great a share
Of hazard as of honour, due alike
To him who Reigns, and so much to him due
Of hazard more, as he above the rest   455
High honour'd sits?   Go therefore mighty Powers,
Terror of Heav'n, though fall'n; intend at home,
While here shall be our home, what best may ease
The present misery, and render Hell
More tolerable; if there be cure or charm   460
To respite or deceive, or slack the pain
Of this ill Mansion: intermit no watch
Against a wakeful Foe, while I abroad
Through all the Coasts of dark destruction seek
Deliverance for us all: this enterprise   465
None shall partake with me.   Thus saying rose
The Monarch, and prevented all reply,
Prudent, lest from his resolution rais'd
Others among the chief might offer now
(Certain to be refus'd) what erst they fear'd;   470
And so refus'd might in opinion stand
His Rivals, winning cheap the high repute

---

tation of *abortive*, which may mean "aborted" (*i.e.*, lifeless) or "monstrous" and "terrifying," or "abortion-causing" (*i.e.*, deadly to an intruder).

457. *intend* has its Latin force of "attend to," "consider."

461. *deceive* has its Latin force of "elude" or "beguile."

462. *Mansion* has its Latin meaning, which is identical with that of "seat" in 347.

468. *rais'd*, emboldened.

Which he through hazard huge must earn. But they
Dreaded not more th' adventure than his voice
Forbidding; and at once with him they rose;   475
Thir rising all at once was as the sound
Of Thunder heard remote. Towards him they bend
With awful reverence prone; and as a God
Extol him equal to the highest in Heav'n:
Nor fail'd they to express how much they prais'd,   480
That for the general safety he despis'd
His own: for neither do the Spirits damn'd
Lose all thir virtue; lest bad men should boast
Thir specious deeds on earth, which glory excites,
Or close ambition varnisht o'er with zeal.   485
Thus they thir doubtful consultations dark
Ended rejoicing in their matchless Chief:
As when from mountain tops the dusky clouds
Ascending, while the North wind sleeps, o'erspread
Heav'n's cheerful face, the low'ring Element   490
Scowls o'er the dark'n'd lantskip Snow, or show'r;
If chance the radiant Sun with farewell sweet
Extend his ev'ning beam, the fields revive,
The birds thir notes renew, and bleating herds
Attest thir joy, that hill and valley rings.   495
O shame to men! Devil with Devil damn'd
Firm concord holds, men only disagree
Of Creatures rational, though under hope
Of heavenly Grace; and God proclaiming peace,
Yet live in hatred, enmity, and strife   500
Among themselves, and levy cruel wars,
Wasting the Earth, each other to destroy:
As if (which might induce us to accord)
Man had not hellish foes anow besides,
That day and night for his destruction wait.   505
     The *Stygian* Council thus dissolv'd; and forth

---

478. *awful*, full of awe or reverence.

485. *close*, secret or lying.

490. *Element*, the atmosphere. Compare the "faery vision of some
gay creatures of the element." (*Comus*, 298–9.)

491. *lantskip*, landscape. The form of this technical term, which was
borrowed from Holland about 1600, was still unsettled.

In order came the grand infernal Peers,
Midst came thir mighty Paramount, and seem'd
Alone th' Antagonist of Heav'n, nor less
Than Hell's dread Emperor with pomp Supreme,   510
And God-like imitated State; him round
A Globe of fiery Seraphim inclos'd
With bright imblazonry, and horrent Arms.
Then of thir Session ended they bid cry
With Trumpet's regal sound the great result: 515
Toward the four winds four speedy Cherubim
Put to thir mouths the sounding Alchymy
By Herald's voice explain'd: the hollow Abyss
Heard far and wide, and all the host of Hell
With deaf'ning shout, return'd them loud acclaim.   520
Thence more at ease thir minds and somewhat rais'd
By false presumptuous hope, the ranged powers
Disband, and wand'ring, each his several way
Pursues, as inclination or sad choice
Leads him perplext, where he may likeliest find   525
Truce to his restless thoughts, and entertain
The irksome hours, till his great Chief return.
Part on the Plain, or in the Air sublime
Upon the wing, or in swift Race contend,
As at th' Olympian Games or *Pythian* fields;   530

507. *Peers:* Milton thought of an analogy to the House of Peers, or
Lords, in Parliament, for only the highest devils in the hierarchy took
part in the debate, presided over by their Paramount, Satan.

512. *Globe,* a solid body of soldiers. The meaning is a Latinism,
parallel to our military "square." *N. E. D.* cites Giles Fletcher's *Christ's
Triumph After Death,* xiii:

> Out there flies
> A globe of winged angels, swift as thought.

513. Like noblemen in armour, the seraphs have heraldic devices or
blazons on their shields.

517. *Alchymy,* or alchemy gold, was an alloy like brass, used in wind
instruments.

522. *powers,* armies.

530. The sports of the demons are an interlude like Virgil's funeral
games at the tomb of Anchises (*Aen.* V, 103–603) and Homer's at the
pyre of Patroclus (*Il.* XXIII, 283, ff.), but they include contests in music
and oratory, like the pan-Hellenic games held quadrennially at Olympia,
and like the Pythian Games at Delphi.

Part curb thir fiery Steeds, or shun the Goal
With rapid wheels, or fronted Brígads form.
As when to warn proud Cities war appears
Wag'd in the troubl'd Sky, and Armies rush
To Battle in the Clouds, before each Van   535
Prick forth the Aery Knights, and couch thir spears
Till thickest Legions close; with feats of Arms
From either end of Heav'n the welkin burns.
Others with vast *Typhœan* rage more fell
Rend up both Rocks and Hills, and ride the Air   540
In whirlwind; Hell scarce holds the wild uproar.
As when *Alcides* from *Oechalia* Crown'd
With conquest, felt th' envenom'd robe, and tore
Through pain up by the roots *Thessalian* Pines,
And *Lichas* from the top of *Oeta* threw   545
Into th' *Euboic* Sea.   Others more mild,
Retreated in a silent valley, sing
With notes Angelical to many a Harp
Thir own Heroic deeds and hapless fall
By doom of Battle; and complain that Fate   550
Free Virtue should enthrall to Force or Chance.
Thir song was partial, but the harmony

531. Milton thought of Roman charioteers swinging their teams around the turning posts in the arena.

534. Perhaps the allusion is to the "chariots and troops of soldiers in their armour running about among the clouds" which Josephus mentions among the portents seen by the Jews before the fall of Jerusalem. (*Wars* VI, v.)

539. *Typhœan.* Compare the note on I, 197. The name of the Titan, Typhon (or Typhœus, the form used in Ovid's account of the Titans' assault on the Gods, *Met.*, V, 321–6) signified a whirlwind and the Greek word has modified the English "typhoon," which is of Arabian or Persian origin. In Milton's time there could not "happen a storm . . . but the multitude will have the devil in it." (Glanvill, *Vanity*, 116.)

542. *Alcides,* Hercules, the story of whose death, caused by a poisoned robe which his friend, Lichas, ignorantly brought to him when he was returning from a victory in Oechalia to the island of Euboea, northeast of Athens, Milton knew in Sophocles' tragedy, the *Trachiniae,* and in Seneca's melodrama, *Hercules Oetaeus.* Ovid's account (*Met.* IX, 134, ff.), which makes Mt. Otea in Thessaly, rather than Euboea, the scene of the whole action, is the most definite influence here.

552. *Thir song was partial* to their own view of their quarrel with God as a struggle of Virtue against the tyranny of Force and Chance.

(What could it less when Spirits immortal sing?)
Suspended Hell, and took with ravishment
The thronging audience. In discourse more sweet   555
(For Eloquence the Soul, Song charms the Sense,)
Others apart sat on a Hill retir'd,
In thoughts more elevate, and reason'd high
Of Providence, Foreknowledge, Will, and Fate,
Fixt Fate, free will, foreknowledge absolute,   560
And found no end, in wand'ring mazes lost.
Of good and evil much they argu'd then,
Of happiness and final misery,
Passion and Apathy, and glory and shame,
Vain wisdom all, and false Philosophie: 565
Yet with a pleasing sorcery could charm
Pain for a while or anguish, and excite
Fallacious hope, or arm th' obdured breast
With stubborn patience as with triple steel.
Another part in Squadrons and gross Bands,   570
On bold adventure to discover wide
That dismal World, if any Clime perhaps
Might yield them easier habitation, bend
Four ways thir flying March, along the Banks
Of four infernal Rivers that disgorge   575
Into the burning Lake thir baleful streams;
Abhorred *Styx* the flood of deadly hate,
Sad *Acheron* of Sorrow, black and deep;
Cocytus, nam'd of lamentation loud
Heard on the rueful stream; fierce *Phlegeton*   580
Whose waves of torrent fire inflame with rage.

---

564. *Apathy* was the Stoic ideal of complete freedom from passion. In
C. D., II, x, Milton condemned it as vainglorious.

565. Like Henry More (*Immortality of the Soul,* III, xvii, 8), Milton
was struck by Cardan's report that "there are Students of philosophy"
among the demons, who "are divided into sects and opinions, as we are
here."

577. Milton himself explains the literal Greek meanings of the four
infernal rivers. Although he makes them flow into "the burning lake"
of St. John's *Apocalypse* (Rev. XX, 10), he thought of them, like Virgil
(*Aen.* VI, 656-9), as vaguely bounding hell. "The bitter (*i.e.,* hateful)
wave of Styx" (*F. Q.* II, viii, 20), Cocytus, whose sad waves echoed
with "piteous cryes and yelling shrightes" (*Ibid.,* II, vii, 57), "flaming
Phlegethon" (*Ibid.,* II, vi, 50) and the "bitter waves of Acheron" (*Ibid.,*
I, v, 33) were already familiar to readers of Spenser.

Far off from these a slow and silent stream,
Lethe the River of Oblivion rolls
Her wat'ry Labyrinth, whereof who drinks,
Forthwith his former state and being forgets,   585
Forgets both joy and grief, pleasure and pain.
Beyond this flood a frozen Continent
Lies dark and wild, beat with perpetual storms
Of Whirlwind and dire Hail, which on firm land
Thaws not, but gathers heap, and ruin seems   590
Of ancient pile; all else deep snow and ice,
A gulf profound as that *Serbonian* Bog
Betwixt *Damiata* and mount *Casius* old,
Where Armies whole have sunk: the parching Air
Burns frore, and cold performs th' effect of Fire.   595
Thither by harpy-footed Furies hal'd,
At certain revolutions all the damn'd
Are brought: and feel by turns the bitter change
Of fierce extremes, extremes by change more fierce,
From Beds of raging Fire to starve in Ice   600
Thir soft Ethereal warmth, and there to pine
Immovable, infixt, and frozen round,
Periods of time, thence hurried back to fire.
They ferry over this *Lethean* Sound

583. See the note on 74 above.

590. The accumulated hail seems like the ruin of a marble pile, *i.e.* building.

595. The frozen torments of the damned in the ninth canto of Dante's *Inferno* are the most famous expression of the medieval belief in a frozen as well as a burning hell. A popular belief that the spirits of the damned alternated between frost and fire inspired Claudio with the fear that his soul might have to

> bathe in fiery floods, or to reside
> In thrilling regions of thick-ribbed ice.
> (*Measure for Measure* III, i, 121–2.)

596. The Furies, or Eumenides, goddesses who avenged crimes like the parricide of Orestes, are "telescoped" with the "claw-handed" Harpies (*Aen.* III, 217), monstrous birds with women's faces which Homer imagined as kidnapping men. Telemachus suspected them of carrying off his father, Ulysses (*Od.* I, 241) and Penelope prayed that they might snatch her away from her suitors (*Ibid.* XX, 77).

600. *starve,* in Scottish, still keeps the meaning "to die of cold" as well as "to die of hunger." Here the verb is transitive and means "to inflict the pain of death by freezing," upon their naturally warm bodies.

Both to and fro, thir sorrow to augment,   605
And wish and struggle, as they pass, to reach
The tempting stream, with one small drop to lose
In sweet forgetfulness all pain and woe,
All in one moment, and so near the brink;
But fate withstands, and to oppose th' attempt   610
Medusa with *Gorgonian* terror guards
The Ford, and of itself the water flies
All taste of living wight, as once it fled
The lip of *Tantalus*. Thus roving on
In confus'd march forlorn, th' advent'rous Bands   615
With shudd'ring horror pale, and eyes aghast
View'd first thir lamentable lot, and found
No rest: through many a dark and dreary Vale
They pass'd, and many a Region dolorous,
O'er many a Frozen, many a Fiery Alp,   620
Rocks, Caves, Lakes, Fens, Bogs, Dens, and shades of death,
A Universe of death, which God by curse *Mostly Spondees*
Created evil, for evil only good,
Where all life dies, death lives, and Nature breeds,
Perverse, all monstrous, all prodigious things,   625
Abominable, inutterable, and worse
Than Fables yet have feign'd, or fear conceiv'd,
Gorgons and *Hydras,* and *Chimeras* dire.

611. The myths about the three Gorgons were, as Milton implies (627
below), inconsistent, but he preferred to imagine them here, like Homer
(*Od.* XI, 633), as monsters of the infernal world.

614. By putting Tantalus in Lethe Milton altered the familiar allegory
of "thirsty Tantalus hung by the chin" (*F. Q.* I, v, 35) in a stream
bordered by fruit trees, as a punishment for his greed when he ban-
queted with the gods.

620. *Alp,* any high mountain.

621. See the note on 948 below.

628. Compare the note on 611. The hydras are vague monsters rather
than exactly such creatures as the Lernean Hydra whose nine proliferat-
ing heads Hercules seared off; and the chimeras are not to be taken
literally as like the Chimera which Bellerophon killed. (*Il.,* VI, 180.)
They are symbolic like the "unnumbered spectres" of Virgil's hell, where

> "horrid Hydra stands,
> And Briareus with all his hundred hands;
> Gorgons, Geryon with his triple frame;
> And vain Chimera vomits empty flame.
>   (*Aen.* VI, 287–9. Dryden's translation.)

Meanwhile the Adversary of God and Man,
Satan with thoughts inflam'd of highest design,   630
Puts on swift wings, and toward the Gates of Hell
Explores his solitary flight; sometimes
He scours the right hand coast, sometimes the left,
Now shaves with level wing the Deep, then soars
Up to the fiery concave tow'ring high.   635
As when far off at Sea a Fleet descri'd
Hangs in the Clouds, by *Equinoctial* Winds
Close sailing from *Bengala,* or the Isles
Of *Ternate* and *Tidore,* whence Merchants bring
Thir spicy Drugs: they on the Trading Flood   640
Through the wide *Ethiopian* to the Cape
Ply stemming nightly toward the Pole.   So seem'd
Far off the flying Fiend: at last appear
Hell bounds high reaching to the horrid Roof,
And thrice threefold the Gates; three folds were Brass,   645
Three Iron, three of Adamantine Rock,
Impenetrable, impal'd with circling fire,
Yet unconsum'd.   Before the Gates there sat
On either side a formidable shape;
The one seem'd Woman to the waist, and fair,   650
But ended foul in many a scaly fold
Voluminous and vast, a Serpent arm'd

---

629. In Job (i, 6) the Adversary, or Satan, is one of the Sons of God, but in I Peter (v, 8) the Adversary is described as a "roaring lion," walking "about, seeking whom he may devour."

635. Compare the note on 434 above.

639. The simile is filled with the excitement of the new trade with Bengal and the Moluccas, or Spice Islands, of which Tarenate (Ternate) and its tiny neighbour, Tidore, were the best known.

641. The classical name for the Indian Ocean off Africa, through which Milton's fleet ploughs toward the Cape of Good Hope and the south pole, was the Ethiopian Sea.

650. In part Sin resembles Spenser's monster, Error,

> Halfe like a serpent horribly displaide,
> But th'other halfe did womans shape retaine;—
> (*F. Q.* I, i, 14.)

but her belt of hell-hounds, barking like Cerberus, is a reminiscence of Ovid's account of Circe's bewitching of the nymph, Scylla. (*Met.* XIV, 65.) In Phineas Fletcher's *Apollyonists* (I, 10–14) Sin is the portress of hell.

With mortal sting: about her middle round
A cry of Hell Hounds never ceasing bark'd
With wide *Cerberean* mouths full loud, and rung   655
A hideous Peal: yet, when they list, would creep,
If aught disturb'd thir noise, into her womb,
And kennel there, yet there still bark'd and howl'd
Within unseen. Far less abhorr'd than these
Vex'd *Scylla* bathing in the Sea that parts   660
Calabria from the hoarse *Trinacrian* shore:
Nor uglier follow the Night-Hag, when call'd
In secret, riding through the Air she comes
Lur'd with the smell of infant blood, to dance
With *Lapland* Witches, while the labouring Moon   665
Eclipses at thir charms. The other shape,
If shape it might be call'd that shape had none
Distinguishable in member, joint, or limb,
Or substance might be call'd that shadow seem'd,
For each seem'd either; black it stood as Night,   670

---

660. Again Milton thought of Circe's transformation of Scylla into the
surf-washed reef between Calabria (the "toe" of the Italian "boot") and
Trinacria (Sicily), whose raging waves were the basis for the mythical
barking dogs; but he thought also of a traditional allegory, represented
by Spenser's Rock of Foul Reproach, with its "shivered ships" and
"carcasses exanimate"

> "Of such, as having all their substance spent
> In wanton joyes and lustes intemperate,
> Did afterwards make shipwrack violent."
> (*F. Q.* II, xii, 7.)

662. The *Night-Hag* is, probably, Hecate, whose charms were used
by Circe to bewitch Scylla (*Met.* XIV, 44). Popular superstition represented her as queen of the witches, as in *Macbeth* (III, v, and IV, i).

665. Lapland was so notorious as the home of witchcraft that "a Lapland" in the seventeenth century meant "a Lapland witch."
labouring, eclipsing. (Compare Virgil's *Georg.* II, 478.) From China
to Greece and Italy popular superstition has attributed eclipses of the
moon to witchcraft.

667. Everywhere in Renaissance literature Milton found the negative-
ness of death's horror stressed. Compare Bacon's Essay *Of Death*, or
Spenser's picture:

> "Death with most grim and griesly visage seen,
> Yet is he nought but parting of the breath;
> Ne ought to see, but like a shade to ween,
> Unbodied, unsoul'd, unheard, unseen."
> (*F. Q.* VII, vii, 46.)

Fierce as ten Furies, terrible as Hell,
And shook a dreadful Dart; what seem'd his head
The likeness of a Kingly Crown had on.
Satan was now at hand, and from his seat
The Monster moving onward came as fast,   675
With horrid strides, Hell trembled as he strode.
Th' undaunted Fiend what this might be admir'd,
Admir'd, not fear'd; God and his Son except,
Created thing naught valu'd he nor shunn'd;
And with disdainful look thus first began.   680
   Whence and what art thou, execrable shape,
That dar'st, though grim and terrible, advance
Thy miscreated Front athwart my way
To yonder Gates? through them I mean to pass,
That be assured, without leave askt of thee: 685
Retire, or taste thy folly, and learn by proof,
Hell-born, not to contend with Spirits of Heav'n.
   To whom the Goblin full of wrath repli'd,
Art thou that Traitor Angel, art thou hee,
Who first broke peace in Heav'n and Faith, till then   690
Unbrok'n, and in proud rebellious Arms
Drew after him the third part of Heav'n's Sons
Conjur'd against the highest, for which both Thou
And they outcast from God, are here condemn'd
To waste Eternal days in woe and pain?   695
And reck'n'st thou thyself with Spirits of Heav'n,
Hell-doom'd, and breath'st defiance here and scorn,
Where I reign King, and to enrage thee more,
Thy King and Lord?   Back to thy punishment,
False fugitive, and to thy speed add wings,   700
Lest with a whip of Scorpions I pursue
Thy ling'ring, or with one stroke of this Dart

---

   673. Milton thought of St. John's vision of the king of terrors, when "a crown was given unto him, and he went forth conquering, and to conquer." (Rev. vi, 2.)

   677. *admir'd* has its Latin force of "wonder" or "observe."

   692. *The third part of Heaven's Sons* alludes to St. John's dragon, whose "tail drew the third part of the stars of heaven, and did cast them to earth." (Rev. xii, 3–4.)

   693. *Conjur'd,* bound together by an oath. The word keeps its Latin meaning literally.

Strange horror seize thee, and pangs unfelt before.
  So spake the grisly terror, and in shape,
So speaking and so threat'ning, grew tenfold   705
More dreadful and deform: on th' other side
Incens't with indignation *Satan* stood
Unterrifi'd, and like a Comet burn'd,
That fires the length of *Ophiucus* huge
In th' Arctic Sky, and from his horrid hair   710
Shakes Pestilence and War.   Each at the Head
Levell'd his deadly aim; thir fatal hands
No second stroke intend, and such a frown
Each cast at th' other, as when two black Clouds
With Heav'n's Artillery fraught, come rattling on   715
Over the *Caspian,* then stand front to front
Hov'ring a space, till Winds the signal blow
To join thir dark Encounter in mid air:
So frown'd the mighty Combatants, that Hell
Grew darker at thir frown, so matcht they stood;   720
For never but once more was either like
To meet so great a foe: and now great deeds
Had been achiev'd, whereof all Hell had rung,
Had not the Snaky Sorceress that sat
Fast by Hell Gate, and kept the fatal Key,   725
Ris'n, and with hideous outcry rush'd between.
  O Father, what intends thy hand, she cri'd,
Against thy only Son?   What fury O Son,
Possesses thee to bend that mortal Dart
Against thy Father's head? and know'st for whom;   730
For him who sits above and laughs the while
At thee ordain'd his drudge, to execute

---

708. Perhaps this is a reminiscence of Aeneas in his armour, shining
like a comet which portended disaster, as his ship bore down upon
Turnus.   (*Aen.* X, 272–5.)

709. *Ophiuchus,* "the serpent-bearer," is one of the largest constellations.

716. As early as Horace (*Odes,* II, 9, 2) the Caspian was proverbially
stormy.

722. The great foe of both, of course, is Christ, whose "last enemy
that shall be destroyed is death."   (I Cor. xv, 26.)

725. Below (774, 850 and 871) there seems to be deliberate stress
ʋpon the allegory that Sin has the keys of hell.

Whate'er his wrath, which he calls Justice, bids,
His wrath which one day will destroy ye both.
   She spake, and at her words the hellish Pest   735
Forbore, then these to her *Satan* return'd:
   So strange thy outcry, and thy words so strange
Thou interposest, that my sudden hand
Prevented spares to tell thee yet by deeds
What it intends; till first I know of thee,   740
What thing thou art, thus double-form'd, and why
In this infernal Vale first met thou call'st
Me Father, and that Phantasm call'st my Son?
I know thee not, nor ever saw till now
Sight more detestable than him and thee.   745
   T' whom thus the Portress of Hell Gate repli'd:
Hast thou forgot me then, and do I seem
Now in thine eye so foul, once deem'd so fair
In Heav'n, when at th' Assembly, and in sight
Of all the Seraphim with thee combin'd   750
In bold conspiracy against Heav'n's King,
All on a sudden miserable pain
Surpris'd thee, dim thine eyes, and dizzy swum
In darkness, while thy head flames thick and fast
Threw forth, till on the left side op'ning wide,   755
Likest to thee in shape and count'nance bright,
Then shining heav'nly fair, a Goddess arm'd
Out of thy head I sprung; amazement seiz'd
All th' Host of Heav'n; back they recoil'd afraid
At first, and call'd me *Sin,* and for a Sign   760
Portentous held me; but familiar grown,
I pleas'd, and with attractive graces won
The most averse, thee chiefly, who full oft
Thyself in me thy perfect image viewing
Becam'st enamour'd, and such joy thou took'st   765

---

752. At the moment when "lust conceived" in Satan's mind Milton imagines Sin as being born, as Minerva was said to have sprung, fully armed, from the head of Jupiter. He felt nothing incongruous in combining that myth with St. James's teaching (i, 15) that "when lust hath conceived, it bringeth forth sin; and sin, when it is finished, bringeth forth death." This verse was the basis of a medieval allegory which shaped the idea of Sin as the daughter of Satan and, by him, the mother of the Seven Deadly Sins, in John Gower's *Mirrour de l'Omme.* (205–237.)

With me in secret, that my womb conceiv'd
A growing burden.   Meanwhile War arose,
And fields were fought in Heav'n; wherein remain'd
(For what could else) to our Almighty Foe
Clear Victory, to our part loss and rout   770
Through all the Empyrean: down they fell
Driv'n headlong from the Pitch of Heaven, down
Into this Deep, and in the general fall
I also; at which time this powerful Key
Into my hand was giv'n, with charge to keep   775
These Gates for ever shut, which none can pass
Without my op'ning.   Pensive here I sat
Alone, but long I sat not, till my womb
Pregnant by thee, and now excessive grown
Prodigious motion felt and rueful throes.   780
At last this odious offspring whom thou seest
Thine own begotten, breaking violent way
Tore through my entrails, that with fear and pain
Distorted, all my nether shape thus grew
Transform'd: but he my inbred enemy   785
Forth issu'd, brandishing his fatal Dart
Made to destroy: I fled, and cri'd out *Death;*
Hell trembl'd at the hideous Name, and sigh'd
From all her Caves, and back resounded *Death.*
I fled, but he pursu'd (though more, it seems,   790
Inflam'd with lust than rage) and swifter far,
Mee overtook his mother all dismay'd,
And in embraces forcible and foul
Ingend'ring with me, of that rape begot
These yelling Monsters that with ceaseless cry   795
Surround me, as thou saw'st, hourly conceiv'd
And hourly born, with sorrow infinite
To me, for when they list into the womb

---

768. For the use of *field* to mean a "battle" compare I, 105.
798. Both the allegory and the details recall Spenser's Error:

> Of her there bred
> A thousand yong ones, which she dayly fed,
> Sucking upon her poisnous dugs, . . .
> Soone as that uncouth light upon them shone,
> Into her mouth they crept, and suddain all were gone.
> (*F. Q.* I, i, 15.)

That bred them they return, and howl and gnaw
My Bowels, thir repast; then bursting forth   800
Afresh with conscious terrors vex me round,
That rest or intermission none I find.
Before mine eyes in opposition sits
Grim *Death* my Son and foe, who sets them on,
And me his Parent would full soon devour   805
For want of other prey, but that he knows
His end with mine involv'd; and knows that I
Should prove a bitter Morsel, and his bane,
Whenever that shall be; so Fate pronounc'd.
But thou O Father, I forewarn thee, shun   810
His deadly arrow; neither vainly hope
To be invulnerable in those bright Arms,
Though temper'd heav'nly, for that mortal dint,
Save he who reigns above, none can resist.
 She finish'd, and the subtle Fiend his lore   815
Soon learn'd, now milder, and thus answer'd smooth.
Dear Daughter, since thou claim'st me for thy Sire,
And my fair Son here show'st me, the dear pledge
Of dalliance had with thee in Heav'n, and joys
Then sweet, now sad to mention, through dire change   820
Befall'n us unforeseen, unthought of, know
I come no enemy, but to set free
From out this dark and dismal house of pain,
Both him and thee, and all the heav'nly Host
Of Spirits that in our just pretenses arm'd   825
Fell with us from on high: from them I go
This uncouth errand sole, and one for all
Myself expose, with lonely steps to tread
Th' unfounded deep, and through the void immense
To search with wand'ring quest a place foretold   830
Should be, and, by concurring signs, ere now
Created vast and round, a place of bliss
In the Purlieus of Heav'n, and therein plac't
A race of upstart Creatures, to supply
Perhaps our vacant room, though more remov'd,   835

818. *pledge* has its Latin meaning of "a child," as a piedge of love.
825. *pretenses,* legal or diplomatic claims.
829. *unfounded,* without foundations or bottom.
deep, Chaos.

Lest Heav'n surcharg'd with potent multitude
Might hap to move new broils: Be this or aught
Than this more secret now design'd, I haste
To know, and this once known, shall soon return,
And bring ye to the place where Thou and Death   840
Shall dwell at ease, and up and down unseen
Wing silently the buxom Air, imbalm'd
With odours; there ye shall be fed and fill'd
Immeasurably, all things shall be your prey.
He ceas'd, for both seem'd highly pleas'd, and Death   845
Grinn'd horrible a ghastly smile, to hear
His famine should be fill'd, and blest his maw
Destin'd to that good hour: no less rejoic'd
His mother bad, and thus bespake her Sire.

    The key of this infernal Pit by due,   850
And by command of Heav'n's all-powerful King
I keep, by him forbidden to unlock
These Adamantine Gates; against all force
Death ready stands to interpose his dart,
Fearless to be o'ermatcht by living might.   855
But what owe I to his commands above
Who hates me, and hath hither thrust me down
Into this gloom of *Tartarus* profound,
To sit in hateful Office here confin'd,
Inhabitant of Heav'n, and heav'nly-born,   860
Here in perpetual agony and pain,
With terrors and with clamors compasst round
Of mine own brood, that on my bowels feed:
Thou art my Father, thou my Author, thou
My being gav'st me; whom should I obey   865
But thee, whom follow? thou wilt bring me soon
To that new world of light and bliss, among
The Gods who live at ease, where I shall Reign
At thy right hand voluptuous, as beseems

---

840. Satan's promise is fulfilled in X, 397–409.

842. *buxom*, unresisting.

847. Compare Eve's dread of Death's "ravenous maw." (X, 991.)

868. *The Gods who live at ease* is a translation of the Homeric account of the Olympians. (*Il.* VI, 138, and *Od.* IV, 805.)

869. Sin imagines herself enthroned with Satan like the Son of God at his Father's right hand. Compare III, 63, and its note.

Thy daughter and thy darling, without end.   870
  Thus saying, from her side the fatal Key,
Sad instrument of all our woe, she took;
And towards the Gate rolling her bestial train,
Forthwith the huge Portcullis high up drew,
Which but herself not all the *Stygian* powers   875
Could but once have mov'd; then in the key-hole turns
Th' intricate wards, and every Bolt and Bar
Of massy Iron or solid Rock with ease
Unfast'ns: on a sudden op'n fly
With impetuous recoil and jarring sound   880
Th' infernal doors, and on thir hinges grate
Harsh Thunder, that the lowest bottom shook
Of *Erebus*.   She op'n'd, but to shut
Excell'd her power; the Gates wide op'n stood,
That with extended wings a Banner'd Host   885
Under spread Ensigns marching might pass through
With Horse and Chariots rankt in loose array;
So wide they stood, and like a Furnace mouth
Cast forth redounding smoke and ruddy flame.
Before thir eyes in sudden view appear   890
The secrets of the hoary deep, a dark

---

  883. *Erebus;* the basic meaning is "darkness." Though Milton used it, like Tartarus, as a synonym for hell, its Homeric meaning was that of a distinct region of darkness under ground, but above Hades.

  891. Milton's treatment of Chaos as a place, the Deep, and as a person, the ancestor, with Night, of all things, and also as the lord of the Deep, combines suggestions from the classics all the way from Hesiod's *Theogony* (116) to the description of Chaos which opens Ovid's *Metamorphoses*. The "embryon atoms" are Ovid's "seeds of things" (*Met.,* I, 9) and the conception of the universe as afloat in Chaos resembles Ovid's "earth supported in the surrounding air by its own weight" (*Met.* I, 12-13). Compare Milton's "self-balanced earth" (VII, 242). The war of the four elements was a doctrine going back to Empedocles, which neo-platonizing poets had christianized by representing them as brought into harmony in the universe,

> As their Almightie Maker first ordained,
> And bound them with inviolable bands;
> Else would the waters overflow the lands,
> And fire devour the ayre, and hell them quight.
>   (*F. Q.* IV, x, 35.)

Even the fanatically orthodox Du Bartas, who insisted on God's creation of the universe out of nothing, made much of "the brawl of atoms."

Illimitable Ocean without bound,
Without dimension, where length, breadth, and highth,
And time and place are lost; where eldest Night
And *Chaos,* Ancestors of Nature, hold   895
Eternal *Anarchy,* amidst the noise
Of endless wars, and by confusion stand.
For hot, cold, moist, and dry, four Champions fierce
Strive here for Maistry, and to Battle bring
Thir embryon Atoms; they around the flag   900
Of each his Faction, in thir several Clans,
Light-arm'd or heavy, sharp, smooth, swift or slow,
Swarm populous, unnumber'd as the Sands
Of *Barca* or *Cyrene's* torrid soil,
Levied to side with warring Winds, and poise   905
Thir lighter wings. To whom these most adhere,
Hee rules a moment; *Chaos* Umpire sits,
And by decision more imbroils the fray
By which he Reigns: next him high Arbiter
Chance governs all. Into this wild Abyss,   910
The Womb of nature and perhaps her Grave,
Of neither Sea, nor Shore, nor Air, nor Fire,
But all these in thir pregnant causes mixt
Confus'dly, and which thus must ever fight,
Unless th' Almighty Maker them ordain   915
His dark materials to create more Worlds,
Into this wild Abyss the wary fiend
Stood on the brink of Hell and look'd a while,
Pondering his Voyage: for no narrow frith
He had to cross. Nor was his ear less peal'd   920
With noises loud and ruinous (to compare

---

904. *Barca* is the desert between Egypt and Tunis. *Cyrene* was the ancient city near the site of modern Tripoli.

911. The end of the world was a Christian doctrine strenuously defended against the Aristotelian theory of a perpetual universe. Du Bartas said positively that

> This *world* to *Chaos* shall again *return.*
> (*du Bartas,* 226, lt.)

In C. D. I, 33, Milton hesitated whether he should believe in the absolute annihilation of the matter of which the universe is made or in a fundamental change in its constituent atoms after the final conflagration.

920. *peal'd,* struck by noise. Compare III, 329.

Great things with small) than when *Bellona* storms,
With all her battering Engines bent to rase
Some Capital City, or less than if this frame
Of Heav'n were falling, and these Elements   925
In mutiny had from her Axle torn
The steadfast Earth.   At last his Sail-broad Vans
He spreads for flight, and in the surging smoke
Uplifted spurns the ground, thence many a League
As in a cloudy Chair ascending rides   930
Audacious, but that seat soon failing, meets
A vast vacuity: all unawares
Flutt'ring his pennons vain plumb down he drops
Ten thousand fadom deep, and to this hour
Down had been falling, had not by ill chance   935
The strong rebuff of some tumultuous cloud
Instinct with Fire and Nitre hurried him
As many miles aloft: that fury stay'd,
Quencht in a Boggy *Syrtis,* neither Sea,
Nor good dry Land: nigh founder'd on he fares,   940
Treading the crude consistence, half on foot,
Half flying; behoves him now both Oar and Sail.
As when a Gryfon through the Wilderness
With winged course o'er Hill or moory Dale,
Pursues the *Arimaspian,* who by stealth   945
Had from his wakeful custody purloin'd
The guarded Gold: So eagerly the fiend
O'er bog or steep, through strait, rough, dense, or rare,
With head, hands, wings, or feet pursues his way,

---

922. *Bellona,* the Roman goddess of war.

934. *fadom* represents Milton's preference for the primitive spelling
and pronunciation of "fathom."

939. *Syrtis* was the name given to two gulfs near Tripoli which were
famous for quicksands.

945. Milton had read Herodotus' story of the gold in "the north of
Europe," which "it is said the Arimaspians, a one-eyed people, steal from
the griffons." (Herodotus, III, 116.)

948. Both the artifice and art of Milton's monosyllabic lines appear in
contrast with the abuse of the device by Sir William Alexander, a favourable example of whose treatment of it is his account of Jonathan and
Nahas, Ammon's Lord, engaged in a single combat in which they

"Urg'd, shunn'd, forc'd, fayn'd, bow'd, rais'd,
hand, leg, left, right, . . . (*Jonathan,* 556.)

And swims or sinks, or wades, or creeps, or flies: 950
At length a universal hubbub wild
Of stunning sounds and voices all confus'd
Borne through the hollow dark assaults his ear
With loudest vehemence: thither he plies,
Undaunted to meet there whatever power   955
Or Spirit of the nethermost Abyss
Might in that noise reside, of whom to ask
Which way the nearest coast of darkness lies
Bordering on light; when straight behold the Throne
Of *Chaos,* and his dark Pavilion spread   960
Wide on the wasteful Deep; with him Enthron'd
Sat Sable-vested Night, eldest of things,
The Consort of his Reign; and by them stood
Orcus and *Ades,* and the dreaded name
Of *Demogorgon; Rumor* next and *Chance,*   965
And *Tumult* and *Confusion* all imbroil'd,
And *Discord* with a thousand various mouths.
   T' whom *Satan* turning boldly, thus.   Ye Powers
And Spirits of this nethermost Abyss,
Chaos and *ancient Night,* I come no Spy,   970
With purpose to explore or to disturb
The secrets of your Realm, but by constraint
Wand'ring this darksome Desert, as my way
Lies through your spacious Empire up to light,
Alone, and without guide, half lost, I seek   975
What readiest path leads where your gloomy bounds

   962. In Hesiod's *Theogony* (123) Night seems to be the child of
Chaos, but the Orphic Hymns and Platonic tradition made her the "most
ancient grandmother of all."   (*F. Q.* I, v, 22.)

   964. *Orcus,* Hell. *Ades,* Hades, or Pluto. Like *Chaos,* Hades was
used for either the realm or its king.

   965. Demogorgon first entered literature as a mysterious infernal deity
mentioned in a scholium to Statius' *Thebaid,* IV, 516; but it was to
Boccaccio's *Genealogy of the Gods,* I, i, that the Renaissance was indebted for the notion of him which Spenser gives when he situates the
home of the Fates

> "Farre under ground from tract of living went,
>   Downe in the bottome of the deepe Abysse,
>   Where Demogorgon, in dull darknesse pent,
>   Farre from the view of gods and heavens blis,
>   The hideous Chaos keepes."
>   (*F. Q.* IV, ii, 47.)

Confine with Heav'n; or if some other place
From your Dominion won, th' Ethereal King
Possesses lately, thither to arrive
I travel this profound, direct my course;   980
Directed, no mean recompence it brings
To your behoof, if I that Region lost,
All usurpation thence expell'd, reduce
To her original darkness and your sway
(Which is my present journey) and once more   985
Erect the Standard there of *ancient Night;*
Yours be th' advantage all, mine the revenge.
      Thus *Satan;* and him thus the Anarch old
With falt'ring speech and visage incompos'd
Answer'd. I know thee, stranger, who thou art,   990
That mighty leading Angel, who of late
Made head against Heav'n's King, though overthrown.
I saw and heard, for such a numerous Host
Fled not in silence through the frighted deep
With ruin upon ruin, rout on rout,   995
Confusion worse confounded; and Heav'n Gates
Pour'd out by millions her victorious Bands
Pursuing. I upon my Frontiers here
Keep residence; if all I can will serve,
That little which is left so to defend   1000
Encroacht on still through our intestine broils
Weak'ning the Sceptre of old Night: first Hell
Your dungeon stretching far and wide beneath;
Now lately Heaven and Earth, another World
Hung o'er my Realm, link'd in a golden Chain   1005
To that side Heav'n from whence your Legions fell:
If that way be your walk, you have not far;
So much the nearer danger; go and speed;
Havoc and spoil and ruin are my gain.
      He ceas'd; and *Satan* stay'd not to reply,   1010

977. *Confine,* border with.

988. *the Anarch,* Chaos as lord of misrule.

989. *incompos'd,* not composed; a more significant word than "discomposed."

1005. For the use made of the golden chain by which Homer said that Zeus drew up the gods, the earth and sea and the whole universe, see the Introduction, §10.

But glad that now his Sea should find a shore,
With fresh alacrity and force renew'd
Springs upward like a Pyramid of fire
Into the wild expanse, and through the shock
Of fighting Elements, on all sides round   1015
Environ'd wins his way; harder beset
And more endanger'd, than when *Argo* pass'd
Through *Bosporus* betwixt the justling Rocks:
Or when *Ulysses* on the Larboard shunn'd
Charybdis, and by th' other whirlpool steer'd.   1020
So he with difficulty and labour hard
Mov'd on, with difficulty and labour hee;
But hee once past, soon after when man fell,
Strange alteration! Sin and Death amain
Following his track, such was the will of Heav'n,   1025
Pav'd after him a broad and beat'n way
Over the dark Abyss, whose boiling Gulf
Tamely endur'd a Bridge of wondrous length
From Hell continu'd reaching th' utmost Orb
Of this frail World; by which the Spirits perverse   1030
With easy intercourse pass to and fro
To tempt or punish mortals, except whom
God and good Angels guard by special grace.
But now at last the sacred influence
Of light appears, and from the walls of Heav'n   1035
Shoots far into the bosom of dim Night
A glimmering dawn; here Nature first begins
Her fardest verge, and *Chaos* to retire
As from her outmost works a brok'n foe

1017. The *Argo* was the ship in which Jason and the Argonauts in quest of the Golden Fleece escaped from the floating islands in the Bosporus (Bosphorus), now the Straits of Constantinople.

1020. *Charybdis* was the whirlpool on the Sicilian side of the Straits of Messina, opposite Scylla.

1026. Compare X, 293–324.

1033. The Attendant Spirit in *Comus,* Raphael (in Books V–VIII), and Michael (in Books XI–XII) attest the imaginative depth of the belief in good angels which Milton stated in *C. D.,* I, ix.

1037. The *glimmering dawn* both announces the empyreal heaven (1047) and prepares for the invocation to Light in Book III.

1039. *her* refers to Nature.

With tumult less and with less hostile din,   1040
That *Satan* with less toil, and now with ease
Wafts on the calmer wave by dubious light
And like a weather-beaten Vessel holds
Gladly the Port, though Shrouds and Tackle torn;
Or in the emptier waste, resembling Air,   1045
Weighs his spread wings, at leisure to behold
Far off th' Empyreal Heav'n, extended wide
In circuit, undetermin'd square or round,
With Opal Tow'rs and Battlements adorn'd
Of living Sapphire, once his native Seat;   1050
And fast by hanging in a golden Chain
This pendant world, in bigness as a Star
Of smallest Magnitude close by the Moon.
Thither full fraught with mischievous revenge,
Accurst, and in a cursed hour he hies.   1055

The End of the Second Book.

1050. There is a vague recollection of St. John's statement that the second foundation of the wall (of heaven) was a sapphire (Rev. xxi, 19).

1051. For Milton's contemporaries the *golden Chain* meant not only the chain with which Zeus controlled the gods (*Il.* VIII, 18–26) but also its many allegorizations from that of Plato in the *Theætetus* (153, c) to that of Chaucer in the *Knight's Tale* (I (A) 2987–2993):

> "The Firste Moevere of the cause above,
> Whan he first made the faire cheyne of love,
> Greet was th'effect, and heigh was his entente.
> Wel wiste he why, and what thereof he mente;
> For with that faire cheyne of love he bond
> The fyr, the eyr, the water, and the lond
> In certeyn boundes, that they may nat flee."

For Conti (p. 138) also the golden chain of Zeus symbolized both the physical and the moral bonds by which the universe is united. Compare the Introduction, §18.

1052. The pendent world is not merely the earth but the entire created universe within its "convex," which Satan has yet to penetrate. Compare III, 418–429.

BOOK III

THE ARGUMENT

God *sitting on his Throne sees* Satan *flying towards this world, then newly created; shows him to the Son who sat at his right hand; foretells the success of* Satan *in perverting mankind; clears his own Justice and Wisdom from all imputation, having created Man free and able enough to have withstood his Tempter; yet declares his purpose of grace towards him, in regard he fell not of his own malice, as did* Satan, *but by him seduc't. The Son of God renders praises to his Father for the manifestation of his gracious purpose towards Man; but God again declares, that Grace cannot be extended towards Man without the satisfaction of divine Justice; Man hath offended the majesty of God by aspiring to Godhead, and therefore with all his Progeny devoted to death must die, unless some one can be found sufficient to answer for his offence, and undergo his Punishment. The Son of God freely offers himself a Ransom for Man: the Father accepts him, ordains his incarnation, pronounces his exaltation above all Names in Heaven and Earth; commands all the Angels to adore him; they obey, and hymning to thir Harps in full Quire, celebrate the Father and the Son. Meanwhile* Satan *alights upon the bare convex of this World's outermost Orb; where wand'ring he first finds a place since call'd The Limbo of Vanity; what persons and things fly up thither; thence comes to the Gate of Heaven, describ'd ascending by stairs, and the waters above the Firmament that flow about it: His passage thence to the Orb of the Sun; he finds there* Uriel *the Regent of that Orb, but first changes himself into the shape of a meaner Angel; and pretending a zealous desire to behold the new Creation and Man whom God had plac't here, inquires of him the place of his habitation, and is directed; alights first on Mount* Niphates.

HAIL holy Light, offspring of Heav'n first-born,
Or of th' Eternal Coeternal beam

---

1. Ultimately, the conception of God as light may go back beyond Zoroastrianism. From Plato's *Republic* and *Timaeus* it entered Christian

77

May I express thee unblam'd? since God is light,
And never but in unapproached light
Dwelt from Eternity, dwelt then in thee, 5
Bright effluence of bright essence increate.
Or hear'st thou rather pure Ethereal stream,
Whose Fountain who shall tell? before the Sun,
Before the Heavens thou wert, and at the voice
Of God, as with a Mantle didst invest 10
The rising world of waters dark and deep,
Won from the void and formless infinite.
Thee I revisit now with bolder wing,

---

thought early, for I John (i, 5) affirms that, "God is light." For Dante light was God's creative power as well as an aspect of his essence, something to be thought of Platonically as the first of His creative ideas, and also as His Son,

> that Idea, which our Sovereign Sire
> Engendreth loving; for that lively light,
> Which passeth from his brightness, not disjoin'd
> From Him, nor from His love triune with them,
> Doth, through His bounty, congregate itself,
> Mirror'd, as 'twere in new existences,
> Itself unalterable and ever one.
> (*Paradiso*, xiii, 50–56, Cary's translation.)

St. Augustine's distinction between "the light which is God and the other light which God has made," M. Saurat suggests (*Milton*, p. 302), was obscured by Neo-Stoic and Cabbalistic influences when Milton's early contemporary, Robert Flud, asked in words almost identical with these lines whether "light is increate or created by an increate light." Milton's meaning may have been little more definite than Sir Thomas Browne's idea that "light is the shadow of God" (*Garden of Cyrus*, iv), but it is significantly less conventional and more philosophical than Du Bartas' invocation:

> All-hail pure Lamp, bright, sacred and excelling;
> Sorrow and Care, Darkness and Dread repelling:
> Thou World's great Taper, Wicked men's just Terror,
> Mother of Truth, true Beautie's only Mirror,
> God's eldest Daughter. . . .
> (*First Day*, 536–540.)

3. *express*, name. Because the more significant names of God in the Old Testament were mysteries, Milton hesitates to invoke light as the divine essence.

7. *hear'st thou rather*, would'st thou rather be called a heavenly effluence than a direct emanation from God.

8. The story of the creation of light before the sun (Gen. i, 3–5) is repeated (VII, 243–52).

Escap't the *Stygian* Pool, though long detain'd
In that obscure sojourn, while in my flight   15
Through utter and through middle darkness borne
With other notes than to th' *Orphean* Lyre
I sung of *Chaos* and *Eternal Night,*
Taught by the heav'nly Muse to venture down
The dark descent, and up to reascend,   20
Though hard and rare: thee I revisit safe,
And feel thy sovran vital Lamp; but thou
Revisit'st not these eyes, that roll in vain
To find thy piercing ray, and find no dawn;
So thick a drop serene hath quencht thir Orbs,   25
Or dim suffusion veil'd.   Yet not the more
Cease I to wander where the Muses haunt
Clear Spring, or shady Grove, or Sunny Hill,
Smit with the love of sacred song; but chief
Thee *Sion* and the flow'ry Brooks beneath   30
That wash thy hallow'd feet, and warbling flow,
Nightly I visit: nor sometimes forget
Those other two equall'd with me in Fate,
So were I equall'd with them in renown,

---

16. *utter and middle darkness,* Hell and Chaos.   Compare I, 72 and
V, 614.

18. Milton may have thought of the Orphic Hymn to Night although
Night is treated there as a beneficent goddess.   He certainly thought of
the tradition that Orpheus was the first interpreter of the physical and
spiritual secrets of hell and heaven, "a man most learned in divinity."
(Conti, p. 767.)

19. Compare I, 62; VII, 1, and IX, 21.

21. *safe:* The word is used here as it is in III, 197, to mean the spiritual security of those who see "light after light," *i.e.,* earthly and
heavenly light.

25. *drop serene* translates *gutta serena,* the technical Latin for "all
blindness in which the eye retains a normal appearance." (Brown,
Blindness, p. 22.)   Dim suffusion describes Milton's state less technically,
while both terms indicate his pleasure in the fact that his eyes, as the
portrait-frontispiece to his poem proved, betrayed so little "external appearance of injury, that they are as unclouded and bright as the eyes of
those who distinctly see." (*P. W.* I, p. 235.)

27. Milton does not repudiate the Muses (*i.e.,* Greek literature), but
he prefers Urania, Sion and Siloam again, as in I, 10–13.

32. Here and again in VII, 29 and IX, 22, Milton corroborates the
tradition that he composed *P. L.* at night.

Blind *Thamyris* and blind *Mæonides,*   35
And *Tiresias* and *Phineus* Prophets old.
Then feed on thoughts, that voluntary move
Harmonious numbers; as the wakeful Bird
Sings darkling, and in shadiest Covert hid
Tunes her nocturnal Note.   Thus with the Year   40
Seasons return, but not to me returns
Day, or the sweet approach of Ev'n or Morn,
Or sight of vernal bloom, or Summer's Rose,
Or flocks, or herds, or human face divine;
But cloud instead, and ever-during dark   45
Surrounds me, from the cheerful ways of men
Cut off, and for the Book of knowledge fair
Presented with a Universal blanc
Of Nature's works to mee expung'd and ras'd,
And wisdom at one entrance quite shut out.   50
So much the rather thou Celestial light

---

35. *Maeonides,* Homer.   Among the obscure myths about Thamyris,
whom Homer mentions (*Il.* II, 102–9), Milton remembered that he
was blind and perhaps also that Plutarch's book *On Music* said that
he was the author of a poem about the war of the Titans against the
Gods.   (Conti, p. 619.)

36. The tradition that the greatest prophets of antiquity were blind
was the basis of Milton's youthful allusion to Tiresias, the sage who
speaks for the gods in Sophocles' *Oedipus Rex* and *Antigone,* as "the
Theban seer whose blindness proved his great illumination." (*De Idea
Platonica,* 25–6.)   Speaking of his own blindness in the *Second Defense*
(*P.W.* I, 236) he quoted Apollonius' *Argonautica* about Tiresias:

> Fearless, though Jove might rage, he showed
> The arcane purposes of heaven to us;
> Endless old age the gods on him bestowed
> And made him strong, but blind and piteous.

Phineus, a Thracian prophet, according to one obscure legend, chose a
miraculously long old age of blindness rather than a short and happy
life.   He was stricken blind by the Sun.   (Conti, p. 730.)

38. *numbers,* technically, feet in a verse of poetry; but here the meaning is verse or poetry itself.

39. *darkling,* not a participle but an adverb.   Compare *Lear* I, iv, 240:
"So out went the candle, and we were left darkling."

48. *blanc:* Milton regularly spelled thus when he used the word in its
primitive meaning of "white" or "grey."   Here his spelling corresponds
with his account of the sensation of dim light in his blind eyes.

51. Milton's imperfect distinction between celestial light and the physical light of the universe, toward which Satan is moving through

Shine inward, and the mind through all her powers
Irradiate, there plant eyes, all mist from thence
Purge and disperse, that I may see and tell
Of things invisible to mortal sight.   55
    Now had the Almighty Father from above,
From the pure Empyrean where he sits
High Thron'd above all highth, bent down his eye,
His own works and their works at once to view:
About him all the Sanctities of Heaven   60
Stood thick as Stars, and from his sight receiv'd
Beatitude past utterance; on his right
The radiant image of his Glory sat,
His only Son; On Earth he first beheld
Our two first Parents, yet the only two   65
Of mankind, in the happy Garden plac't,
Reaping immortal fruits of joy and love,
Uninterrupted joy, unrivall'd love
In blissful solitude; he then survey'd
Hell and the Gulf between, and *Satan* there   70

Chaos, recalls Bacon's belief that "the first form that was created was
light, which hath a relation and correspondence in nature and corporeal
things to knowledge in spirits and incorporate things." (*Advancement*,
I, vi, 4). For Milton physical light was "the first of things" (VII, 244),
and its making was the second step in the creation of the universe
(III, 712); but he was influenced by Neo-Platonic theories which related
the "lucid essence" of God with the sun, on the one hand, and with
the human mind, on the other. Such theories assumed a scientific guise
in Flud's *History of Both Worlds* (Tome II, tractatus I, section 1, p. 167)
and were stamped expressly as orthodox by Melancthon in his chapter
on *The Image of God in Man* (*De anima*, p. 169).

57. *Empyrean* to Milton, vividly conscious of its Greek etymology,
meant the "realm of fire," or "of light," and not merely "Heaven."

60. *the Sanctities of Heaven,* the angelic hierarchies. Medieval practice referred to the angels as "saints."

62. See note on I, 684. The *C.D.* (I, 33) speaks of the perfect happiness of the righteous in Heaven as arising chiefly from the divine vision.

63. Hebrews (i, 2–3) is quoted in *C.D.* (I, v) as the amplest account
of God's Son; "by whom he made the worlds. Who being the brightness of his glory, and the express image of his person, . . . sat down on
the right hand of the majesty on high."

70. Satan flies *sublime* (aloft) through the upper limits of Chaos and
Night, close to the wall of Heaven, in a twilit atmosphere (*dun air*),
ready to *stoop* (pounce like a bird of prey) upon the outer shell of the
universe.

Coasting the wall of Heav'n on this side Night
In the dun Air sublime, and ready now
To stoop with wearied wings, and willing feet
On the bare outside of this World, that seem'd
Firm land imbosom'd without Firmament,   75
Uncertain which, in Ocean or in Air.
Him God beholding from his prospect high,
Wherein past, present, future he beholds,
Thus to his only Son foreseeing spake.

Only begotten Son, seest thou what rage   80
Transports our adversary, whom no bounds
Prescrib'd, no bars of Hell, nor all the chains
Heapt on him there, nor yet the main Abyss
Wide interrupt can hold; so bent he seems
On desperate revenge, that shall redound   85
Upon his own rebellious head. And now
Through all restraint broke loose he wings his way
Not far off Heav'n, in the Precincts of light,
Directly towards the new created World,
And Man there plac't, with purpose to assay   90
If him by force he can destroy, or worse,
By some false guile pervert; and shall pervert;
For man will heark'n to his glozing lies,
And easily transgress the sole Command,
Sole pledge of his obedience: So will fall   95
Hee and his faithless Progeny: whose fault?
Whose but his own? ingrate, he had of mee

---

74. *World,* not the earth, but the outer shell of the universe as viewed
from the outside. Milton describes the firmament in VII, 261–7.

76. *Uncertain,* an impersonal and absolute construction, "it is uncertain." Milton did not know whether Chaos, in which his island universe floated, was comparable to sea or air.

84. *interrupt* is felt as the Latin perfect passive participle from which
it is derived, and the thought is of the vast Abyss (*i.e.,* Chaos), broken
wide between Heaven and Hell.

90. *assay,* make trial.

94. *sole Command,* the prohibition to touch the Tree of Life.

96. *faithless,* because when Adam broke faith all his posterity were
involved—not that his sin is arbitrarily visited on his descendants, but in
a mystical yet actual sense, perhaps because the sin involved "insensibility to the welfare of their offspring," "all sinned in Adam." (*C.D.,*
I, xi.) Compare III, 209.

All he could have; I made him just and right,
Sufficient to have stood, though free to fall.
Such I created all th' Ethereal Powers   100
And Spirits, both them who stood and them who fail'd;
Freely they stood who stood, and fell who fell.
Not free, what proof could they have giv'n sincere
Of true allegiance, constant Faith or Love,
Where only what they needs must do, appear'd,   105
Not what they would? what praise could they receive?
What pleasure I from such obedience paid,
When Will and Reason (Reason also is choice)
Useless and vain, of freedom both despoil'd,
Made passive both, had serv'd necessity,   110
Not mee. They therefore as to right belong'd,
So were created, nor can justly accuse
Thir maker, or thir making, or thir Fate;
As if predestination over-rul'd
Thir will, dispos'd by absolute Decree   115
Or high foreknowledge; they themselves decreed
Thir own revolt, not I: if I foreknew,
Foreknowledge had no influence on their fault,
Which had no less prov'd certain unforeknown.
So without least impulse or shadow of Fate,   120
Or aught by me immutably foreseen,
They trespass, Authors to themselves in all

---

100. In the *C.D.* (I, iii), urging God's freedom from responsibility in spite of his foreknowledge of the rebellion of both angels and men, Milton wrote "that, in assigning the gift of free will, God suffered both men and angels to stand or fall at their own uncontrolled choice, . . . not necessitating the evil consequences which ensued, but leaving them contingent." Compare Satan's confession (IV, 63-8) and the stress on the angels' guilt (V, 525-43).

106. Arguing that the miracle of God's grace is enhanced, not impaired, by belief in the freedom of the will, Milton insisted that "The acceptableness of duties done under a law of necessity is diminished, or rather is annihilated altogether." (*C.D.*, I, iv.) Compare III, 173-189.

108. "Reason is but choosing," Milton said of God's gift of reason to Adam. (*Areopagitica,* P.W., II, 79.)

119. Milton devotes a long chapter in *C.D.* (I, iv) to proving that "the prescience of God seems to have no connection with the principle or essence of predestination."

120. See Introduction, §14.

Both what they judge and what they choose; for so
I form'd them free, and free they must remain,
Till they enthrall themselves: I else must change   125
Thir nature, and revoke the high Decree
Unchangeable, Eternal, which ordain'd
Thir freedom, they themselves ordain'd thir fall.
The first sort by thir own suggestion fell,
Self-tempted, self-deprav'd: Man falls deceiv'd   130
By the other first: Man therefore shall find grace,
The other none: in Mercy and Justice both,
Through Heav'n and Earth, so shall my glory excel,
But Mercy first and last shall brightest shine.
   Thus while God spake, ambrosial fragrance fill'd   135
All Heav'n, and in the blessed Spirits elect
Sense of new joy ineffable diffus'd:
Beyond compare the Son of God was seen
Most glorious, in him all his Father shone
Substantially express'd, and in his face   140
Divine compassion visibly appear'd,
Love without end, and without measure Grace,
Which uttering thus he to his Father spake.
   O Father, gracious was that word which clos'd
Thy sovran sentence, that Man should find grace;   145

---

128. The thought is paralleled by Descartes' *Passions of the Soul* (*Les passions de l'âme*, I, 47 and III, 152), and by *C.D.* (I, iii), where Milton insists that "God is not mutable, so long as he decrees nothing absolutely which could happen otherwise through the liberty assigned to man. He would indeed be mutable, . . . if he were to obstruct by another decree that liberty which he had already decreed, or were to darken it with the least shadow of necessity."

129. *The first sort:* The angels who revolted.
suggestion, temptation.

135. *ambrosial,* delicious. See note on II, 245.

136. *elect:* Milton's term for the good angels. (Compare III, 360, VI, 374.) In *C.D.* (I, ix) he challenges "the opinion that the good angels are now upheld, not as much by their own strength, as by the grace of God," and adds that "the elect angels" of I Tim. v, 21, means "those who have not revolted." *Elect* is used of men in the same sense in III, 184.

140. In *C.D.* (I, v) Milton draws the inference from Hebrews i, 2–3, that "it must be understood from this that God imparted to the Son as much as he pleased of the divine nature, nay of the divine substance itself."

For which both Heav'n and Earth shall high extol
Thy praises, with th' innumerable sound
Of Hymns and sacred Songs, wherewith thy Throne
Encompass'd shall resound thee ever blest.
For should Man finally be lost, should Man   150
Thy creature late so lov'd, thy youngest Son
Fall circumvented thus by fraud, though join'd
With his own folly? that be from thee far,
That far be from thee, Father, who art Judge
Of all things made, and judgest only right.   155
Or shall the Adversary thus obtain
His end, and frustrate thine, shall he fulfil
His malice, and thy goodness bring to naught,
Or proud return though to his heavier doom,
Yet with revenge accomplish't and to Hell   160
Draw after him the whole Race of mankind,
By him corrupted? or wilt thou thyself
Abolish thy Creation, and unmake,
For him, what for thy glory thou hast made?
So should thy goodness and thy greatness both   165
Be question'd and blasphem'd without defence.
    To whom the great Creator thus repli'd.
O Son, in whom my Soul hath chief delight,
Son of my bosom, Son who art alone
My word, my wisdom, and effectual might,   170
All hast thou spok'n as my thoughts are, all
As my Eternal purpose hath decreed:
Man shall not quite be lost, but sav'd who will,
Yet not of will in him, but grace in me
Freely voutsaf't; once more I will renew   175

---

156. See note on II, 629, and compare "foe" in III, 179.

166. *blasphem'd* has its primitive Greek force of "evil-speaking," not of "impiety."

168. Compare the words from heaven at Christ's baptism, "This is my beloved Son, in whom I am well pleased." (Matt. iii, 17.)

170. *C.D.* (I, v) interprets John i, 1, as meaning that the Word, Christ, was not "in the beginning God, but was in the beginning with God; that he might show him to be God only by proximity and love, not in essence."

might: The titles *wisdom* and *might* recall Paul's saying that to the elect Christ is "the power of God and the wisdom of God." (I Cor. i, 24.)

His lapsed powers, though forfeit and enthrall'd
By sin to foul exorbitant desires;
Upheld by me, yet once more he shall stand
On even ground against his mortal foe,
By me upheld, that he may know how frail   180
His fall'n condition is, and to me owe
All his deliv'rance, and to none but me.
Some I have chosen of peculiar grace
Elect above the rest; so is my will:
The rest shall hear me call, and oft be warn'd   185
Thir sinful state, and to appease betimes
Th' incensed Deity while offer'd grace
Invites; for I will clear thir senses dark,
What may suffice, and soft'n stony hearts
To pray, repent, and bring obedience due.   190
To Prayer, repentance, and obedience due,
Though but endeavour'd with sincere intent,
Mine ear shall not be slow, mine eye not shut.
And I will place within them as a guide
My Umpire *Conscience,* whom if they will hear,   195
Light after light well us'd they shall attain,
And to the end persisting, safe arrive.
This my long sufferance and my day of grace
They who neglect and scorn, shall never taste;
But hard be hard'n'd, blind be blinded more,   200
That they may stumble on, and deeper fall;
And none but such from mercy I exclude.
But yet all is not done; Man disobeying,
Disloyal breaks his fealty, and sins
Against the high Supremacy of Heav'n,   205

---

176. *lapsed,* "fallen," is appropriately used of the effect of Adam's "fall."

forfeit, "forfeited," suggests the legal view of the "fall" which becomes explicit in III, 210.

180. Compare David's prayer to know his human frailty. (Psalms, xxxix, 4.)

184. *C.D.* (I, iv) reconciles God's "election" of men and angels by his "grace" with the freedom of the will by insisting that "God has plainly declared that predestination [*i.e.,* election] is the effect of his mercy, and love, and grace, and wisdom in Christ," and that "it is to these qualities that we ought to attribute it, and not, as is generally done, to his absolute and secret will."

197. Compare note on III, 21.

Affecting God-head, and so losing all,
To expiate his Treason hath naught left,
But to destruction sacred and devote,
He with his whole posterity must die,
Die hee or Justice must; unless for him   210
Some other able, and as willing, pay
The rigid satisfaction, death for death.
Say Heav'nly Powers, where shall we find such love,
Which of ye will be mortal to redeem
Man's mortal crime, and just th' unjust to save,   215
Dwells in all Heaven charity so dear?
   He ask'd, but all the Heav'nly Quire stood mute,
And silence was in Heav'n: on man's behalf
Patron or Intercessor none appear'd,
Much less that durst upon his own head draw   220
The deadly forfeiture, and ransom set.
And now without redemption all mankind
Must have been lost, adjudg'd to Death and Hell
By doom severe, had not the Son of God,
In whom the fulness dwells of love divine,   225
His dearest mediation thus renew'd.
   Father, thy word is past, man shall find grace;
And shall grace not find means, that finds her way,
The speediest of thy winged messengers,
To visit all thy creatures, and to all   230

------

206. It is to be a "Goddess among Gods, . . . served by Angels numberless" (IX, 547–8) that Satan tempts Eve.

208. *sacred* and *devote* both have their Latin force of "dedicated to a deity for destruction."

216. *charity* has the Greek force, "love," which is usual in the New Testament.

218. So St. John says that there was silence in heaven when the seventh seal was opened. (Rev. viii, 1.)

219. *Patron* has its Latin meaning of a legal defender. Christ is constantly represented as an intercessor or mediator between God and man: "for this cause he is the Mediator of the new testament, that by means of [his] death . . . they which are called might receive the promise of eternal inheritance." (Heb. ix, 15.)

225. Discussing the relation of Christ, the Mediator, to God in *C.D.* (I. v), Milton quotes John iii, 35: "The Father loveth the Son, and hath given all things into his hand."

226. *dearest,* earnest or cordial.

Comes unprevented, unimplor'd, unsought?
Happy for man, so coming; he her aid
Can never seek, once dead in sins and lost;
Atonement for himself or offering meet,
Indebted and undone, hath none to bring: 235
Behold mee then, mee for him, life for life
I offer, on mee let thine anger fall;
Account mee man; I for his sake will leave
Thy bosom, and this glory next to thee
Freely put off, and for him lastly die   240
Well pleas'd, on me let Death wreck all his rage;
Under his gloomy power I shall not long
Lie vanquisht; thou hast giv'n me to possess
Life in myself for ever, by thee I live,
Though now to Death I yield, and am his due   245
All that of me can die, yet that debt paid,
Thou wilt not leave me in the loathsome grave
His prey, nor suffer my unspotted Soul
For ever with corruption there to dwell;
But I shall rise Victorious, and subdue   250
My vanquisher, spoil'd of his vaunted spoil;
Death his death's wound shall then receive, and stoop
Inglorious, of his mortal sting disarm'd.

---

231. *unprevented* has its Latin force of "unanticipated."   Lines 227–31
recall Spenser's paean (*F. Q.* II, viii, I), to

> "Th' exceeding grace
> Of Highest God, that loves his creatures so,
> And all his workes with mercy doth embrace,
> That blessed angels, he sends to and fro,
> To serve to wicked man, to serve his wicked foe!"

233. St. Paul speaks of Christ's quickening those "dead in sins."   (Col.
ii, 13.)

247. Following Acts ii, 27, Milton attributes to Christ David's boast
that (Ps. xvi, 10): "Thou wilt not leave my soul in hell; neither wilt
thou suffer thine Holy One to see corruption."

253. It is not safe to infer from passages like this that Milton was
swept away by enthusiasm for the Bible.   Here he seems to have been
influenced by the Italian poet, Sannazaro, in the first book of whose
epic on the birth of Christ, *De Partu Virginis,* he found a similar net-
work of texts forming a prophecy which is put into the mouth of David.
David foresees Pluto (*i.e.,* Satan) led captive to Tartarus and Christ
vanquishing the powers of the air and subduing Death and Hell.

I through the ample Air in Triumph high
Shall lead Hell Captive maugre Hell, and show   255
The powers of darkness bound. Thou at the sight
Pleas'd, out of Heaven shalt look down and smile,
While by thee rais'd I ruin all my Foes,
Death last, and with his Carcass glut the Grave:
Then with the multitude of my redeem'd   260
Shall enter Heaven long absent, and return,
Father, to see thy face, wherein no cloud
Of anger shall remain, but peace assur'd,
And reconcilement; wrath shall be no more
Thenceforth, but in thy presence Joy entire.   265
    His words here ended, but his meek aspéct
Silent yet spake, and breath'd immortal love
To mortal men, above which only shone
Filial obedience: as a sacrifice
Glad to be offer'd, he attends the will   270
Of his great Father. Admiration seiz'd
All Heav'n, what this might mean, and whither tend
Wond'ring; but soon th' Almighty thus repli'd:
    O thou in Heav'n and Earth the only peace
Found out for mankind under wrath, O thou   275
My sole complacence! well thou know'st how dear,
To me are all my works, nor Man the least
Though last created, that for him I spare
Thee from my bosom and right hand, to save,
By losing thee a while, the whole Race lost.   280
Thou therefore whom thou only canst redeem,
Thir Nature also to thy Nature join;
And be thyself Man among men on Earth,

---

254. The lines paraphrase Psalm lxviii, 18: "Thou hast ascended on
high, thou hast led captivity captive."

255. *maugre,* in spite of.

259. Compare "The last enemy to be destroyed is death." (I Cor.
xv, 26.)

270. *attends,* waits for an expression of his Father's will.

271. *Admiration.* Compare II, 677–8.

274. *peace,* means of peace.

275. *under wrath,* subject to God's anger.

276. *complacence,* satisfaction, ground of pleasure.

Made flesh, when time shall be, of Virgin seed,
By wondrous birth: Be thou in *Adam's* room   285
The Head of all mankind, though *Adam's* Son.
As in him perish all men, so in thee
As from a second root shall be restor'd,
As many as are restor'd, without thee none.
His crime makes guilty all his Sons, thy merit   290
Imputed shall absolve them who renounce
Thir own both righteous and unrighteous deeds,
And live in thee transplanted, and from thee
Receive new life. So Man, as is most just,
Shall satisfy for Man, be judg'd and die,   295
And dying rise, and rising with him raise
His Brethren, ransom'd with his own dear life.
So Heav'nly love shall outdo Hellish hate,
Giving to death, and dying to redeem,
So dearly to redeem what Hellish hate   300
So easily destroy'd, and still destroys
In those who, when they may, accept not grace.
Nor shalt thou by descending to assume
Man's Nature, less'n or degrade thine own.
Because thou hast, though Thron'd in highest bliss   305
Equal to God, and equally enjoying
God-like fruition, quitted all to save
A World from utter loss, and hast been found
By Merit more than Birthright Son of God,
Found worthiest to be so by being Good,   310
Far more than Great or High; because in thee
Love hath abounded more than Glory abounds,

---

284. The prophecy in Isaiah (vii, 14), "Behold, a virgin shall conceive,
and bear a son, and shall call his name Immanuel," was interpreted
(Compare Matt, i, 23) as referring definitely to Christ. Compare x, 74.

287. So St. Paul: "For as in Adam all die, even so in Christ shall all
be made alive." (1 Cor. xv, 22.)

291. *Imputed*. C.D. (I, xxii) explains that "Christ paid the ransom
of our sins, which he took upon himself by imputation, . . . whereas
man, paying nothing on his part, . . . receives as a gift the imputed
righteousness of Christ."

306. In *C.D.* (I, v) Milton insists that the passages in which Christ
seems to assert equality (John v, 18) or unity (John x, 30) with God
are in contexts in which "he distinctly denies that he made himself one
with God."

Therefore thy Humiliation shall exalt
With thee thy Manhood also to this Throne;
Here shalt thou sit incarnate, here shalt Reign   315
Both God and Man, Son both of God and Man,
Anointed universal King; all Power
I give thee, reign for ever, and assume
Thy Merits; under thee as Head Supreme
Thrones, Princedoms, Powers, Dominions I reduce: 320
All knees to thee shall bow, of them that bide
In Heaven, or Earth, or under Earth in Hell;
When thou attended gloriously from Heav'n
Shalt in the Sky appear, and from thee send
The summoning Arch-Angels to proclaim   325
Thy dread Tribunal: forthwith from all Winds
The living, and forthwith the cited dead
Of all past Ages to the general Doom
Shall hast'n, such a peal shall rouse thir sleep.
Then all thy Saints assembl'd, thou shalt judge   330
Bad men and Angels, they arraign'd shall sink
Beneath thy Sentence; Hell, her numbers full,
Thenceforth shall be for ever shut. Meanwhile
The World shall burn, and from her ashes spring
New Heav'n and Earth, wherein the just shall dwell   335
And after all thir tribulations long
See golden days, fruitful of golden deeds,
With Joy and Love triumphing, and fair Truth.

---

320. Exigencies of metre rather than their sequence in the ninefold
heavenly hierarchy determine the order of the names. Compare
Colossians i, 16.

321. The promise repeats Philippians ii, 10. "That at the name of
Jesus every knee should bow, of things in heaven, and things in earth,
and things under the earth."

324. The details of Christ's appearance for the last judgement are
drawn from Matthew xxiv, 30-1, and I Thessalonians iv, 16.

326. *from all Winds,* from all directions.

334. *C. D.* (I, 33) affirms "The destruction of the present unclean and
polluted world itself, namely, *its final conflagration."*

335. The new heaven and new earth of Revelation (xxi, 1) meant to
Milton "The renovation of heaven and earth, and of all things therein
adapted to our service or delight, to be possessed by us in perpetuity.
Isaiah lxv, 17." (*C. D.,* I, 33.)

Then thou thy regal Sceptre shalt lay by,
For regal Sceptre then no more shall need,   340
God shall be All in All. But all ye Gods,
Adore him, who to compass all this dies,
Adore the Son, and honour him as mee.
    No sooner had th' Almighty ceas't, but all
The multitude of Angels with a shout   345
Loud as from numbers without number, sweet
As from blest voices, uttering joy, Heav'n rung
With Jubilee, and loud Hosannas fill'd
Th' eternal Regions: lowly reverent
Towards either Throne they bow, and to the ground   350
With solemn adoration down they cast
Thir Crowns inwove with Amarant and Gold,
Immortal Amarant, a Flow'r which once
In Paradise, fast by the Tree of Life
Began to bloom, but soon for man's offence   355
To Heav'n remov'd where first it grew, there grows,
And flow'rs aloft shading the Fount of Life,
And where the river of Bliss through midst of Heav'n
Rolls o'er *Elysian* Flow'rs her Amber stream;
With these that never fade the Spirits elect   360
Bind thir resplendent locks inwreath'd with beams,
Now in loose Garlands thick thrown off, the bright
Pavement that like a Sea of Jasper shone
Impurpl'd with Celestial Roses smil'd.
Then Crown'd again thir gold'n Harps they took,   365
Harps ever tun'd, that glittering by thir side

---

341. Compare I Corinthians xv, 28: "And when all things shall be
subdued unto him, then shall the Son also himself be subject unto him
that put all things under him, that God may be all in all."

344. *all . . . uttering joy,* The absolute construction means, "because
all uttered joy."

352. *Amarant:* The Greek name means literally an "unfading flower."
Compare XI, 78.

358. *The river of Bliss* is St. John's "pure river of water of life, clear
as crystal" (Rev. xxii, 1), although it flows through the Elysian Fields
and is the haunt of spirits singing paeans, as Virgil describes the Elysian
river. (*Aen.* VI, 656–9.)

363. "And before the throne was a sea of glass, like unto crystal."
(Rev. iv, 6)

Like Quivers hung, and with Preamble sweet
Of charming symphony they introduce
Thir sacred Song, and waken raptures high;
No voice exempt, no voice but well could join   370
Melodious part, such concord is in Heav'n.
  Thee Father first they sung Omnipotent,
Immutable, Immortal, Infinite,
Eternal King; thee Author of all being,
Fountain of Light, thyself invisible   375
Amidst the glorious brightness where thou sit'st
Thron'd inaccessible, but when thou shad'st
The full blaze of thy beams, and through a cloud
Drawn round about thee like a radiant Shrine,
Dark with excessive bright thy skirts appear,   380
Yet dazzle Heav'n, that brightest Seraphim
Approach not, but with both wings veil thir eyes.
Thee next they sang of all Creation first,
Begotten Son, Divine Similitude,
In whose conspicuous count'nance, without cloud   385
Made visible, th' Almighty Father shines,
Whom else no Creature can behold; on thee
Impresst the effulgence of his Glory abides,
Transfus'd on thee his ample Spirit rests.
Hee Heav'n of Heavens and all the Powers therein   390
By thee created, and by thee threw down

---

371. *part:* a constituent melody in a harmony.

373. Taylor (*Du Bartas,* p. 42) compares the idea of God in *The Divine Weekes:*

> Before all Time, all Matter, Form, and Place,
> God *all in all,* and *all in God it was:*
> *Immutable, immortal, infinite,*
> Incomprehensible, all spirit all *light,*
> All *Majestie,* all-self-*Omnipotent,*
> *Invisible.*

(D. B., 1 rb.)

382. *C. D.* (I, ii) says, finally that "God must be styled by us wonderful and incomprehensible." Milton makes the seraphs in heaven veil their eyes before Him as they do in Isaiah's vision. (vi, 1–2.)

384. The analysis of the Son of God in *C. D.* (I, v) is based upon the saying that the Son is *the first born of every creature* and the *beginning of the creation of God,* and on the passage in Hebrews (i, 2–3) which is quoted in the note on III, 63.

Th' aspiring Dominations: thou that day
Thy Father's dreadful Thunder didst not spare,
Nor stop thy flaming Chariot wheels, that shook
Heav'n's everlasting Frame, while o'er the necks   395
Thou drov'st of warring Angels disarray'd.
Back from pursuit thy Powers with loud acclaim
Thee only extoll'd, Son of thy Father's might,
To execute fierce vengeance on his foes,
Not so on Man; him through their malice fall'n,   400
Father of Mercy and Grace, thou didst not doom
So strictly, but much more to pity incline:
No sooner did thy dear and only Son
Perceive thee purpos'd not to doom frail Man
So strictly, but much more to pity inclin'd,   405
He to appease thy wrath, and end the strife
Of Mercy and Justice in thy face discern'd,
Regardless of the Bliss wherein hee sat
Second to thee, offer'd himself to die
For man's offence. O unexampl'd love,   410
Love nowhere to be found less than Divine!
Hail Son of God, Saviour of Men, thy Name
Shall be the copious matter of my Song
Henceforth, and never shall my Harp thy praise
Forget, nor from thy Father's praise disjoin.   415
    Thus they in Heav'n, above the starry Sphere,
Thir happy hours in joy and hymning spent.
Meanwhile upon the firm opacous Globe
Of this round World, whose first convex divides
The luminous inferior Orbs, enclos'd   420
From *Chaos* and th' inroad of Darkness old,

---

392. This passage, like I, 93–4, prepares the reader for the account of
the war in heaven in VI.
    Dominations here refers to the rebel angels.

413. Throughout *P. L.,* as the invocations to the Heavenly Muse imply,
Milton regards himself as almost a member of the choir of angels. So
he uses *my Song* and *Harp* with a certain impersonality, for he speaks as
a representative of the City of God both in heaven and on earth.

416. *The starry Sphere* means nothing more precise than the stars
themselves. The term is still more loosely used to include the planets
with the fixed stars.

418. *opacous,* shadowy. The shell of the universe encloses the sun's
light and is itself immersed in Chaos.

Satan alighted walks: a Globe far off
It seem'd, now seems a boundless Continent
Dark, waste, and wild, under the frown of Night
Starless expos'd, and ever-threat'ning storms   425
Of *Chaos* blust'ring round, inclement sky;
Save on that side which from the wall of Heav'n,
Though distant far, some small reflection gains
Of glimmering air less vext with tempest loud:
Here walk'd the Fiend at large in spacious field.   430
As when a Vultur on *Imaus* bred,
Whose snowy ridge the roving *Tartar* bounds,
Dislodging from a Region scarce of prey
To gorge the flesh of Lambs or yeanling Kids
On Hills where Flocks are fed, flies toward the Springs   435
Of *Ganges* or *Hydaspes, Indian* streams;
But in his way lights on the barren Plains
Of *Sericana,* where *Chineses* drive
With Sails and Wind thir cany Waggons light:
So on this windy Sea of Land, the Fiend   440
Walk'd up and down alone bent on his prey,
Alone, for other Creature in this place

---

422. For Milton's cosmic scheme see the Introduction, §§ 8–12.

431. Even more distinctly than leviathan in the simile at I, 201, the
vulture represents Satan.   The simile is both a relief from the story and
a symbol of the incident which it relieves.   *Imaus,* which Pliny (VI, 17)
says "signifies in the local language 'full of snow,'" was the name given
to the mountains extending from Afghanistan, across Tartary, to the Arctic.

436. *Hydaspes:* the modern Jehlam.

438. *Sericana:* Serica or Seres was placed by Purchas (*Pilgrimage,* p.
452) east of Scythia beyond Imaus and north of India beyond the Ganges
Chineses, the regular plural in the seventeenth century.

439. Editors quote Heylin's *Cosmography* (1662): ". . . The country
[China] is so plain and level, that they have carts and coaches driven
with sails."

442. *this place,* the Limbo of Vanity or Paradise of Fools (495).   The
conception is based upon Ariosto's *Orlando Furioso,* canto 34, of which
Milton translated a quatrain in *Of Reformation in England* (*P. W.* II.
383).   Ariosto brings Astolfo, the English knight, up into the moon
where St. John, as he feigns, met him.

> And, to be short, at last his guide him brings
> Into a goodly valley where he sees
> A mighty mass of things strangely confus'd,
> Things that on earth were lost, or were abus'd.

Living or lifeless to be found was none,
None yet, but store hereafter from the earth
Up hither like Aereal vapours flew   445
Of all things transitory and vain, when Sin
With vanity had fill'd the works of men:
Both all things vain, and all who in vain things
Built their fond hopes of Glory or lasting fame,
Or happiness in this or th' other life;   450
All who have thir reward on Earth, the fruits
Of painful Superstition and blind Zeal,
Naught seeking but the praise of men, here find
Fit retribution, empty as thir deeds;
All th' unaccomplisht works of Nature's hand,   455
Abortive, monstrous, or unkindly mixt,
Dissolv'd on earth, fleet hither, and in vain,
Till final dissolution, wander here,
Not in the neighbouring Moon, as some have dream'd;
Those argent Fields more likely habitants,   460
Translated Saints, or middle Spirits hold
Betwixt th' Angelical and Human kind:
Hither of ill-join'd Sons and Daughters born
First from the ancient World those Giants came
With many a vain exploit, though then renown'd: 465
The builders next of *Babel* on the Plain
Of *Sennaar,* and still with vain design
New *Babels,* had they wherewithal, would build:
Others came single; hee who to be deem'd

---

456. *unkindly,* unnaturally.   Kind and nature were synonymous words.

459. Rejecting Ariosto's "dream," Milton placed Fools' Paradise just outside the shell of his universe, and instead of Ariosto's humorous satire of various human futilities he wrote an invective of the Roman Church as unexpected as his attack upon the venal clergy in *Lycidas.*

460. *argent* has its Latin meaning of "silver."

461. Giordano Bruno, Cardan and many Renaissance thinkers speculated boldly about spirit inhabitants of the moon and stars   Milton suggests that "translated saints," *i.e.,* good men "taken" out of the world alive like Enoch (Gen. v, 24), and "middle spirits" like the "mighty men" who were born of "the sons of God" (*i.e.,* angels) and of "the daughters of men," or like the giants who preceded them on earth (Gen. vi, 4), are in the moon.

467. *Sennaar,* Shinar, the Babylonian plain where the tower of Babel was built. (Gen. xi, 2–9.)

A God, leap'd fondly into *Ætna* flames,   470
Empedocles, and hee who to enjoy
Plato's Elysium, leap'd into the Sea,
Cleombrotus, and many more too long,
Embryos, and Idiots, Eremites and Friars
White, Black and Grey, with all thir trumpery.   475
Here Pilgrims roam, that stray'd so far to seek
In *Golgotha* him dead, who lives in Heav'n;
And they who to be sure of Paradise
Dying put on the weeds of *Dominic,*
Or in *Franciscan* think to pass disguis'd;   480
They pass the Planets seven, and pass the fixt,
And that Crystalline Sphere whose balance weighs
The Trepidation talkt, and that first mov'd;
And now Saint *Peter* at Heav'n's Wicket seems
To wait them with his Keys, and now at foot   485
Of Heav'n's ascent they lift thir Feet, when lo
A violent cross wind from either Coast
Blows them transverse ten thousand Leagues awry

---

471. Empedocles, who is said to have tried vainly to win posthumous honours as a god by jumping into the crater of Aetna, may be mentioned because Milton had in mind his theory that certain spirits are forever driven from sky to sea, and from earth to the sun and back again. (Conti, p. 112.)

473. Cleombrotus of Ambracia in Epirus is said to have been a suicide because he was too seriously convinced by Plato's *Phaedo* (68, B) that a true philosopher "will confidently believe that he will find wisdom nowhere else than in the other world."

474. *Eremites,* hermits.

475. The white friars are the Carmelites, the black, the Dominicans and the grey the Franciscans, all of whom had long been popularly known as White, Black and Grey Friars respectively.

477. *Golgotha,* where Christ was buried (John xix, 17) is still the goal of many pilgrims.

479. A widespread medieval superstition made many persons don the habits of the Black or Grey Friars on their deathbeds.

481. *the fixt,* the fixed stars.

483. *Trepidation,* "a libration of the eighth (or ninth) sphere, added to the system of Ptolemy by the Arab astronomer Thabet ben Korrah, c. 950, . . . to account for certain phenomena . . . really due to the rotation of the earth's axis." *N.E.D.*

that first mov'd is the *primum mobile,* or outermost heavenly sphere, which "Ptolemaic" astronomers imagined as moving the other spheres.

Into the devious Air; then might ye see
Cowls, Hoods and Habits with thir wearers tost   490
And flutter'd into Rags, then Reliques, Beads,
Indulgences, Dispenses, Pardons, Bulls,
The sport of Winds: all these upwhirl'd aloft
Fly o'er the backside of the World far off
Into a *Limbo* large and broad, since call'd   495
The Paradise of Fools, to few unknown
Long after, now unpeopl'd, and untrod;
All this dark Globe the Fiend found as he pass'd,
And long he wander'd, till at last a gleam
Of dawning light turn'd thither-ward in haste   500
His travell'd steps; far distant he descries
Ascending by degrees magnificent
Up to the wall of Heaven a Structure high,
At top whereof, but far more rich appear'd
The work as of a Kingly Palace Gate   505
With Frontispiece of Diamond and Gold
Imbellisht, thick with sparkling orient Gems
The Portal shone, inimitable on Earth
By Model, or by shading Pencil drawn.
The Stairs were such as whereon *Jacob* saw   510
Angels ascending and descending, bands
Of Guardians bright, when he from *Esau* fled
To *Padan-Aram* in the field of *Luz,*
Dreaming by night under the open Sky,
And waking cri'd, *This is the Gate of Heav'n.*   515
Each Stair mysteriously was meant, nor stood

491. *Reliques,* personal remains of saints.
Beads, of the rosary.

492. *Indulgences,* papal or episcopal remissions of punishment due for
sin.
Dispenses, dispensations from vows or other canonical obligations.
Pardons, absolutions from sin.
Bulls, papal edicts.

502. The *degrees, i.e.,* steps, of this description indicate that Milton
now thinks of the bond between Heaven and the universe not as the
golden chain of II, 1005, but as Jacob's ladder.

506. *Frontispiece,* the decorated façade of a building.

510. This and the lines following repeat the story of Jacob's vision told
in Genesis (xxviii, 10–19).

516. *mysteriously was meant,* had a mystic significance.

There always, but drawn up to Heav'n sometimes
Viewless, and underneath a bright Sea flow'd
Of Jasper, or of liquid Pearl, whereon
Who after came from Earth, sailing arriv'd,   520
Wafted by Angels, or flew o'er the Lake
Rapt in a Chariot drawn by fiery Steeds.
The Stairs were then let down, whether to dare
The Fiend by easy ascent, or aggravate
His sad exclusion from the doors of Bliss.   525
Direct against which op'n'd from beneath,
Just o'er the blissful seat of Paradise,
A passage down to th' Earth, a passage wide,
Wider by far than that of after-times
Over Mount *Sion,* and, though that were large,   530
Over the *Promis'd Land* to God so dear,
By which, to visit oft those happy Tribes,
On high behests his Angels to and fro
Pass'd frequent, and his eye with choice regard
From *Paneas* the fount of *Jordan's* flood   535
To *Beërsaba,* where the *Holy Land*
Borders on *Egypt* and the *Arabian* shore;
So wide the op'ning seem'd, where bounds were set
To darkness, such as bound the Ocean wave.
Satan from hence now on the lower stair   540
That scal'd by steps of Gold to Heav'n Gate
Looks down with wonder at the sudden view
Of all this World at once. As when a Scout
Through dark and desert ways with peril gone
All night; at last by break of cheerful dawn   545

---

518. The jasper sea is the crystalline sphere of Ptolemaic astronomy.
Compare VII, 619.

521. Milton compares the carrying of the beggar, Lazarus, to heaven
by angels, as related in Christ's parable (Luke xvi, 22), with Elijah's
being caught up in a fiery chariot (II Kings ii, 11).

528. Milton imagines a passage directly from heaven to God's temple
on Mt. Sion in Jerusalem and another opening to all parts of the Promised
Land of Canaan, for the angels whose visits to men are described in the
Old Testament.

535. Dan, later known as Paneas, was the northernmost city of Palestine.

536. *Beërsaba,* for the biblical form Beersheba. Compare the unaspirated form in I, 398.

Obtains the brow of some high-climbing Hill,
Which to his eye discovers unaware
The goodly prospect of some foreign land
First seen, or some renown'd Metropolis
With glistering Spires and Pinnacles adorn'd,   550
Which now the Rising Sun gilds with his beams.
Such wonder seiz'd, though after Heaven seen,
The Spirit malign, but much more envy seiz'd
At sight of all this World beheld so fair.
Round he surveys, and well might, where he stood   555
So high above the circling Canopy
Of Night's extended shade; from Eastern Point
Of *Libra* to the fleecy Star that bears
Andromeda far off *Atlantic* Seas
Beyond th' *Horizon;* then from Pole to Pole   560
He views in breadth, and without longer pause
Down right into the World's first Region throws
His flight precipitant, and winds with ease
Through the pure marble Air his oblique way
Amongst innumerable Stars, that shone   565
Stars distant, but nigh hand seem'd other Worlds,
Or other Worlds they seem'd, or happy Isles,
Like those *Hesperian* Gardens fam'd of old,
Fortunate Fields, and Groves and flow'ry Vales,
Thrice happy Isles, but who dwelt happy there   570
He stay'd not to enquire: above them all
The golden Sun in splendor likest Heaven
Allur'd his eye: Thither his course he bends
Through the calm Firmament; but up or down

552. *though after Heaven seen,* although he had seen heaven.

555. Satan is just entering the universe through the only opening in its outer envelope, at the "top," directly beneath Heaven.

558. *Libra,* the sign of the Scales in the Zodiac.
The fleecy Star is the opposite sign of the ram, which stands immediately beneath the constellation of Andromeda.

562. Compare the note on I, 516.

564. *marble,* luminous or shining like marble.

567. The happy islands were supposed by the Greeks to lie far west in the Atlantic, while the Hesperides lay close to the African coast. To the former the spirits of some fortunate men went without dying.

574. *Firmament* here means simply the expanse or vault of the sky.
up or down, north or south.

By centre, or eccentric, hard to tell,   575
Or Longitude, where the great Luminary
Aloof the vulgar Constellations thick,
That from his Lordly eye keep distance due,
Dispenses Light from far; they as they move
Thir Starry dance in numbers that compute   580
Days, months, and years, towards his all-cheering Lamp
Turn swift their various motions, or are turn'd
By his Magnetic beam, that gently warms
The Universe, and to each inward part
With gentle penetration, though unseen,   585
Shoots invisible virtue even to the deep:
So wondrously was set his Station bright.
There lands the Fiend, a spot like which perhaps
Astronomer in the Sun's lucent Orb
Through his glaz'd Optic Tube yet never saw.   590
The place he found beyond expression bright,
Compar'd with aught on Earth, Metal or Stone;
Not all parts like, but all alike inform'd
With radiant light, as glowing Iron with fire;
If metal, part seem'd Gold, part Silver clear;   595
If stone, Carbuncle most or Chrysolite,
Ruby or Topaz, to the Twelve that shone
In *Aaron's* Breastplate, and a stone besides
Imagin'd rather oft than elsewhere seen,
That stone, or like to that which here below   600

---

575. *By centre or eccentric,* toward or away from the centre, *i.e.,* the earth. Milton seems to intend to leave it a question whether the sun or earth is the centre of the universe, as he does again in 582–3.

576. *Longitude,* east and west extent of the celestial sphere.

577. *Aloof,* a preposition. In the Ptolemaic astronomy the sun in its sphere is below that of the fixed stars and midway from the earth among the planetary spheres.

580. VII, 341–2 paraphrases the passage in Genesis (I, 14) of which Milton thought here.

588. Galileo's discovery of sun spots in 1609 was one of the most exciting astronomical events of the century.

598. The twelve precious stones prescribed for Aaron's breastplate as High Priest (Exod. xxviii, 17–24) include all those mentioned in the preceding lines.

600. The philosopher's stone, which the alchemists sought, was supposed to have the power to turn baser metals into gold and also to heal

Philosophers in vain so long have sought,
In vain, though by thir powerful Art they bind
Volatile *Hermes,* and call up unbound
In various shapes old *Proteus* from the Sea,
Drain'd through a Limbec to his Native form.   605
What wonder then if fields and regions here
Breathe forth *Elixir* pure, and Rivers run
Potable Gold, when with one virtuous touch
Th' Arch-chemic Sun so far from us remote
Produces with Terrestrial Humour mixt   610
Here in the dark so many precious things
Of colour glorious and effect so rare?
Here matter new to gaze the Devil met
Undazzl'd, far and wide his eye commands,
For sight no obstacle found here, nor shade,   615
But all Sun-shine, as when his Beams at Noon

---

all wounds. For that reason R. Scot speaks of "the philosophers stone, called Alixer." (*Discoverie,* xiv, ii.) Below (607), *Elixir,* which primarily meant a medicament for wounds, is used of the influence of the sun as felt in the upper region of the air in all its strength, for the sun's rays were supposed to transform earthly substances into gems and precious metals.

603. *Hermes,* Mercury, here used to mean quicksilver, whose solidification was one of the objects of the alchemists. Verity quotes Ben Jonson's *Mercury Vindicated from the Alchemists:* "Stay, see! our *Mercury* is coming forth . . . He will be gone, he will evaporate. . . . Precious, golden Mercury; be fixt; be not so *volatile."*

604. The myth of Proteus, the Old Man of the Sea who refused to answer any summons and, when caught, transformed himself into every shape in order to escape, was treated by Bacon in *The Wisdom of the Ancients* as a symbol of the basic substance in matter which he believed might be obtained by heating various materials in alembics, or air-tight vessels. "For like as . . . Proteus (never) changed shapes till he was straitened and held fast, so the passages and variations of nature cannot appear so fully in the liberty of nature as in the trials and vexations of art." (*Works,* VI, p. 188.)

605. *Limbec,* alembic.

607. Physicians and alchemists spoke of an elixir of life supposed to be borne in *Potable Gold*.

608. *virtuous* has its alchemical force of power to transform physical substances, which was similar to the power to heal diseases.

609. *Arch-chemic,* supremely powerful to work "chemical" changes.

610. *Humour* is here equivalent to moisture.

613. *gaze,* admire.

Culminate from th' *Equator,* as they now
Shot upward still direct, whence no way round
Shadow from body opaque can fall, and the Air,
Nowhere so clear, sharp'n'd his visual ray   620
To objects distant far, whereby he soon
Saw within ken a glorious Angel stand,
The same whom *John* saw also in the Sun:
His back was turn'd, but not his brightness hid;
Of beaming sunny Rays, a golden tiar   625
Circl'd his Head, nor less his Locks behind
Illustrious on his Shoulders fledge with wings
Lay waving round; on some great charge imploy'd
He seem'd, or fixt in cogitation deep.
Glad was the Spirit impure; as now in hope   630
To find who might direct his wand'ring flight
To Paradise the happy seat of Man,
His journey's end and our beginning woe.
But first he casts to change his proper shape,
Which else might work him danger or delay: 635
And now a stripling Cherub he appears,
Not of the prime, yet such as in his face
Youth smil'd Celestial, and to every Limb
Suitable grace diffus'd, so well he feign'd;
Under a Coronet his flowing hair   640
In curls on either cheek play'd, wings he wore
Of many a colour'd plume sprinkl'd with Gold,
His habit fit for speed succinct, and held
Before his decent steps a Silver wand.

---

617. *Culminate* is used because the position in the zenith is called the sun's culmination.

620. Satan, standing on the sun, looks out over the universe in every direction and can see no shadow. His *visual ray* means his faculty of sight. "Eye beam" was a frequent equivalent term.

622. Uriel, the angel in the sun, is identified with the angel whom St. John saw "standing in the sun." (Rev. xix, 17.)

625. *tiar,* tiara, a crown or mitre.

627. *fledge,* fledged, feathered.

628. *charge,* duty, task.

637. *prime;* compare "prime in Manhood where Youth ended", XI, 245–6, and the contrast of "manly prime" with youth in *Comus,* 289.

He drew not nigh unheard, the Angel bright,   645
Ere he drew nigh, his radiant visage turn'd,
Admonisht by his ear, and straight was known
Th' Arch-Angel *Uriel,* one of the sev'n
Who in God's presence, nearest to his Throne
Stand ready at command, and are his Eyes   650
That run through all the Heav'ns, or down to th' Earth
Bear his swift errands over moist and dry,
O'er Sea and Land; him *Satan* thus accosts.

　　Uriel, for thou of those sev'n Spirits that stand
In sight of God's high Throne, gloriously bright,   655
The first art wont his great authentic will
Interpreter through highest Heav'n to bring,
Where all his Sons thy Embassy attend;
And here art likeliest by supreme decree
Like honour to obtain, and as his Eye   660
To visit oft this new Creation round;
Unspeakable desire to see, and know
All these his wondrous works, but chiefly Man,
His chief delight and favour, him for whom
All these his works so wondrous he ordain'd,   665
Hath brought me from the Quires of Cherubim
Alone thus wand'ring.   Brightest Seraph tell
In which of all these shining Orbs hath Man
His fixed seat, or fixed seat hath none,
But all these shining Orbs his choice to dwell;   670

---

648. Though Uriel is not mentioned in the Bible, rabbinical tradition made him one of Zechariah's angelic "eyes of the Lord, which run to and fro through the whole earth" (iv, 10). The name was supposed to mean the "fire" or "light" of "God," and the *Midrasch Rabba to the book of Numbers* (cited by Fletcher, *Rabbinical Readings*, p. 244) explains that "the Holy One blessed-be-He through Uriel (as through the Sun) spreads his light over Israel and over [other nations], as it is said (Isaiah lx, 1) *Arise, shine for thy light is come."* Milton calls him an archangel here, but a seraph in 667; and in VI, 363 he ranks with Raphael, Gabriel and Michael as one of the four supreme seraphs.

658. Like the writer of Job (ii, 1), Milton called the angels Sons of God and thought of them as living scattered through the provinces of heaven, except on the special days when they "came to present themselves before the Lord."

659. *here,* in the sun, Uriel's station as supervisor of the universe.

666. The cherubs were the second rank of the first angelic order, the seraphs the first.

That I may find him, and with secret gaze,
Or open admiration him behold
On whom the great Creator hath bestow'd
Worlds, and on whom hath all these graces pour'd;
That both in him and all things, as is meet,   675
The Universal Maker we may praise;
Who justly hath driv'n out his Rebel Foes
To deepest Hell, and to repair that loss
Created this new happy Race of Men
To serve him better: wise are all his ways.   680
    So spake the false dissembler unperceiv'd;
For neither Man nor Angel can discern
Hypocrisy, the only evil that walks
Invisible, except to God alone,
By his permissive will, through Heav'n and Earth: 685
And oft though wisdom wake, suspicion sleeps
At wisdom's Gate, and to simplicity
Resigns her charge, while goodness thinks no ill
Where no ill seems: Which now for once beguil'd
Uriel, though Regent of the Sun, and held   690
The sharpest-sighted Spirit of all in Heav'n;
Who to the fraudulent Impostor foul
In his uprightness answer thus return'd.
Fair Angel, thy desire which tends to know
The works of God, thereby to glorify   695
The great Work-Master, leads to no excess
That reaches blame, but rather merits praise
The more it seems excess, that led thee hither
From thy Empyreal Mansion thus alone,
To witness with thine eyes what some perhaps   700
Contented with report hear only in heav'n:
For wonderful indeed are all his works,
Pleasant to know, and worthiest to be all
Had in remembrance always with delight;

---

685. The distinction between God's *permissive* and his active will
avoided making Him responsible for evil.

696. It was a principle of Renaissance Neo-Platonism (*e. g.,* The *Heroic
Madnesses,* I, ii, of Giordano Bruno) that excess in the contemplation of
God and his works did not violate Aristotle's law that all extremes are
vicious.

702. Several Psalms are echoed, *e.g.,* viii and cxi, 4.

But what created mind can comprehend   705
Thir number, or the wisdom infinite
That brought them forth, but hid thir causes deep.
I saw when at his Word the formless Mass,
This world's material mould, came to a heap:
Confusion heard his voice, and wild uproar   710
Stood rul'd, stood vast infinitude confin'd;
Till at his second bidding darkness fled,
Light shone, and order from disorder sprung:
Swift to thir several Quarters hasted then
The cumbrous Elements, Earth, Flood, Air, Fire,   715
And this Ethereal quintessence of Heav'n
Flew upward, spirited with various forms,
That roll'd orbicular, and turn'd to Stars
Numberless, as thou seest, and how they move;
Each had his place appointed, each his course,   720
The rest in circuit walls this Universe.
Look downward on that Globe whose hither side

---

706. The word *wisdom* in the passage in Proverbs (iii, 19) to which
Milton alludes—"The Lord by wisdom hath founded the earth; by
understanding hath he established the heavens"—was sometimes understood as referring to Christ, the creator in the great passage in VII, 208–
221; for which this is a preparation.

709. For the conception of the creation as moulding of preëxistent
matter see the Introduction, §19.

710. *Confusion* and uproar are half personified, like Chaos, whom
they represent.

712. The second step in the story of creation in Genesis (i, 2) is God's
command, "Let there be light."

713. The broad resemblance of Milton's conception of the creation to
that of Plato is polarized in this line, which seems like a deliberate
translation of the *Timaeus,* 30 A.

715. Compare II, 925.

716. The aether or incandescent substance, of which Aristotle supposed
the heavens and the stars to be made, was contrasted with the four
terrestrial elements (earth, water, air and fire) as a "fifth essence" or
"quintessence."

718. The *Timaeus* of Plato and still more the forgery known as the
Timaeus Locrus were responsible for the conception of the heavenly
bodies as living spirits and for the belief that, since the most perfect
form is the sphere, their shape, like that of all perfect spirits, is spherical.

721. The residue of the quintessence, remaining after the heavens and
the stars were made, formed the envelope of the universe.

With light from hence, though but reflected, shines;
That place is Earth the seat of Man, that light
His day, which else as th' other Hemisphere   725
Night would invade, but there the neighbouring Moon
(So call that opposite fair Star) her aid
Timely interposes, and her monthly round
Still ending, still renewing through mid Heav'n,
With borrow'd light her countenance triform   730
Hence fills and empties to enlighten the Earth,
And in her pale dominion checks the night.
That spot to which I point is *Paradise,*
Adam's abode, those lofty shades his Bow'r.
Thy way thou canst not miss, me mine requires.   735
   Thus said, he turn'd, and *Satan* bowing low,
As to superior Spirits is wont in Heav'n,
Where honour due and reverence none neglects,
Took leave, and toward the coast of Earth beneath,
Down from th' Ecliptic, sped with hop'd success,   740
Throws his steep flight in many an Aery wheel,
Nor stay'd, till on *Niphates'* top he lights.

The End of the Third Book.

---

730. *triform,* is a reminiscence of Horace's term, the "triform goddess" (*Odes,* III, 22, 4), which alludes both to the fact that the moon has
three phases and was known as three different divinities, Luna, Diana
and Hecate.

734. Paradise and Adam's bower are to be the focus of the next six
books.

740. The earth is the centre of the universe and Satan descends to it
from the sun's position at midday on its path, the ecliptic.

742. Mt. Niphates was in the Taurus range in Armenia, near Assyria;
as Milton says (IV, 126). There is irony in the fact that he later (XI,
381, and *P. R.,* III, 252–265, and IV, 26, 236) made Niphates the mountain where Satan vainly tempted Christ with a view of the kingdoms of
this world.

BOOK IV

THE ARGUMENT

Satan *now in prospect of* Eden, *and nigh the place where he must now attempt the bold enterprise which he undertook alone against God and Man, falls into many doubts with himself, and many passions, fear, envy, and despair; but at length confirms himself in evil, journeys on to Paradise, whose outward prospect and situation is described, overleaps the bounds, sits in the shape of a Cormorant on the Tree of life, as highest in the Garden to look about him. The Garden describ'd;* Satan's *first sight of* Adam *and* Eve; *his wonder at thir excellent form and happy state, but with resolution to work thir fall; overhears thir discourse, thence gathers that the Tree of knowledge was forbidden them to eat of, under penalty of death; and thereon intends to found his Temptation, by seducing them to transgress: then leaves them a while, to know further of thir state by some other means. Meanwhile* Uriel *descending on a Sun-beam warns* Gabriel, *who had in charge the Gate of Paradise, that some evil spirit had escap'd the Deep, and past at Noon by his Sphere in the shape of a good Angel down to Paradise, discovered after by his furious gestures in the Mount.* Gabriel *promises to find him ere morning. Night coming on,* Adam *and* Eve *discourse of going to thir rest: thir Bower describ'd; thir Evening worship.* Gabriel *drawing forth his Bands of Night-watch to walk the round of Paradise, appoints two strong Angels to* Adam's *Bower, lest the evil spirit should be there doing some harm to* Adam *or* Eve *sleeping; there they find him at the ear of* Eve, *tempting her in a dream, and bring him, though unwilling, to* Gabriel; *by whom question'd, he scornfully answers, prepares resistance, but hinder'd by a Sign from Heaven, flies out of Paradise.*

O FOR that warning voice, which he who saw
Th' *Apocalypse*, heard cry in Heav'n aloud,

---

1. Milton's opening is based on a passage in St. John's Apocalypse prophesying the triumph of the early Christians over their spiritual foes

Then when the Dragon, put to second rout,
Came furious down to be reveng'd on men,
Woe to the inhabitants on Earth! that now,   5
While time was, our first Parents had been warn'd
The coming of thir secret foe, and scap'd
Haply so scap'd his mortal snare; for now
Satan, now first inflam'd with rage, came down,
The Tempter ere th' Accuser of man-kind,   10
To wreck on innocent frail man his loss
Of that first Battle, and his flight to Hell:
Yet not rejoicing in his speed, though bold,
Far off and fearless, nor with cause to boast,
Begins his dire attempt, which nigh the birth   15
Now rolling, boils in his tumultuous breast,
And like a devilish Engine back recoils
Upon himself; horror and doubt distract
His troubl'd thoughts, and from the bottom stir
The Hell within him, for within him Hell   20
He brings, and round about him, nor from Hell
One step no more than from himself can fly
By change of place: Now conscience wakes despair

It represents the approaching defeat of the "dragon," Satan, as a defeat
of the "serpent" who tempted Eve and of the "accuser" who tempted
Job. "And there was war in heaven: Michael and his angels fought
against the dragon; and the dragon fought and his angels, And prevailed
not; neither was their place found any more in heaven. And the great
dragon was cast out, that old serpent, called the Devil, and Satan, which
deceiveth the whole world: he was cast out into the earth, and his
angels were cast out with him. And I heard a loud voice saying in
heaven, . . . The accuser of our brethren is cast down, which accused
them before our God day and night. . . . Woe to the inhabiters of the
earth and of the sea! for the devil is come down unto you, having great
wrath, because he knoweth that he hath but a short time." (Rev. xii,
7–12.)

17. *a devilish Engine,* a cannon.   Compare the note on VI, 518.

20. The thought was a favourite with Protestant mystics.   "We are of
God's substance: we have heaven and hell in ourselves," said Boehme
(*Threefold Life of Man,* xiv, 72), and Benjamin Whichcote preached
that, "The Jewel of *Tophet* burning is the guiltiness of man's conscience, malignity, and a naughty disposition against goodness and holi-
ness; and God's withdrawing because the person is incapable of His
communication." (*Sermons,* III, p. 153.)   Orthodox Catholic doctrine
regarded the devils as suffering wherever they went.   Compare the note
on I, 255

That slumber'd, wakes the bitter memory
Of what he was, what is, and what must be   25
Worse; of worse deeds worse sufferings must ensue.
Sometimes towards *Eden* which now in his view
Lay pleasant, his griev'd look he fixes sad,
Sometimes towards Heav'n and the full-blazing Sun,
Which now sat high in his Meridian Tow'r: 30
Then much revolving, thus in sighs began.
　　O thou that with surpassing Glory crown'd,
Look'st from thy sole Dominion like the God
Of this new World; at whose sight all the Stars
Hide thir diminisht heads; to thee I call,   35
But with no friendly voice, and add thy name
O Sun, to tell thee how I hate thy beams
That bring to my remembrance from what state
I fell, how glorious once above thy Sphere;
Till Pride and worse Ambition threw me down   40
Warring in Heav'n against Heav'n's matchless King:
Ah wherefore! he deserv'd no such return

---

25. Editors compare Francesca's cry to Dante, "No greater pain than recollection of happiness in misery" (*Inf.*, V, 121–3)—words which Dante attributed to the "philosopher," *i. e.*, Boethius. (*Consolation of Philosophy*, II, pr. iv.)　See also Pandarus' translation of Boethius:
> The worste kynde of infortune is this,
> A man to han ben in prosperitee,
> And it remembren, whan it passed is.
> (*Troilus and Criseyde*, III, 1626–8.)

The commonplace was applied to hell's pains by St. Thomas Aquinas (*Summa Theologica*, II, 2, 36, 1) and to the fallen devils by Sir Thomas Browne. (*Christian Morals*, II, 10.)

32. Satan's address to the sun was originally written as Lucifer's first words in the projected drama of *Adam Unparadised*. The form of the drama was to have been Greek and there may be an echo here of Prometheus' appeal in his first speech in Aeschylus' tragedy:
> ". . . Thou bright round
> Of the all-seeing Sun, you I invoke!"

Compare the address to the sun in Euripides' *Phoenissae*, 1–6.

40. Perhaps in this confession of pride and ambition, where Satan so objectively accuses himself, we have a speech such as Milton planned to put into the mouth of Conscience, who was to appear "in a shape" as a speaking actor in his tragedy.　In Elizabethan drama, however, bad men such as Claudius in *Hamlet* (III, iii), are no less searchingly objective with themselves in their soliloquies.

From me, whom he created what I was
In that bright eminence, and with his good
Upbraided none; nor was his service hard.   45
What could be less than to afford him praise,
The easiest recompense, and pay him thanks,
How due! yet all his good prov'd ill in me,
And wrought but malice; lifted up so high
I sdein'd subjection, and thought one step higher   50
Would set me highest, and in a moment quit
The debt immense of endless gratitude,
So burthensome, still paying, still to owe;
Forgetful what from him I still receiv'd,
And understood not that a grateful mind   55
By owing owes not, but still pays, at once
Indebted and discharg'd; what burden then?
O had his powerful Destiny ordain'd
Me some inferior Angel, I had stood
Then happy; no unbounded hope had rais'd   60
Ambition. Yet why not? some other Power
As great might have aspir'd, and me though mean
Drawn to his part; but other Powers as great
Fell not, but stand unshak'n, from within
Or from without, to all temptations arm'd.   65
Hadst thou the same free Will and Power to stand?
Thou hadst: whom hast thou then or what to accuse,
But Heav'n's free Love dealt equally to all?
Be then his Love accurst, since love or hate,
To me alike, it deals eternal woe.   70
Nay curs'd be thou; since against his thy will
Chose freely what it now so justly rues.
Me miserable! which way shall I fly

---

43. Here Satan recognizes that he is God's creature, but when he urges
his followers to revolt in heaven he argues that the angels were "self-
begot." (V, 860.)

45. *Upbraided*, taxed, rebuked (for ingratitude).

50. *sdein'd*, disdained.

51. *quit*, dispose of.

54. *still*, continually.

66. Compare God's statement that the devils fell "freely" (III, 102)
and Raphael's insistence on the free obedience of the good angels. (V,
535.)

Infinite wrath, and infinite despair?
Which way I fly is Hell; myself am Hell;   75
And in the lowest deep a lower deep
Still threat'ning to devour me opens wide,
To which the Hell I suffer seems a Heav'n.
O then at last relent: is there no place
Left for Repentance, none for Pardon left?   80
None left but by submission; and that word
Disdain forbids me, and my dread of shame
Among the spirits beneath, whom I seduc'd
With other promises and other vaunts
Than to submit, boasting I could subdue   85
Th' Omnipotent. Ay me, they little know
How dearly I abide that boast so vain,
Under what torments inwardly I groan:
While they adore me on the Throne of Hell,
With Diadem and Sceptre high advanc'd   90
The lower still I fall, only Supreme
In misery; such joy Ambition finds.
But say I could repent and could obtain
By Act of Grace my former state; how soon
Would highth recall high thoughts, how soon unsay   95
What feign'd submission swore: ease would recant
Vows made in pain, as violent and void.
For never can true reconcilement grow
Where wounds of deadly hate have pierc'd so deep:
Which would but lead me to a worse relapse,   100
And heavier fall: so should I purchase dear
Short intermission bought with double smart.
This knows my punisher; therefore as far
From granting hee, as I from begging peace:

---

76. In *Doctrine of Divorce* (II, iii) Milton, arguing that even the
pagans understood that the appropriate punishment for sin was the
sinner's depravity, wrote: "To banish forever into a local hell, whether
in the air or in the centre, or in that uttermost and bottomless gulf of
chaos, deeper from holy bliss than the world's diameter multiplied; they
thought not a punishing so proper and proportionate for God to inflict
as to punish sin with sin."

79. Compare Hebrews xii, 17, where the story of Esau is used to
warn erring Christians that they may find "no place of repentance."

94. *Act of Grace,* a formal pardon.

97. A promise made under violence is void in law.

All hope excluded thus, behold instead   105
Of us out-cast, exil'd, his new delight,
Mankind created, and for him this World.
So farewell Hope, and with Hope farewell Fear,
Farewell Remorse: all Good to me is lost;
Evil be thou my Good; by thee at least   110
Divided Empire with Heav'n's King I hold
By thee, and more than half perhaps will reign;
As Man ere long, and this new World shall know.
    Thus while he spake, each passion dimm'd his face,
Thrice chang'd with pale, ire, envy and despair,   115
Which marr'd his borrow'd visage, and betray'd
Him counterfeit, if any eye beheld.
For heav'nly minds from such distempers foul
Are ever clear. Whereof hee soon aware,
Each perturbation smooth'd with outward calm,   120
Artificer of fraud; and was the first
That practis'd falsehood under saintly show,
Deep malice to conceal, couch't with revenge:

---

110. In a later soliloquy Satan is driven to acknowledge that all good
has become evil for him. (IX, 122-3.)

112. *reign,* govern. Satan is undisputed lord of hell and intends to
take "this new World" from God, leaving him less than half of the
Universe, namely, heaven.

115. *pale,* paleness, recurring three times as the three passions shake
Satan. Paleness might be caused by any passion, while a "sanguine
complexion" was generally regarded as indicating "the members [of the
body] so qualified by mixture of elements, as all conspire together in
due proportion, [which] breedeth an indifferencie to all passions."
(Timothy Bright's *A Treatise of Melancholy,* 1613, p. 118.)

116. Satan's "borrow'd visage" was that of a stripling cherub (III,
636), young and, presumably, "sanguine."

120. The stoic term, perturbation, for passion, was acclimated in
poetry by Spenser:

> Who ever doth to temperaunce apply
> His stedfast life, and all his actions frame,
> Trust me, shal find no greater enimy,
> Then stubborne perturbation, to the same.
>
>   (*F. Q.* II, V, 1.)

121. *Artificer of fraud* renders Satan's title of "father of lies." Compare III, 683.

123. *couch't,* lying concealed.

Yet not anough had practis'd to deceive
Uriel once warn'd; whose eye pursu'd him down   125
The way he went, and on th' *Assyrian* mount
Saw him disfigur'd, more than could befall
Spirit of happy sort: his gestures fierce
He mark'd and mad demeanour, then alone,
As he suppos'd, all unobserv'd, unseen.   130
So on he fares, and to the border comes
Of *Eden,* where delicious Paradise,
Now nearer, Crowns with her enclosure green,
As with a rural mound the champaign head
Of a steep wilderness, whose hairy sides   135
With thicket overgrown, grotesque and wild,
Access deni'd; and over head up grew
Insuperable highth of loftiest shade,
Cedar, and Pine, and Fir, and branching Palm,
A Silvan Scene, and as the ranks ascend   140
Shade above shade, a woody Theatre
Of stateliest view. Yet higher than thir tops
The verdurous wall of Paradise up sprung:
Which to our general Sire gave prospect large
Into his nether Empire neighbouring round.   145
And higher than that Wall a circling row
Of goodliest Trees loaden with fairest Fruit,
Blossoms and Fruits at once of golden hue
Appear'd, with gay enamell'd colours mixt:
On which the Sun more glad impress'd his beams   150
Than in fair Evening Cloud, or humid Bow,
When God hath show'r'd the earth; so lovely seem'd

---

126. *Assyrian mount,* Niphates.   Compare III, 742.

132. Satan seems to be flying across western Asia into the region
called Eden (which is bounded below, 210–4), toward Paradise, the
garden which "God planted . . . eastward in Eden." (Gen. ii, 8.)

134. *champaign head,* plateau. Paradise is described in further detail
in VIII, 300–11. One of the accepted, medieval locations for the
Earthly Paradise was the top of a mountain supposed to have towered
above the waters of Noah's flood. Dante puts it at the summit of the
mount of Purgatory. (*Purgatorio,* xxviii.)

141. The circling ranks of trees which surround the garden are like
the terraced seats of a Greek theatre.

151. *humid Bow,* the rainbow.

That Lantskip: And of pure now purer air
Meets his approach, and to the heart inspires
Vernal delight and joy, able to drive   155
All sadness but despair: now gentle gales
Fanning thir odoriferous wings dispense
Native perfúmes, and whisper whence they stole
Those balmy spoils. As when to them who sail
Beyond the *Cape of Hope,* and now are past   160
Mozambic, off at Sea North-East winds blow
Sabean Odours from the spicy shore
Of *Araby* the blest, with such delay
Well pleas'd they slack thir course, and many a League
Cheer'd with the grateful smell old Ocean smiles.   165
So entertain'd those odorous sweets the Fiend
Who came thir bane, though with them better pleas'd
Than *Asmodeus* with the fishy fume,

---

153. *Lantskip,* landscape. Compare II, 491.

of pure: The Greek construction of preposition and adjective instead
of preposition and abstract noun (*pure* for pureness) is illustrated in
VIII, 433; X, 720, 723.

160. *Cape of Hope,* Cape of Good Hope.

161. *Mozambic,* or Mozambique is the name of a province of
Portuguese East Africa and its island capital. The region was famous
for its fertility and because "all the Armadas and Fleetes that sayle from
Portugall to the Indies, if they cannot finish and performe their Voyage,
will goe and Winter . . . in this Iland of Mozambique." (Purchas,
Pilgrimes, II, 1023.)

162. Saba, "which in the Greeke tongue signifieth a secret mysterie"
(Pliny, Holland's translation, 12, 14), was an inaccessible region famous
for its incense, in southern Arabia. *Arabia Felix,* "Araby the blest." "In
the springtime," Milton read in Diodorus Siculus (3, 45), "the winds
from off that land waft the air, perfumed with sweet odours of myrrh
and other odoriferous plants, to the adjacent parts of the sea."

167. *bane,* harm, destruction. In Old English the word means "a mur-
derer."

168. Milton shared the extraordinary interest of his time in the
apocryphal Book of Tobit—an interest responsible for Savoldo's painting
of "the sociable spirit," Raphael (V, 221) accompanying young Tobias,
Tobit's son, in Media. There Tobias, by Raphael's advice, married Sara,
who had previously lost seven husbands, all of them murdered on their
wedding night by "the destroyer," Asmodeus, or Asmadai, as Milton
calls him when he stands opposed to Raphael in battle in heaven (VI,
365). Asmodeus was in love with Sara and would have killed Tobias
on his marriage night, if Raphael had not instructed him to burn the
heart and liver of a fish in his chamber. "The which smell when the

That drove him, though enamour'd, from the Spouse
Of *Tobit's* Son, and with a vengeance sent   170
From *Media* post to *Egypt,* there fast bound.
  Now to th' ascent of that steep savage Hill
Satan had journey'd on, pensive and slow;
But further way found none, so thick entwin'd,
As one continu'd brake, the undergrowth   175
Of shrubs and tangling bushes had perplext
All path of Man or Beast that pass't that way:
One Gate there only was, and that look'd East
On th' other side: which when th' arch-felon saw
Due entrance he disdain'd, and in contempt,   180
At one slight bound high overleap'd all bound
Of Hill or highest Wall, and sheer within
Lights on his feet. As when a prowling Wolf,
Whom hunger drives to seek new haunt for prey,
Watching where Shepherds pen thir Flocks at eve   185
In hurdl'd Cotes amid the field secure,
Leaps o'er the fence with ease into the Fold:
Or as a Thief bent to unhoard the cash
Of some rich Burgher, whose substantial doors,
Cross-barr'd and bolted fast, fear no assault,   190
In at the window climbs, or o'er the tiles:
So clomb this first grand Thief into God's Fold:
So since into his Church lewd Hirelings climb.
Thence up he flew, and on the Tree of Life,

---

evil spirit had smelled, he fled into the utmost parts of Egypt, and the
angel bound him." (Tobit, viii, 3.)

178. It was "east of the garden of Eden" (*i. e.,* the garden *in* Eden)
that God posted the cherubs to prevent Adam and Eve from reëntering
after their banishment. (Gen. iii, 24.)

181. The pun on *bound* expresses the contempt that Satan feels for the
ramparts of Paradise.

183. St. John's warning (x, 1) against the thief climbing into the
sheepfold inspires this Virgilian simile. (*Aen.,* IX, 566.)

193. Milton echoes the thought of his pamphlet on *The likeliest Means
to remove Hirelings out of the Church,* and the language of his attack
in *Lycidas* (115) on the dishonest clergy who

"Creep, and intrude and climb into the fold."

194. According to Genesis (ii, 9), God made all pleasant trees grow
in Paradise; "The tree of life also in the midst of the garden, and the
tree of knowledge of good and evil." Compare 218–22.

The middle Tree and highest there that grew,   195
Sat like a Cormorant; yet not true Life
Thereby regain'd, but sat devising Death
To them who liv'd; nor on the virtue thought
Of that life-giving Plant, but only us'd
For prospect, what well us'd had been the pledge   200
Of immortality. So little knows
Any, but God alone, to value right
The good before him, but perverts best things
To worst abuse, or to thir meanest use.
Beneath him with new wonder now he views   205
To all delight of human sense expos'd
In narrow room Nature's whole wealth, yea more,
A Heaven on Earth: for blissful Paradise
Of God the Garden was, by him in the East
Of *Eden* planted; *Eden* stretch'd her Line   210
From *Auran* Eastward to the Royal Tow'rs
Of Great *Seleucia,* built by *Grecian* Kings,
Or where the Sons of *Eden* long before
Dwelt in *Telassar:* in this pleasant soil
His far more pleasant Garden God ordain'd;   215
Out of the fertile ground he caus'd to grow

196. Satan is compared to a cormorant for the same reason that he is
compared to a vulture in III, 431; but here he seems to be actually
transformed, as he was later to embody himself in the serpent. X, 516.

198. *virtue* means the medicinal quality in a plant. Milton seems to
have been loosely contrasting Satan's abuse of the Tree of Life with
its symbolic value to Adam and Eve as the pledge of their immortality.

203. That few recognize true good is a maxim found in Juvenal, X,
2-3.

209. Compare note on 132 above.

211. *Auran* is probably Auranitis on the Euphrates. Gilbert cites
Purchas' statement that Auranitis is "easily declined from Heden [Eden]
mentioned after Moses' time in II Kings xix, 12 and Isaiah xxxvii, 12."
(*Pilgrimage,* p. 19.)

212. Alexander's general, Seleucus, founded Seleucia, the seat of the
Greek kingdom in Western Asia from 312 to about 65 B.C., on the
Tigris about fifteen miles below modern Bagdad.

214. Milton must have had in his mind the question put in II Kings
xix, 12 and repeated in Isaiah, xxxvii, 12: "Have the gods of the
nations delivered them which my fathers have destroyed; . . . the children of Eden which were in Thelasar?" Telassar seems to have been
regarded as a city of Eden.

All Trees of noblest kind for sight, smell, taste;
And all amid them stood the Tree of Life,
High eminent, blooming Ambrosial Fruit
Of vegetable Gold; and next to Life   220
Our Death the Tree of Knowledge grew fast by,
Knowledge of Good bought dear by knowing ill.
Southward through *Eden* went a River large,
Nor chang'd his course, but through the shaggy hill
Pass'd underneath ingulft, for God had thrown   225
That Mountain as his Garden mould high rais'd
Upon the rapid current, which through veins
Of porous Earth with kindly thirst up-drawn,
Rose a fresh Fountain, and with many a rill
Water'd the Garden; thence united fell   230
Down the steep glade, and met the nether Flood,
Which from his darksome passage now appears,
And now divided into four main Streams,
Runs diverse, wand'ring many a famous Realm
And Country whereof here needs no account,   235
But rather to tell how, if Art could tell,
How from that Sapphire Fount the crisped Brooks,
Rolling on Orient Pearl and sands of Gold,
With mazy error under pendant shades
Ran Nectar, visiting each plant, and fed   240
Flow'rs worthy of Paradise which not nice Art

---

217. Compare 194 above, and its note.

220. Perhaps there is a vague comparison intended with the golden apples of the Hesperides, for classical tradition put the earthly paradise in those islands.

223. The marvellous river rests upon the biblical account of a rainless world irrigated by nightly mists and of "a river [which] went out of Eden to water the garden; and from thence it was parted, and became into four heads." (Gen. ii, 10.)

226. *mould*, a compact mass of earth, not merely "soil."

228. *kindly*, natural.

234. *wand'ring*, traversing.

237. *crisped*, rippling.

239. *error* keeps its Latin force of "wandering." *N. E. D.* cites Ben Jonson's *Discoveries*, speaking of Aeneas' journeying as "his error by sea."

240. *Nectar*, the drink of the gods, corresponds with flowers worthy of Paradise.

In Beds and curious Knots, but Nature boon
Pour'd forth profuse on Hill and Dale and Plain,
Both where the morning Sun first warmly smote
The open field, and where the unpierc't shade   245
Imbrown'd the noontide Bow'rs: Thus was this place,
A happy rural seat of various view:
Groves whose rich Trees wept odorous Gums and Balm,
Others whose fruit burnisht with Golden Rind
Hung amiable, *Hesperian* Fables true,   250
If true, here only, and of delicious taste:
Betwixt them Lawns, or level Downs, and Flocks
Grazing the tender herb, were interpos'd,
Or palmy hillock, or the flow'ry lap
Of some irriguous Valley spread her store,   255
Flow'rs of all hue, and without Thorn the Rose:
Another side, umbrageous Grots and Caves
Of cool recess, o'er which the mantling vine
Lays forth her purple Grape, and gently creeps
Luxuriant; meanwhile murmuring waters fall   260
Down the slope hills, disperst, or in a Lake,
That to the fringed Bank with Myrtle crown'd,
Her crystal mirror holds, unite thir streams.
The Birds thir quire apply; airs, vernal airs,
Breathing the smell of field and grove, attune   265
The trembling leaves, while Universal *Pan*
Knit with the *Graces* and the *Hours* in dance

242. *boon,* liberal, bountiful.

246. *Imbrown'd,* darkened. The word is an italianism.

247. *view,* appearance.

250. Compare 220 above, and III, 568.

255. *irriguous,* well-watered.

256. Herrick's epigram, *The Rose,* repeats the tradition that
              "Before man's fall the Rose was born,
                  St. Ambrose says, without the thorn."

264. *apply,* contribute, make use of.

266. The Orphic Hymn underlies the conception of Pan (whose name
means "all") as the god of universal nature, enthroned with the hours.
Conti (p. 458) identified him with nature itself, proceeding from and
created by the divine providence and mind. Comparison with Botticelli's
Spring is inevitable.

267. Euphrosyne, Aglaia and Thalia, the three goddesses who em-
bodied the amenities of life, were the Graces.

Led on th' Eternal Spring. Not that fair field
Of *Enna,* where *Proserpin* gath'ring flow'rs
Herself a fairer Flow'r by gloomy *Dis*   270
Was gather'd, which cost *Ceres* all that pain
To seek her through the world; nor that sweet Grove
Of *Daphne* by *Orontes,* and th' inspir'd
Castalian Spring might with this Paradise
Of *Eden* strive; nor that *Nyseian* Isle   275
Girt with the River *Triton,* where old *Cham,*
Whom Gentiles *Ammon* call and *Lybian Jove,*
Hid *Amalthea* and her Florid Son,

---

268. Why spring was eternal in Eden Milton explains in X, 678–9.
Not that . . . nor . . . etc., The excursion to the mysterious and
lovely places of ancient story provides contrast to prove the supreme
beauty of Adam's Paradise. Compare the treatment of the serpent that
tempted Eve, IX, 503–10.

269. Milton thought of Ovid's account of the perpetual spring in the
Sicilian fields of Enna, where Dis (Pluto) kidnapped Proserpina (*Met.*
V, 385–91), and of the Homeric *Hymn to Demeter,* which describes
Ceres' quest of her daughter, how she "wandered nine days through the
earth with flaming torches in her hands, nor did she once taste of am-
brosia or sweet nectar in her grief, nor refresh her body with the bath."
The story had been a symbol with him since he wrote from Horton to
Charles Diodati, "Ceres never sought her daughter Proserpine . . . with
greater ardour than I do this Idea of Beauty."

273. The gardens of Daphne at Antioch in Syria, on the river Orontes,
had a temple of Apollo and a spring which was called after the Castalian
spring on Mt. Parnassus, near Delphi, in Greece. Milton calls it "inspired" because tradition says that the waters gave oracles by putting
marks on the leaves dipped into them by enquirers.

275. Nysa was a lovely island in the river Triton, in modern Tunis.
There, as a famous passage of Diodorus Siculus (3, 67, translated
literally by Conti, pp. 510–11) reports, Saturn's son Ammon, "fearing the
jealous anger of Rhea," hid his son, "young Bacchus," the child whom
a nymph called Amalthea bore to him.

276. *Cham* is the spelling of the name of Noah's second son, Ham, in
the Septuagint (Gen. v, 32). Tradition said that after the flood he
settled in Africa, and the likeness of the names led to his identification
with the Egyptian god, Ammon, who became known as Zeus-Ammon or
Jupiter-Ammon when the Greeks and Romans penetrated Egypt. Probably Milton, like Sir Walter Raleigh (*History of the World,* i, 6, 6),
believed that "the Egyptians, even after the flood, began . . . to entitle
Cham, . . . Jupiter Chammon, or Hammon."

277. *Gentiles,* non-Jewish races.

278. *Florid,* rubicund, red-faced. Bacchus is god of wine.

Young *Bacchus,* from his Stepdame *Rhea's* eye;
Nor where *Abassin* Kings thir issue Guard,   280
Mount *Amara,* though this by some suppos'd
True Paradise under the *Ethiop* Line
By *Nilus* head, enclos'd with shining Rock,
A whole day's journey high, but wide remote
From this *Assyrian* Garden, where the Fiend   285
Saw undelighted all delight, all kind
Of living Creatures new to sight and strange:
Two of far nobler shape erect and tall,
Godlike erect, with native Honour clad
In naked Majesty seem'd Lords of all,   290
And worthy seem'd, for in thir looks Divine
The image of thir glorious Maker shone,
Truth, Wisdom, Sanctitude severe and pure,
Severe, but in true filial freedom plac't;
Whence true autority in men; though both   295
Not equal, as their sex not equal seem'd;
For contemplation hee and valour form'd,
For softness shee and sweet attractive Grace,
Hee for God only, shee for God in him:
His fair large Front and Eye sublime declar'd   300

---

280. *Abassin,* Abassynian.
issue, children.

281. Milton's romantic impression of Mt. Amara may have been drawn from the enthusiastic description in Purchas' *Pilgrimage* (pp. 843–6) or from Peter Heylin's *Cosmographie* (iv, 64): "The hill of Amara is a day's journey high, on the top whereof are thirty-four palaces in which the younger sons of the Emperor are continually enclosed to avoid sedition; . . . though not much distant from the Equator if not plainly under it, yet blessed with such a temperate air that some have taken it for the place of Paradise."

282. *Ethiop Line,* the equator.

283. *Nilus head,* the source of the Nile.

285. *Assyrian Garden,* Adam's Paradise.

288. Compare VII, 506-11, where Milton makes a point of man's upright stance and reason in contrast with the "prone," unreasonable beasts.

296. "Who can be ignorant, that woman was created for man, and not man for woman?" Milton asks in *Doctrine of Divorce,* II, xv, where St. Paul's treatment of women is as influential as it is in this passage.

300. *Front,* forehead.
sublime, raised, upward looking.

Absolute rule; and Hyacinthine Locks
Round from his parted forelock manly hung
Clust'ring, but not beneath his shoulders broad:
Shee as a veil down to the slender waist
Her unadorned golden tresses wore   305
Dishevell'd, but in wanton ringlets wav'd
As the Vine curls her tendrils, which impli'd
Subjection, but requir'd with gentle sway,
And by her yielded, by him best receiv'd,
Yielded with coy submission, modest pride,   310
And sweet reluctant amorous delay.
Nor those mysterious parts were then conceal'd,
Then was not guilty shame: dishonest shame
Of nature's works, honour dishonorable,
Sin-bred, how have ye troubl'd all mankind   315
With shows instead, mere shows of seeming pure,
And banisht from man's life his happiest life,
Simplicity and spotless innocence.
So pass'd they naked on, nor shunn'd the sight
Of God or Angel, for they thought no ill: 320
So hand in hand they pass'd, the loveliest pair
That ever since in love's imbraces met,
Adam the goodliest man of men since born
His Sons, the fairest of her Daughters *Eve.*
Under a tuft of shade that on a green   325
Stood whispering soft, by a fresh Fountain side
They sat them down, and after no more toil
Of thir sweet Gard'ning labour than suffic'd
To recommend cool *Zephyr,* and made ease
More easy, wholesome thirst and appetite   330
More grateful, to thir Supper Fruits they fell,

---

301. *Hyacinthine.* The comparison of hair to the colour of the hyacinth is a recollection of Homer. (*Od.* VI, 231 and XXIII, 158.)

303. Milton's authority is St. Paul in I Corinthians, xi, 14–15: ". . . if
a man have long hair, it is a shame unto him, But if a woman have
long hair, it is a glory to her; for her hair is given her for a covering."

310. *coy,* shy.

313. *dishonest,* unchaste.

329. *Zephyr,* the northwest wind. Homer describes it as blowing
gently in the Elysian Fields. (*Od.* IV, 567.)

Nectarine Fruits which the compliant boughs
Yielded them, side-long as they sat recline
On the soft downy Bank damaskt with flow'rs:
The savoury pulp they chew, and in the rind   335
Still as they thirsted scoop the brimming stream;
Nor gentle purpose, nor endearing smiles
Wanted, nor youthful dalliance as beseems
Fair couple, linkt in happy nuptial League,
Alone as they. About them frisking play'd   340
All Beasts of th' Earth, since wild, and of all chase
In Wood or Wilderness, Forest or Den;
Sporting the Lion ramp'd, and in his paw
Dandl'd the Kid; Bears, Tigers, Ounces, Pards
Gamboll'd before them, th' unwieldy Elephant   345
To make them mirth us'd all his might, and wreath'd
His Lithe Proboscis; close the Serpent sly
Insinuating, wove with Gordian twine
His braided train, and of his fatal guile
Gave proof unheeded; others on the grass   350
Coucht, and now fill'd with pasture gazing sat,
Or Bedward ruminating; for the Sun
Declin'd was hasting now with prone career
To th' Ocean Isles, and in th' ascending Scale
Of Heav'n the Stars that usher Evening rose: 355
When *Satan* still in gaze, as first he stood,
Scarce thus at length fail'd speech recover'd sad.

---

332. *compliant,* pliant.

333. *recline,* reclining.

334. *damaskt,* richly figured, like the elaborate silks once woven in Damascus.

337. *purpose,* conversation.

338. *Wanted,* were absent.

344. *Ounce,* lynx.
Pard, leopard, or panther.

348. *Insinuating,* knotting or winding itself up.
Gordian twine, a tangle like the Gordian knot—which Alexander cut.

349. *braided train,* writhing, coiled body. Compare the "voluble-bold serpent" of IX, 436, which is not "prone," "with indented wave," (496), but erect and coiled.

352. *Bedward ruminating,* chewing the cud on the way to bed.

354. *Ocean Isles,* The Azores, as 592 below indicates.

357. *fail'd speech,* the speech that had failed him.

O Hell! what do mine eyes with grief behold,
Into our room of bliss thus high advanc't
Creatures of other mould, earth-born perhaps,   360
Not Spirits, yet to heav'nly Spirits bright
Little inferior; whom my thoughts pursue
With wonder, and could love, so lively shines
In them Divine resemblance, and such grace
The hand that form'd them on thir shape hath pour'd.   365
Ah gentle pair, yee little think how nigh
Your change approaches, when all these delights
Will vanish and deliver ye to woe,
More woe, the more your taste is now of joy;
Happy, but for so happy ill secur'd   370
Long to continue, and this high seat your Heav'n
Ill fenc't for Heav'n to keep out such a foe
As now is enter'd; yet no purpos'd foe
To you whom I could pity thus forlorn
Though I unpitied: League with you I seek,   375
And mutual amity so strait, so close,
That I with you must dwell, or you with me
Henceforth; my dwelling haply may not please
Like this fair Paradise, your sense, yet such
Accept your Maker's work; he gave it me,   380
Which I as freely give; Hell shall unfold,
To entertain you two, her widest Gates,
And send forth all her Kings; there will be room,
Not like these narrow limits, to receive
Your numerous offspring; if no better place,   385

359. *our room of bliss,* our happy position or rank.

360. *mould,* material, substance.

362. Satan is paraphrasing the Psalm (viii, 5) which says that God has made man "a little lower than the angels."

368. *ye,* you. *ye* and *thee* were often used as objects of the verb.

374. *forlorn,* undefended.

375. *Though I unpitied:* Though he is beyond God's pity himself, Satan feels the impulse of pity.

376. *strait,* intimate.

382. The lines gather force from their echo of Isaiah's prophecy (xiv, 9): "Hell from beneath is moved for thee to meet thee at thy coming; . . . it hath raised up from their thrones all the kings of the nations."

Thank him who puts me loath to this revenge
On you who wrong me not for him who wrong'd.
And should I at your harmless innocence
Melt, as I do, yet public reason just,
Honour and Empire with revenge enlarg'd,   390
By conquering this new World, compels me now
To do what else though damn'd I should abhor.
　So spake the Fiend, and with necessity,
The Tyrant's plea, excus'd his devilish deeds.
Then from his lofty stand on that high Tree   395
Down he alights among the sportful Herd
Of those fourfooted kinds, himself now one,
Now other, as thir shape serv'd best his end
Nearer to view his prey, and unespi'd
To mark what of thir state he more might learn   400
By word or action markt: about them round
A Lion now he stalks with fiery glare,
Then as a Tiger, who by chance hath spi'd
In some Purlieu two gentle Fawns at play,
Straight couches close, then rising changes oft   405
His couchant watch, as one who chose his ground
Whence rushing he might surest seize them both
Gript in each paw: when *Adam* first of men
To first of women *Eve* thus moving speech,
Turn'd him all ear to hear new utterance flow.   410
　Sole partner and sole part of all these joys,
Dearer thyself than all; needs must the Power
That made us, and for us this ample World
Be infinitely good, and of his good

---

389. *public reason*, reason of state.　Bacon speaks of the time-serving which "The Italians call *ragioni di stato*, whereof . . . Pius Quintus could not hear spoken with patience, terming them inventions against religion and the moral virtues." (*Advancement*, I, ii, 3.)

393. Necessity had been the plea of Charles I for some of his acts of "tyranny."

398. *end*, object.

404. *purlieu*, a tract on the edge of a forest.

405. *couches*, lies.

406. *couchant*, lying down.　The word which we now use only as a term in heraldry was commonly applied to wild animals.

409. *moving speech*, speaking.

As liberal and free as infinite,   415
That rais'd us from the dust and plac't us here
In all this happiness, who at his hand
Have nothing merited, nor can perform
Aught whereof hee hath need, hee who requires
From us no other service than to keep   420
This one, this easy charge, of all the Trees
In Paradise that bear delicious fruit
So various, not to taste that only Tree
Of knowledge, planted by the Tree of Life,
So near grows Death to Life, whate'er Death is,   425
Some dreadful thing no doubt; for well thou know'st
God hath pronounc't it death to taste that Tree,
The only sign of our obedience left
Among so many signs of power and rule
Conferr'd upon us, and Dominion giv'n   430
Over all other Creatures that possess
Earth, Air, and Sea. Then let us not think hard
One easy prohibition, who enjoy
Free leave so large to all things else, and choice
Unlimited of manifold delights: 435
But let us ever praise him, and extol
His bounty, following our delightful task
To prune these growing Plants, and tend these Flow'rs,
Which were it toilsome, yet with thee were sweet.
    To whom thus *Eve* repli'd. O thou for whom   440
And from whom I was form'd flesh of thy flesh,
And without whom am to no end, my Guide
And Head, what thou hast said is just and right.
For wee to him indeed all praises owe,
And daily thanks, I chiefly who enjoy   445
So far the happier Lot, enjoying thee
Preëminent by so much odds, while thou
Like consort to thyself canst nowhere find.
That day I oft remember, when from sleep

---

424. Compare the note on 194 above.

430. Compare Genesis I, 26. "And God said, Let us make man in
our image, . . . and let them have dominion over the fish of the sea,
and over the fowl of the air, and over the cattle, and over all the earth."

443. Compare St. Paul's words "The head of the woman is the man."
(I Cor. xi, 3.) Compare 483 below, and its note.

I first awak't, and found myself repos'd   450
Under a shade on flow'rs, much wond'ring where
And what I was, whence thither brought, and how.
Not distant far from thence a murmuring sound
Of waters issu'd from a Cave and spread
Into a liquid Plain, then stood unmov'd   455
Pure as th' expanse of Heav'n; I thither went
With unexperienc't thought, and laid me down
On the green bank, to look into the clear
Smooth Lake, that to me seem'd another Sky.
As I bent down to look, just opposite,   460
A Shape within the wat'ry gleam appear'd
Bending to look on me, I started back,
It started back, but pleas'd I soon return'd,
Pleas'd it return'd as soon with answering looks
Of sympathy and love; there I had fixt   465
Mine eyes till now, and pin'd with vain desire,
Had not a voice thus warn'd me, What thou seest,
What there thou seest fair Creature is thyself,
With thee it came and goes: but follow me,
And I will bring thee where no shadow stays   470
Thy coming, and thy soft imbraces, hee
Whose image thou art, him thou shall enjoy
Inseparably thine, to him shalt bear
Multitudes like thyself, and thence be call'd
Mother of human Race: what could I do,   475
But follow straight, invisibly thus led?
Till I espi'd thee, fair indeed and tall,
Under a Platan, yet methought less fair,
Less winning soft, less amiably mild,
Than that smooth wat'ry image; back I turn'd,   480
Thou following cri'd'st aloud, Return fair *Eve*,
Whom fli'st thou? whom thou fli'st, of him thou art,

---

461. So Ovid describes Narcissus lying down beside a beautiful pool, fascinated with his reflection, but pining away and dying because he never finds out that what he sees is himself. (*Met.* III, 402–510.)

470. *stays,* waits for.

475. Compare XI, 159.

478. *Platan,* plane tree.
methought, it seemed to me.

His flesh, his bone; to give thee being I lent
Out of my side to thee, nearest my heart
Substantial Life, to have thee by my side   485
Henceforth an individual solace dear;
Part of my Soul I seek thee, and thee claim
My other half: with that thy gentle hand
Seiz'd mine, I yielded, and from that time see
How beauty is excell'd by manly grace   490
And wisdom, which alone is truly fair.
   So spake our general Mother, and with eyes
Of conjugal attraction unreprov'd,
And meek surrender, half imbracing lean'd
On our first Father, half her swelling Breast   495
Naked met his under the flowing Gold
Of her loose tresses hid: he in delight
Both of her Beauty and submissive Charms
Smil'd with superior Love, as *Jupiter*
On *Juno* smiles, when he impregns the Clouds   500
That shed *May* Flowers; and press'd her Matron lip
With kisses pure: aside the Devil turn'd
For envy, yet with jealous leer malign
Ey'd them askance, and to himself thus plain'd.
   Sight hateful, sight tormenting! thus these two   505
Imparadis't in one another's arms
The happier *Eden,* shall enjoy thir fill
Of bliss on bliss, while I to Hell am thrust,
Where neither joy nor love, but fierce desire,
Among our other torments not the least,   510
Still unfulfill'd with pain of longing pines;

---

   483. The line paraphrases Adam's words in Genesis (ii, 23), after Eve
is created from the rib taken out of his body.

   486. *individual* has its basic Latin meaning of "inseparable" or "un-
dividable."

   493. *unreprov'd,* not blamable, innocent. The use of the perfect passive participle in this sense is a Greek construction. Compare *unremov'd*
in 987 below.

   499. Jupiter was lord of the sky "and Juno of the ayre." (*F. Q.* VII
vii, 26.)

   500. *impregns,* impregnates.

   504. *plain'd,* complained.

   511. *pines,* makes (me) pine.

Yet let me not forget what I have gain'd
From thir own mouths; all is not theirs it seems:
One fatal Tree there stands of Knowledge call'd,
Forbidden them to taste: Knowledge forbidd'n?   515
Suspicious, reasonless.   Why should thir Lord
Envy them that? can it be sin to know,
Can it be death? and do they only stand
By Ignorance, is that thir happy state,
The proof of thir obedience and thir faith?   520
O fair foundation laid whereon to build
Thir ruin!   Hence I will excite thir minds
With more desire to know, and to reject
Envious commands, invented with design
To keep them low whom knowledge might exalt   525
Equal with Gods; aspiring to be such,
They taste and die: what likelier can ensue?
But first with narrow search I must walk round
This Garden, and no corner leave unspi'd;
A chance but chance may lead where I may meet   530
Some wand'ring Spirit of Heav'n, by Fountain side,
Or in thick shade retir'd, from him to draw
What further would be learnt.   Live while ye may,
Yet happy pair; enjoy, till I return,
Short pleasures, for long woes are to succeed.   535
    So saying, his proud step he scornful turn'd,
But with sly circumspection, and began
Through wood, through waste, o'er hill, o'er dale his roam.
Meanwhile in utmost Longitude, where Heav'n
With Earth and Ocean meets, the setting Sun   540
Slowly descended, and with right aspect
Against the eastern Gate of Paradise

---

512. A work of Moses Barcephas, published in 1569 (according to
Todd), may have given Milton the Talmudic tradition that Satan over-
heard Adam tell Eve about the taboo of the Tree of Knowledge.   In the
dramatic form in which he first planned *P. L.* the situation would have
been doubly effective.

526. Compare III, 206 and IX, 547–8.

539. *utmost longitude,* farthest west.   Compare III, 574–6.

541. *right aspect,* direct view.   The setting sun shines straight upon
the inner face of the gate on the east side of Paradise, illuminating it
from the point of view of those inside the garden.

Levell'd his ev'ning Rays: it was a Rock
Of Alablaster, pil'd up to the Clouds,
Conspicuous far, winding with one ascent   545
Accessible from Earth, one entrance high;
The rest was craggy cliff, that overhung
Still as it rose, impossible to climb.
Betwixt these rocky Pillars *Gabriel* sat
Chief of th' Angelic Guards, awaiting night;   550
About him exercis'd Heroic Games
Th' unarmed Youth of Heav'n, but nigh at hand
Celestial Armory, Shields, Helms, and Spears
Hung high with Diamond flaming, and with Gold.
Thither came *Uriel,* gliding through the Even   555
On a Sun-beam, swift as a shooting Star
In *Autumn* thwarts the night, when vapours fir'd
Impress the Air, and shows the Mariner
From what point of his Compass to beware
Impetuous winds: he thus began in haste.   560
  Gabriel, to thee thy course by Lot hath giv'n
Charge and strict watch that to this happy place
No evil thing approach or enter in;
This day at highth of Noon came to my Sphere
A Spirit, zealous, as he seem'd, to know   565
More of th' Almighty's works, and chiefly Man
God's latest Image: I describ'd his way
Bent all on speed, and markt his Aery Gait;
But in the Mount that lies from *Eden* North,
Where he first lighted, soon discern'd his looks 570
Alien from Heav'n, with passions foul obscur'd:
Mine eye pursu'd him still, but under shade

544. Alablaster was the prevailing form of the word "alabaster."

549. In the Bible, Gabriel is the interpreter of Daniel's vision (viii, 16 and ix, 21) and the bearer of the news of John the Baptist's impending birth to Zacharias (Luke i, 19). Rabbinical tradition explains Milton's treatment of him as a warrior angel who has a divinely appointed post *in the east.* Fletcher (*Rabbinical Readings,* p. 237) cites Buxtorf's *Lexicon:* "Gabriel stands before his [*i. e.,* God's] face towards the kingdom of Judah . . . which was toward the east." Compare 778–85 below.

557. *thwarts,* flies across.
vapours fir'd, "heat lightning."

567. Christ is the first "divine similitude" (III, 383–4). Compare 430 above and its note.

Lost sight of him; one of the banisht crew
I fear, hath ventur'd from the deep, to raise
New troubles; him thy care must be to find.   575
    To whom the winged Warrior thus return'd:
Uriel, no wonder if thy perfet sight,
Amid the Sun's bright circle where thou sitst,
See far and wide: in at this Gate none pass
The vigilance here plac't, but such as come   580
Well known from Heav'n; and since Meridian hour
No Creature thence: if Spirit of other sort,
So minded, have o'erleapt these earthy bounds
On purpose, hard thou know'st it to exclude
Spiritual substance with corporeal bar.   585
But if within the circuit of these walks
In whatsoever shape he lurk, of whom
Thou tell'st, by morrow dawning I shall know.
    So promis'd hee, and *Uriel* to his charge
Return'd on that bright beam, whose point now rais'd   590
Bore him slope downward to the Sun now fall'n
Beneath th' *Azores;* whither the prime Orb,
Incredible how swift, had thither roll'd
Diurnal, or this less volúbil Earth
By shorter flight to th' East, had left him there   595
Arraying with reflected Purple and Gold
The Clouds that on his Western Throne attend:
Now came still Ev'ning on, and Twilight gray
Had in her sober Livery all things clad;
Silence accompanied, for Beast and Bird,   600
They to thir grassy Couch, these to thir Nests
Were slunk, all but the wakeful Nightingale;

---

580. *vigilance:* the abstract word put for Gabriel himself and his squad
of angels.

585. On spiritual substance see the Introduction, §17.

591. Uriel slides *down* the sunbeam to the sun, which is now below
the horizon and therefore, in a Ptolemaic universe, *lower* than the earth.

592. Compare line 354, and its note.
Prime Orb, the sun.

593. Milton shared Donne's wonder "that so vast and immense a
body as the Sun, should run so many miles, in a minute." (*Sermon at
St. Pauls,* Easter, 1627.) But what appears to be the more credible
alternative—the rotation of the *volubil* (turning) earth—is mentioned
quite impartially. Compare 661–4 below, and VIII, 25–38.

She all night long her amorous descant sung;
Silence was pleas'd: now glow'd the Firmament
With living Sapphires: *Hesperus* that led   605
The starry Host, rode brightest, till the Moon
Rising in clouded Majesty, at length
Apparent Queen unveil'd her peerless light,
And o'er the dark her Silver Mantle threw.

   When *Adam* thus to *Eve:* Fair Consort, th' hour   610
Of night, and all things now retir'd to rest
Mind us of like repose, since God hath set
Labour and rest, as day and night to men
Successive, and the timely dew of sleep
Now falling with soft slumbrous weight inclines   615
Our eye-lids; other Creatures all day long
Rove idle unimploy'd, and less need rest;
Man hath his daily work of body or mind
Appointed, which declares his Dignity,
And the regard of Heav'n on all his ways;   620
While other Animals unactive range,
And of thir doings God takes no account.
Tomorrow ere fresh Morning streak the East
With first approach of light, we must be ris'n,
And at our pleasant labour, to reform   625
Yon flow'ry Arbours, yonder Alleys green,
Our walk at noon, with branches overgrown,
That mock our scant manuring, and require
More hands than ours to lop thir wanton growth:
Those Blossoms also, and those dropping Gums,   630
That lie bestrown unsightly and unsmooth,

---

   603. *descant,* a warbled song. The word was often used of birds'
music.

   604. Compare the personification of Silence, enchanted by the Lady's
song in *Comus,* 557–60, and again in *Il Penseroso,* 55–6:

              And the mute Silence hist along,
              Less *Philomel* will deign a song.

   605. *Hesperus,* The evening star. Compare IX, 49.

   608. *Apparent Queen,* a manifest or visible queen.

   620. *regard,* attention, oversight.

   628. *manuring* has its Latin force of "working with the hands," *i. e.,*
cultivating.

Ask riddance, if we mean to tread with ease;
Meanwhile, as Nature wills, Night bids us rest.
　　To whom thus *Eve* with perfet beauty adorn'd.
My Author and Disposer, what thou bidd'st   635
Unargu'd I obey; so God ordains,
God is thy Law, thou mine: to know no more
Is woman's happiest knowledge and her praise.
With thee conversing I forget all time,
All seasons and thir change, all please alike.   640
Sweet is the breath of morn, her rising sweet,
With charm of earliest Birds; pleasant the Sun
When first on this delightful Land he spreads
His orient Beams, on herb, tree, fruit, and flow'r,
Glist'ring with dew; fragrant the fertile earth   645
After soft showers; and sweet the coming on
Of grateful Ev'ning mild, then silent Night
With this her solemn Bird and this fair Moon,
And these the Gems of Heav'n, her starry train:
But neither breath of Morn when she ascends   650
With charm of earliest Birds, nor rising Sun
On this delightful land, nor herb, fruit, flow'r,
Glist'ring with dew, nor fragrance after showers,
Nor grateful Ev'ning mild, nor silent Night
With this her solemn Bird, nor walk by Moon,   655
Or glittering Star-light without thee is sweet.
But wherefore all night long shine these, for whom
This glorious sight, when sleep hath shut all eyes?
　　To whom our general Ancestor repli'd.
Daughter of God and Man, accomplisht *Eve*,   660
Those have thir course to finish, round the Earth,
By morrow Ev'ning, and from Land to Land

632. *Ask*, demand, require.

635. Eve calls Adam her *Author* because she had been created out of
his body. Compare Adam's title for her in 660.

640. Since there is no change of seasons in Paradise, Eve must refer
to the time of day.

642. *charm*, a name regularly given to the blended singing of birds.

660. *accomplisht*, full of "accomplishments" or of fine, personal at-
tainments. Compare Samson's ironical description of Dalila,

　　"That specious Monster, my accomplished snare." (*S. A.*, 230.)

661. Compare line 593 above and its note.

In order, though to Nations yet unborn,
Minist'ring light prepar'd, they set and rise;
Lest total darkness should by Night regain   665
Her old possession, and extinguish life
In Nature and all things, which these soft fires
Not only enlighten, but with kindly heat
Of various influence foment and warm,
Temper or nourish, or in part shed down   670
Thir stellar virtue on all kinds that grow
On Earth, made hereby apter to receive
Perfection from the Sun's more potent Ray.
These then, though unbeheld in deep of night,
Shine not in vain, nor think, though men were none,   675
That heav'n would want spectators, God want praise;
Millions of spiritual Creatures walk the Earth
Unseen, both when we wake, and when we sleep:
All these with ceaseless praise his works behold
Both day and night: how often from the steep   680
Of echoing Hill or Thicket have we heard
Celestial voices to the midnight air,
Sole, or responsive each to other's note
Singing thir great Creator: oft in bands
While they keep watch, or nightly rounding walk   685
With Heav'nly touch of instrumental sounds
In full harmonic number join'd, thir songs
Divide the night, and lift our thoughts to Heaven.
    Thus talking hand in hand alone they pass'd

---

665. *total darkness,* the darkness of Chaos which was banished first of
all at the creation.

668. *kindly,* natural.

669. In *Doctrine of Divorce* (I, x) Milton displayed a sceptical interest
in astrological theories of the "proper star" by which individual tempera-
ments were supposed to be fixed, and in "the supernal influence of
schemes and angular aspects" on which the importance of an individual's
horoscope was supposed to depend. In less degree all the stars were
believed to "rain influence" upon the earth as Milton says that the sun
does in III, 606–12.

682. Contrast the diabolic "airy tongues, that syllable mens names" of
Comus, 208. Compare the Introduction, §16.

685. *rounding,* walking the rounds, as sentries.

688. *Divide the night, i. e.,* into watches. This military term is a
Latinism.

On to thir blissful Bower; it was a place   690
Chos'n by the sovran Planter, when he fram'd
All things to man's delightful use; the roof
Of thickest covert was inwoven shade
Laurel and Myrtle, and what higher grew
Of firm and fragrant leaf; on either side   695
Acanthus, and each odorous bushy shrub
Fenc'd up the verdant wall; each beauteous flow'r,
Iris all hues, Roses, and Jessamin
Rear'd high thir flourisht heads between, and wrought
Mosaic; underfoot the Violet,   700
Crocus, and Hyacinth with rich inlay
Broider'd the ground, more colour'd than with stone
Of costliest Emblem: other Creature here
Beast, Bird, Insect, or Worm durst enter none;
Such was thir awe of Man. In shadier Bower   705
More sacred and sequester'd, though but feign'd,
Pan or *Silvanus* never slept, nor Nymph,
Nor *Faunus* haunted. Here in close recess
With Flowers, Garlands, and sweet-smelling Herbs
Espoused *Eve* deckt first her nuptial Bed,   710
And heav'nly Quires the Hymenæan sung,
What day the genial Angel to our Sire
Brought her in naked beauty more adorn'd
More lovely than *Pandora,* whom the Gods

702. *stone Of costliest Emblem,* stone decorated with precious metal
inlaid.

705. *In shadier Bower:* The construction and thought resemble those
in 268 above, where Milton lists the earthly paradises of the "Gentiles"
to compare them unfavourably with Paradise.

706. *feign'd,* imagined by poets. "For the truest poetry is the most
feigning." (*As You Like It,* I!I, iii, 21–22.)

707. *Pan.* Compare the note on 266 above.
Sylvanus and *Faunus, like the Nymphs,* were deities of groves and
forests.

708. *close,* secret.

711. *Hymenaean,* marriage song.

712. *genial,* nuptial. The term is given as a kind of title to the angel
sent to preside over the marriage.

714. Pandora was the deceptive gift brought by Hermes to Epimetheus
(*After*-thought), "unwiser" than his brother Prometheus (Fore-thought),
whose capture of fire from heaven for men the gods resented. Epimetheus married her and opened the casket that the gods sent with her.

Endow'd with all thir gifts, and O too like   715
In sad event, when to the unwiser Son
Of *Japhet* brought by *Hermes,* she ensnar'd
Mankind with her fair looks, to be aveng'd
On him who had stole *Jove's* authentic fire.

   Thus at thir shady Lodge arriv'd, both stood,   720
Both turn'd, and under op'n Sky ador'd
The God that made both Sky, Air, Earth and Heav'n
Which they beheld, the Moon's resplendent Globe
And starry Pole: Thou also mad'st the Night,
Maker Omnipotent, and thou the Day,   725
Which we in our appointed work imploy'd
Have finisht happy in our mutual help
And mutual love, the Crown of all our bliss
Ordain'd by thee, and this delicious place
For us too large, where thy abundance wants   730
Partakers, and uncropt falls to the ground.
But thou hast promis'd from us two a Race
To fill the Earth, who shall with us extol
Thy goodness infinite, both when we wake,
And when we seek, as now, thy gift of sleep.   735
   This said unanimous, and other Rites
Observing none, but adoration pure
Which God likes best, into thir inmost bower
Handed they went; and eas'd the putting off
These troublesome disguises which wee wear,   740
Straight side by side were laid, nor turn'd I ween
Adam from his fair Spouse, nor *Eve* the Rites

It proved to contain all the evils of life. "Plato and Chryssippus,"
Milton wrote in *Doctrine of Divorce,* II, iii, "knew not what a consummate and most adorned Pandora was bestowed upon Adam, to be the
nurse . . . of his native innocence and perfection, which might have
kept him from being our true Epimetheus."

   717. *Japhet,* one of the Titans, the father of Prometheus and Epimetheus.

   719. *authentic,* genuine.

   724. *Pole,* The sky generally; a Latinism, depending upon the use of
the word in astronomy to mean the north and south celestial poles.

   730. *wants,* lacks, needs.

   735. Both the classics and the Bible call sleep a divine gift. Milton
may have thought of Psalms cxxvii, 2: "he giveth his beloved sleep":
or of Aeneas' allusion to the quiet of evening coming most gratefully
with the gift of the gods. (*Aen.* II, 269.)

Mysterious of connubial Love refus'd:
Whatever Hypocrites austerely talk
Of purity and place and innocence,   745
Defaming as impure what God declares
Pure, and commands to some, leaves free to all.
Our Maker bids increase, who bids abstain
But our destroyer, foe to God and Man?
Hail wedded Love, mysterious Law, true source   750
Of human offspring, sole propriety,
In Paradise of all things common else.
By thee adulterous lust was driv'n from men
Among the bestial herds to range, by thee
Founded in Reason, Loyal, Just, and Pure,   755
Relations dear, and all the Charities
Of Father, Son, and Brother first were known.
Far be it, that I should write thee sin or blame,
Or think thee unbefitting holiest place,
Perpetual Fountain of Domestic sweets,   760
Whose bed is undefil'd and chaste pronounc't,
Present, or past, as Saints and Patriarchs us'd.
Here Love his golden shafts imploys, here lights
His constant Lamp, and waves his purple wings,
Reigns here and revels; not in the bought smile   765
Of Harlots, loveless, joyless, unindear'd,
Casual fruition, nor in Court Amours,
Mixt Dance, or wanton Mask, or Midnight Ball,

---

743. Compare Milton's justification of the "intelligible flame, not in Paradise to be resisted," in *Doctrine of Divorce*, I, iv. Milton calls it mysterious because St. Paul calls marriage "a great mystery" (Ephes. v, 32), and in *Colasterion* he bitterly attacked an opponent who objected to his calling marriage "The mystery of joy."

744. The hypocrites represent "that church of antichrist" which Milton attacks in *Doctrine of Divorce*, I, xiv, for "wilfully forbidding" some classes to marry.

748. "Be fruitful, and multiply, and replenish the earth" (Gen. i, 28), God's first command to Adam and Eve, is echoed here and in line 733 above.

763. Ovid (*Met.* I, 468) was the source of the idea that Cupid had two arrows, one "all of gold, with point full sharp and bright," which inspired love, and the other which banished love, of lead.

768. Compare Milton's attack on the bishops for instigating to "gaming, jigging, wassailing, and mixed dancing, . . . a horror to think." (*Of Reformation*, II, P. W., II, 402.)

Or Serenate, which the starv'd Lover sings
To his proud fair, best quitted with disdain.   770
These lull'd by Nightingales imbracing slept,
And on thir naked limbs the flow'ry roof
Show'r'd Roses, which the Morn repair'd. Sleep on,
Blest pair; and O yet happiest if ye seek
No happier state, and know to know no more.   775
    Now had night measur'd with her shadowy Cone
Half way up Hill this vast Sublunar Vault,
And from thir Ivory Port the Cherubim
Forth issuing at th' accustom'd hour stood arm'd
To thir night watches in warlike Parade,   780
When *Gabriel* to his next in power thus spake.
    Uzziel, half these draw off, and coast the South
With strictest watch; these other wheel the North,
Our circuit meets full West. As flame they part
Half wheeling to the Shield, half to the Spear.   785
From these, two strong and subtle Spirits he call'd
That near him stood, and gave them thus in charge.
    Ithuriel and *Zephon,* with wing'd speed
Search through this Garden, leave unsearcht no nook,
But chiefly where those two fair Creatures Lodge,   790

---

769. *Serenate,* serenade.
starv'd, dead of cold or disappointment. Compare II, 600.

770. *quitted,* repaid.

773. *repair'd,* supplied the loss of (with fresh roses).

775. *know to know no more,* be wise enough not to be tempted to
seek more knowledge (*i. e.,* of good and evil).

776. The cone of the earth's shadow, cast by the sun below the
horizon at an angle of 45° against heaven, indicates that it is nine
o'clock. When the point of the cone is in the zenith, it will be midnight.

778. *Port,* gate, *i. e.,* of Paradise.

782. In the Bible *Uzziel* is a human, but not an angelic name, meaning "Strength of God." (*e. g.,* Exod. vi, 18 and Num. iii, 19.)
Fletcher (*Rabbinical Readings,* p. 252) cites Buxtorf's *Lexicon* as recog-
nizing Uzziel (Usiel) as an angel and as one of the sons of God who
loved the daughters of men (Gen. vi, 4), but it is not yet clear why
Milton made him Gabriel's lieutenant.

788. Milton's ground for the two angels' names is a mystery. Ithuriel,
which means in Hebrew "Discovery of God," does not occur at all in
the Bible, and Zephon, "Searcher," occurs only as a human name.
(Num. xxvi, 15.)

Now laid perhaps asleep secure of harm.
This Ev'ning from the Sun's decline arriv'd
Who tells of some infernal Spirit seen
Hitherward bent (who could have thought?) escap'd
The bars of Hell, on errand bad no doubt: 795
Such where ye find, seize fast, and hither bring.
  So saying, on he led his radiant Files,
Dazzling the Moon; these to the Bower direct
In search of whom they sought: him there they found
Squat like a Toad, close at the ear of *Eve;*   800
Assaying by his Devilish art to reach
The Organs of her Fancy, and with them forge
Illusions as he list, Phantasms and Dreams,
Or if, inspiring venom, he might taint
Th' animal Spirits that from pure blood arise   805
Like gentle breaths from Rivers pure, thence raise
At least distemper'd, discontented thoughts,
Vain hopes, vain aims, inordinate desires
Blown up with high conceits ingend'ring pride.
Him thus intent *Ithuriel* with his Spear   810
Touch'd lightly; for no falsehood can endure
Touch of Celestial temper, but returns
Of force to its own likeness: up he starts
Discover'd and surpris'd. As when a spark
Lights on a heap of nitrous Powder, laid   815
Fit for the Tun some Magazin to store

---

797. *Files,* ranks (of warrior angels).

802. In attributing Eve's dream to the devil working through her imagination and animal spirits, Milton followed old and well-established tradition. The sixteenth-century Italian, Mario Equicola, wrote in his *Book of Love:* "The ancient theologians attribute all our irrational acts to the demons, believing that aeriel spirits move the humours in our bodies and excite some of our imaginings." (Ed. of 1525, Mantua, p. 48 *verso.*) To converse with men, said Henry More (*Immortality of the Soul,* III, viii, 3) the demons "are disposed to turn themselves into several bestial forms."

804. *inspiring,* has its literal, Latin meaning, "breathing in."

805. Compare V, 484–5, and its note.

813. *Of force,* by compulsion.

815. *nitrous Powder,* gunpowder.

816. *Tun,* barrel (for storage).
Magazin, powder magazine.

Against a rumor'd War, the Smutty grain
With sudden blaze diffus'd, inflames the Air:
So started up in his own shape the Fiend.
Back stept those two fair Angels half amaz'd   820
So sudden to behold the grisly King;
Yet thus, unmov'd with fear, accost him soon.
    Which of those rebel Spirits adjudg'd to Hell
Com'st thou, escap'd thy prison, and transform'd,
Why satst thou like an enemy in wait   825
Here watching at the head of these that sleep?
    Know ye not then said *Satan,* fill'd with scorn,
Know ye not mee? ye knew me once no mate
For you, there sitting where ye durst not soar;
Not to know mee argues yourselves unknown,   830
The lowest of your throng; or if ye know,
Why ask ye, and superfluous begin
Your message, like to end as much in vain?
To whom thus *Zephon,* answering scorn with scorn.
Think not, revolted Spirit, thy shape the same,   835
Or undiminisht brightness, to be known
As when thou stood'st in Heav'n upright and pure;
That Glory then, when thou no more wast good,
Departed from thee, and thou resembl'st now
Thy sin and place of doom obscure and foul.   840
But come, for thou, be sure, shalt give account
To him who sent us, whose charge is to keep
This place inviolable, and these from harm.
    So spake the Cherub, and his grave rebuke
Severe in youthful beauty, added grace   845
Invincible: abasht the Devil stood,
And felt how awful goodness is, and saw
Virtue in her shape how lovely, saw, and pin'd
His loss; but chiefly to find here observ'd

---

817. *Against,* in anticipation of.
828. *mate,* equal.
830. *argues,* proves.
832. *superfluous,* with needless words.
840. *obscure,* has its Latin force of "dark."
843. *these,* The sleeping Adam and Eve.
848. In *Comus* (214–16) the Platonic conception that the virtues have

His lustre visibly impair'd; yet seem'd   850
Undaunted. If I must contend, said he,
Best with the best, the Sender not the sent,
Or all at once; more glory will be won,
Or less be lost. Thy fear, said *Zephon* bold,
Will save us trial what the least can do   855
Single against thee wicked, and thence weak.
    The Fiend repli'd not, overcome with rage;
But like a proud Steed rein'd, went haughty on,
Champing his iron curb: to strive or fly
He held it vain; awe from above had quell'd   860
His heart, not else dismay'd. Now drew they nigh
The western Point, where those half-rounding guards
Just met, and closing stood in squadron join'd
Awaiting next command. To whom thir Chief
Gabriel from the Front thus call'd aloud.   865
    O friends, I hear the tread of nimble feet
Hasting this way, and now by glimpse discern
Ithuriel and *Zephon* through the shade,
And with them comes a third of Regal port,
But faded splendor wan; who by his gait   870
And fierce demeanour seems the Prince of Hell,
Not likely to part hence without contést;
Stand firm, for in his look defiance low'rs.
    He scarce had ended, when those two approach'd
And brief related whom they brought, where found,   875
How busied, in what form and posture coucht.
    To whom with stern regard thus *Gabriel* spake.
Why hast thou, *Satan*, broke the bounds prescrib'd
To thy transgressions, and disturb'd the charge

─────────────────────

forms or shapes is more distinctly expressed in the Lady's glimpse of
Hope as a "hovering angel girt with golden wings" and her cry,

> ". . . Thou unblemish't form of Chastity!
>   I see ye visibly."

pin'd, pined in consequence of.

862. *Point,* the point of the compass, due west from Gabriel's station
in the east, at the gate of Paradise.
    half-rounding, completing the half-circle, some having swung north,
the others south, so as to meet in the west.

877. *regard,* look.

879. *charge,* Adam and Eve, with whose protection Gabriel's troop is
charged.

Of others, who approve not to transgress   880
By thy example, but have power and right
To question thy bold entrance on this place;
Imploy'd it seems to violate sleep, and those
Whose dwelling God hath planted here in bliss?
   To whom thus *Satan,* with contemptuous brow.   885
Gabriel, thou hadst in Heav'n th' esteem of wise,
And such I held thee; but this question askt
Puts me in doubt.   Lives there who loves his pain?
Who would not, finding way, break loose from Hell,
Though thither doom'd?   Thou wouldst thyself, no doubt,
And boldly venture to whatever place   891
Farthest from pain, where thou might'st hope to change
Torment with ease, and soonest recompense
Dole with delight, which in this place I sought;
To thee no reason; who know'st only good,   895
But evil hast not tri'd: and wilt object
His will who bound us? let him surer bar
His Iron Gates, if he intends our stay
In that dark durance: thus much what was askt.
The rest is true, they found me where they say;   900
But that implies not violence or harm.
   Thus hee in scorn.   The warlike Angel mov'd,
Disdainfully half smiling thus repli'd.
O loss of one in Heav'n to judge of wise,
Since *Satan* fell, whom folly overthrew,   905
And now returns him from his prison scap't,
Gravely in doubt whether to hold them wise
Or not, who ask what boldness brought him hither
Unlicens't from his bounds in Hell prescrib'd;
So wise he judges it to fly from pain   910
However, and to scape his punishment.

-----

886. *esteem,* reputation (of being wise).

894. *Dole,* has its Latin meaning of pain.   Compare "dolorous."

896. *object,* raise the legal objection (that the devils are confined to
hell by God's will).

904. *O loss,* O what a loss (to lose a judge of wisdom like Satan in
heaven).   The irony influences the elliptical construction.

906. *returns him,* returns.   This verb was often used reflexively.

911. *However,* howsoever, by whatever means.

So judge thou still, presumptuous, till the wrath,
Which thou incurr'st by flying, meet thy flight
Sevenfold, and scourge that wisdom back to Hell,
Which taught thee yet no better, that no pain   915
Can equal anger infinite provok't.
But wherefore thou alone? wherefore with thee
Came not all Hell broke loose? is pain to them
Less pain, less to be fled, or thou than they
Less hardy to endure? courageous Chief,   920
The first in flight from pain, had'st thou alleg'd
To thy deserted host this cause of flight,
Thou surely hadst not come sole fugitive.
    To which the Fiend thus answer'd frowning stern.
Not that I less endure, or shrink from pain,   925
Insulting Angel, well thou know'st I stood
Thy fiercest, when in Battle to thy aid
The blasting volley'd Thunder made all speed
And seconded thy else not dreaded Spear.
But still thy words at random, as before,   930
Argue thy inexperience what behooves
From hard assays and ill successes past
A faithful Leader, not to hazard all
Through ways of danger by himself untri'd.
I therefore, I alone first undertook   935
To wing the desolate Abyss, and spy
This new created World, whereof in Hell
Fame is not silent, here in hope to find
Better abode, and my afflicted Powers
To settle here on Earth, or in mid Air;   940
Though for possession put to try once more

---

912. *still,* always.

926. *stood,* withstood, or confronted, "stood up against."

928. Another anticipation of the battle to be finally described in Book VI.

931. *inexperience what behooves:* an elliptical construction meaning "betray thy ignorance of the duty of a loyal leader to his followers when they have suffered a reverse."

938. *Fame* has its Latin force of "report," "rumour."

939. *Powers,* armies.

940. Satan was known as "the prince of the power of the air." (Ephes. ii, 2.)

What thou and thy gay Legions dare against;
Whose easier business were to serve thir Lord
High up in Heav'n, with songs to hymn his Throne,
And practis'd distances to cringe, not fight.   945
   To whom the warrior Angel soon repli'd.
To say and straight unsay, pretending first
Wise to fly pain, professing next the Spy,
Argues no Leader, but a liar trac't,
Satan, and couldst thou faithful add? O name,   950
O sacred name of faithfulness profan'd!
Faithful to whom? to thy rebellious crew?
Army of Fiends, fit body to fit head;
Was this your discipline and faith ingag'd,
Your military obedience, to dissolve   955
Allegiance to th' acknowledg'd Power supreme?
And thou sly hypocrite, who now wouldst seem
Patron of liberty, who more than thou
Once fawn'd, and cring'd, and servilely ador'd
Heav'n's awful Monarch? wherefore but in hope   960
To dispossess him, and thyself to reign?
But mark what I arede thee now, avaunt;
Fly thither whence thou fledd'st: if from this hour
Within these hallow'd limits thou appear,
Back to th' infernal pit I drag thee chain'd,   965
And Seal thee so, as henceforth not to scorn
The facile gates of hell too slightly barr'd.
   So threatn'd hee, but *Satan* to no threats
Gave heed, but waxing more in rage repli'd.
   Then when I am thy captive talk of chains,   970
Proud limitary Cherub, but ere then
Far heavier load thyself expect to feel

954. *faith ingag'd,* plighted word, oath of allegiance.

958. *Patron,* champion.

962. *Arede,* advise.

avaunt, be gone.

965. The recurrent stress upon the chaining of Satan is due to the apocalyptic visions in the New Testament of Satan "reserved in everlasting chains, under darkness, unto the judgment of the great day." (Jude i, 6.)

971. *limitary,* "boundary protecting" is the main force of the term, but there is an overtone in the word which suggests that Gabriel is presuming too much in setting bounds to Satan's freedom.

From my prevailing arm, though Heaven's King
Ride on thy wings, and thou with thy Compeers,
Us'd to the yoke, draw'st his triumphant wheels   975
In progress through the road of Heav'n Star-pav'd.
    While thus he spake, th' Angelic Squadron bright
Turn'd fiery red, sharp'ning in mooned horns
Thir Phalanx, and began to hem him round
With ported Spears, as thick as when a field   980
Of *Ceres* ripe for harvest waving bends
Her bearded Grove of ears, which way the wind
Sways them; the careful Plowman doubting stands
Lest on the threshing floor his hopeful sheaves
Prove chaff. On th' other side *Satan* alarm'd   985
Collecting all his might dilated stood,
Like *Teneriff* or *Atlas* unremov'd:
His stature reacht the Sky, and on his Crest
Sat horror Plum'd; nor wanted in his grasp
What seem'd both Spear and Shield: now dreadful deeds 990
Might have ensu'd, nor only Paradise
In this commotion, but the Starry Cope

---

975. Compare the chariots of God which seem to be the wings of
the cherubs, VI, 770–1.

978. *mooned,* crescent-shaped.

980. *ported,* a military term meaning that the spear was held across
the breast in both hands so as to be easily carried (ported) or brought
down for a thrust.

981. *Ceres* is used for the grain of which she is patroness as Bacchus
is used for wine.

983. *careful,* thoughtful, meditating.

987. *Teneriff,* the great peak in the Canary Islands.
Atlas, the range of mountains in northwestern Africa, a bird's-eye-view
of which Virgil describes Hermes as enjoying:

> "Now sees the top of Atlas as he flies,
> Whose brawny back supports the starry skies—
> Atlas, whose head, with piny forests crown'd,
> Is beaten by the winds—with foggy vapours bound.
> Snows hide his shoulders: from beneath his chin
> The founts of rolling streams their race begin:
> A beard of ice on his large breast depends—
>   (*Aen.* IV, 246–51.   Dryden's translation.*)*

unremov'd, irremovable, unshakable.

992. *Cope,* which is related to "cape," was often used to express the
idea of "the covering sky."

Of Heav'n perhaps, or all the Elements
At least had gone to rack, disturb'd and torn
With violence of this conflict, had not soon   995
Th' Eternal to prevent such horrid fray
Hung forth in Heav'n his golden Scales, yet seen
Betwixt *Astrea* and the *Scorpion* sign,
Wherein all things created first he weigh'd,
The pendulous round Earth with balanc't Air   1000
In counterpoise, now ponders all events,
Battles and Realms: in these he put two weights
The sequel each of parting and of fight;
The latter quick up flew, and kickt the beam;
Which *Gabriel* spying, thus bespake the Fiend.   1005
     Satan, I know thy strength, and thou know'st mine,
Neither our own but giv'n; what folly then
To boast what Arms can do, since thine no more
Than Heav'n permits, nor mine, though doubl'd now
To trample thee as mire: for proof look up,   1010
And read thy Lot in yon celestial Sign
Where thou art weigh'd, and shown how light, how weak,
If thou resist. The Fiend lookt up and knew
His mounted scale aloft: nor more; but fled
Murmuring, and with him fled the shades of night.   1015

The End of the Fourth Book.

---

997. Milton remembered the golden scales in which Zeus weighed the
destinies of the Greeks against those of the Trojans (*Il.* VIII, 69–72),
and of Hector against Achilles (*Il.* XXII, 209) or the weighing of
Aeneas' fate against that of Turnus (*Aen.* XII, 725–7), but he gives the
conception cosmic scope by identifying the scales with the constellation
of *Libra,* or the Scales, which stands between the Virgin and the
Scorpion in the Zodiac.

999. Compare Isaiah xl, 12, God is he "Who hath measured the
waters in the hollow of his hand, and meted out heaven with the
span, and comprehended the dust of the earth in a measure, and weighed
the mountains in scales, and the hills in a balance?"

1001. *ponders* has its literal, Latin meaning, "weighs."

1003. *sequel,* consequence.

1012. Milton repeats a phrase from the record in Daniel (v, 27) of
God's use of the figure of the scales to warn the Babylonian king, Bel-
shazzar: "Thou art weighed in the balance, and art found wanting."

1015. Like Book II, Book IV ends with a transition from darkness to
day.

BOOK V

THE ARGUMENT

Morning approach't, Eve *relates to* Adam *her troublesome dream; he likes it not, yet comforts her: They come forth to thir day labours: Thir Morning Hymn at the Door of thir Bower. God to render Man inexcusable sends* Raphael *to admonish him of his obedience, of his free estate, of his enemy near at hand; who he is, and why his enemy, and whatever else may avail* Adam *to know. Raphael comes down to Paradise, his appearance describ'd, his coming discern'd by* Adam *afar off sitting at the door of his Bower; he goes out to meet him, brings him to his lodge, entertains him with the choicest fruits of Paradise got together by* Eve; *thir discourse at Table:* Raphael *performs his message, minds* Adam *of his state and of his enemy; relates at* Adam's *request who that enemy is, and how he came to be so, beginning from his first revolt in Heaven, and the occasion thereof; how he drew his Legions after him to the parts of the North, and there incited them to rebel with him, persuading all but only* Abdiel *a Seraph, who in Argument dissuades and opposes him, then forsakes him.*

Now Morn her rosy steps in th' Eastern Clime
Advancing, sow'd the Earth with Orient Pearl,
When *Adam* wak't, so custom'd, for his sleep
Was Aery light, from pure digestion bred,
And temperate vapours bland, which th' only sound   5
Of leaves and fuming rills, *Aurora's* fan,
Lightly dispers'd, and the shrill Matin Song
Of Birds on every bough; so much the more
His wonder was to find unwak'n'd *Eve*

---

4. Compare the "grosser sleep" of Adam and Eve after the fall (IX, 1049–50).

5. *vapours,* a definite medical term meaning the exhalations from food in digestion, which were transformed into the humours of the body.

6. *Aurora's fan,* the leaves stirred by the morning breeze.

With Tresses discompos'd, and glowing Cheek,   10
As through unquiet rest: he on his side
Leaning half-rais'd, with looks of cordial Love
Hung over her enamour'd, and beheld
Beauty, which whether waking or asleep,
Shot forth peculiar Graces; then with voice   15
Mild, as when *Zephyrus* on *Flora* breathes,
Her hand soft touching, whisper'd thus. Awake
My fairest, my espous'd, my latest found,
Heav'n's last best gift, my ever new delight,
Awake, the morning shines, and the fresh field   20
Calls us, we lose the prime, to mark how spring
Our tended Plants, how blows the Citron Grove,
What drops the Myrrh, and what the balmy Reed,
How Nature paints her colours, how the Bee
Sits on the Bloom extracting liquid sweet.   25
   Such whispering wak'd her, but with startl'd eye
On *Adam,* whom imbracing, thus she spake.
   O Sole in whom my thoughts find all repose,
My Glory, my Perfection, glad I see
Thy face, and Morn return'd, for I this Night,   30
Such night till this I never pass'd, have dream'd,
If dream'd, not as I oft am wont, of thee,
Works of day past, or morrow's next design,
But of offence and trouble, which my mind
Knew never till this irksome night; methought   35
Close at mine ear one call'd me forth to walk
With gentle voice, I thought it thine; it said,
Why sleep'st thou *Eve?* now is the pleasant time,
The cool, the silent, save where silence yields
To the night-warbling Bird, that now awake   40

---

15. *peculiar,* belonging solely (to Eve).

16. *Zephyrus,* Zephyr, the mild west wind. Compare IV, 329.
Flora, the goddess of flowers. Compare the use of *Ceres* in IV, 271.

21. *prime,* the first hour of the day. Compare 170 below.

22. *blows,* blooms.

23. *balmy Reed,* reed or plant which produces balm.

40. Compare the nightingale as Night's "solemn bird" (IV, 648, 655
and VII, 435) and also:
            "Sweet bird, that shunn'st the noise of folly,
                Most musical, most melancholy."   (*Il Penseroso,* 61–2.)

Tunes sweetest his love-labour'd song; now reigns
Full Orb'd the Moon, and with more pleasing light
Shadowy sets off the face of things; in vain,
If none regard; Heav'n wakes with all his eyes,
Whom to behold but thee, Nature's desire,   45
In whose sight all things joy, with ravishment
Attracted by thy beauty still to gaze.
I rose as at thy call, but found thee not;
To find thee I directed then my walk;
And on, methought, alone I pass'd through ways   50
That brought me on a sudden to the Tree
Of interdicted Knowledge: fair it seem'd,
Much fairer to my Fancy than by day:
And as I wond'ring lookt, beside it stood
One shap'd and wing'd like one of those from Heav'n   55
By us oft seen; his dewy locks distill'd
Ambrosia; on that Tree he also gaz'd;
And O fair Plant, said he, with fruit surcharg'd,
Deigns none to ease thy load and taste thy sweet,
Nor God, nor Man; is Knowledge so despis'd?   60
Or envy, or what reserve forbids to taste?
Forbid who will, none shall from me withhold
Longer thy offer'd good, why else set here?
This said he paus'd not, but with vent'rous Arm
He pluckt, he tasted; mee damp horror chill'd   65
At such bold words voucht with a deed so bold:

---

44. *regard,* see.
   eyes: compare Giles Fletcher: "Heaven awaken'd all his eyes." (*Christ's Victorie,* I, 78.)

45. *desire,* object of desire, *i. e.,* loveliest thing in nature.

51. This passage, like the anticipation of a theme to be developed later in a symphony, prepares for the actual temptation in IX, 494–833.

57. *Ambrosia,* The perfume of ambrosia. Compare II, 245. Milton remembered Virgil's description of Venus'
"dishevell'd hair,
Which flowing from her shoulders reach'd the ground,
And widely spread ambrosial scents around."
                              (*Aen.* I, 403–4. Dryden's translation.)

61. *or . . . or.* The construction is a Latin one, meaning, "Does either envy or," etc.?

65. *damp horror,* the sweat of fear.

66. *voucht,* supported, corroborated.

But he thus overjoy'd, O Fruit Divine,
Sweet of thyself, but much more sweet thus cropt,
Forbidd'n here, it seems, as only fit
For Gods, yet able to make Gods of Men: 70
And why not Gods of Men, since good, the more
Communicated, more abundant grows,
The Author not impair'd, but honour'd more?
Here, happy Creature, fair Angelic *Eve*,
Partake thou also; happy though thou art,   75
Happier thou may'st be, worthier canst not be:
Taste this, and be henceforth among the Gods
Thyself a Goddess, not to Earth confin'd,
But sometimes in the Air, as wee, sometimes
Ascend to Heav'n, by merit thine, and see   80
What life the Gods live there, and such live thou.
So saying, he drew nigh, and to me held,
Even to my mouth of that same fruit held part
Which he had pluckt; the pleasant savoury smell
So quick'n'd appetite, that I, methought,   85
Could not but taste. Forthwith up to the Clouds
With him I flew, and underneath beheld
The Earth outstretcht immense, a prospect wide
And various: wond'ring at my flight and change
To this high exaltation; suddenly   90
My Guide was gone, and I, methought, sunk down,
And fell asleep; but O how glad I wak'd
To find this but a dream! Thus *Eve* her Night
Related, and thus *Adam* answer'd sad.
  Best Image of myself and dearer half,   95
The trouble of thy thoughts this night in sleep
Affects me equally; nor can I like

---

71. So Du Bartas has Satan promise Eve that the Tree of Knowledge will

        ". . . make you seem
    Excelling us, even equal Gods to him."
                        (92 lt, Taylor, *Du Bartas,* p. 81.)
Compare IX, 705–712.

  90. The semicolon after *exaltation,* like the colon before *wond'ring,*
is the original and probably deliberate punctuation. The subject of
wond'ring is *I,* in 91, but Milton did not hesitate to separate it from
its subject by a semicolon to mark the pause in the swift, broken narrative.

This uncouth dream, of evil sprung I fear;
Yet evil whence? in thee can harbour none,
Created pure.   But know that in the Soul   100
Are many lesser Faculties that serve
Reason as chief; among these Fancy next
Her office holds; of all external things,
Which the five watchful Senses represent,
She forms Imaginations, Aery shapes,   105
Which Reason joining or disjoining, frames
All what we affirm or what deny, and call
Our knowledge or opinion; then retires
Into her private Cell when Nature rests.
Oft in her absence mimic Fancy wakes   110
To imitate her; but misjoining shapes,
Wild work produces oft, and most in dreams,
Ill matching words and deeds long past or late.
Some such resemblances methinks I find
Of our last Ev'ning's talk, in this thy dream,   115
But with addition strange; yet be not sad.
Evil into the mind of God or Man
May come and go, so unapprov'd, and leave

---

98. *uncouth,* unfamiliar, inexplicable.

100. "If we receive the soul immediately from God, it must be pure," Milton argued in *C.D.,* I, vii, where his point was that only Adam and Eve, of all men, received their souls directly from God.

102. Even in the descendants of Adam and Eve Milton held that "the gift of reason has been implanted in all, by which they may of themselves resist bad desires." (*C.D.,* I, iv.)

The distinction between fancy or imagination, the faculty which received and combined the impressions of the senses, and reason, which should control both the imagination and the passions, was a medieval inheritance of the Renaissance. Milton here thinks of the fancy, like Spenser, as the source of

> "idle thoughts and fantasies,
> Devices, dreames, opinions unsound,
> Shewes, visions, sooth-sayes, and prophesies;
> And all that fained is, as leasings, tales, and lies."
> *(F.Q.* II, ix, 51.)

108. In sleep reason relaxes its censorship of fancy, which is free to invent whatever dreams it likes.

115. Adam, overheard by Satan, had explained that the Tree of Knowledge was prohibited.   (IV, 411-39.)

118. *so unapproved,* condemned so positively (that no spot is left).

No spot or blame behind: Which gives me hope
That what in sleep thou didst abhor to dream,   120
Waking thou never wilt consent to do:
Be not disheart'n'd then, nor cloud those looks
That wont to be more cheerful and serene
Than when fair Morning first smiles on the World,
And let us to our fresh imployments rise   125
Among the Groves, the Fountains, and the Flow'rs
That open now thir choicest bosom'd smells
Reserv'd from night, and kept for thee in store.
   So cheer'd he his fair Spouse, and she was cheer'd,
But silently a gentle tear let fall   130
From either eye, and wip'd them with her hair;
Two other precious drops that ready stood,
Each in thir chrystal sluice, hee ere they fell
Kiss'd as the gracious signs of sweet remorse
And pious awe, that fear'd to have offended.   135
   So all was clear'd, and to the Field they haste.
But first from under shady arborous roof,
Soon as they forth were come to open sight
Of day-spring, and the Sun, who scarce up risen
With wheels yet hov'ring o'er the Ocean brim,   140
Shot parallel to the earth his dewy ray,
Discovering in wide Lantskip all the East
Of Paradise and *Eden's* happy Plains,
Lowly they bow'd adoring, and began
Thir Orisons, each Morning duly paid   145
In various style, for neither various style
Nor holy rapture wanted they to praise
Thir Maker, in fit strains pronounc't or sung
Unmeditated, such prompt eloquence

   137. *arborous,* arbour-like, tree-made.

   139. *day-spring,* the dawn.

   140. So Milton, thinking of an English scene, wrote that
                 "the gilded Car of Day
              His glowing Axle doth allay
              In the steep *Atlantic* stream."   (*Comus,* 95–7.)

   142. *lantskip:* compare the note on II, 491.

   146. Here, as in *C.D.,* II, iv, Milton stresses "the superfluousness of
set forms of worship; seeing that, with Christ for our master, and the
Holy Spirit for our assistant in prayer, we can have no need of any
human aid."

Flow'd from thir lips, in Prose or numerous Verse,   150
More tuneable than needed Lute or Harp
To add more sweetness, and they thus began.
   These are thy glorious works, Parent of good,
Almighty, thine this universal Frame,
Thus wondrous fair; thyself how wondrous then!   155
Unspeakable, who sit'st above these Heavens
To us invisible or dimly seen
In these thy lowest works, yet these declare
Thy goodness beyond thought, and Power Divine:
Speak yee who best can tell, ye Sons of light,   160
Angels, for yee behold him, and with songs
And choral symphonies, Day without Night,
Circle his Throne rejoicing, yee in Heav'n,
On Earth join all ye Creatures to extol
Him first, him last, him midst, and without end.   165
Fairest of Stars, last in the train of Night,
If better thou belong not to the dawn,
Sure pledge of day, that crown'st the smiling Morn

150. *numerous,* harmonious or musical. Compare the "harmonious numbers" of III, 38. *Numbers* was a familiar term for verse.

154. *frame:* Compare Hamlet's "goodly frame, the earth." (*Hamlet*, II, ii, 310.)

157. The theme of the hymn—God's mysteriousness and his manifestation of himself in nature—was a medieval conception which had wide currency in the Renaissance and later. Du Bartas' *Divine Weekes*, for example, are written very largely around the thought that

> God, of himself, incapable to sense,
> In's Works reveals him t'our intelligence.
>
> (2 rc, Taylor, *Du Bartas*, p. 82.)

161. This hymn is a kind of amplification of Psalm cxlviii, especially verses 2–4 and 8–10:

"Praise ye him, all his angels: praise ye him, all his hosts.
Praise ye him, sun and moon: praise ye him, all ye stars of light.

. . . .

Fire, and hail: snow, and vapour: stormy wind fulfilling his word:
Mountains, and all hills: fruitful trees, and all cedars:
Beasts, and all cattle; creeping things, and flying fowl."

162. Raphael explains to Adam (642–6 below) that night brings no deep darkness in heaven.

165. Compare II, 324, and its note.

166. *Fairest of stars,* Venus, called Lucifer, the light-bringer, when it is a morning star, and Hesperus when it shines in the evening. Homer calls it the fairest star in heaven. (*Il.,* XXII, 318.)

With thy bright Circlet, praise him in thy Sphere
While day arises, that sweet hour of Prime.   170
Thou Sun, of this great World both Eye and Soul,
Acknowledge him thy Greater, sound his praise
In thy eternal course, both when thou climb'st,
And when high Noon hast gain'd, and when thou fall'st.
Moon, that now meet'st the orient Sun, now fli'st   175
With the fixt Stars, fixt in thir Orb that flies,
And yee five other wand'ring Fires that move
In mystic Dance not without Song, resound
His praise, who out of Darkness call'd up Light.
Air, and ye Elements the eldest birth   180
Of Nature's Womb, that in quaternion run
Perpetual Circle, multiform; and mix
And nourish all things, let your ceaseless change
Vary to our great Maker still new praise.
Ye Mists and Exhalations that now rise   185
From Hill or steaming Lake, dusky or grey,
Till the Sun paint your fleecy skirts with Gold,
In honour to the World's great Author rise,
Whether to deck with Clouds the uncolour'd sky,
Or wet the thirsty Earth with falling showers,   190

---

171. Spenser's comparison of Una's face to "the great eye of heaven"
and Shakespeare's "Eye of heaven" are two among Milton's many precedents here. The conception of the sun as the soul of the world, which
goes back to Pliny (*Nat. Hist.*, II, 4), was developed by the mythographer,
Conti (p. 543), into an allegorical interpretation of all the solar myths
as representing the sun as "lord of the stars and of light and giver of
life to mortals, since he is the author of light to the other stars and
since it is by his course that all living beings flourish." Compare VII,
364–6.

175. In its last phase the moon meets the orient (rising) sun, and when
it is full it shines in the dark hours with the stars.

176. *orb*, sphere. For the meaning of the term see the Introduction,
§13.

177. *wandering Fires*, the planets. The Greek word which "planet"
transliterates means "a wanderer."

178. For the dance and music of the spheres see the Introduction, §13.

181. The four elements had been supposed, as far back as Plato
(*Timaeus*, 49, C) to be transformed into one another, water to be produced from earth, from water air, and from air fire, in a reversible
process. Compare 415–426 below.

189. *uncolour'd*, without diversity of colours, of one hue.

Rising or falling still advance his praise.
His praise ye Winds, that from four Quarters blow,
Breathe soft or loud; and wave your tops, ye Pines,
With every Plant, in sign of Worship wave.
Fountains and yee, that warble, as ye flow,   195
Melodious murmurs, warbling tune his praise.
Join voices all ye living Souls, ye Birds,
That singing up to Heaven Gate ascend,
Bear on your wings and in your notes his praise;
Yee that in Waters glide, and yee that walk   200
The Earth, and stately tread, or lowly creep;
Witness if I be silent, Morn or Even,
To Hill, or Valley, Fountain, or fresh shade
Made vocal by my Song, and taught his praise.
Hail universal Lord, be bounteous still   205
To give us only good; and if the night
Have gathered aught of evil or conceal'd,
Disperse it, as now light dispels the dark.
   So pray'd they innocent, and to thir thoughts
Firm peace recover'd soon and wonted calm.   210
On to thir morning's rural work they haste
Among sweet dews and flow'rs; where any row
Of Fruit-trees overwoody reach'd too far
Thir pamper'd boughs, and needed hands to check
Fruitless imbraces: or they led the Vine   215
To wed her Elm; she spous'd about him twines

---

192. *four Quarters,* the points of the compass.

202. The emphatic *I* seems to mean that each speaker individually invokes every creature to watch his fidelity to God's praise, night and morning, somewhat as the Psalmist (cxxxvii, 6) prays that, if he forgets Zion, his tongue may cleave to the roof of his mouth.

206. *give us only good:* Milton may have recollected, as Newton thought, "that celebrated prayer in Plato": "O Zeus, give us good things, whether we pray for them or not; and remove from us all evil things, even though we pray for them." So the famous Platonic prayer of Cardinal Bembo in Castiglione's *Courtier* (p. 321) asks the Lord to "correct the falsehood of the senses, and after long wandering in vanitie, give us the right and sound joy."

216. Milton expands a favourite fancy of Horace (*Odes,* II, xv. 4 and IV, v, 31) which gave Spenser his phrase, "the vine-propt elme" (*F.Q.* I, i, 8) and Shakespeare's Adriana her cry:

> "Thou art an elm, my husband, I a vine."
> (*Comedy of Errors,* II, ii, 179.)

Her marriageable arms, and with her brings
Her dow'r th' adopted Clusters, to adorn
His barren leaves. Them thus imploy'd beheld
With pity Heav'n's high King, and to him call'd   220
Raphael, the sociable Spirit, that deign'd
To travel with *Tobias,* and secur'd
His marriage with the seven-times-wedded Maid.

    Raphael, said hee, thou hear'st what stir on Earth
Satan from Hell scap't through the darksome Gulf   225
Hath rais'd in Paradise, and how disturb'd
This night the human pair, how he designs
In them at once to ruin all mankind.
Go therefore, half this day as friend with friend
Converse with *Adam,* in what Bow'r or shade   230
Thou find'st him from the heat of Noon retir'd,
To respite his day-labour with repast,
Or with repose; and such discourse bring on,
As may advise him of his happy state,
Happiness in his power left free to will,   235
Left to his own free Will, his Will though free,
Yet mutable; whence warn him to beware
He swerve not too secure: tell him withal
His danger, and from whom, what enemy
Late fall'n himself from Heaven, is plotting now   240
The fall of others from like state of bliss;
By violence, no, for that shall be withstood,
But by deceit and lies; this let him know,
Lest wilfully transgressing he pretend
Surprisal, unadmonisht, unforewarn'd.   245
    So spake th' Eternal Father, and fulfill'd
All Justice: nor delay'd the winged Saint

---

221. Compare IV, 168 and its note on Raphael, Tobias and Sara.

230. *what,* whatever.

234. *advise,* inform.

235. Again Milton underscores his belief that "God suffered both men and angels to stand or fall at their own uncontrolled choice." (*C.D.* I, iii.) Compare III, 96–134; IV, 63–8; and V, 520–43.

238. *secure,* confident of safety. Literally, "careless." Compare IV, 186.

247. *Saint* was applied to any citizen of the City of God, either angel or man. Compare III, 330.

After his charge receiv'd; but from among
Thousand Celestial Ardors, where he stood
Veil'd with his gorgeous wings, up springing light   250
Flew through the midst of Heav'n; th' angelic Quires
On each hand parting, to his speed gave way
Through all th' Empyreal road; till at the Gate
Of Heav'n arriv'd, the gate self-open'd wide
On golden Hinges turning, as by work   255
Divine the sovran Architect had fram'd.
From hence, no cloud, or, to obstruct his sight,
Star interpos'd, however small he sees,
Not unconform to other shining Globes,
Earth and the Gard'n of God, with Cedars crown'd   260
Above all Hills. As when by night the Glass
Of *Galileo,* less assur'd, observes
Imagin'd Lands and Regions in the Moon:
Or Pilot from amidst the *Cyclades*
Delos or *Samos* first appearing kens   265
A cloudy spot. Down thither prone in flight
He speeds, and through the vast Ethereal Sky
Sails between worlds and worlds, with steady wing
Now on the polar winds, then with quick Fan
Winnows the buxom Air; till within soar   270
Of Tow'ring Eagles, to all the Fowls he seems

---

249. *Thousand,* myriad, countless.

Ardors, flames, *i.e.,* the angels of Psalm civ, 4: "Who maketh his angels spirits; his ministers a flaming fire."

259. *Not unconform,* not unlike. See the Introduction, §§ 9, 11, 12.

261. A Galileo glass was a usual name for a telescope. Compare I, 287-91.

264. *Cyclades,* the circular archipelago in the Aegean Sea of which Delos is the centre. Samos is a large island lying outside the Cyclades to the northeast.

266. *prone,* downward moving. The picture is deliberately made more splendid than the epic descriptions of Mercury flying on Jove's errands over sea and land. (*Il.,* XXIV, 341, and *Aen.,* IV, 241.)

269. *fan,* wing.

270. One pole of Milton's universe was at the point closest to the empyrean heaven, near where Raphael entered. Milton thought of the whole interior of his universe as full of an atmosphere like air.

270. *buxom,* yielding.

A *Phœnix,* gaz'd by all, as that sole Bird
When to enshrine his reliques in the Sun's
Bright Temple, to *Egyptian Thebes* he flies.
At once on th' Eastern cliff of Paradise   275
He lights, and to his proper shape returns
A Seraph wing'd; six wings he wore, to shade
His lineaments Divine; the pair that clad
Each shoulder broad, came mantling o'er his breast
With regal Ornament; the middle pair   280
Girt like a Starry Zone his waist, and round
Skirted his loins and thighs with downy Gold
And colours dipt in Heav'n; the third his feet
Shadow'd from either heel with feather'd mail
Sky-tinctur'd grain. Like *Maia's* son he stood,   285
And shook his Plumes, that Heav'nly fragrance fill'd
The circuit wide. Straight knew him all the Bands
Of Angels under watch; and to his state,
And to his message high in honour rise;
For on some message high they guess'd him bound.   290
Thir glittering Tents he pass'd, and now is come

272. Milton was familiar with many accounts of the Phoenix, the
unique bird which Ovid describes as immolating itself once in five
hundred years on a pyre of spices and being reborn from its ashes to
"carry its own cradle and its father's tomb to the city of the sun."
(*Met.* XV, 391–407.) Milton changed "the city of the sun," *i. e.,* Heli-
opolis, to the neighbouring Egyptian city of Thebes. Perhaps his conception is drawn from the poem *On the Phœnix,* attributed to Lactantius, for it ends with the new-created Phoenix glorious in full flight, "a
thing to gaze at" for both birds and men. In Tasso's Poem, *The
Phoenix,* he found an imaginative treatment of ideas about the bird from
many classical poets.

276. Raphael drops the disguised shape of the Phoenix to assume
his "proper" (*i.e.,* his own) shape as a seraph, for which Milton drew
upon Isaiah's seraphs, each with "six wings; with twain he covered his
face, and with twain he covered his feet, and with twain did he fly."
(Isaiah vi, 2.)

281. *zone,* belt.

285. *sky tinctur'd grain,* azure dye, sky-blue colour.
Maia's son, Hermes or Mercury, the son and messenger of Jove. Milton thought of the apparitions of Mercury in the masques at the court
of James I and Charles I, *e.g.,* the opening scene in Thomas Carew's
Coelum Britannicum.

288. *state,* majesty, splendour. Compare Adam's *state* in 353 below
289. *message,* commission (as God's ambassador).

Into the blissful field, through Groves of Myrrh,
And flow'ring Odours, Cassia, Nard, and Balm;
A Wilderness of sweets; for Nature here
Wanton'd as in her prime, and play'd at will   295
Her Virgin Fancies, pouring forth more sweet,
Wild above Rule or Art, enormous bliss.
Him through the spicy Forest onward come
Adam discern'd, as in the door he sat
Of his cool Bow'r, while now the mounted Sun   300
Shot down direct his fervid Rays, to warm
Earth's inmost womb, more warmth than *Adam* needs;
And *Eve* within, due at her hour prepar'd
For dinner savoury fruits, of taste to please
True appetite, and not disrelish thirst   305
Of nectarous draughts between, from milky stream,
Berry or Grape: to whom thus *Adam* call'd.
   Haste hither *Eve,* and worth thy sight behold
Eastward among those Trees, what glorious shape
Comes this way moving; seems another Morn   310
Ris'n on mid-noon; some great behest from Heav'n
To us perhaps he brings, and will voutsafe
This day to be our Guest. But go with speed,
And what thy stores contain, bring forth and pour
Abundance, fit to honour and receive   315
Our Heav'nly stranger; well we may afford
Our givers thir own gifts, and large bestow
From large bestow'd, where Nature multiplies
Her fertile growth, and by disburd'ning grows
More fruitful, which instructs us not to spare.   320
   To whom thus *Eve. Adam,* earth's hallow'd mould,
Of God inspir'd, small store will serve, where store,
All seasons, ripe for use hangs on the stalk;
Save what by frugal storing firmness gains

---

292. *blissful field,* Paradise. Compare *bliss* in 297 below.

299. So Abraham, sitting in the door of his tent, saw the Lord coming and ordered his wife to prepare a meal. (Gen. xviii.)

308. *worth thy sight,* worth seeing.

322. *inspired,* inspirited, *i.e.,* made alive by the spirit inbreathed by God.

Store, stock, is played off against *store,* abundance, and against *storing,* preserving in the technical sense of "curing."

To nourish, and superfluous moist consumes: 325
But I will haste and from each bough and brake,
Each Plant and juiciest Gourd will pluck such choice
To entertain our Angel guest, as hee
Beholding shall confess that here on Earth
God hath dispenst his bounties as in Heav'n.   330
    So saying, with dispatchful looks in haste
She turns, on hospitable thoughts intent
What choice to choose for delicacy best,
What order, so contriv'd as not to mix
Tastes, not well join'd, inelegant, but bring   335
Taste after taste upheld with kindliest change,
Bestirs her then, and from each tender stalk
Whatever Earth all-bearing Mother yields
In *India* East or West, or middle shore
In *Pontus* or the *Punic* Coast, or where   340
Alcinoüs reign'd, fruit of all kinds, in coat,
Rough, or smooth rin'd, or bearded husk, or shell
She gathers, Tribute large, and on the board
Heaps with unsparing hand; for drink the Grape
She crushes, inoffensive must, and meaths   345
From many a berry, and from sweet kernels prest
She tempers dulcet creams, nor these to hold
Wants her fit vessels pure, then strews the ground
With Rose and Odours from the shrub unfum'd.
Meanwhile our Primitive great Sire, to meet   350
His god-like Guest, walks forth, without more train
Accompani'd than with his own complete

---

336. *kindliest,* in perfect accord with nature.

339. *India East or West,* tropical Asia or tropical America.
middle shore, the coast of the "middle sea," *i.e.,* the Mediterranean.

340. Pontus is on the south shore of the Black Sea.
The Punic, or Carthaginian coast is on the south shore of the Mediterranean.

341. Around Alcinoüs' palace Ulysses found a garden where springtime and harvest were both perpetual (*Od.* VII, 125–8), as they were in Paradise.

345. *must,* unfermented wine.
meath, mead; Milton used the word vaguely, not remembering that mead was made of honey and water.

349. *the shrub unfum'd,* unburnt. The perfume came from fresh flowers rather than from burnt incense.

Perfections, in himself was all his state,
More solemn than the tedious pomp that waits
On Princes, when thir rich Retinue long   355
Of Horses led, and Grooms besmear'd with Gold
Dazzles the crowd, and sets them all agape.
Nearer his presence *Adam* though not aw'd,
Yet with submiss approach and reverence meek,
As to a superior Nature, bowing low,   360
  Thus said.   Native of Heav'n, for other place
None can than Heav'n such glorious shape contain;
Since by descending from the Thrones above,
Those happy places thou hast deign'd a while
To want, and honour these, voutsafe with us   365
Two only, who yet by sovran gift possess
This spacious ground, in yonder shady Bow'r
To rest, and what the Garden choicest bears
To sit and taste, till this meridian heat
Be over, and the Sun more cool decline.   370
  Whom thus the Angelic Virtue answer'd mild.
Adam, I therefore came, nor art thou such
Created, or such place hast here to dwell,
As may not oft invite, though Spirits of Heav'n
To visit thee; lead on then where thy Bow'r   375
O'ershades; for these mid-hours, till Ev'ning rise
I have at will.   So to the Silvan Lodge
They came, that like *Pomona's* Arbour smil'd
With flow'rets deck't and fragrant smells; but *Eve*
Undeckt, save with herself more lovely fair   380
Than Wood-Nymph, or the fairest Goddess feign'd
Of three that in Mount *Ida* naked strove,
Stood to entertain her guest from Heav'n; no veil

---

365. *want,* do without.

371. Because, as a seraph, Raphael belongs to the supreme rank in the
heavenly hierarchy, he seems to enjoy the titles of all the inferior
ranks.   The Virtues stood fifth, between the Dominations and the Powers.

374. *though Spirits of Heaven,* even the spirits of heaven.

378. Pomona was the Roman goddess of fruit-trees.

382. The three who strove naked on Mt. Ida (in the range of hills
overlooking Troy) are, of course, Hera, Aphrodite and Athena, to the
second of whom Paris awarded the golden apple which the goddess of
strife had inscribed, "For the fairest."

Shee needed, Virtue-proof, no thought infirm
Alter'd her cheek. On whom the Angel *Hail*   385
Bestow'd, the holy salutation us'd
Long after to blest *Mary,* second *Eve.*

    Hail Mother of Mankind, whose fruitful Womb
Shall fill the World more numerous with thy Sons
Than with these various fruits the Trees of God   390
Have heap'd this Table. Rais'd of grassy turf
Thir Table was, and mossy seats had round,
And on her ample Square from side to side
All *Autumn* pil'd, though *Spring* and *Autumn* here
Danc'd hand in hand. A while discourse they hold;   395
No fear lest Dinner cool; when thus began
Our Author. Heav'nly stranger, please to taste
These bounties which our Nourisher, from whom
All perfet good unmeasur'd out, descends,
To us for food and for delight hath caus'd   400
The Earth to yield; unsavoury food perhaps
To spiritual Natures; only this I know,
That one Celestial Father gives to all.

    To whom the Angel. Therefore what he gives
(Whose praise be ever sung) to man in part   405
Spiritual, may of purest Spirits be found
No ingrateful food: and food alike those pure
Intelligential substances require

----

    384. *Virtue-proof,* proof (against evil) by her virtue.

    385. *Hail* is the greeting of the angel in the Annunciation to Mary
(Luke i, 28). Mary is the "second Eve" as "Jesus Son of Mary,
second Eve" (X, 183) is "the last Adam" (I Cor. xv, 45).

    388. Compare XI, 159.

    394. *Autumn,* the fruits of autumn. The allusion to Alcinoüs' gar-
den (341 above) was a reminder that Paradise enjoyed all the seasons,
except winter, simultaneously.

    399. Milton glances at James i, 17: "Every good gift and every per-
fect gift is from above, and cometh down from the Father of lights."

    407. Compare 633 below, where Raphael speaks of the banquets of
the angels in heaven. In Psalm lxxviii, 25, "angels' food" is mentioned as if it had actually fallen to earth as the manna which the Israelites gathered in the wilderness. The "mellifluous dews" and "pearly
grain" (429–30 below) which Raphael says cover the trees of heaven
every morning seem like manna.

As doth your Rational; and both contain
Within them every lower faculty   410
Of sense, whereby they hear, see, smell, touch, taste,
Tasting concoct, digest, assimilate,
And corporeal to incorporeal turn.
For know, whatever was created, needs
To be sustain'd and fed; of Elements   415
The grosser feeds the purer, Earth the sea,
Earth and the Sea feed Air, the Air those Fires
Ethereal, and as lowest first the Moon;
Whence in her visage round those spots, unpurg'd
Vapours not yet into her substance turn'd.   420
Nor doth the Moon no nourishment exhale
From her moist Continent to higher Orbs.
The Sun that light imparts to all, receives
From all his alimental recompense
In humid exhalations, and at Even   425
Sups with the Ocean: though in Heav'n the Trees
Of life ambrosial fruitage bear, and vines
Yield Nectar, though from off the boughs each Morn
We brush mellifluous Dews, and find the ground
Cover'd with pearly grain: yet God hath here   430
Varied his bounty so with new delights,
As may compare with Heaven; and to taste
Think not I shall be nice. So down they sat,

---

409. Milton believed that "spirit being the more excellent substance,
virtually and essentially contains within itself the inferior (*i.e.,* physical)
one; as the spiritual and rational faculty contains the corporeal." (*C.D.*
I, vii.) Henry More, who developed similar views in the *Immortality
of the Soul* (p. 177), dared write: "to speak freely my mind, it will be
a very hard thing to disprove that they [the angels] have not something
analogical to *smell* and *taste.*"

412. *concoct* was the regular term for the first process in digestion.

415. The ancient theory that the grosser elements "feed" the purer
and the inferior planets the superior was illustrated by Robert Flud
with an engraving of the sun seeming to "sup" on the ocean at sunset.
(*Historia* I, v, 6.) In return the "arch-chemic Sun" (III, 609) infused
its creative elixir into the earth. Plato's conception of the four elements
as "passing into one another in an unbroken circle of birth" (*Timaeus,*
49c) descended through many channels to become a "scientific" commonplace in the Renaissance. Milton may have met it first in a handbook
like *Batman upon Bartholome.* (IV, i.)

433. *nice,* fastidious.

And to thir viands fell, nor seemingly
The Angel, nor in mist, the common gloss   435
Of Theologians, but with keen dispatch
Of real hunger, and concoctive heat
To transubstantiate; what redounds, transpires
Through Spirits with ease; nor wonder; if by fire
Of sooty coal the Empiric Alchemist   440
Can turn, or holds it possible to turn
Metals of drossiest Ore to perfet Gold
As from the Mine.   Meanwhile at Table *Eve*
Minister'd naked, and thir flowing cups
With pleasant liquors crown'd: O innocence   445
Deserving Paradise! if ever, then,
Then had the Sons of God excuse to have been
Enamour'd at that sight; but in those hearts
Love unlibidinous reign'd, nor jealousy
Was understood, the injur'd Lover's Hell.   450
    Thus when with meats and drinks they had suffic'd
Not burd'n'd Nature, sudden mind arose
In *Adam,* not to let th' occasion pass
Given him by this great Conference to know
Of things above his World, and of thir being   455
Who dwell in Heav'n, whose excellence he saw
Transcend his own so far, whose radiant forms
Divine effulgence, whose high Power so far
Exceeded human, and his wary speech
Thus to th' Empyreal Minister he fram'd.   460
    Inhabitant with God, now know I well
Thy favour, in this honour done to man,
Under whose lowly roof thou hast voutsaf't

    438. *redounds,* is excessive or unassimilable. Compare the explana-
tion of the angels' immunity to "surfeit" at their heavenly banquets
(639 below).

    439. Milton thought of the angels as "ardors" (249 above), literally
composed of celestial fire, with power to refine all baser elements in
themselves as the alchemist's fire transmutes base metals into gold.

    440. *Empiric,* experimenter. The word generally meant a medical
or alchemical shyster and it is not used respectfully here.

    445. *crown'd,* filled to overflowing.
    Compare the note on XI, 574.

    451. Compare the temperate feasts of the angels (639 below) and
Michael's warning to Adam against "gluttonous delight." (XI, 533.)

To enter, and these earthly fruits to taste,
Food not of Angels, yet accepted so,   465
As that more willingly thou couldst not seem
At Heav'n's high feasts to have fed: yet what compare?
  To whom the winged Hierarch repli'd.
O *Adam,* one Almighty is, from whom
All things proceed, and up to him return,   470
If not deprav'd from good, created all
Such to perfection, one first matter all,
Indu'd with various forms, various degrees
Of substance, and in things that live, of life;
But more refin'd, more spiritous, and pure,   475
As nearer to him plac't or nearer tending
Each in thir several active Spheres assign'd,
Till body up to spirit work, in bounds
Proportion'd to each kind. So from the root
Springs lighter the green stalk, from thence the leaves   480
More aery, last the bright consummate flow'r
Spirits odorous breathes: flow'rs and thir fruit
Man's nourishment, by gradual scale sublim'd
To vital Spirits aspire, to animal,
To intellectual, give both life and sense,   485
Fancy and understanding, whence the Soul

---

467. *yet what compare:*   What comparison is possible between heavenly and earthly feasts?

470. "Matter," Milton said in *C.D.* I, vii, "like the form and nature of the angels itself, proceeded incorruptible from God; and even since the fall it remains incorruptible as far as concerns its essence."

479. Milton is evoking a great Platonic doctrine which goes back to a saying in the *Timaeus* (90, A) that heaven has given each of us a spiritual guardian, the soul or reasoning faculty, which lifts us, "since we are not an earthly but a heavenly plant, from earth to our kinsfolk in heaven."

484. Burton (*Anatomy,* I, i, 2, 2) explains the theory of the three "spirits"; natural, vital, animal. "The *natural* are begotten in the *liver,* and thence dispersed through the veins . . . . The *vital spirits* are made in the heart. . . . The *animal* [*i.e.,* spiritual, from Latin *anima,* soul] *spirits* formed of the *vital,* brought up to the brain, and diffused by the nerves, to the subordinate members, give sense and motion to them all." The German reformer, Melancthon, explained that, "what is more wonderful, the divine spirit itself mixes with the animal spirits in pious men, . . . so that their impulses toward God are more ardent." (*De anima,* pp. 88–89.)

Reason receives, and reason is her being,
Discursive, or Intuitive; discourse
Is oftest yours, the latter most is ours,
Differing but in degree, of kind the same.   490
Wonder not then, what God for you saw good
If I refuse not, but convert, as you,
To proper substance; time may come when men
With Angels may participate, and find
No inconvenient Diet, nor too light Fare: 495
And from these corporal nutriments perhaps
Your bodies may at last turn all to Spirit,
Improv'd by tract of time, and wing'd ascend
Ethereal, as wee, or may at choice
Here or in Heav'nly Paradises dwell;   500
If ye be found obedient, and retain
Unalterably firm his love entire
Whose progeny you are.   Meanwhile enjoy
Your fill what happiness this happy state
Can comprehend, incapable of more.   505
    To whom the Patriarch of mankind repli'd.
O favourable spirit, propitious guest,
Well hast thou taught the way that might direct
Our knowledge, and the scale of Nature set
From centre to circumference, whereon   510
In contemplation of created things
By steps we may ascend to God.   But say,
What meant that caution join'd, *if ye be found
Obedient?* can wee want obedience then

---

488. Compare Raphael's distinction of the intuitive intellect of
angels from "your rational" (408–9 above. *Discourse, i.e.,* of reason,
means literally the "running to and fro" of the mind in the effort to
penetrate something which intuitive perception comprehends instan-
taneously.

493. *proper,* (my) own. Compare 276 above.

498. *tract,* extent.

509. *the scale of Nature* stretched from the "centre," the earth, to
which the heaviest elements gravitated, to the spheres of the sun and
the other planets, the fixed stars and the outermost sphere of the
created universe. Compare IX, 112.

511. The "Cherub Contemplation" of *Il Penseroso* (54) already represented both the medieval, mystical life and the new ideal of con-
templating God in his works which is fundamental in *P.L.*

To him, or possibly his love desert   515
Who form'd us from the dust, and plac'd us here
Full to the utmost measure of what bliss
Human desires can seek or apprehend?
    To whom the Angel.   Son of Heav'n and Earth,
Attend: That thou art happy, owe to God;   520
That thou continu'st such, owe to thyself,
That is, to thy obedience; therein stand.
This was that caution giv'n thee; be advis'd.
God made thee perfet, not immutable;
And good he made thee, but to persevere   525
He left it in thy power, ordain'd thy will
By nature free, not over-rul'd by Fate
Inextricable, or strict necessity;
Our voluntary service he requires,
Not our necessitated, such with him   530
Finds no acceptance, nor can find, for how
Can hearts, not free, be tri'd whether they serve
Willing or no, who will but what they must
By Destiny, and can no other choose?
Myself and all th' Angelic Host that stand   535
In sight of God enthron'd, our happy state
Hold, as you yours, while our obedience holds;
On other surety none; freely we serve,
Because wee freely love, as in our will
To love or not; in this we stand or fall: 540
And some are fall'n, to disobedience fall'n,
And so from Heav'n to deepest Hell; O fall
From what high state of bliss into what woe!
    To whom our great Progenitor.   Thy words
Attentive, and with more delighted ear   545
Divine instructer, I have heard, than when

---

521. Raphael's argument is not a mere repetition of that in III, 96-128.
The angel defends God dramatically, with Milton's belief in *C.D.*, I, iii,
that it would be "unworthy of God that man should nominally enjoy
a liberty of which he was virtually deprived, which would be the case
were that liberty to be oppressed or even obscured under the pretext
of some sophistical necessity of immutability."

540. Compare Milton's assertion in *C.D.*, I, iii, that "in assigning the
gift of free will, God suffered both men and angels to stand or fall
at their own uncontrolled choice."

Cherubic Songs by night from neighbouring Hills
Aereal Music send: nor knew I not
To be both will and deed created free;
Yet that we never shall forget to love   550
Our maker, and obey him whose command
Single, is yet so just, my constant thoughts
Assur'd me and still assure: though what thou tell'st
Hath past in Heav'n, some doubt within me move,
But more desire to hear, if thou consent,   555
The full relation, which must needs be strange,
Worthy of Sacred silence to be heard;
And we have yet large day, for scarce the Sun
Hath finisht half his journey, and scarce begins
His other half in the great Zone of Heav'n.   560
     Thus *Adam* made request, and *Raphaël*
After short pause assenting, thus began.
     High matter thou injoin'st me, O prime of men,
Sad task and hard, for how shall I relate
To human sense th' invisible exploits   565
Of warring Spirits; how without remorse
The ruin of so many glorious once
And perfet while they stood; how last unfold
The secrets of another world, perhaps
Not lawful to reveal? yet for thy good   570
This is dispens't, and what surmounts the reach
Of human sense, I shall delineate so,
By lik'ning spiritual to corporal forms,

---

547. Compare the "celestial voices" of IV, 682.

558. The story to be told by Raphael in the remaining "large day"
includes the war in heaven (Book VI), the creation of the universe
(Book VII) and a short account of the movements of the stars (Book
VIII, 1–178). There have been constant allusions to the war in heaven
which prepare the reader for this long account by a participant, and
the creation story has been adumbrated by Uriel's account to Satan
(III, 693–732).

563. The words are like Aeneas' beginning of the story of the fall
of Troy, a story which, though it is supposed to be told after a banquet,
fills two books of the *Aeneid*. Addressing Dido, Aeneas says:

> "Great Queen, what you command me to relate
> Renews the sad remembrance of our fate.
> An empire from its old foundations rent,
> And every woe the Trojans underwent."
>   (*Aen.* II, 3–6. Dryden's translation.)

As may express them best, though what if Earth
Be but the shadow of Heav'n, and things therein   575
Each to other like, more than on earth is thought?
   As yet this world was not, and *Chaos* wild
Reign'd where these Heav'ns now roll, where Earth now rests
Upon her Centre pois'd, when on a day
(For Time, though in Eternity, appli'd   580
To motion, measures all things durable
By present, past, and future) on such day
As Heav'n's great Year brings forth, th' Empyreal Host
Of Angels by Imperial summons call'd,
Innumerable before th' Almighty's Throne   585
Forthwith from all the ends of Heav'n appear'd
Under thir Hierarchs in orders bright;
Ten thousand thousand Ensigns high advanc'd,
Standards and Gonfalons, twixt Van and Rear
Stream in the Air, and for distinction serve   590
Of Hierarchies, of Orders, and Degrees;
Or in thir glittering Tissues bear imblaz'd
Holy Memorials, acts of Zeal and Love
Recorded eminent. Thus when in Orbs

---

574. The Platonic conception of earth as the shadow of heaven was supported by thinkers like Servetus and Henry More as well as by Rabbinical works such as Ben Gerson's *Understanding and her Relation to the Plan of Creation.*

579. Milton's thought here went beyond Ovid's picture of the earth as floating on its centre (*Met.* I, 12–14) to Aristotle's basic conception of the earth as firmly founded at the centre of the universe. (*De coelo,* II, xiv. Compare II, 895, note.)

580. Arguing in *C.D.,* I, vii, that "it seems even probable, that the apostasy which caused the expulsion of so many thousands from heaven, took place before the foundations of the world were laid," Milton attacked "the common opinion that motion and time (which is the measure of motion) could not, according to the ratio of priority and subsequence, have existed before this world was made; since Aristotle, who teaches that no ideas of motion and time can be formed except in reference to this world, nevertheless pronounces the world itself to be eternal."

583. The Platonic Great Year—supposed to be the period between two returns of all the heavenly bodies to the same relative positions and variously estimated from 600 to more than 49,000 years—was often used as a vague measure of time. Milton used the term with double vagueness of time in heaven before the creation of the stars.

594. *orbs,* circles, or concentric spheres of angels ranked according to their hierarchies.

Of circuit inexpressible they stood,   595
Orb within Orb, the Father infinite,
By whom in bliss imbosom'd sat the Son,
Amidst as from a flaming Mount, whose top
Brightness had made invisible, thus spake.
    Hear all ye Angels, Progeny of Light,   600
Thrones, Dominations, Princedoms, Virtues, Powers,
Hear my Decree, which unrevok't shall stand.
This day I have begot whom I declare
My only Son, and on this holy Hill
Him have anointed, whom ye now behold   605
At my right hand; your Head I him appoint;
And by my Self have sworn to him shall bow
All knees in Heav'n, and shall confess him Lord:
Under his great Vice-gerent Reign abide
United as one individual Soul   610
For ever happy: him who disobeys
Mee disobeys, breaks union, and that day
Cast out from God and blessed vision, falls
Into utter darkness, deep ingulft, his place
Ordain'd without redemption, without end.   615
    So spake th' Omnipotent, and with his words
All seem'd well pleas'd, all seem'd, but were not all.
That day, as other solemn days, they spent
In song and dance about the sacred Hill,
Mystical dance, which yonder starry Sphere   620

    599. Compare II, 264 and its note.
    603. A rabbinical doctrine that creation was instantaneous and that
only gradually did the true natures of created things become manifest
seems to underly the apparently flagrant inconsistency of this passage
with III, 383-91 and with 833-45 below. The Son was really the first
born of every creature, as *C.D.*, I, vii, acknowledges; but, just as it was
only in the fulness of time that he was born of Mary, so it was only
in the fulness of time that God proclaimed, "Yet have I set my king
upon my holy hill of Zion. I will declare the decree: the Lord hath
said unto me, Thou art my son; this day have I begotten thee."
(Ps. ii, 6-7.)
    607. *by myself have sworn*: compare God's oath by himself to Abra-
ham. (Gen. xxii, 16.)
    613. Compare I, 684 and its note. Milton's conviction of the
beatific vision appears in his conclusion to *Of Reformation in England*
with a prophecy of the leaders of the reform "in supereminence of
beatific vision, progressing the dateless and irrevoluble circle of eternity."

Of Planets and of fixt in all her Wheels
Resembles nearest, mazes intricate,
Eccentric, intervolv'd, yet regular
Then most, when most irregular they seem:
And in thir motions harmony Divine   625
So smooths her charming tones, that God's own ear
Listens delighted. Ev'ning now approach'd
(For wee have also our Ev'ning and our Morn,
Wee ours for change delectable, not need)
Forthwith from dance to sweet repast they turn   630
Desirous; all in Circles as they stood,
Tables are set, and on a sudden pil'd
With Angels' Food, and rubied Nectar flows:
In Pearl, in Diamond, and massy Gold,
Fruit of delicious Vines, the growth of Heav'n.   635
On flow'rs repos'd, and with fresh flow'rets crown'd,
They eat, they drink, and in communion sweet
Quaff immortality and joy, secure
Of surfeit where full measure only bounds
Excess, before th' all bounteous King, who show'r'd   640
With copious hand, rejoicing in thir joy.
Now when ambrosial Night with Clouds exhal'd
From that high mount of God, whence light and shade
Spring both, the face of brightest Heav'n had chang'd
To grateful Twilight (for Night comes not there   645

---

625. Compare the reference to the music of the spheres in 178 above,
and 793 below. Their dance is a conception of Plato. (*Timaeus*,
40, C.)

633. Nectar is regularly described in the *Iliad* as red.

637. Compare the "fellowships of joy" of the "Sons of Light" in XI, 80,
and the "sweet societies" of heaven in *Lycidas*, 179.

638. Compare Psalms xxxvi, 8–9: "They shall be abundantly satisfied
with the fatness of thy house; and thou shalt make them drink of the
river of thy pleasures. For with thee is the fountain of life."

642. *ambrosial,* fragrant. Compare 57 above.

643. Milton thought it "more reasonable to conceive . . . of the
heaven of heavens, the throne and habitation of God, than to imagine
that God should have been without a heaven till the first of the six
days of creation." And the highest heaven he called "the supreme
citadel and habitation of God." (*C.D.,* I, vii.)

645. The mild darkness of heaven which cannot be called night
corresponds to the prophecy in Revelation xxi, 25, that "there shall be
no night there."

In darker veil) and roseate Dews dispos'd
All but the unsleeping eyes of God to rest,
Wide over all the Plain, and wider far
Than all this globous Earth in Plain outspread,
(Such are the Courts of God) Th' Angelic throng   650
Disperst in Bands and Files thir Camp extend
By living Streams among the Trees of Life,
Pavilions numberless, and sudden rear'd,
Celestial Tabernacles, where they slept
Fann'd with cool Winds, save those who in thir course   655
Melodious Hymns about the sovran Throne
Alternate all night long: but not so wak'd
Satan, so call him now, his former name
Is heard no more in Heav'n; he of the first,
If not the first Arch-Angel, great in Power,   660
In favour and preëminence, yet fraught
With envy against the Son of God, that day
Honour'd by his great Father, and proclaim'd
Messiah King anointed, could not bear
Through pride that sight, and thought himself impair'd.   665
Deep malice thence conceiving and disdain,
Soon as midnight brought on the dusky hour
Friendliest to sleep and silence, he resolv'd
With all his Legions to dislodge, and leave
Unworshipt, unobey'd the Throne supreme,   670
Contemptuous, and his next subordinate
Awak'ning, thus to him in secret spake.
    Sleep'st thou, Companion dear, what sleep can close
Thy eye-lids? and rememb'rest what Decree
Of yesterday, so late hath past the lips   675

647. God is unsleeping, for "he that keepeth Israel shall neither slumber nor sleep." (Ps. cxxi, 4.)

659. Compare I, 82 and 361 and its note. In *C.D.,* I, iv, Milton remarked that "mention is frequently made . . . of the book of life, but never of the book of death." Only a change of name after his revolt could symbolize the erasure of his former name from the book of life.

664. *Messiah* is literally translated by "anointed." Compare the translation of *Moloch* as King (I, 392).

665. *impair'd,* injured, lowered in rank.

671. *his next subordinate:* Beëlzebub. Compare II, 299-300.

Of Heav'n's Almighty.   Thou to me thy thoughts
Wast wont, I mine to thee was wont to impart;
Both waking we were one; how then can now
Thy sleep dissent? new Laws thou see'st impos'd;
New Laws from him who reigns, new minds may raise   680
In us who serve, new Counsels, to debate
What doubtful may ensue, more in this place
To utter is not safe.   Assemble thou
Of all those Myriads which we lead the chief;
Tell them that by command, ere yet dim Night   685
Her shadowy Cloud withdraws, I am to haste,
And all who under me thir Banners wave,
Homeward with flying march where we possess
The Quarters of the North, there to prepare
Fit entertainment to receive our King   690
The great *Messiah,* and his new commands,
Who speedily through all the Hierarchies
Intends to pass triumphant, and give Laws.
    So spake the false Arch-Angel, and infus'd
Bad influence into th' unwary breast   695
Of his Associate; hee together calls,
Or several one by one, the Regent Powers,
Under him Regent, tells, as he was taught,
That the most High commanding, now ere Night,
Now ere dim Night had disincumber'd Heav'n,   700
The great Hierarchal Standard was to move;
Tells the suggested cause, and casts between
Ambiguous words and jealousies, to sound
Or taint integrity; but all obey'd
The wonted signal, and superior voice   705
Of thir great Potentate; for great indeed

---

689. The idea that Satan was lord of the north is partly due to
Isaiah xiv, 13, where Lucifer is accused of having said in his heart,
"I will ascend into heaven, I will exalt my throne above the stars of
God: I will sit also upon the mount of the congregation, in the sides
of the north."

696. *hee,* i.e., Beëlzebub.

697. *several,* severally, separately.

Regent Powers, governing angels, holding commands subordinate to
Satan.

704. *but all obey'd,* i.e., the unanimity was unexpected.

His name, and high was his degree in Heav'n;
His count'nance, as the Morning Star that guides
The starry flock, allur'd them, and with lies
Drew after him the third part of Heav'n's Host: 710
Meanwhile th' Eternal eye, whose sight discerns
Abstrusest thoughts, from forth his holy Mount
And from within the golden Lamps that burn
Nightly before him, saw without thir light
Rebellion rising, saw in whom, how spread   715
Among the sons of Morn, what multitudes
Were banded to oppose his high Decree;
And smiling to his only Son thus said.

    Son, thou in whom my glory I behold
In full resplendence, Heir of all my might,   720
Nearly it now concerns us to be sure
Of our Omnipotence, and with what Arms
We mean to hold what anciently we claim
Of Deity or Empire, such a foe
Is rising, who intends to erect his Throne   725
Equal to ours, throughout the spacious North;
Nor so content, hath in his thought to try
In battle, what our Power is, or our right.
Let us advise, and to this hazard draw
With speed what force is left, and all imploy   730
In our defence, lest unawares we lose
This our high place, our Sanctuary, our Hill.

    To whom the Son with calm aspect and clear

----

708. The allusion is again to Isaiah xiv, 12: "How art thou fallen
from heaven, O Lucifer, son of the morning."

710. Compare II, 692 and its note. The proportion was uncertain,
but not the vast number. Spenser wrote,

        The brightest angell, even the Child of Light,
        Drew millions more against their God to fight.
                    (*Hymne of Heavenly Love,* 83–4.)

713. Milton referred to the "seven lamps of fire burning before the
throne" (Rev. iv, 5) and to the "unsleeping eyes of God" (compare
647 above), passages which he perhaps related to the seven angelic
eyes of Zechariah's prophecy. (iii, 9.)   Compare III, 648.

716. Milton first used the phrase in the *Nativity Ode,* 119:
        "But when of old the sons of morning sung."

719. Compare III, 63.

Light'ning Divine, ineffable, serene,
Made answer. Mighty Father, thou thy foes   735
Justly hast in derision, and secure
Laugh'st at thir vain designs and tumults vain,
Matter to mee of Glory, whom thir hate
Illustrates, when they see all Regal Power
Giv'n me to quell thir pride, and in event   740
Know whether I be dext'rous to subdue
Thy Rebels, or be found the worst in Heav'n.
      So spake the Son, but *Satan* with his Powers
Far was advanc't on winged speed, an Host
Innumerable as the Stars of Night,   745
Or Stars of Morning, Dew-drops, which the Sun
Impearls on every leaf and every flower.
Regions they pass'd, the mighty Regencies
Of Seraphim and Potentates and Thrones
In thir triple Degrees, Regions to which   750
All thy Dominion, *Adam,* is no more
Than what this Garden is to all the Earth,
And all the Sea, from one entire globose
Stretcht into Longitude; which having pass'd
At length into the limits of the North   755
They came, and *Satan* to his Royal seat
High on a Hill, far blazing, as a Mount
Rais'd on a Mount, with Pyramids and Tow'rs
From Diamond Quarries hewn, and Rocks of Gold,
The Palace of great *Lucifer,* (so call   760
That Structure in the Dialect of men

---

734. The Son is the "Similitude" of the invisible "Fountain of Light."
III, 375–84.

736. Compare II, 191 and its note.

739. *Illustrates,* makes illustrate or glorious. The word is used
with a reminiscence of its basic Latin meaning of "light."

740. *event* has its Latin force of "outcome."

743. *Powers,* armies. The word is not used here, as in 601 above,
to mean a definite rank in the heavenly hierarchy.

748. *Regencies,* provinces. See note on 792 below.

749. The three ranks are chosen at random from the four highest
hierarchal ranks. See the Introduction, §7.

753. *globose.* sphere. Milton thought of the projections of the two
hemispheres which cartographers were perfecting.

Interpreted) which not long after, hee
Affecting all equality with God,
In imitation of that Mount whereon
Messiah was declar'd in sight of Heav'n,   765
The Mountain of the Congregation call'd;
For thither he assembl'd all his Train,
Pretending so commanded to consult
About the great reception of thir King,
Thither to come, and with calumnious Art   770
Of counterfeited truth thus held thir ears.
   Thrones, Dominations, Princedoms, Virtues, Powers,
If these magnific Titles yet remain
Not merely titular, since by Decree
Another now hath to himself ingross't   775
All Power, and us eclipst under the name
Of King anointed, for whom all this haste
Of midnight march, and hurried meeting here,
This only to consult how we may best
With what may be devis'd of honours new   780
Receive him coming to receive from us
Knee-tribute yet unpaid, prostration vile,
Too much to one, but double how endur'd,
To one and to his image now proclaim'd?
But what if better counsels might erect   785
Our minds and teach us to cast off this Yoke?
Will ye submit your necks, and choose to bend
The supple knee? ye will not, if I trust
To know ye right, or if ye know yourselves
Natives and Sons of Heav'n possest before   790
By none, and if not equal all, yet free,
Equally free; for Orders and Degrees

763. *affecting,* pretending to.

766. Compare note on 689 above.

768. Pretending that they were so assembled to consult, *etc.*

777. Compare note on 664 above.

784. Compare III, 63 and its note.

790. *possest,* in possession, *i.e.,* of heaven

792. In *Reason of Church Government,* I, 1, Milton saw his conception of liberty and order exemplified among "the angels themselves, in whom no disorder is feared, as the apostle that saw them in
his rapture describes, . . . distinguished and quaternioned into their

Jar not with liberty, but well consist.
Who can in reason then or right assume
Monarchy over such as live by right   795
His equals, if in power and splendor less,
In freedom equal? or can introduce
Law and Edict on us, who without law
Err not, much less for this to be our Lord,
And look for adoration to th' abuse   800
Of those Imperial Titles which assert
Our being ordain'd to govern, not to serve?
    Thus far his bold discourse without control
Had audience, when among the Seraphim
Abdiel, than whom none with more zeal ador'd   805
The Deity, and divine commands obey'd,
Stood up, and in a flame of zeal severe
The current of his fury thus oppos'd.
    O argument blasphémous, false and proud!
Words which no ear ever to hear in Heav'n   810
Expected, least of all from thee, ingrate
In place thyself so high above thy Peers.
Canst thou with impious obloquy condemn
The just Decree of God, pronounc't and sworn,
That to his only Son by right endu'd   815
With Regal Sceptre, every Soul in Heav'n
Shall bend the knee, and in that honour due
Confess him rightful King? unjust thou say'st

---

celestial princedoms and satrapies, according as God himself has writ
his imperial decrees through the great provinces of heaven."

793. *Jar not,* are not inconsistent with. The term meant a discord
in music and corresponds with the conception in 625 above.
    consist, are consistent with.

798. Satan argues that the angels need no law because they have
committed no sins in the past.

799. *to be* cannot be definitely related to any verb; *much less* seems
to compare the idea of a lord, or law-giver with the only less obnoxious
idea of laws.

804. *audience,* a hearing, *i.e.,* toleration.

805. The name Abdiel, meaning "servant of God," occurs only as a
human name in the Bible (I Chron. v, 15).

807. Compare 249 above and its note.

815. Compare the assertion of Messiah's right of merit in VI, 43 and
:75–8.

Flatly unjust, to bind with Laws the free,
And equal over equals to let Reign,   820
One over all with unsucceeded power.
Shalt thou give Law to God, shalt thou dispute
With him the points of liberty, who made
Thee what thou art, and form'd the Pow'rs of Heav'n
Such as he pleas'd, and circumscrib'd thir being?   825
Yet by experience taught we know how good,
And of our good, and of our dignity
How provident he is, how far from thought
To make us less, bent rather to exalt
Our happy state under one Head more near   830
United. But to grant it thee unjust,
That equal over equals Monarch Reign:
Thyself though great and glorious dost thou count,
Or all Angelic Nature join'd in one,
Equal to him begotten Son? By whom   835
As by his Word the mighty Father made
All things, ev'n thee, and all the Spirits of Heav'n
By him created in thir bright degrees,
Crown'd them with Glory, and to thir Glory nam'd
Thrones, Dominations, Princedoms, Virtues, Powers,   840
Essential Powers, nor by his Reign obscur'd,
But more illustrious made, since he the Head
One of our number thus reduc't becomes,
His Laws our Laws, all honour to him done
Returns our own. Cease then this impious rage,   845
And tempt not these; but hast'n to appease
Th' incensed Father, and th' incensed Son,
While Pardon may be found in time besought.
    So spake the fervent Angel, but his zeal
None seconded, as out of season judg'd,   850
Or singular and rash, whereat rejoic'd

_____

834. *all Angelic Nature,* all that part of nature represented by the
angels, all the angels, together.

835. In *C.D.,* I, vii, Milton interprets the verses in Colossians (i, 15–
17) to which he alludes here. There his attempt is to prove that all
created things were made *through* Christ, who is "the first born of every
creature," both in the sense that he existed before all other creatures,
and also in the sense that he excels all his fellow creatures and stands
nearest to God, from whom all created things ultimately come.

Th' Apostate, and more haughty thus repli'd.
That we were form'd then say'st thou? and the work
Of secondary hands, by task transferr'd
From Father to his Son? strange point and new!   855
Doctrine which we would know whence learnt: who saw
When this creation was? remember'st thou
Thy making, while the Maker gave thee being?
We know no time when we were not as now;
Know none before us, self-begot, self-rais'd   860
By our own quick'ning power, when fatal course
Had circl'd his full Orb, the birth mature
Of this our native Heav'n, Ethereal Sons.
Our puissance is our own, our own right hand
Shall teach us highest deeds, by proof to try   865
Who is our equal: then thou shalt behold
Whether by supplication we intend
Address, and to begirt th' Almighty Throne
Beseeching or besieging. This report,
These tidings carry to th' anointed King;   870
And fly, ere evil intercept thy flight.
    He said, and as the sound of waters deep
Hoarse murmur echo'd to his words applause
Through the infinite Host, nor less for that
The flaming Seraph fearless, though alone   875
Encompass'd round with foes, thus answer'd bold.
    O alienate from God, O spirit accurst,
Forsak'n of all good; I see thy fall
Determin'd, and thy hapless crew involv'd
In this perfidious fraud, contagion spread   880
Both of thy crime and punishment: henceforth

---

853. Compare IV, 43 and its note, and Milton's statement in *C.D.,* I,
vii: "That the angels were created at some particular period, we have the
testimony of Numb. xvi, 22 and xxvii, 16."

857. The apparent facts, as Milton has indicated them in his account
of the begetting of the Son in Book III, justify Satan's rhetorical question. His error consists in denying what Milton calls in *C.D.,* I, vii, the
"superlative" and "partitive" senses in which the Messiah is the first-
born of every creature and the channel through which God's creative
power reaches all other creatures.

860. Compare I, 116 ff.

870. *Anointed King.* Compare 664.

No more be troubl'd how to quit the yoke
Of God's *Messiah:* those indulgent Laws
Will not be now voutsaf'd, other Decrees
Against thee are gone forth without recall;   885
That Golden Sceptre which thou didst reject
Is now an Iron Rod to bruise and break
Thy disobedience. Well thou didst advise,
Yet not for thy advice or threats I fly
These wicked Tents devoted, lest the wrath   890
Impendent, raging into sudden flame
Distinguish not: for soon expect to feel
His Thunder on thy head, devouring fire.
Then who created thee lamenting learn,
When who can uncreate thee thou shalt know.   895
   So spake the Seraph *Abdiel* faithful found,
Among the faithless, faithful only hee;
Among innumerable false, unmov'd,
Unshak'n, unseduc'd, unterrifi'd
His Loyalty he kept, his Love, his Zeal;   900
Nor number, nor example with him wrought
To swerve from truth, or change his constant mind
Though single. From amidst them forth he pass'd,
Long way through hostile scorn, which he sustain'd
Superior, nor of violence fear'd aught;   905
And with retorted scorn his back he turn'd
On those proud Tow'rs to swift destruction doom'd.

The End of the Fifth Book.

---

887. Compare II, 327 and its note. Abdiel's words are like Milton's
assertion in *Of Reformation,* Book II, that he who rejects "the meek
censure of the church" must "fear to fall under the iron sceptre of
[Christ's] anger, that will dash him to pieces like a potsherd."

890. *devoted* has its Latin force of "doomed to destruction."

906. *retorted* has its literal Latin force of "turned back."

BOOK VI

THE ARGUMENT

Raphael *continues to relate how* Michael *and* Gabriel *were sent forth to Battle against* Satan *and his Angels. The first Fight describ'd:* Satan *and his Powers retire under Night: He calls a Council, invents devilish Engines, which in the second day's Fight put* Michael *and his Angels to some disorder; but they at length pulling up Mountains overwhelm'd both the force and Machines of* Satan: *Yet the Tumult not so ending, God on the third day sends* Messiah *his Son, for whom he had reserv'd the glory of that Victory: Hee in the Power of his Father coming to the place, and causing all his Legions to stand still on either side, with his Chariot and Thunder driving into the midst of his Enemies, pursues them unable to resist towards the wall of Heaven; which opening, they leap down with horror and confusion into the place of punishment prepar'd for them in the Deep:* Messiah *returns with triumph to his Father.*

ALL night the dreadless Angel unpursu'd
Through Heav'n's wide Champaign held his way, till Morn,
Wak't by the circling Hours, with rosy hand
Unbarr'd the gates of Light.   There is a Cave

---

1. *the dreadless Angel,* the fearless angel, Abdiel.

2. *Champaign,* plain.   At heaven's centre lay the Mount of God (V, 643) and in the north the Mountain of the Congregation (V, 766), but Milton visualized the "regions" of heaven as a wide plain.

Morn is the goddess of the dawn, Aurora, Spenser's "rosy fingred Morning faire" (*F.Q.,* I, ii, 7).   The epithet "rosy-fingered" is inherited from Homer and Hesiod.

3. Homer (*Il.,* V, 749) is finally the source of the personified Hours, "faire daughters of high Jove" who guarded

> "the charge to them fore-shewed
> By mighty Jove; who did them porters make
> Of heavens gate."   (*F.Q.,* VII, vii, 45.)

4. The cave inhabited by Light and Darkness may owe something to the abysm which Hesiod made the alternate home of Day and Night. (*Theog.,* 736–57.)

Within the Mount of God, fast by his Throne,   5
Where light and darkness in perpetual round
Lodge and dislodge by turns, which makes through Heav'n
Grateful vicissitude, like Day and Night;
Light issues forth, and at the other door
Obsequious darkness enters, till her hour   10
To veil the Heav'n, though darkness there might well
Seem twilight here; and now went forth the Morn
Such as in highest Heav'n, array'd in Gold
Empyreal, from before her vanisht Night,
Shot through with orient Beams: when all the Plain   15
Cover'd with thick embattl'd Squadrons bright,
Chariots and flaming Arms, and fiery Steeds
Reflecting blaze on blaze, first met his view:
War he perceiv'd, war in procinct, and found
Already known what he for news had thought   20
To have reported: gladly then he mixt
Among those friendly Powers who him receiv'd
With joy and acclamations loud, that one
That of so many Myriads fall'n, yet one
Return'd not lost: On to the sacred hill   25
They led him high applauded, and present
Before the seat supreme; from whence a voice
From midst a Golden Cloud thus mild was heard.
     Servant of God, well done, well hast thou fought
The better fight, who single hast maintain'd   30

---

8. *vicissitude,* change. Compare VII, 351.

10. *Obsequious* always has a favourable connotation in Milton. Compare Eve's "obsequious majesty" when she yields to Adam's wooing in VIII, 509.

12. Compare V, 645–6.

14. *Empyreal* is used with conscious reference to its derivation from the Greek word for "fire" and to the distinction of heavenly from earthly fire. Compare the note on II, 139.

19. To illustrate this technical military term *N.E.D.* quotes Chapman's *Iliad*, XII, 88–9: ". . . gave up each chariot and steed . . . to be kept in all procinct of warre." "Readiness" is the meaning.

29. *Servant of God* simply translates the Hebrew name Abdiel. Compare V, 805. The greeting, "Well done, thou good and faithful servant," to the man in Christ's parable of judgement (Matt. xxv, 21) who is told to "enter into the joy of thy lord," mingles here with St. Paul's cry, "I have fought a good fight." (II Tim. iv, 7.)

Against revolted multitudes the Cause
Of Truth, in word mightier than they in Arms;
And for the testimony of Truth hast borne
Universal reproach, far worse to bear
Than violence: for this was all thy care   35
To stand approv'd in sight of God, though Worlds
Judg'd thee perverse: the easier conquest now
Remains thee, aided by this host of friends,
Back on thy foes more glorious to return
Than scorn'd thou didst depart, and to subdue   40
By force, who reason for thir Law refuse,
Right reason for thir Law, and for thir King
Messiah, who by right of merit Reigns.
Go *Michael* of Celestial Armies Prince,
And thou in Military prowess next,   45
Gabriel, lead forth to Battle these my Sons

---

32. *Truth* is used in *Areopagitica* as if it meant an ultimate and living reality, "strong, next to the Almighty." Milton's Messiah was conceived as the "true light" of St. John (i, 9), who made Christ identify himself with Truth (xiv, 6).

33. Throughout the later books of the Old Testament the prophets treated the exiled nation of the Jews with the allegory of a man who for God's sake has "borne reproach." (Ps. lxix, 7.)

34. Spenser used the thought as if it were a maxim:
    "For evill deedes may better then bad words be bore."
                                        (*F.Q.,* IV, iv, 4.)

41. Milton's conception of Truth as strong next to the Almighty implied that ultimately force is the servant, not the foe of reason.

42. The early Greek Stoics used *right reason* as a criterion of truth and it became one of the great principles of Renaissance humanism. In *C.D.,* I, ii, Milton identifies it with conscience and appeals to it as a proof of the existence of God.

43. Compare I, 98, which seems like deliberate preparation for this line.

44. Michael is introduced as commander of the celestial forces because he appears generally in Christian tradition "to be one who presides over the rest of the good angels." He is introduced, Milton says in *C.D.,* I, ix, as "the leader of the angels, . . . in the capacity of a hostile commander waging war with the prince of the devils, the armies on both sides being drawn out in battle array. Rev. xii, 7;8." The name *Michael* seems to mean "godlike" and Milton calls him prince because he appears in Daniel xii, 1, as "the great prince which standeth for the children of thy people."

46. Although Gabriel is mentioned (IV, 971) as a cherub, belonging to the second rank of the heavenly hierarchy, while Michael is never

Invincible, lead forth my armed Saints
By Thousands and by Millions rang'd for fight;
Equal in number to that Godless crew
Rebellious, them with Fire and hostile Arms   50
Fearless assault, and to the brow of Heav'n
Pursuing drive them out from God and bliss,
Into thir place of punishment, the Gulf
Of *Tartarus,* which ready opens wide
His fiery *Chaos* to receive thir fall.   55
    So spake the Sovran voice, and Clouds began
To darken all the Hill, and smoke to roll
In dusky wreaths, reluctant flames, the sign
Of wrath awak't: nor with less dread the loud
Ethereal Trumpet from on high gan blow: 60
At which command the Powers Militant,
That stood for Heav'n, in mighty Quadrate join'd
Of Union irresistible, mov'd on
In silence thir bright Legions, to the sound
Of instrumental Harmony that breath'd   65
Heroic Ardor to advent'rous deeds
Under thir God-like Leaders, in the Cause
Of God and his *Messiah.* On they move
Indissolubly firm; nor obvious Hill,
Nor strait'ning Vale, nor Wood, nor Stream divides   70

---

mentioned as more than an archangel, Christian tradition ranked them
both with Raphael and Milton ranked them with Raphael and Uriel,
who are seraphs of the first order. Michael, the warrior angel so often
painted, is represented as prince of the four equal leaders of the heavenly
host. Compare IV, 549, and III, 648, and notes.

47. *Saints* here refers to the angels. Michael was most familiar in
popular tradition as "Saint Michael" and Milton calls Raphael a
"winged saint" (V, 247).

54. Compare II, 69.

57. The picture is like that of Mt. Sinai in Exodus xix, 18, "altogether
on a smoke, because the Lord descended upon it in fire; and the smoke
thereof ascended as the smoke of a furnace."

58. *reluctant,* struggling, *i.e.,* through the smoke.

62. *Quadrate,* a square phalanx of soldiers. Another such military
term is "globe" in II, 512. Compare the devils moving "in perfect
phalanx" to Dorian strains in I, 550.

69. *obvious* has its literal Latin meaning, "in the way."

70. *strait'ning,* confining.

Thir perfet ranks; for high above the ground
Thir march was, and the passive Air upbore
Thir nimble tread; as when the total kind
Of Birds in orderly array on wing
Came summon'd over *Eden* to receive   75
Thir names of thee; so over many a tract
Of Heav'n they march'd, and many a Province wide
Tenfold the length of this terrene: at last
Far in th' Horizon to the North appear'd
From skirt to skirt a fiery Region, stretcht   80
In battailous aspect, and nearer view
Bristl'd with upright beams innumerable
Of rigid Spears, and Helmets throng'd, and Shields
Various, with boastful Argument portray'd,
The banded Powers of *Satan* hasting on   85
With furious expedition; for they ween'd
That selfsame day by fight, or by surprise
To win the Mount of God, and on his Throne
To set the envier of his State, the proud
Aspirer, but thir thoughts prov'd fond and vain   90
In the mid way: though strange to us it seem'd
At first, that Angel should with Angel war,
And in fierce hosting meet, who wont to meet
So oft in Festivals of joy and love
Unanimous, as sons of one great Sire   95
Hymning th' Eternal Father: but the shout

---

74. Similarly Homer (*Il.*, II, 459–63) and Vergil (*Aen.*, VII, 699–701) compare mustering troops to flocks of birds.

75. The allusion to Adam's naming of the animals looks forward to VII, 493.

79. Compare V, 689 and its note.

81. *battailous*, warlike.
aspect, appearance.
nearer view is felt adverbially, "when seen more nearly."

84. *Argument: i.e.,* the boastful inscriptions which the demons carried on their shields instead of the idealistic emblems which were traditional on the shields of Knights.

86. *expedition* has its Latin meaning of "haste."

93. *hosting* was a term already obsolescent, meaning the rallying of popular forces to a leader's standard.
wont, were wonted or accustomed.

Of Battle now began, and rushing sound
Of onset ended soon each milder thought.
High in the midst exalted as a God
Th' Apostate in his Sun-bright Chariot sat   100
Idol of Majesty Divine, enclos'd
With Flaming Cherubim, and golden Shields;
Then lighted from his gorgeous Throne, for now
'Twixt Host and Host but narrow space was left,
A dreadful interval, and Front to Front   105
Presented stood in terrible array
Of hideous length: before the cloudy Van,
On the rough edge of battle ere it join'd,
Satan with vast and haughty strides advanc't,
Came tow'ring, arm'd in Adamant and Gold;   110
Abdiel that sight endur'd not, where he stood
Among the mightiest, bent on highest deeds,
And thus his own undaunted heart explores.

O Heav'n! that such resemblance of the Highest
Should yet remain, where faith and realty   115
Remain not; wherefore should not strength and might
There fail where Virtue fails, or weakest prove
Where boldest; though to sight unconquerable?
His puissance, trusting in th' Almighty's aid,
I mean to try, whose Reason I have tri'd   120
Unsound and false; nor is it aught but just,
That he who in debate of Truth hath won,
Should win in Arms, in both disputes alike
Victor; though brutish that contest and foul,
When Reason hath to deal with force, yet so   125
Most reason is that Reason overcome.

So pondering, and from his armed Peers

---

100. *Apostate* means literally "one who stands out" or "withdraws."

101. *Idol,* which literally means an "image" of any kind, combines
the ideas that Satan pretends to be God and enjoys the worship of
his idolatrous followers.

115. *realty,* if it is not a misprint for "lealty" or "fealty," is a contraction of "reality," the want of which Abdiel may naturally charge
to the empty "idol," Satan.

118. *to sight,* in appearance.

120. *try,* put to a test.
tri'd, proved by trial.

Forth stepping opposite, half way he met
His daring foe, at this prevention more
Incens't, and thus securely him defi'd.   130
    Proud, art thou met? thy hope was to have reacht
The highth of thy aspiring unoppos'd,
The Throne of God unguarded, and his side
Abandon'd at the terror of thy Power
Or potent tongue; fool, not to think how vain   135
Against th' Omnipotent to rise in Arms;
Who out of smallest things could without end
Have rais'd incessant Armies to defeat
Thy folly; or with solitary hand
Reaching beyond all limit, at one blow   140
Unaided could have finisht thee, and whelm'd
Thy Legions under darkness; but thou seest
All are not of thy Train; there be who Faith
Prefer, and Piety to God, though then
To thee not visible, when I alone   145
Seem'd in thy World erroneous to dissent
From all: my Sect thou seest, now learn too late
How few sometimes may know, when thousands err.
    Whom the grand foe with scornful eye askance
Thus answer'd. Ill for thee, but in wisht hour   150
Of my revenge, first sought for thou return'st
From flight, seditious Angel, to receive
Thy merited reward, the first assay
Of this right hand provok't, since first that tongue

---

129. *prevention* has its Latin force of "coming before," "confrontation."

130. *securely,* confidently.

138. *incessant,* unceasing, *i.e.,* both inexhaustible in numbers and everlasting.

143. *there be,* there are those.
faith, loyalty, faithfulness.

146. *erroneous,* erring. In Satan's world truth seems like error.

147. *Sect* and *sectary* were common terms of reproach among the Royalists for the divisions into which the English Nonconformists broke up and for their adherents. In *Areopagitica* Milton asserted his belief in the value of all sects of opinion in the quest of truth. When he wrote *P.L.* he was himself a despised sectary in Charles II's London.

153. *assay,* trial of strength.

Inspir'd with contradiction durst oppose   155
A third part of the Gods, in Synod met
Thir Deities to assert, who while they feel
Vigor Divine within them, can allow
Omnipotence to none. But well thou com'st
Before thy fellows, ambitious to win   160
From me some Plume, that thy success may show
Destruction to the rest: this pause between
(Unanswer'd lest thou boast) to let thee know;
At first I thought that Liberty and Heav'n
To heav'nly Souls had been all one; but now   165
I see that most through sloth had rather serve,
Minist'ring Spirits, train'd up in Feast and Song;
Such hast thou arm'd, the Minstrelsy of Heav'n,
Servility with freedom to contend,
As both thir deeds compar'd this day shall prove.   170
    To whom in brief thus *Abdiel* stern repli'd.
Apostate, still thou err'st, nor end wilt find
Of erring, from the path of truth remote:
Unjustly thou deprav'st it with the name
Of *Servitude* to serve whom God ordains,   175
Or Nature; God and Nature bid the same,
When he who rules is worthiest, and excels
Them whom he governs. This is servitude,
To serve th' unwise, or him who hath rebell'd
Against his worthier, as thine now serve thee,   180
Thyself not free, but to thyself enthrall'd;

---

156. *Synod,* assembly. Compare II, 391.

157. Compare Satan's temptation of Eve to become a goddess. (IX, 547.)

161. *success,* as in II, 123, has no connotation of good fortune. Here it implies failure.
show, show the way to, prepare for.

162. *rest, i.e.,* of angels on Abdiel's side.
this pause between, i.e., I pause between meeting you and attacking you to reply to you.

169. *Servility,* like *Minstrelsy,* stands for the loyal angels; *freedom* for the apostates.

174. *deprav'st,* pervert'st. The word keeps its Latin meaning.

178. This definition of servitude reappears in such key passages as XII, 90–101, and *P.R.* II, 463–472.

Yet lewdly dar'st our minist'ring upbraid.
Reign thou in Hell thy Kingdom, let mee serve
In Heav'n God ever blest, and his Divine
Behests obey, worthiest to be obey'd,   185
Yet Chains in Hell, not Realms expect: meanwhile
From mee return'd, as erst thou said'st, from flight,
This greeting on thy impious Crest receive.
    So saying, a noble stroke he lifted high,
Which hung not, but so swift with tempest fell   190
On the proud Crest of *Satan,* that no sight,
Nor motion of swift thought, less could his Shield
Such ruin intercept: ten paces huge
He back recoil'd; the tenth on bended knee
His massy Spear upstay'd; as if on Earth   195
Winds under ground or waters forcing way
Sidelong, had push't a Mountain from his seat
Half sunk with all his Pines. Amazement seiz'd
The Rebel Thrones, but greater rage to see
Thus foil'd thir mightiest, ours joy fill'd, and shout,   200
Presage of Victory and fierce desire
Of Battle: whereat *Michaël* bid sound
Th' Arch-angel trumpet; through the vast of Heav'n
It sounded, and the faithful Armies rung
Hosanna to the Highest: nor stood at gaze   205
The adverse Legions, nor less hideous join'd
The horrid shock: now storming fury rose,
And clamor such as heard in Heav'n till now
Was never, Arms on Armor clashing bray'd
Horrible discord, and the madding Wheels   210
Of brazen Chariots rag'd; dire was the noise

---

187. *as erst thou said'st* recalls the words of Ascanius when replying
to his enemy's threats. (*Aen.,* IX, 599, 635.) Very often the taunts exchanged between the angels and the demons resemble the boasts of the
champions in the battles described by Homer and Vergil.

196. For the belief that subterranean winds cause earthquakes compare the note on I, 230.

199. *Thrones,* the lowest order in the highest triad in the heavenly
hierarchy. The term is used loosely to mean all the angels on Satan's
side.

205. *Hosanna,* save, pray. Compare the note on II, 243.

206. *adverse,* opposed.

Of conflict; over head the dismal hiss
Of fiery Darts in flaming volleys flew,
And flying vaulted either Host with fire.
So under fiery Cope together rush'd   215
Both Battles main, with ruinous assault
And inextinguishable rage; all Heav'n
Resounded, and had Earth been then, all Earth
Had to her Centre shook. What wonder? when
Millions of fierce encount'ring Angels fought   220
On either side, the least of whom could wield
These Elements, and arm him with the force
Of all thir Regions: how much more of Power
Army against Army numberless to raise
Dreadful combustion warring, and disturb,   225
Though not destroy, thir happy Native seat;
Had not th' Eternal King Omnipotent
From his strong hold of Heav'n high over-rul'd
And limited thir might; though number'd such
As each divided Legion might have seem'd   230
A numerous Host, in strength each armed hand
A Legion; led in fight, yet Leader seem'd
Each Warrior single as in Chief, expert
When to advance, or stand, or turn the sway
Of Battle, open when, and when to close   235
The ridges of grim War; no thought of flight,
None of retreat, no unbecoming deed
That argu'd fear; each on himself reli'd,

---

215. *Cope,* covering. The sky, darkened with missiles, is meant.
Compare the note on IV, 992.

216. *Both Battles main,* the main parts of both armies.

222. *These Elements* are the four elements of earth, imagined as not
yet created. Compare the note on II, 275.

229. *number'd such,* so numerous.

231. *in strength each armed hand a Legion,* though every armed
hand, *i.e.,* every individual, among the devils had the strength of a
legion of soldiers.

232. *led in fight, etc.,* although they were led, each individual seemed
to have the skill of a leader.

233. *expert,* knowing by experience.

236. *ridges,* ranks.

As only in his arm the moment lay
Of victory; deeds of eternal fame   240
Were done, but infinite: for wide was spread
That War and various; sometimes on firm ground
A standing fight, then soaring on main wing
Tormented all the Air; all Air seem'd then
Conflicting Fire: long time in even scale   245
The Battle hung; till *Satan,* who that day
Prodigious power had shown, and met in Arms
No equal, ranging through the dire attack
Of fighting Seraphim confus'd, at length
Saw where the Sword of *Michael* smote, and fell'd   250
Squadrons at once, with huge two-handed sway
Brandisht aloft the horrid edge came down
Wide wasting; such destruction to withstand
He hasted, and oppos'd the rocky Orb
Of tenfold Adamant, his ample Shield   255
A vast circumference: At his approach
The great Arch-Angel from his warlike toil
Surceas'd, and glad as hoping here to end
Intestine War in Heav'n, the arch foe subdu'd
Or Captive dragg'd in Chains, with hostile frown   260
And visage all inflam'd first thus began.
      Author of evil, unknown till thy revolt,
Unnam'd in Heav'n, now plenteous, as thou seest
These Acts of hateful strife, hateful to all,
Though heaviest by just measure on thyself   265
And thy adherents: how hast thou disturb'd
Heav'n's blessed peace, and into Nature brought
Misery, uncreated till the crime

---

239. *moment* inherited from Latin the meaning of a weight just
sufficient to turn the scales. Compare X, 45.

250. In hell the fear of Michael's sword wrought still in the demons.
(II, 293-5.)

254. *Orb,* the round of Satan's shield is called rocky because it is
made of adamant, which meant either loadstone, diamond, or steel.

259. *Intestine War,* civil war.
  the arch foe subdu'd, "when the arch foe should be subdued," an
absolute construction.

267. Here, as in 176 above, *Nature* means the moral constitution of
reality.

Of thy Rebellion? how hast thou instill'd
Thy malice into thousands, once upright   270
And faithful, now prov'd false. But think not here
To trouble Holy Rest; Heav'n casts thee out
From all her Confines. Heav'n the seat of bliss
Brooks not the works of violence and War.
Hence then, and evil go with thee along   275
Thy offspring, to the place of evil, Hell,
Thou and thy wicked crew; there mingle broils,
Ere this avenging Sword begin thy doom,
Or some more sudden vengeance wing'd from God
Precipitate thee with augmented pain.   280
   So spake the Prince of Angels; to whom thus
The Adversary. Nor think thou with wind
Of airy threats to awe whom yet with deeds
Thou canst not. Hast thou turn'd the least of these
To flight, or if to fall, but that they rise   285
Unvanquisht, easier to transact with mee
That thou shouldst hope, imperious, and with threats
To chase me hence? err not that so shall end
The strife which thou call'st evil, but wee style
The strife of Glory: which we mean to win,   290
Or turn this Heav'n itself into the Hell
Thou fablest, here however to dwell free,
If not to reign: meanwhile thy utmost force,
And join him nam'd *Almighty* to thy aid,
I fly not, but have sought thee far and nigh.   **295**
   They ended parle, and both addrest for fight

---

275. *evil . . . thy offspring* seems to be a contemptuous reference to
Sin and Death. Compare II, 648–889 and X, 230–409.

282. Here there is an obvious reason in the circumstances for giving
Satan the name of *Adversary,* which implies also the loss of some more
definite name. Compare the note on I, 361.

286. *easier to transact, etc.,* that thou should'st expect to find it easier
to deal with me.

288. *err not,* do not make the mistake of thinking.

289. *The strife which thou call'st evil:* Michael has called Satan's
"works of violence and war" a crime which must be banished from
heaven.

296. *parle,* parley.
addrest, prepared.

Unspeakable; for who, though with the tongue
Of Angels, can relate, or to what things
Liken on Earth conspicuous, that may lift
Human imagination to such highth   300
Of Godlike Power: for likest Gods they seem'd,
Stood they or mov'd, in stature, motion, arms
Fit to decide the Empire of great Heav'n.
Now wav'd thir fiery Swords, and in the Air
Made horrid Circles; two broad Suns thir Shields   305
Blaz'd opposite, while expectation stood
In horror; from each hand with speed retir'd
Where erst was thickest fight, th' Angelic throng,
And left large field, unsafe within the wind
Of such commotion, such as, to set forth   310
Great things by small, if Nature's concord broke,
Among the Constellations war were sprung,
Two Planets rushing from aspect malign
Of fiercest opposition in mid Sky,
Should combat, and thir jarring Spheres confound.   315
Together both with next to Almighty Arm,
Uplifted imminent one stroke they aim'd
That might determine, and not need repeat,
As not of power, at once; nor odds appear'd

---

306. It is hard to tell whether *expectation* is felt as personified or as
representing the expectant and horrified armies. With the same am-
biguity "expectation" is described in *Antony and Cleopatra* (III, vi) as
fainting, "Longing for what it had not."

311. Milton thought of the traditional concord of nature by which

"the heaven is in his course contained,
And all the world in state unmoved stands,
As their Almightie Maker first ordained,
And bound them with inviolable bands.
                                    (*F.Q.*, IV, x, 35.)

313. Compare the reference in X, 658–9, to the opposite aspects, or
positions of the planets, in which they were thought to be hostile, because their rays then collided, with malignant effects on the earth.

315. The planets Milton imagines as grating together and destroying
the music of the spheres with their jar. Compare the note on *jar* in
V, 793.

318. *determine,* end the matter.
repeat, repetition.

319. *as not of power,* as if of insufficient power.

In might or swift prevention; but the sword   320
Of *Michael* from the Armory of God
Was giv'n him temper'd so, that neither keen
Nor solid might resist that edge: it met
The sword of *Satan* with steep force to smite
Descending, and in half cut sheer, nor stay'd,   325
But with swift wheel reverse, deep ent'ring shar'd
All his right side; then *Satan* first knew pain,
And writh'd him to and fro convolv'd; so sore
The griding sword with discontinuous wound
Pass'd through him, but th' Ethereal substance clos'd   330
Not long divisible, and from the gash
A stream of Nectarous humour issuing flow'd
Sanguine, such as Celestial Spirits may bleed,
And all his Armor stain'd erewhile so bright.
Forthwith on all sides to his aid was run   335
By Angels many and strong, who interpos'd
Defence, while others bore him on thir Shields
Back to his Chariot; where it stood retir'd
From off the files of war: there they him laid
Gnashing for anguish and despite and shame   340
To find himself not matchless, and his pride
Humbl'd by such rebuke, so far beneath
His confidence to equal God in power.

---

320. *prevention,* speed or skill to anticipate an opponent's blows.

326. *shar'd,* cut or clove.

327. Compare the "lasting pain" which is a part of the "lost happiness" of the demons in Book I, 55, and the pain inflicted on Moloch (362 below) and the other rebellious angels. The pure spiritual substance of the angels is incapable of pain, but the demons are already beginning their transformation into the grosser elements of matter.

329. *Discontinuous wound* is said in allusion to the old definition of a wound, that it separates the continuity of the parts. (Newton.)

330. Burton parallels Milton's treatment of the demons with traditions that the "Devils . . are corporeal, and have aerial bodies, . . . that they are nourished and have excrements, that they feel pain if they be hurt . . or stroken; &, if their bodies be cut, with admirable celerity they come together again." (*Anatomy,* I, ii, 1, 2.)

332. *Nectarous humours:* Milton thought of the clear ichor which Homer attributed to the gods instead of blood.

335. *was run:* the construction is impersonal. Milton used this Latin form of words again in X, 229.

Yet soon he heal'd; for Spirits that live throughout
Vital in every part, not as frail man   345
In Entrails, Heart or Head, Liver or Reins,
Cannot but by annihilating die;
Nor in thir liquid texture mortal wound
Receive, no more than can the fluid Air:
All Heart they live, all Head, all Eye, all Ear,   350
All Intellect, all Sense, and as they please,
They Limb themselves, and colour, shape or size
Assume, as likes them best, condense or rare.
    Meanwhile in other parts like deeds deserv'd
Memorial, where the might of *Gabriel* fought,   355
And with fierce Ensigns pierc'd the deep array
Of *Moloch* furious King, who him defi'd,
And at his Chariot wheels to drag him bound
Threat'n'd, nor from the Holy One of Heav'n
Refrain'd his tongue blasphémous; but anon   360
Down clov'n to the waist, with shatter'd Arms
And uncouth pain fled bellowing.   On each wing
Uriel and *Raphaël* his vaunting foe,
Though huge, and in a Rock of Diamond Arm'd,
Vanquish'd *Adramelech,* and *Asmadai,*   365
Two potent Thrones, that to be less than Gods
Disdain'd, but meaner thoughts learn'd in thir flight,

---

348. *liquid,* like *fluid,* was often applied to the air.   Compare Mar-
cellus' protest against any show of violence to the ghost in *Hamlet*
(I, i, 145–6),
              "For it is, as the air, invulnerable,
               And our vain blows malicious mockery."

351. Compare the note on I, 423.

355. *the might of Gabriel,* the mighty Gabriel.   Another example of
this Greek and Latin construction occurs at 371–2 below.

357. Compare I, 392, and its note.

360. Milton adapted Isaiah's question (II Kings xix, 22), "Whom hast
thou reproached and blasphemed? . . the Holy One of Israel."

365. *Adramelech,* whose name means "mighty king," was one of the
local phases of the Babylonian sun god.   II Kings xvii, 31, says that
children were offered to him as burnt offerings.
Asmadai is identical with the *Asmodeus* of IV, 168, but medieval
tradition, which ranked him as head of the fourth order of fallen
angels (according to Thomas Heywood, *Hierarchy,* p. 436), contributes
to his appearance as a commander of the rebellious legions here.

Mangl'd with ghastly wounds through Plate and Mail
Nor stood unmindful *Abdiel* to annoy
The Atheist crew, but with redoubl'd blow   370
Ariel and *Arioch,* and the violence
Of *Ramiel* scorcht and blasted overthrew.
I might relate of thousands, and thir names
Eternize here on Earth; but those elect
Angels contented with thir fame in Heav'n   375
Seek not the praise of men; the other sort
In might though wondrous and in Acts of War,
Nor of Renown less eager, yet by doom
Cancell'd from Heav'n and sacred memory,
Nameless in dark oblivion let them dwell.   380
For strength from Truth divided and from Just,
Illaudable, naught merits but dispraise
And ignominy, yet to glory aspires
Vain-glorious, and through infamy seeks fame:
Therefore Eternal silence be thir doom.   385
    And now thir Mightiest quell'd, the battle swerv'd,
With many an inroad gor'd; deformed rout
Enter'd, and foul disorder; all the ground

---

368. *Plate and mail,* solid armour made of metal moulded to fit the
body and armour made of meshed links of steel.

370. *Atheist* was regularly used to mean an enemy of God rather
than a disbeliever. Here both meanings may be involved.

371. The name *Ariel,* meaning "lion of God," is found as a kind
of epithet of Jerusalem in Isaiah xxix, 1. Rabbinical commentary on
Isaiah xxxiii, 7, where "valiant ones" translates the same Hebrew word,
and on similar passages elsewhere, explains how it acquired such meanings as "hero," "champion," "mighty warrior" and "angel" or "messenger" (Harris Fletcher, *Milton's Rabbinical Readings,* p. 271), but his
position among the demons is still a mystery. The Ariel of Shakespeare's *Tempest* is a quite different spirit.
    The name *Arioch,* "lion-like," is not given to an angel anywhere in
the Bible, but some light is thrown on Milton's conception by a com-
ment of the Rabbi Rashi on Daniel ii, 14 (cited by Fletcher, *op. cit.,*
p. 276), making Arioch, the captain of the royal guard, an executioner,
and by the appearance of the name once as that of an angel in the
Book of the Secrets of Enoch.

372. *Ramiel* is interpreted by Fletcher (p. 278, as signifying "the
thunder of God" (translated by Milton, perhaps, in *violence*). In the
Book of Enoch Ramiel is an angel in charge of the thunder.

379. Compare 282 above and I, 361, notes.

387. *deformed* has its Latin meaning of "ugly," "malformed."

With shiver'd armor strown, and on a heap
Chariot and Charioter lay overturn'd   390
And fiery foaming Steeds; what stood, recoil'd
O'erwearied, through the faint Satanic Host
Defensive scarce, or with pale fear surpris'd,
Then first with fear surpris'd and sense of pain
Fled ignominious, to such evil brought   395
By sin of disobedience, till that hour
Not liable to fear or flight or pain.
Far otherwise th' inviolable Saints
In Cubic Phalanx firm advanc't entire,
Invulnerable, impenetrably arm'd: 400
Such high advantages thir innocence
Gave them above thir foes, not to have sinn'd,
Not to have disobey'd; in fight they stood
Unwearied, unobnoxious to be pain'd
By wound, though from thir place by violence mov'd.   405
    Now Night her course began, and over Heav'n
Inducing darkness, grateful truce impos'd,
And silence on the odious din of War:
Under her Cloudy covert both retir'd,
Victor and Vanquisht: on the foughten field   410
Michaël and his Angels prevalent
Encamping, plac'd in Guard thir Watches round,
Cherubic waving fires: on th' other part
Satan with his rebellious disappear'd,
Far in the dark dislodg'd, and void of rest,   415
His Potentates to Council call'd by night;
And in the midst thus undismay'd began.
    O now in danger tri'd, now known in Arms

391. *what stood*, those who stood.

393. *Defensive scarce*, hardly able to stand on the defensive.

398. *inviolable Saints*, the angels, who are immune to wounds.

404. *unobnoxious*, not subject to harm. The word regularly had this
Latin meaning which is almost the reverse of its modern force.

407. *inducing* keeps its literal Latin meaning of "leading in."
grateful, welcome.

410. *foughten*, the obsolete perfect passive participle of "fight."

411. *prevalent*, prevailing, victorious.

415. *dislodg'd*, driven from their lodging or position.
void of rest, deprived of rest.

Not to be overpow'r'd, Companions dear,
Found worthy not of Liberty alone,   420
Too mean pretense, but what we more affect,
Honour, Dominion, Glory, and renown,
Who have sustain'd one day in doubtful fight,
(And if one day, why not Eternal days?)
What Heaven's Lord had powerfullest to send   425
Against us from about his Throne, and judg'd
Sufficient to subdue us to his will,
But proves not so: then fallible, it seems,
Of future we may deem him, though till now
Omniscient thought.   True is, less firmly arm'd,   430
Some disadvantage we endur'd and pain,
Till now not known, but known as soon contemn'd,
Since now we find this our Empyreal form
Incapable of mortal injury
Imperishable, and though pierc'd with wound,   435
Soon closing, and by native vigor heal'd.
Of evil then so small as easy think
The remedy; perhaps more valid Arms,
Weapons more violent, when next we meet,
May serve to better us, and worse our foes,   440
Or equal what between us made the odds,
In Nature none: if other hidden cause
Left them Superior, while we can preserve
Unhurt our minds, and understanding sound,
Due search and consultation will disclose.   445
     He sat; and in th' assembly next upstood
Nisroch, of Principalities the prime;
As one he stood escap't from cruel fight,
Sore toil'd, his riv'n Arms to havoc hewn,
And cloudy in aspect thus answering spake.   450

---

421. *Too mean pretense,* too moderate an object or ambition.

429. *of future,* in future.

432. *known as soon contemn'd,* despised as soon as known.

447. *Nisroch* was an Assyrian deity in whose temple at Nineveh
Sennacherib was murdered (II Kings xix, 37 and Isaiah xxxvii, 38). Milton may have derived the word from the Hebrew *nesher,* "eagle,"
or have made the mistake of identifying Nisroch with the vulture-god
of the Assyrian bas-reliefs.

449. *toil'd:* compare "overworked."

Deliverer from new Lords, leader to free
Enjoyment of our right as Gods; yet hard
For Gods, and too unequal work we find
Against unequal arms to fight in pain,
Against unpain'd, impassive; from which evil　　　455
Ruin must needs ensue; for what avails
Valour or strength, though matchless, quell'd with pain
Which all subdues, and makes remiss the hands
Of Mightiest. Sense of pleasure we may well
Spare out of life perhaps, and not repine,　　　460
But live content, which is the calmest life:
But pain is perfet misery, the worst
Of evils, and excessive, overturns
All patience. He who therefore can invent
With what more forcible we may offend　　　465
Our yet unwounded Enemies, or arm
Ourselves with like defence, to mee deserves
No less than for deliverance what we owe.

　　Whereto with look compos'd *Satan* repli'd.
Not uninvented that, which thou aright　　　470
Believ'st so main to our success, I bring;
Which of us who beholds the bright surface
Of this Ethereous mould whereon we stand,
This continent of spacious Heav'n, adorn'd
With Plant, Fruit, Flow'r Ambrosial, Gems and Gold,　　　475
Whose Eye so superficially surveys
These things, as not to mind from whence they grow
Deep under ground, materials dark and crude,
Of spiritous and fiery spume, till toucht
With Heav'n's ray, and temper'd they shoot forth　　　480
So beauteous, op'ning to the ambient light.

---

455. *impassive,* not subject to passion or painful sensation.

458. *remiss,* has its literal Latin force of "loose," "relaxed."

465. *offend* has its literal Latin meaning of "strike at."

467. *to mee,* seems to me (to deserve no less than we would owe to any deliverer).

471. *main,* important.

480. The crude materials in the soil of heaven seem to be transformed by "Heav'n's ray" as Milton says that "terrestrial humour" was transmuted by the sun into precious things. (III, 609–612.)

These in thir dark Nativity the Deep
Shall yield us, pregnant with infernal flame,
Which into hollow Engines long and round
Thick. ramm'd, at th' other bore with touch of fire   485
Dilated and infuriate shall send forth
From far with thund'ring noise among our foes
Such implements of mischief as shall dash
To pieces, and o'erwhelm whatever stands
Adverse, that they shall fear we have disarm'd   490
The Thunderer of his only dreaded bolt.
Nor long shall be our labour, yet ere dawn,
Effect shall end our wish.   Meanwhile revive;
Abandon fear; to strength and counsel join'd
Think nothing hard, much less to be despair'd.   495
He ended, and his words thir drooping cheer
Enlight'n'd, and thir languisht hope reviv'd.
Th' invention all admir'd, and each, how hee
To be th' inventor miss'd, so easy it seem'd
Once found, which yet unfound most would have thought
Impossible: yet haply of thy Race   501
In future days, if Malice should abound,
Some one intent on mischief, or inspir'd
With dev'lish machination might devise
Like instrument to plague the Sons of men   505
For sin, on war and mutual slaughter bent.
Forthwith from Council to the work they flew,
None arguing stood, innumerable hands
Were ready, in a moment up they turn'd
Wide the Celestial soil, and saw beneath   510

482. The *dark Nativity* is the origin or birthplace of metals in the
Deep, which means here, as it does in the reference to
          "The unadorned bosom of the Deep"
in *Comus* (23), the depths of the earth.

484. Milton—at least as a poet—seems to have agreed with Ariosto
(*Orlando Furioso* IX, 91) and Spenser that cannon were a
          "divelish yron engin wrought
     In deepest hell, and framd by furies skill."
                    (*F.Q.,* I, vii, 13.)

493. *Effect,* performance shall fulfil our wish.

494. *to strength, etc.,* do not despair of anything which is exposed to
strength and wisdom.

Th' originals of Nature in thir crude
Conception; Sulphurous and Nitrous Foam
They found, they mingl'd, and with subtle Art,
Concocted and adusted they reduc'd
To blackest grain, and into store convey'd: 515
Part hidd'n veins digg'd up (nor hath this Earth
Entrails unlike) of Mineral and Stone,
Whereof to found thir Engines and thir Balls
Of missive ruin; part incentive reed
Provide, pernicious with one touch to fire.   520
So all ere day-spring, under conscious Night
Secret they finish'd, and in order set,
With silent circumspection unespi'd.
Now when fair Morn Orient in Heav'n appear'd
Up rose the Victor Angels, and to Arms   525
The matin Trumpet Sung: in Arms they stood
Of Golden Panoply, refulgent Host,
Soon banded; others from the dawning Hills
Look'd round, and Scouts each Coast light-armed scour,
Each quarter, to descry the distant foe,   530
Where lodg'd, or whither fled, or if for fight,
In motion or in alt: him soon they met
Under spread Ensigns moving nigh, in slow
But firm Battalion; back with speediest Sail

---

512. With *Foam* compare *spume* in 479 above. Milton was thinking
of the contemporary name for molybditis, which was called "the foam"
or "spume of lead."

514. *concocted* has its Latin force of "cook" or "bake."
adusted was most familiar as a medical term with the basic, Latin
meaning of "burnt," "reduced to ashes."

518. *Engines,* cannon. The word was common in this sense.

519. *missive ruin:* both words keep their literal Latin meaning of
"destruction capable of being sent."
incentive, another Latinism, means "kindling."
Incentive reed is Milton's name for a gunner's match.

520. *pernicious* here has the Latin force of "swift," *i.e.,* swift in its
response to the spark.

521. *conscious:* night is half personified and imagined as watching
the work. The phrase is a Latinism (*e.g.,* Ovid's *Met.,* XIII, 15).

523. *circumspection:* compare the use of the word in IV, 537.

532. *alt,* a halt.

Zophiel, of Cherubim the swiftest wing,   535
Came flying, and in mid Air aloud thus cri'd.

  Arm, Warriors, Arm for fight, the foe at hand,
Whom fled we thought, will save us long pursuit
This day, fear not his flight; so thick a Cloud
He comes, and settl'd in his face I see   540
Sad resolution and secure: let each
His Adamantine coat gird well, and each
Fit well his Helm, gripe fast his orbed Shield,
Borne ev'n or high, for this day will pour down,
If I conjecture aught, no drizzling show'r,   545
But rattling storm of Arrows barb'd with fire.
So warn'd he them aware themselves, and soon
In order, quit of all impediment;
Instant without disturb they took Alarm,
And onward move Embattl'd; when behold   550
Not distant far with heavy pace the Foe
Approaching gross and huge; in hollow Cube
Training his devilish Enginry, impal'd
On every side with shadowing Squadrons Deep,
To hide the fraud. At interview both stood   555
A while, but suddenly at head appear'd
Satan: And thus was heard Commanding loud.

  Vanguard, to Right and Left the Front unfold;
That all may see who hate us, how we seek
Peace and composure, and with open breast   ·   560
Stand ready to receive them, if they like

  535. *Zophiel,* which signifies in Hebrew "the spy of God," has not
been traced to any source.

  540. *He,* the foe, is a collective idea and can appropriately be called a
Cloud. Compare the host of blasphemers in II Peter, ii, 17, who are
called "clouds carried with a tempest."

  541. *Sad,* firm.
  secure, fearless.

  548. *quit of all impediment,* unencumbered of all baggage.
  impediment keeps its meaning as a technical, Latin military term.

  549. *Instant* has its Latin force of "forward," "urgent."
  disturb, disturbance.

  553. *Training,* dragging.
  impal'd, surrounded.

  555. *interview,* mutual view, confrontation.

  560. *composure,* composition, settlement.

Our overture, and turn not back perverse;
But that I doubt; however witness Heaven,
Heav'n witness thou anon, while we discharge
Freely our part: yee who appointed stand   565
Do as you have in charge, and briefly touch
What we propound, and loud that all may hear.
  So scoffing in ambiguous words, he scarce
Had ended; when to Right and Left the Front
Divided, and to either Flank retir'd.   570
Which to our eyes discover'd new and strange,
A triple-mounted row of Pillars laid
On Wheels (for like to Pillars most they seem'd
Or hollow'd bodies made of Oak or Fir
With branches lopt, in Wood or Mountain fell'd)   575
Brass, Iron, Stony mould, had not thir mouths
With hideous orifice gap't on us wide,
Portending hollow truce; at each behind
A Seraph stood, and in his hand a Reed
Stood waving tipt with fire; while we suspense,   580
Collected stood within our thoughts amus'd,
Not long, for sudden all at once thir Reeds
Put forth, and to a narrow vent appli'd
With nicest touch. Immediate in a flame,
But soon obscur'd with smoke, all Heav'n appear'd,   585
From those deep-throated Engines belcht, whose roar
Embowell'd with outrageous noise the Air,
And all her entrails tore, disgorging foul
Thir devilish glut, chain'd Thunderbolts and Hail
Of Iron Globes, which on the Victor Host   590
Levell'd, with such impetuous fury smote,
That whom they hit, none on thir feet might stand,
Though standing else as Rocks, but down they fell
By thousands, Angel on Arch-Angel roll'd;

---

576. *mould,* substance. Compare III, 709 and IV, 226.

578. *hollow:* the pun on the moral and physical senses of this word
is so bad that it almost escapes notice.

580. *suspense* keeps its force as a Latin participle, "suspended," *i.e.,*
with curiosity.

581. *amus'd,* in a muse or daze.

587. *Embowell'd,* crammed, filled.

The sooner for thir Arms, unarm'd they might   595
Have easily as Spirits evaded swift
By quick contraction or remove; but now
Foul dissipation follow'd and forc't rout;
Nor serv'd it to relax thir serried files.
What should they do? if on they rusht, repulse   600
Repeated, and indecent overthrow
Doubl'd, would render them yet more despis'd,
And to thir foes a laughter; for in view
Stood rankt of Seraphim another row
In posture to displode thir second tire   605
Of Thunder: back defeated to return
They worse abhorr'd. *Satan* beheld thir plight,
And to his Mates thus in derision call'd.
    O Friends, why come not on these Victors proud?
Erewhile they fierce were coming, and when wee,   610
To entertain them fair with open Front
And Breast, (what could we more?) propounded terms
Of composition, straight they chang'd thir minds,
Flew off, and into strange vagaries fell,
As they would dance, yet for a dance they seem'd   615
Somewhat extravagant and wild, perhaps
For joy of offer'd peace: but I suppose
If our proposals once again were heard
We should compel them to a quick result.

___

597. *quick contraction or remove*: in I, 429, the spirits are said to be able to dilate or condense their bodies at will and to move swiftly about their "aery purposes."

598. *dissipation* keeps its Latin, military meaning of "scatter," "disperse," "rout."

599. *serv'd*, "help'd," "served the turn."

601. *indecent* keeps its Latin meaning of "ugly," "disgraceful."

605. *displode*, explode, fire.
tire, discharge, volley.

607. A strange light is thrown upon Milton's account of the plight of the angels and upon this entire passage by Donne's remark that "by the benefit of this light of reason, [men] have found out *Artillery*, by which warres come to quicker ends than heretofore, and the great expense of bloud is avoyded: for the numbers of men slain now, since the invention of Artillery, are much lesse than before, when the sword was the executioner." (*Sermon at St. Paul's*, Christmas, 1621.)

615. Satan's irony has Homeric justification in Patroclus' praise of the skilful "dance" of Hector's stricken charioteer. (*Il.*, XVI, 745-50.)

To whom thus *Belial* in like gamesome mood.   620
Leader, the terms we sent were terms of weight,
Of hard contents, and full of force urg'd home,
Such as we might perceive amus'd them all,
And stumbl'd many; who receives them right,
Had need from head to foot well understand;   625
Not understood, this gift they have besides,
They show us when our foes walk not upright.
  So they among themselves in pleasant vein
Stood scoffing, highth'n'd in thir thoughts beyond
All doubt of Victory, eternal might   630
To match with thir inventions they presum'd
So easy, and of his Thunder made a scorn,
And all his Host derided, while they stood
A while in trouble; but they stood not long,
Rage prompted them at length, and found them arms   635
Against such hellish mischief fit to oppose.
Forthwith (behold the excellence, the power
Which God hath in his mighty Angels plac'd)
Thir Arms away they threw, and to the Hills
(For Earth hath this variety from Heav'n   640
Of pleasure situate in Hill and Dale)
Light as the Lightning glimpse they ran, they flew,
From thir foundations loos'ning to and fro
They pluckt the seated Hills with all thir load,
Rocks, Waters, Woods, and by the shaggy tops   645
Uplifting bore them in thir hands: Amaze,
Be sure, and terror seiz'd the rebel Host,

---

625. The pun is on the familiar, metaphorical meaning of *understand* and its now obsolete meaning of "support." So Viola says, "My legs do better understand me, sir, than I understand what you mean." (*Twelfth Night*, III, i, 90.)

635. *Rage . . . found them arms*, like the stone-throwing mob in *Aen.*, I, 150.

640. *from Heav'n*, in conformity with heaven, like heaven.

642. *Light*, swift because light in weight.

644. Like the giants who fought for Zeus against the titans in Hesiod's *Theogony* (713–20), the angels pluck up the hills and overwhelm their enemies. Throughout *P.L.* Milton felt that Hesiod's story significantly paralleled his own, but his treatment of it elsewhere is more reticent than it is in the emphatic details here. Compare the note on I, 50.

646. *Amaze*, amazement.

When coming towards them so dread they saw
The bottom of the Mountains upward turn'd,
Till on those cursed Engines' triple-row   650
They saw them whelm'd, and all thir confidence
Under the weight of Mountains buried deep,
Themselves invaded next, and on thir heads
Main Promontories flung, which in the Air
Came shadowing, and opprest whole Legions arm'd,   655
Thir armor help'd thir harm, crush't in and bruis'd
Into thir substance pent, which wrought them pain
Implacable, and many a dolorous groan,
Long struggling underneath, ere they could wind
Out of such prison, though Spirits of purest light,   660
Purest at first, now gross by sinning grown.
The rest in imitation to like Arms
Betook them, and the neighbouring Hills uptore;
So Hills amid the Air encounter'd Hills
Hurl'd to and fro with jaculation dire,   665
That under ground they fought in dismal shade:
Infernal noise; War seem'd a civil Game
To this uproar; horrid confusion heapt
Upon confusion rose: and now all Heav'n
Had gone to wrack, with ruin overspread,   670
Had not th' Almighty Father where he sits
Shrin'd in his Sanctuary of Heav'n secure,
Consulting on the sum of things, foreseen
This tumult, and permitted all, advis'd:
That his great purpose he might so fulfil,   675
To honour his Anointed Son aveng'd
Upon his enemies, and to declare
All power on him transferr'd: whence to his Son
Th' Assessor of his Throne he thus began.

---

655. *opprest,* crushed.

665. *jaculation,* throwing, hurling.

667. *civil* seems to be used in the sense which is opposed to "military."

673. *sum of things,* the whole universe. The term is borrowed from
Lucretius (*De rerum natura,* V, 361).

674. *advis'd,* with mind made up in advance.

679. *Assessor* is still used in law as a term for judges or committee-
men who are "sharers of the seat" of a chief judge or of some other
official.

Effulgence of my Glory, Son belov'd,   680
Son in whose face invisible is beheld
Visibly, what by Deity I am,
And in whose hand what by Decree I do,
Second Omnipotence, two days are past,
Two days, as we compute the days of Heav'n,   685
Since *Michael* and his Powers went forth to tame
These disobedient; sore hath been thir fight,
As likeliest was, when two such Foes met arm'd;
For to themselves I left them, and thou know'st,
Equal in their Creation they were form'd,   690
Save what sin hath impair'd, which yet hath wrought
Insensibly, for I suspend thir doom;
Whence in perpetual fight they needs must last
Endless, and no solution will be found:
War wearied hath perform'd what War can do,   695
And to disorder'd rage let loose the reins,
With Mountains as with Weapons arm'd, which makes
Wild work in Heav'n, and dangerous to the main.
Two days are therefore past, the third is thine;
For thee I have ordain'd it, and thus far   700
Have suffer'd, that the Glory may be thine
Of ending this great War, since none but Thou
Can end it. Into thee such Virtue and Grace
Immense I have transfus'd, that all may know
In Heav'n and Hell thy Power above compare,   705
And this perverse Commotion govern'd thus,
To manifest thee worthiest to be Heir
Of all things, to be Heir and to be King

---

682. The chapter on "The Son of God" in *C.D.* opens with a reference to the verse which is echoed here: "Who is the image of the invisible God." (Col. i, 15.)

684. Milton's discussion of the Son's omnipotence quotes John v, 19: "The Son can do nothing of himself, but what he seeth the Father do."

692. *Insensibly*, imperceptibly.

695. *War wearied, etc.*: those who are worn out by fighting have done everything that can be done by fighting.

698. *main*, continent or whole extent of heaven.

700. *thus far Have suffer'd*, have allowed matters to run their course until now.

706. *govern'd*, controlled, managed.

By Sacred Unction, thy deserved right.
Go then thou Mightiest in thy Father's might,   710
Ascend my Chariot, guide the rapid Wheels
That shake Heav'n's basis, bring forth all my War,
My Bow and Thunder, my Almighty Arms
Gird on, and Sword upon thy puissant Thigh;
Pursue these sons of Darkness, drive them out   715
From all Heav'n's bounds into the utter Deep:
There let them learn, as likes them, to despise
God and *Messiah* his anointed King.
   He said, and on his Son with Rays direct
Shone full, he all his Father full exprest   720
Ineffably into his face receiv'd,
And thus the filial Godhead answering spake.
   O Father, O Supreme of heav'nly Thrones,
First, Highest, Holiest, Best, thou always seek'st
To glorify thy Son, I always thee,   725
As is most just; this I my Glory account,
My exaltation, and my whole delight,
That thou in me well pleas'd declar'st thy will
Fulfill'd, which to fulfil is all my bliss.
Sceptre and Power, thy giving, I assume,   730
And gladlier shall resign, when in the end
Thou shalt be All in All, and I in thee
For ever, and in mee all whom thou lov'st;

---

709. *Sacred Unction* refers to the meaning of Messiah, "anointed king."
Compare V, 664.

712. *War,* troops.

716. *utter,* outer.   Compare I, 72.

717. *as likes them,* however they please, as best they can.

723. The words of the Messiah here are woven out of several New
Testament passages which support Milton's insistent argument in *C.D.,*
I, v, that "the Father does not alienate his glory from himself in impart-
ing it to the Son, inasmuch as the Son uniformly glorifies the Father."

725. The thought is taken from the prayer of Christ before the passion, "Father, the hour is come; glorify thy Son, that thy Son also may
glorify thee." (John xvii, 1.)

728. Compare the voice from heaven at Christ's baptism and again
at the transfiguration, "This is my beloved Son, in whom I am well
pleased." (Matt. iii, 17 and xvii, 5.)

732. Compare III, 341, and its note.

But whom thou hat'st, I hate, and can put on
Thy terrors, as I put thy mildness on,   735
Image of thee in all things; and shall soon,
Arm'd with thy might, rid heav'n of these rebell'd,
To thir prepar'd ill Mansion driven down
To chains of darkness, and th' undying Worm,
That from thy just obedience could revolt,   740
Whom to obey is happiness entire.
Then shall thy Saints unmixt, and from th' impure
Far separate, circling thy holy Mount
Unfeigned *Halleluiahs* to thee sing,
Hymns of high praise, and I among them chief.   745
So said, he o'er his Sceptre bowing, rose
From the right hand of Glory where he sat,
And the third sacred Morn began to shine
Dawning through Heav'n: forth rush'd with whirl-wind sound
The Chariot of Paternal Deity,   750
Flashing thick flames, Wheel within Wheel, undrawn,
Itself instinct with Spirit, but convoy'd
By four Cherubic shapes, four Faces each
Had wondrous, as with Stars thir bodies all
And Wings were set with Eyes, with Eyes the wheels   755
Of Beryl, and careering Fires between;
Over thir heads a crystal Firmament,

739. In IV, 965, similar use is made of John's vision of "an angel come down from heaven, having the key of the bottomless pit and a great chain in his hand. And he laid hold on the dragon, that old serpent, which is the Devil, and Satan, and bound him." (Rev. xx, 1–2. Compare II Pet. ii, 4, and Jude i, 6.)

The *undying Worm* is a remnant of the conventional Old Testament symbolism of hell which survives in Mark ix, 44.

748. *sacred Morn* is an Homeric phrase (*Il.* XI, 84), used here perhaps because its context is a scene of universal war directly commanded by the gods.

750. The chariot is Milton's interpretation of Ezekiel's vision of "a great cloud, and a fire infolding itself, . . . and out of the midst thereof as the colour of amber. . . . Also out of the midst thereof came the likeness of four living creatures. . . . And every one had four faces, and every one had four wings." (Ezek. i, 4–6.) From the same chapter come the idea that the chariot moves of itself because it is pure spirit, the mysterious wheels, the play of colours and precious stones, and the darting eyes.

752. *instinct* (adj.) has its basic Latin force of "excited" or "moved."

Whereon a Sapphire Throne, inlaid with pure
Amber, and colours of the show'ry Arch.
Hee in Celestial Panoply all arm'd   760
Of radiant *Urim,* work divinely wrought,
Ascended, at his right hand Victory
Sat Eagle-wing'd, beside him hung his Bow
And Quiver with three-bolted Thunder stor'd,
And from about him fierce Effusion roll'd   765
Of smoke and bickering flame, and sparkles dire;
Attended with ten thousand thousand Saints,
He onward came, far off his coming shone,
And twenty thousand (I thir number heard)
Chariots of God, half on each hand were seen: 770
Hee on the wings of Cherub rode sublime
On the Crystálline Sky, in Sapphire Thron'd.
Illustrious far and wide, but by his own
First seen, them unexpected joy surpris'd,
When the great Ensign of *Messiah* blaz'd   775
Aloft by Angels borne, his Sign in Heav'n:
Under whose Conduct *Michael* soon reduc'd
His Army, circumfus'd on either Wing,
Under thir Head imbodied all in one.

761. Milton understood the *Urim,* which were a part of the breastplate of the Jewish high priest (see Exod. xxviii, 30), as symbols of the
judgments or revelations of God. His epithet, "radiant" indicates that
he understood the Hebrew word to mean "light" in the physical as well
as in a mystical sense.

762. *Victory* may be a mere personification, but it seems like the goddess often represented in Greek sculpture on the chariots of warriors.

767. *Saints* signifies the loyal angels with a suggestion of their inviola-
bility or immunity to harm. Compare 398 above, and Psalm lxviii, 17:
"The chariots of God are twenty thousand, even thousands of angels."

771. The line is an echo of a paean of David, exclaiming that God
"rode upon a cherub, and did fly; and he was seen upon the wings of
the wind." (II Sam. xxii, 11.) *sublime,* "aloft," is Milton's translation
of the final phrase.

773. *Illustrious,* glorious, luminous.

776. The *Sign* is a reminiscence of the promise that at the end of the
world "shall appear the sign of the Son of Man in heaven." (Matt. xxiv,
30.)

777. *reduc'd,* led back; a Latinism.

779. Milton thought of Messiah as "the head of the body, the church"
(Col. i, 18), and of a mystical unity of the saints on earth and in heaven

Before him Power Divine his way prepar'd;   780
At his command the uprooted Hills retir'd
Each to his place, they heard his voice and went
Obsequious, Heav'n his wonted face renew'd,
And with fresh Flow'rets Hill and Valley smil'd.
This saw his hapless Foes, but stood obdur'd,   785
And to rebellious fight rallied thir Powers
Insensate, hope conceiving from despair.
In heav'nly Spirits could such perverseness dwell?
But to convince the proud what Signs avail,
Or Wonders move th' obdúrate to relent?   790
They hard'n'd more by what might most reclaim,
Grieving to see his Glory, at the sight
Took envy, and aspiring to his highth,
Stood reimbattl'd fierce, by force or fraud
Weening to prosper, and at length prevail   795
Against God and *Messiah,* or to fall
In universal ruin last, and now
To final Battle drew, disdaining flight,
Or faint retreat; when the great Son of God
To all his Host on either hand thus spake.   800
    Stand still in bright array ye Saints, here stand
Ye Angels arm'd, this day from Battle rest;
Faithful hath been your Warfare, and of God
Accepted, fearless in his righteous Cause,
And as ye have receiv'd, so have ye done   805
Invincibly: but of this cursed crew
The punishment to other hand belongs,
Vengeance is his, or whose he sole appoints;

---

as being "one body in Christ, and every one members one of another."
(Rom. xii, 5.)

783. *Obsequious,* obedient.   Contrast the meaning in 10 above.

785. *obdur'd* has its Latin meaning of "hardened."

788. The line translates Virgil's question at the close of his account of
Juno's malice against Aeneas.   (*Aen.* I, 11.)

797. *last* may mean "at last" or be an adjective modifying *ruin* and
meaning "final."

805. *as ye have receiv'd, etc.,* what you have suffered from your foes
you have reinflicted.

808. The thought recurs often in the Bible (Deut. xxxii, 35; Ps. xciv,
1; Rom. xii, 19; and Heb. x, 30).

Number to this day's work is not ordain'd
Nor multitude, stand only and behold   810
God's indignation on these Godless pour'd
By mee; not you but mee they have despis'd,
Yet envied; against mee is all thir rage,
Because the Father, t'whom in Heav'n supreme
Kingdom and Power and Glory appertains,   815
Hath honour'd me according to his will.
Therefore to mee thir doom he hath assign'd;
That they may have thir wish, to try with mee
In Battle which the stronger proves, they all,
Or I alone against them, since by strength   820
They measure all, of other excellence
Not emulous, nor care who them excels;
Nor other strife with them do I voutsafe.
   So spake the Son, and into terror chang'd
His count'nance too severe to be beheld   825
And full of wrath bent on his Enemies.
At once the Four spread out thir Starry wings
With dreadful shade contiguous, and the Orbs
Of his fierce Chariot roll'd, as with the sound
Of torrent Floods, or of a numerous Host.   830
Hee on his impious Foes right onward drove,
Gloomy as Night; under his burning Wheels
The steadfast Empyrean shook throughout,
All but the Throne itself of God.   Full soon
Among them he arriv'd; in his right hand   835
Grasping ten thousand Thunders, which he sent
Before him, such as in thir Souls infix'd
Plagues; they astonisht all resistance lost,
All courage; down thir idle weapons dropp'd;
O'er Shields and Helms, and helmed heads he rode   840

   828. The vast shadow results from union of the contiguous wings of
the cherubs.
   832. So Hector, though splendidly armed, was "gloomy as night"
(*Il.*, XII, 462), and so, with Apollo's aid, he paralyzed his foes. (*Il.*,
XV, 323.)
   838. *Plagues* has its original Greek force of "blow" or "stroke."
   840. In Ezekiel's vision there is no suggestion of violence, but long
before writing *P.L.*, in *An Apology for Smectymnuus* (*P.W.*, III, 129),
Milton had imagined a "fiery chariot, drawn with two blazing meteors,
figured like beasts, . . . resembling two of those four which Ezekiel and

Of Thrones and mighty Seraphim prostrate,
That wish't the Mountains now might be again
Thrown on them as a shelter from his ire.
Nor less on either side tempestuous fell
His arrows, from the fourfold-visag'd Four,   845
Distinct with eyes, and from the living Wheels,
Distinct alike with multitude of eyes,
One Spirit in them rul'd, and every eye
Glar'd lightning, and shot forth pernicious fire
Among th' accurst, that wither'd all thir strength,   850
And of thir wonted vigor left them drain'd,
Exhausted, spiritless, afflicted, fall'n.
Yet half his strength he put not forth, but check'd
His Thunder in mid Volley, for he meant
Not to destroy, but root them out of Heav'n: 855
The overthrown he rais'd, and as a Herd
Of Goats or timorous flock together throng'd
Drove them before him Thunder-struck, pursu'd
With terrors and with furies to the bounds
And Crystal wall of Heav'n, which op'ning wide,   860
Roll'd inward, and a spacious Gap disclos'd
Into the wasteful Deep; the monstrous sight
Strook them with horror backward, but far worse
Urg'd them behind; headlong themselves they threw
Down from the verge of Heav'n, Eternal wrath   865
Burnt after them to the bottomless pit.
  Hell heard th' unsufferable noise, Hell saw
Heav'n ruining from Heav'n, and would have fled
Affrighted; but strict Fate had cast too deep
Her dark foundations, and too fast had bound.   870
Nine days they fell; confounded *Chaos* roar'd,
And felt tenfold confusion in thir fall

St. John saw"; and in the chariot "Zeal, shaking loosely the slack reins,
drives over the heads of scarlet prelates."

  842. The phrase is an application of the cry of the wicked at the last
judgement; saying "to the mountains and rocks, Fall on us, and hide us
from the face of him that sitteth on the throne." (Rev. vi, 16.)

  864. With this line the chain of events whose last link was given to
the reader in I, 44, ff., is complete.

  868. *ruining* has its Latin meaning of "collapsing," "falling."

  871. Compare the note on I, 50.

Through his wild Anarchy, so huge a rout
Incumber'd him with ruin: Hell at last
Yawning receiv'd them whole, and on them clos'd,   875
Hell thir fit habitation fraught with fire
Unquenchable, the house of woe and pain.
Disburd'n'd Heav'n rejoic'd, and soon repair'd
Her mural breach, returning whence it roll'd.
Sole Victor from th' expulsion of his Foes   880
Messiah his triumphal Chariot turn'd:
To meet him all his Saints, who silent stood
Eye-witnesses of his Almighty Acts,
With Jubilee advanc'd; and as they went,
Shaded with branching Palm, each order bright,   885
Sung Triumph, and him sung Victorious King,
Son, Heir, and Lord, to him Dominion giv'n,
Worthiest to Reign: he celebrated rode
Triumphant through mid Heav'n, into the Courts
And Temple of his mighty Father Thron'd   890
On high; who into Glory him receiv'd,
Where now he sits at the right hand of bliss.
    Thus measuring things in Heav'n by things on Earth
At thy request, and that thou mayst beware
By what is past, to thee I have reveal'd   895
What might have else to human Race been hid:
The discord which befell, and War in Heav'n
Among th' Angelic Powers, and the deep fall
Of those too high aspiring, who rebell'd
With *Satan,* hee who envies now thy state,   900
Who now is plotting how he may seduce
Thee also from obedience, that with him
Bereav'd of happiness thou mayst partake
His punishment, Eternal misery;
Which would be all his solace and revenge,   905
As a despite done against the most High,
Thee once to gain Companion of his woe.
But list'n not to his Temptations, warn

---

879. *mural breach,* breach in the walls.

890. The apocalyptic echoes in this verse paragraph culminate in this
definite, final allusion to St. Paul's vision of the Son "upholding all things
by the word of his power" and sitting down "on the right hand of the
Majesty on high." (Heb. i, 3.)

Thy weaker; let it profit thee to have heard
By terrible Example the reward   910
Of disobedience; firm they might have stood,
Yet fell; remember, and fear to transgress.

The End of the Sixth Book.

---

909. *Thy weaker,* Eve, the "weaker vessel" of I Peter iii, 7. Even the humanist, Vives, could speak of woman as "a frail thing, and of weak discretion, and that may lightly be deceived, which thing our first mother Eve showeth, whom the Devil caught with a light argument." (Richard Hyrde's translation of Vives' *Instruction of a Christian Woman,* ed. by Watson, p. 56.)

BOOK VII

THE ARGUMENT

Raphael *at the request of* Adam *relates how and wherefore this world was first created; that God, after the expelling of* Satan *and his Angels out of Heaven, declar'd his pleasure to create another World and other Creatures to dwell therein; sends his Son with Glory and attendance of Angels to perform the work of Creation in six days: the Angels celebrate with Hymns the performance thereof, and his reascension into Heaven.*

DESCEND from Heav'n *Urania*, by that name
If rightly thou art call'd, whose Voice divine
Following, above th' *Olympian* Hill I soar,
Above the flight of *Pegasean* wing.

---

1. *Descend* is an appeal both for Urania's presence and for her guidance from the scenes of war in heaven down to the created universe and finally to earth.

Urania, in the exordium to Book I, has the double character of a tenth and heavenly Muse and of a kind of aspect of the "Spirit of God" which "moved upon the face of the waters" (Gen. 1, 2) at the Creation. "That is," Milton says in *C.D.,* I, vii, "his divine power, rather than any person." But rabbinical tradition had developed an allegory which taught that "God did not fail to have with him (at Creation) Understanding and Wisdom by means of which the world was made or created." (Ben Gerson, quoted by Fletcher, *Rabbinical Readings,* p. 111.) Long before Milton wrote, Neo-Platonic influences had fused with the biblical tradition to identify Understanding (or Knowledge) with the Urania whom Spenser invoked in *The Teares of the Muses* (499–502) as the patroness of the "knowledge" by which

> "we behold the worlds creation,
> How in his cradle first he fostred was;
> And judge of Natures cunning operation,
> How things she formed of a formelesse mas."

3. The *Olympian Hill,* like the Aonian mount Helicon of I, 15, was a haunt of the pagan Muses whose inspiration Milton intended to outsoar.

4. The allusion to Pegasus, the winged horse of the poets, prepares for the reference to Bellerophon (18 below), who rode on it to fight with the monster, Chimera. (Compare note on II, 628.)

The meaning, not the Name I call: for thou   5
Nor of the Muses nine, nor on the top
Of old *Olympus* dwell'st, but Heav'nly born,
Before the Hills appear'd, or Fountain flow'd,
Thou with Eternal Wisdom didst converse,
Wisdom thy Sister, and with her didst play   10
In presence of th' Almighty Father, pleas'd
With thy Celestial Song. Up led by thee
Into the Heav'n of Heav'ns I have presum'd,
An Earthly Guest, and drawn Empyreal Air,
Thy temp'ring; with like safety guided down   15
Return me to my Native Element:
Lest from this flying Steed unrein'd, (as once
Bellerophon, though from a lower Clime)
Dismounted, on th' *Aleian* Field I fall
Erroneous there to wander and forlorn.   20

---

9. Behind the conception of *Eternal wisdom* playing before God lies
Proverbs viii, 30, where Wisdom tells of her part in the Creation, and
adds, "Then I was by him [God], as one brought up with him: and I
was daily his delight, rejoicing ['playing' in the Vulgate] always before
him." In the *Wisdom of Solomon* vii, 17–18, Milton found Wisdom
gifted with knowledge "how the world was made" and understanding
"the operation of the elements . . . the alteration of the turning of the
sun and the change of the seasons," *etc.* In the Renaissance this quasi-
theological figure gathered prestige from the half-metaphysical wisdom of
classical philosophy, the wisdom which "is knowledge of things divine
and human, and in which is contained the relationships and the society of
men with gods mutually." (Cicero, *De officiis,* I, 143.) Drawing upon
both Hebrew and Neo-Platonic sources, Spenser dedicated *An Hymne
of Heavenly Beautie* to Sapience (*i.e.,* Wisdom),

> "The soveraine dearling of the Deity." (184.)

> "Both heaven and earth obey unto her will,
>   And all the creatures which they both containe:
>   For of her fulnesse, which the world doth fill,
>   They all partake, and do in state remaine,
>   As their great Maker did at first ordaine." (197–201.)

15. *Thy temp'ring,* because thou tempered'st the air of heaven for my
mortal breathing.

16. *Element,* the air of earth.

18. In the myth of Bellerophon's attempt to storm heaven on the
winged horse, Pegasus, Milton saw an allegory of his own boldness in
writing *Paradise Lost.* Zeus punished Bellerophon by throwing him down
onto the Aleian marshes in remotest Lycia, where he wandered, crazed
and (according to Conti, p. 964) blind, until he died.

20. *Erroneous,* wandering, a Latinism.

Half yet remains unsung, but narrower bound
Within the visible Diurnal Sphere;
Standing on Earth, not rapt above the Pole,
More safe I Sing with mortal voice, unchang'd
To hoarse or mute, though fall'n on evil days,   25
On evil days though fall'n, and evil tongues;
In darkness, and with dangers compast round,
And solitude; yet not alone, while thou
Visit'st my slumbers Nightly, or when Morn
Purples the East: still govern thou my Song,   30
Urania, and fit audience find, though few.
But drive far off the barbarous dissonance
Of *Bacchus* and his Revellers, the Race
Of that wild Rout that tore the *Thracian* Bard
In *Rhodope,* where Woods and Rocks had Ears   35
To rapture, till the savage clamor drown'd

---

22. *Diurnal Sphere,* the universe of stars making its diurnal (or daily)
movement around the earth.

23. *rapt* has its literal, Latin force of "caught up."
The *Pole* is the summit of Milton's created universe in the zenith from
the earth and, from the point of view of heaven, the nearest part, where
God's golden chain is made fast.   Compare II, 1005.

25. *evil days* is Milton's name for the Restoration period, when, for a
time, he was in danger of his life and suffered what for him was the
worse misery of *evil tongues,* the hostility of the general public.

27. *In darkness* refers to his blindness, but only—as in III, 21–55—to
contrast it with the inward illumination of Urania.

29. *Nightly:* compare III, 32, and IX, 22.

31. With the same aloofness Milton, in his preface to *Eikonoklastes,*
launched that tract "to find out her own readers: few perhaps, but those
few, such of value and substantial worth, as truth and wisdom, not re-
specting numbers and big names, have been ever wont in all ages to be
contented with."

33. *Bacchus and his Revellers,* a thin disguise for the merrymakers of
London in the first years of Charles II's reign.

34. With very similar feeling Milton had retold Ovid's story (*Met.* XI,
1–43) of the mob murder of the Thracian bard, Orpheus, by the followers of Bacchus in *Lycidas* (57–63).

35. *Rhodope,* a mountain range between Thrace and Macedonia where
Bacchus had a famous shrine.

36. Calliope, the Muse of epic poetry, was the mother of Orpheus; and
Milton saw a grim application to himself in the myth that she could not
save her son from the rage of the bacchantes, although his music had
power even over the woods and rocks.

Both Harp and Voice; nor could the Muse defend
Her Son. So fail not thou, who thee implores:
For thou art Heavn'ly, shee an empty dream.
   Say Goddess, what ensu'd when *Raphaël,*   40
The affable Arch-angel, had forewarn'd
Adam by dire example to beware
Apostasy, by what befell in Heaven
To those Apostates, lest the like befall
In Paradise to *Adam* or his Race,   45
Charg'd not to touch the interdicted Tree,
If they transgress, and slight that sole command,
So easily obey'd amid the choice
Of all tastes else to please thir appetite,
Though wand'ring. He with his consorted *Eve*   50
The story heard attentive, and was fill'd
With admiration, and deep Muse to hear
Of things so high and strange, things to thir thought
So unimaginable as hate in Heav'n,
And War so near the Peace of God in bliss   55
With such confusion: but the evil soon
Driv'n back redounded as a flood on those
From whom it sprung, impossible to mix
With Blessedness. Whence *Adam* soon repeal'd
The doubts that in his heart arose: and now   60
Led on, yet sinless, with desire to know
What nearer might concern him, how this World
Of Heav'n and Earth conspicuous first began,

---

40. Compare *Raphael, the sociable spirit,* of V, 221.

44. Compare *Apostate* in VI, 100.

46. The interdiction on which Milton's story turns is the word of God
to Adam in Paradise: "But of the tree of the knowledge of good and
evil, thou shalt not eat of it: for in the day that thou eatest thereof, thou
shalt surely die." (Gen. ii, 17.)

50. *Though wand'ring,* however freely it may wander.
consorted, associated. "Consort" was a not unusual name for a wife.

52. *admiration,* wondering attention.

57. *redounded,* thrown back. The root of the word is the Latin word
for "wave."

59. *repeal'd* preserves the French meaning of "call back."

63. *Heav'n and Earth conspicuous,* the visible sky and earth. In his
chapter on "Creation" in *C.D.* Milton distinguished between the invisible

When, and whereof created, for what cause,
What within *Eden* or without was done   65
Before his memory, as one whose drouth
Yet scarce allay'd still eyes the current stream,
Whose liquid murmur heard new thirst excites,
Proceeded thus to ask his Heav'nly Guest.

   Great things, and full of wonder in our ears,   70
Far differing from this World, thou hast reveal'd
Divine Interpreter, by favour sent
Down from the Empyrean to forewarn
Us timely of what might else have been our loss,
Unknown, which human knowledge could not reach: 75
For which to the infinitely Good we owe
Immortal thanks, and his admonishment
Receive with solemn purpose to observe
Immutably his sovran will, the end
Of what we are. But since thou hast voutsaf't   80
Gently for our instruction to impart
Things above Earthly thought, which yet concern'd
Our knowing, as to highest wisdom seem'd,
Deign to descend now lower, and relate
What may no less perhaps avail us known,   85
How first began this Heav'n which we behold
Distant so high, with moving Fires adorn'd
Innumerable, and this which yields or fills
All space, the ambient Air wide interfus'd
Imbracing round this florid Earth, what cause   90
Mov'd the Creator in his holy Rest

---

creation of God, the empyrean heaven and the angels, and the visible
creation of this universe.

66. *drouth*, thirst.

72. *Divine Interpreter* is a reminiscence of Virgil's title for Mercury as
the spokesman of the gods (*Aen.* IV, 378), but the word was familiar
enough in Milton's connection for Bunyan to send his Pilgrim to the
house of an interpreter (*i.e.*, of sacred mysteries) before his conflict with
Apolyon (the Devil).

79. *end*, ultimate purpose. Compare the "end" of man of the Cate-
chism.

83. *seem'd*, seemed good, *i.e.*, seemed wise to permit.

90. *florid*, flowery.

Through all Eternity so late to build
In *Chaos,* and the work begun, how soon
Absolv'd, if unforbid thou mayst unfold
What wee, not to explore the secrets ask   95
Of his Eternal Empire, but the more
To magnify his works, the more we know.
And the great Light of Day yet wants to run
Much of his Race though steep, suspense in Heav'n
Held by thy voice, thy potent voice he hears,   100
And longer will delay to hear thee tell
His Generation, and the rising Birth
Of Nature from the unapparent Deep:
Or if the Star of Ev'ning and the Moon
Haste to thy audience, Night with her will bring   105
Silence, and Sleep list'ning to thee will watch,
Or we can bid his absence, till thy Song
End, and dismiss thee ere the Morning shine.
    Thus *Adam* his illustrious Guest besought:
And thus the Godlike Angel answer'd mild.   110
This also thy request with caution askt
Obtain: though to recount Almighty works
What words or tongue of Seraph can suffice,
Or heart of man suffice to comprehend?
Yet what thou canst attain, which best may serve   115
To glorify the Maker, and infer
Thee also happier, shall not be withheld

---

92. To Adam, as to many a medieval Schoolman and rabbi, and to Milton himself (*C.D.* I, vii), it was "not imaginable that God should have been wholly occupied from eternity in decreeing that which was to be created in a period of six days."

94. *Absolv'd,* has its Latin meaning, "finished."

98. *wants,* is short of (having run).

99. *suspense* is used here analogously to its use in VI, 580.

103. The *Deep,* Chaos, is unapparent, *i.e.,* invisible, not only because walled out of Milton's universe by the opaque shell, but also because it was "confused and formless" (*C.D.* I, vii). Milton instinctively thought of creation in terms of the imposition of "forms" (in the Platonic sense) upon absolutely unformed matter. (Compare l. 233 below.)

105. *audience,* hearing.

106. *watch,* stay awake, keep vigil.

116. *infer,* prove, indicate.

Thy hearing, such Commission from above
I have receiv'd, to answer thy desire
Of knowledge within bounds; beyond abstain   120
To ask, nor let thine own inventions hope
Things not reveal'd which th' invisible King,
Only Omniscient hath supprest in Night,
To none communicable in Earth or Heaven:
Anough is left besides to search and know.   125
But Knowledge is as food, and needs no less
Her Temperance over Appetite, to know
In measure what the mind may well contain,
Oppresses else with Surfeit, and soon turns
Wisdom to Folly, as Nourishment to Wind.   130
  Know then, that after *Lucifer* from Heav'n
(So call him, brighter once amidst the Host
Of Angels, than that Star the Stars among)
Fell with his flaming Legions through the Deep
Into his place, and the great Son return'd   135

120. For the principle of *knowledge within bounds* see the Introduction, §21.

121. *inventions* are equivalent to the *Conjecture* of VIII, 76, the guesswork of science.

hope, hope for, expect.

123. Perhaps Milton remembered Virgil's fear over revealing the secrets hid in darkness by the infernal gods. (*Aen.* VI, 267.)

126. To justify this comparison Keightley quoted from Davenant's *Gondibert:*

> "For though books serve as diet for the mind,
>   If knowledge, early got, self-value breeds,
>   By false digestion it is turned to wind,
>   And what should nourish on the eater feeds."
>   (II, viii, 22.)

132. *So call him* is said in allusion to Satan's loss of his angelic name when he revolted. Compare I, 361, and its note.

133. The *Star* is, of course, Venus as the morning star, bringing or announcing the daylight, as the name *Lucifer* literally signifies. Milton, like Spenser, thought of all the angels as

>   "bright,
> All glistring glorious in their Makers light";
>   (*An Hymne of Heavenly Love,* 55–6)

and of Satan as

> "The brightest angell, even the Child of Light."   (83.)

Compare the note on I, 84.

Victorious with his Saints, th' Omnipotent
Eternal Father from his Throne beheld
Thir multitude, and to his Son thus spake.
  At least our envious Foe hath fail'd, who thought
All like himself rebellious, by whose aid   140
This inaccessible high strength, the seat
Of Deity supreme, us dispossest,
He trusted to have seiz'd, and into fraud
Drew many, whom thir place knows here no more;
Yet far the greater part have kept, I see,   145
Thir station, Heav'n yet populous retains
Number sufficient to possess her Realms
Though wide, and this high Temple to frequent
With Ministeries due and solemn Rites:
But lest his heart exalt him in the harm   150
Already done, to have dispeopl'd Heav'n,
My damage fondly deem'd, I can repair
That detriment, if such it be to lose
Self-lost, and in a moment will create
Another World, out of one man a Race   155
Of men innumerable, there to dwell,
Not here, till by degrees of merit rais'd
They open to themselves at length the way
Up hither, under long obedience tri'd,
And Earth be chang'd to Heav'n, and Heav'n to Earth,   160
One Kingdom, Joy and Union without end.
Meanwhile inhabit lax, ye Powers of Heav'n,

---

136. As in VI, 767, *Saints* signifies the loyal angels.

137. The throne is that seen by St. John, "set in heaven, and one sat on the throne." (Rev. iv, 2.)

142. *us dispossest,* after dispossessing us.

143. *fraud* has its Latin meaning of "injury" and "treachery."

144. "Neither shall his place know him any more" is the strong expression for the lot of the dead in Job vii, 10.

154. *Self-lost,* lost with my free consent.

160. Milton imagined the Fall as frustrating God's intention that Adam and his descendants should, little by little, by a process the reverse of that degradation of the rebellious angels into the elements of earth to which Mammon refers in II, 275, develop into beings like the angels.

162. *inhabit lax,* settle widely, a Latinism. It seems that the angels are invited to go and make homes for themselves in the heavenly regions abandoned by Satan's followers.

And thou my Word, begotten Son, by thee
This I perform, speak thou, and be it done:
My overshadowing Spirit and might with thee   165
I send along, ride forth, and bid the Deep
Within appointed bounds be Heav'n and Earth.
Boundless the Deep, because I am who fill
Infinitude, nor vacuous the space.
Though I uncircumscrib'd myself retire,   170
And put not forth my goodness, which is free
To act or not, Necessity and Chance
Approach not mee, and what I will is Fate.
　　So spake th' Almighty, and to what he spake
His Word, the Filial Godhead, gave effect.   175
Immediate are the Acts of God, more swift
Than time or motion, but to human ears

163. In *C.D.* I, v, Milton insisted that the Son was voluntarily begotten
by the Father, that creation was accomplished through the Son by the
Father, and that the Son "in his capacity of creator, is himself called the
first born of every creature." (Col. i, 17. Compare the notes on III,
170 and 384.)

168. Milton argued against the orthodox Christian view that the world
was created out of nothing and insisted that before the creation there
"was a substance, . . . derivable from no other source than from the
fountain of every substance [*i.e.*, God], though at first confused and
formless." (*C.D.*, I, vii.)

170. Anent this retirement of God from creation M. Saurat, who sees in
it an attempt to exculpate God from the imperfection of the material
world, cites the *Zohar:* "When we think that the Holy One (Blessed be
He) is infinite and that he fills everything, it is easily understood that
any creation would have been impossible without the *zimzum* ['retrac-
tion']. . . . Since the Light of God is of such purity and strength that
it eclipses all things, even the higher angels, . . . the Holy One (Blessed
be He), to make possible the existence of celestial and material worlds,
withdrew his almighty Light from a part of himself." (Milton, *Man and
Thinker,* p. 287.) For the essence of the principle, however, we need
go no further than the saying of John Smith that God "is that omnipres-
ent life that penetrates all things. . . . The world is in God, rather than
God in the world." (Quoted by G. P. H. Pawson, *The Cambridge
Platonists,* p. 41.)

176. Milton had the authority of all the rabbinical commentators quoted
in the Buxtorf Bible on the story of the Creation in six days in Genesis, i,
that the creative act was instantaneous, and its consequences unfolded in
accordance with the Bible story. And he had the example of Du Bartas'
line,
　　"The Word and Deed, all in an instant wrought." (551.)

Cannot without procéss of speech be told,
So told as earthly notion can receive.
Great triumph and rejoicing was in Heav'n   180
When such was heard declar'd the Almighty's will;
Glory they sung to the most High, good will
To future men, and in thir dwellings peace:
Glory to him whose just avenging ire
Had driven out th' ungodly from his sight   185
And th' habitations of the just; to him
Glory and praise, whose wisdom had ordain'd
Good out of evil to create, instead
Of Spirits malign a better Race to bring
Into thir vacant room, and thence diffuse   190
His good to Worlds and Ages infinite.
So sang the Hierarchies: Meanwhile the Son
On his great Expedition now appear'd,
Girt with Omnipotence, with Radiance crown'd
Of Majesty Divine, Sapience and Love   195
Immense, and all his Father in him shone.
About his Chariot numberless were pour'd
Cherub and Seraph, Potentates and Thrones,
And Virtues, winged Spirits, and Chariots wing'd,
From the Armory of God, where stand of old   200
Myriads between two brazen Mountains lodg'd
Against a solemn day, harness't at hand,

---

179. *earthly notion,* human intelligence.

182. The song is like that of the angels to the shepherds at Christ's birth (Luke ii, 13–14), but Milton drew his idea that the angels "shouted for joy before God at the creation" from Job xxxviii, 7, a verse which he quoted in *C.D.,* I, vii, to prove that the angels existed before our universe. Compare *Nativity Ode,* 119–21.

194. *Girt;* compare Psalm xviii, 39: "For thou hast girded me with strength unto the battle."

196. Distinguishing the glory of the Son from that of the Father, as inferior, Milton quoted Hebrews i, 3; the Son is "the brightness of his glory, and the express image of his person." *C.D.* I, vii. Compare III, 138–40.

200. *Armoury of God* is a phrase from Jeremiah l, 25.

201. The *brazen Mountains* seem to be a reminiscence of Zechariah's vision of four chariots coming "out from between two mountains; and the mountains were mountains of brass." (Zech. vi, 1.)

202. *Against,* in readiness for.

Celestial Equipage; and now came forth
Spontaneous, for within them Spirit liv'd,
Attendant on thir Lord: Heav'n op'n'd wide   205
Her ever-during Gates, Harmonious sound
On golden Hinges moving, to let forth
The King of Glory in his powerful Word
And Spirit coming to create new Worlds.
On heav'nly ground they stood, and from the shore   210
They view'd the vast immeasurable Abyss
Outrageous as a Sea, dark, wasteful, wild,
Up from the bottom turn'd by furious winds
And surging waves, as Mountains to assault
Heav'n's highth, and with the Centre mix the Pole.   215
  Silence, ye troubl'd waves, and thou Deep, peace,
Said then th' Omnific Word, your discord end:
  Nor stay'd, but on the Wings of Cherubim
Uplifted, in Paternal Glory rode
Far into *Chaos,* and the World unborn;   220
For *Chaos* heard his voice: him all his Train
Follow'd in bright procession to behold
Creation, and the wonders of his might.
Then stay'd the fervid Wheels, and in his hand
He took the golden Compasses, prepar'd   225

204. Compare the note on VI, 750.

205. The opening gates suggested Psalm xxiv, 9: "Lift up your heads,
O ye gates; . . . and the King of glory shall come in."

211. The view of Chaos is comparable to Satan's view of it when the
infernal doors open "and on thir hinges grate Harsh thunder." (II,
881–2.)

217. *Omnific,* all-creating.

218. Compare the divine chariot of the wings of cherubim in VI, 827.

224. *fervid* seems to be a Latinism, used of the wheels that gleam with
motion, but it may be a reminiscence of "the appearance of the wheels"
of the chariot in Ezekiel (i, 16), which "was like unto the colour of a
beryl."

225. Milton thought of Wisdom's account of the Creation in Proverbs
viii, 27: "When he prepared the heavens, I was there: when he set a
compass upon the face of the depth." Here "compass" means a circuit,
but Rabbi Kimchi's commentary in the Buxtorf Bible says that the circle
was actually made "with a compass, for there are two legs to the compass, one standing still and the second going round the circle. And
there is a point in the midst of the circle. And the earth is as the point,
for . . . the heavens surround the earth as a circle." (Quoted by Flet-

In God's Eternal store, to circumscribe
This Universe, and all created things:
One foot he centred, and the other turn'd
Round through the vast profundity obscure,
And said, thus far extend, thus far thy bounds,   230
This be thy just Circumference, O World.
Thus God the Heav'n created, thus the Earth,
Matter unform'd and void: Darkness profound
Cover'd th' Abyss: but on the wat'ry calm
His brooding wings the Spirit of God outspread,   235
And vital virtue infus'd, and vital warmth
Throughout the fluid Mass, but downward purg'd
The black tartareous cold Infernal dregs
Adverse to life; then founded, then conglob'd
Like things to like, the rest to several place   240
Disparted, and between spun out the Air,
And Earth self-balanc't on her Centre hung.
   Let there be Light, said God, and forthwith Light
Ethereal, first of things, quintessence pure

cher, *Rabbinical Readings,* p. 108.)   The divine hand, drawing the circle
in Chaos, was a familiar printer's ornament and must have been etched
on Milton's memory.   Perhaps also he remembered Dante's reference to
him, "who rolled the compass round the limit of the Universe." (*Paradiso* xix, 40–2.)

   233. The conception in Plato's *Timaeus* (50, E) of formless matter
harmonized with the account of the earth as without form and void, with
darkness upon the face of the deep in Genesis i, 2.   From this point
Milton scrupulously follows the account of Creation in Genesis.

   235. Milton thought of "the Spirit of God [which] moved upon the
face of the waters" (Gen. 1, 2) at Creation as a power giving form to the
amorphous elements.   Compare the note on 1 above.

   238. *tartareous* and *cold* seem inconsistent, but Milton thought of the
crudest matter as falling closest to the centre of the earth, where both
Greek and Christian tradition put Tartarus, while the more volatile and
impressionable matter flew up to become air or starry fire.

   239. *founded* and *conglob'd* seem to mean that Messiah established
and moulded the celestial spheres, using homogeneous elements.

   242. The *Earth self-balanc't* derives from Job xxvi, 7:   "He stretcheth
out the north over the empty place, and hangeth the earth upon nothing."
Fletcher (*Rabbinical Readings,* p. 137) cites Ben Gerson's commentary on
"upon nothing"; "that is, on something that has no existence in reality,
and this is the centre of the earth, from which point the earth is suspended."   Compare the Introduction, §9.

   243. *Let there be Light* is God's first creative command.   (Gen. i, 3.)

Sprung from the Deep, and from her Native East   245
To journey through the airy gloom began,
Spher'd in a radiant Cloud, for yet the Sun
Was not; shee in a cloudy Tabernacle
Sojourn'd the while. God saw the Light was good;
And light from darkness by the Hemisphere   250
Divided: Light the Day, and Darkness Night
He nam'd. Thus was the first Day Ev'n and Morn:
Nor past uncelebrated, nor unsung
By the Celestial Quires, when Orient Light
Exhaling first from Darkness they beheld: 255
Birth-day of Heav'n and Earth; with joy and shout
The hollow Universal Orb they fill'd,
And touch't thir Golden Harps, and hymning prais'd
God and his works, Creator him they sung,
Both when first Ev'ning was, and when first Morn.   260
    Again, God said, let there be Firmament
Amid the Waters, and let it divide
The Waters from the Waters: and God made
The Firmament, expanse of liquid, pure,
Transparent, Elemental Air, diffus'd   265

---

247. Milton's conception is illuminated by Rashi's commentary on the
words of Psalm xix, 4, "In them [the heavens] hath he set a tabernacle
for the sun." Fletcher quotes, "On the first day the lights [sun, moon,
and stars] were created, and on the fourth day he [God] ordered them
to be placed in the firmament." (*Rabbinical Readings*, p. 150.) Although "we cannot form any conception of light independent of a
luminary," Milton argued (*C.D.*, I, vii) that "we do not therefore infer
that a luminary is the same as light."

249. Compare Genesis i, 4–5: "And God saw the light that it was
good: and God divided the light from the darkness. And God called
the light Day, and the darkness he called Night. And the evening and
the morning were the first day."

253. Compare the note on 182 above.

261. Compare Genesis i, 6–8: "And God said, Let there be a firmament in the midst of the waters. . . . And God made the firmament, and
divided the waters which were under the firmament from the waters
which were above the firmament. . . . And God called the firmament
heaven. . . ."
    The biblical firmament is imagined as the concave of the shell of the
universe, dividing the waters of the universe from the waves of Chaos
and the "Glassy Sea" (VII, 619) outside. It corresponded to Milton's
conception of Chaos as a kind of vast sea through which Satan voyaged
to the shell of the universe.

In circuit to the uttermost convex
Of this great Round: partition firm and sure,
The Waters underneath from those above
Dividing: for as Earth, so he the World
Built on circumfluous Waters calm, in wide   270
Crystálline Ocean, and the loud misrule
Of *Chaos* far remov'd, lest fierce extremes
Contiguous might distemper the whole frame:
And Heav'n he nam'd the Firmament: So Ev'n
And Morning *Chorus* sung the second Day.   275
     The Earth was form'd, but in the Womb as yet
Of Waters, Embryon immature involv'd,
Appear'd not: over all the face of Earth
Main Ocean flow'd, not idle, but with warm
Prolific humour soft'ning all her Globe,   280
Fermented the great Mother to conceive,
Satiate with genial moisture, when God said
Be gather'd now ye Waters under Heav'n
Into one place, and let dry Land appear.
Immediately the Mountains huge appear   285
Emergent, and thir broad bare backs upheave
Into the Clouds, thir tops ascend the Sky:
So high as heav'd the tumid Hills, so low
Down sunk a hollow bottom broad and deep,
Capacious bed of Waters: thither they   290
Hasted with glad precipitance, uproll'd
As drops on dust conglobing from the dry;
Part rise in crystal Wall, or ridge direct,

---

267. *Round*, the universe.

269. *World*, the universe.

271. *misrule;* compare the "universal hubbub" of II, 951.

280. The *Prolific humour* of the sea fertilizing Mother Earth is less biblical than it is in keeping with Ovid's account of the creation (*Met.*, I, 1–51) and with Lucretius' theory of organic life (*De rerum natura*, V, 783–820), but it is in harmony with Milton's conception of the impregnating spirit brooding on the waters.

282. *genial*, fertilizing, impregnating.

283. Compare Genesis i, 9: "And God said, Let the waters under the heaven be gathered together unto one place, and let the dry land appear."

291. Compare the account of Creation in Psalm civ, 8, where, at God's command, the waters "go up by the mountains; they go down by the valleys unto the place which thou hast founded for them."

For haste; such flight the great command impress'd
On the swift floods: as Armies at the call   295
Of Trumpet (for of Armies thou hast heard)
Troop to thir Standard, so the wat'ry throng,
Wave rolling after Wave, where way they found,
If steep, with torrent rapture, if through Plain,
Soft-ebbing; nor withstood them Rock or Hill,   300
But they, or under ground, or circuit wide
With Serpent error wand'ring, found thir way,
And on the washy Ooze deep Channels wore;
Easy, ere God had bid the ground be dry,
All but within those banks, where Rivers now   305
Stream, and perpetual draw thir humid train.
The dry Land, Earth, and the great receptacle
Of congregated Waters he call'd Seas:
And saw that it was good, and said, Let th' Earth
Put forth the verdant Grass, Herb yielding Seed,   310
And Fruit Tree yielding Fruit after her kind;
Whose Seed is in herself upon the Earth.
He scarce had said, when the bare Earth, till then
Desert and bare, unsightly, unadorn'd,
Brought forth the tender Grass, whose verdure clad   315
Her Universal Face with pleasant green,
Then Herbs of every leaf, that sudden flow'r'd
Op'ning thir various colours, and made gay
Her bosom smelling sweet: and these scarce blown,

---

302. *error,* meandering, twisting, straying (in serpentine coils).

303. *Ooze,* wet mud, especially in the bed of a river.

306. *humid train,* liquid flow.

309. Compare Genesis i, 11: "And God said, Let the earth bring forth
grass, the herb yielding seed, and the fruit tree yielding fruit after his
kind, whose seed is in itself upon the earth."

315. An at least very striking analogue to Milton's thought and lan-
gauge is cited from Du Bartas' (25 rc) by G. C. Taylor:

> "Change, change (quoth he), O fair and firmest Globe,
> Thy mourning weed, to a green gallant Robe;
>
> .   .   .   .
>
> Cheer thy sad brows and stately garnish them
> With a rich fragrant, flow'ry Diadem;
> Lay forth thy locks and paint thee (Lady-like)
> With freshest colours on thy sallow cheek."

Forth flourish't thick the clust'ring Vine, forth crept   320
The smelling Gourd, up stood the corny Reed
Embattl'd in her field: and the humble Shrub,
And Bush with frizzl'd hair implicit: last
Rose as in Dance the stately Trees, and spread
Thir branches hung with copious Fruit: or gemm'd   325
Thir Blossoms: with high Woods the Hills were crown'd,
With tufts the valleys and each fountain side,
With borders long the Rivers. That Earth now
Seem'd like to Heav'n, a seat where Gods might dwell,
Or wander with delight, and love to haunt   330
Her sacred shades: though God had yet not rain'd
Upon the Earth, and man to till the ground
None was, but from the Earth a dewy Mist
Went up and water'd all the ground, and each
Plant of the field, which ere it was in the Earth   335
God made, and every Herb, before it grew
On the green stem; God saw that it was good:
So Ev'n and Morn recorded the Third Day.
   Again th' Almighty spake: Let there be Lights
High in th' expanse of Heaven to divide   340

---

321. *corny Reed,* corn, *i.e.,* grain generally. Compare "balmy Reed"
in V, 23.

322. Observe the comparison of a "field of Ceres" to an army with
ported spears in IV, 980–3.

323. With this use of *frizzl'd* the N. E. D. parallels Browne's *Britan-
nia's Pastorals:*
           "The frizled coates which doe the mountaines hide."
implicit has its Latin meaning of "tangled."

327. *tufts,* groves.

331. Compare Genesis ii, 5–6: ". . . for the Lord God had not
caused it to rain upon the earth, and there was not a man to till the
ground. But there went up a mist from the earth, and watered the
whole face of the ground."

335. The conception in Genesis ii, 5, that God made "every plant of
the field before it was in the earth, and every herb of the field before it
grew," was stressed by rabbinical commentators as evidence that the Creation was a single act, done in an instant; and it harmonized with the
Platonic doctrine that everything in this world has its ideal form or
pattern in the heaven.

339. This and the following thirteen lines are a close paraphrase of
Genesis i, 14–19.

The Day from Night; and let them be for Signs,
For Seasons, and for Days, and circling Years,
And let them be for Lights as I ordain
Thir Office in the Firmament of Heav'n
To give Light on the Earth; and it was so.   345
And God made two great Lights, great for thir use
To Man, the greater to have rule by Day,
The less by Night altern: and made the Stars,
And set them in the Firmament of Heav'n
To illuminate the Earth, and rule the Day   350
In thir vicissitude, and rule the Night,
And Light from Darkness to divide. God saw, ·
Surveying his great Work, that it was good:
For of Celestial Bodies first the Sun
A mighty Sphere he fram'd, unlightsome first,   355
Though of Ethereal Mould: then form'd the Moon
Globose, and every magnitude of Stars,
And sow'd with Stars the Heav'n thick as a field:
Of Light by far the greater part he took,
Transplanted from her cloudy Shrine, and plac'd   360
In the Sun's Orb, made porous to receive
And drink the liquid Light, firm to retain
Her gather'd beams, great Palace now of Light.
Hither as to thir Fountain other Stars
Repairing, in thir gold'n Urns draw Light,   365
And hence the Morning Planet gilds her horns;
By tincture or reflection they augment
Thir small peculiar, though from human sight
So far remote, with diminution seen.
First in his East the glorious Lamp was seen,   370
Regent of Day, and all th' Horizon round

---

351. *vicissitude,* alternation.   Compare VI, 8.

356. *Mould,* substance.

364. The conception of the sun as the fountain of light for all the
other stars goes back to Pliny's *Natural History,* II, iv, 6.

366. *the Morning Planet gilds her horns* is an allusion to the fact
which Galileo had discovered, that Venus has phases like those of the
moon.

367. Either by absorbing (*tincture*) or by reflecting the sun's rays
Milton thought of the planets as increasing their individual (peculiar)
radiance.

Invested with bright Rays, jocund to run
His Longitude through Heav'n's high road: the gray
Dawn, and the *Pleiades* before him danc'd
Shedding sweet influence: less bright the Moon,   375
But opposite in levell'd West was set
His mirror, with full face borrowing her Light
From him, for other light she needed none
In that aspect, and still that distance keeps
Till night, then in the East her turn she shines,   380
Revolv'd on Heav'n's great Axle, and her Reign
With thousand lesser Lights dividual holds,
With thousand thousand Stars, that then appear'd
Spangling the Hemisphere: then first adorn'd
With thir bright Luminaries that Set and Rose,   385
Glad Ev'ning and glad Morn crown'd the fourth day.
    And God said, let the Waters generate
Reptile with Spawn abundant, living Soul:
And let Fowl fly above the Earth, with wings
Display'd on the op'n Firmament of Heav'n.   390
And God created the great Whales, and each
Soul living, each that crept, which plenteously
The waters generated by thir kinds,
And every Bird of wing after his kind;
And saw that it was good, and bless'd them, saying,   395
Be fruitful, multiply, and in the Seas

---

373. *Longitude,* course from east to west (a usage the reverse of ours today).   Compare IV, 539.

374. There is an allusion to "the sweet influences of Pleiades" (Job xxxviii, 31) and perhaps a recollection of Guido Reni's famous picture of the chariot of the sun, with the dawn flying before it, and seven nymphs —who correspond in number at least with the Pleiades—trooping alongside.

376. *levell'd West,* the horizontal west, straight opposite to the sun, whose mirror she is.

379. *aspect,* situation in the sky.

382. *dividual,* which modifies *Reign,* has its Latin meaning of "divided" or "dividable."

387. The next twelve lines closely paraphrase Genesis i, 20–23.

388. *Reptile* is used to mean any reptant, or creeping thing in the broadest sense and obviously includes the fish.
Soul is used in Genesis to mean life, and here it means living things generally.

And Lakes and running Streams the waters fill;
And let the Fowl be multipli'd on the Earth.
Forthwith the Sounds and Seas, each Creek and Bay
With Fry innumerable swarm, and Shoals   400
Of Fish that with thir Fins and shining Scales
Glide under the green Wave, in Sculls that oft
Bank the mid Sea: part single or with mate
Graze the Seaweed thir pasture, and through Groves
Of Coral stray, or sporting with quick glance   405
Show to the Sun thir wav'd coats dropt with Gold,
Or in thir Pearly shells at ease, attend
Moist nutriment, or under Rocks thir food
In jointed Armor watch: on smooth the Seal,
And bended Dolphins play: part huge of bulk   410
Wallowing unwieldy, enormous in thir Gait
Tempest the Ocean: there Leviathan
Hugest of living Creatures, on the Deep
Stretcht like a Promontory sleeps or swims,
And seems a moving Land, and at his Gills   415
Draws in, and at his Trunk spouts out a Sea.
Meanwhile the tepid Caves, and Fens and shores
Thir Brood as numerous hatch, from the Egg that soon
Bursting with kindly rupture forth disclos'd
Thir callow young, but feather'd soon and fledge   420
They summ'd thir Pens, and soaring th' air sublime
With clang despis'd the ground, under a cloud
In prospect; there the Eagle and the Stork
On Cliffs and Cedar tops thir Eyries build:

---

402. *Sculls*, schools.

403. *Bank the mid Sea*, make a bank (with their numbers) in mid-ocean.

409. *on smooth*, on the smooth sea.

412. Compare the simile of the Leviathan in I, 200–205.

419. *kindly*, natural.

420. *callow*, unfledged.
fledge, fledged.

421. *summ'd their Pens*, developed complete plumage.
sublime, aloft.   Compare its use in II, 528, and VI, 771.

422. *under a cloud*, i.e., of the mass of birds (?).

423. *In prospect*, in view (*i.e.*, as seen from above).

Part loosely wing the Region, part more wise   425
In common, rang'd in figure wedge thir way,
Intelligent of seasons, and set forth
Thir Aery Caravan high over Seas
Flying, and over Lands with mutual wing
Easing thir flight; so steers the prudent Crane   430
Her annual Voyage, borne on Winds; the Air
Floats, as they pass, fann'd with unnumber'd plumes:
From Branch to Branch the smaller Birds with song
Solac'd the Woods, and spread thir painted wings
Till Ev'n, nor then the solemn Nightingale   435
Ceas'd warbling, but all night tun'd her soft lays:
Others on Silver Lakes and Rivers Bath'd
Thir downy Breast; the Swan with Arched neck
Between her white wings mantling proudly, Rows
Her state with Oary feet: yet oft they quit   440
The Dank, and rising on stiff Pennons, tow'r
The mid Aereal Sky: Others on ground
Walk'd firm; the crested Cock whose clarion sounds
The silent hours, and th' other whose gay Train
Adorns him, colour'd with the Florid hue   445
Of Rainbows and Starry Eyes. The Waters thus
With Fish replenisht, and the Air with Fowl,
Ev'ning and Morn solémniz'd the Fift day.
   The Sixt, and of Creation last arose
With Ev'ning Harps and Matin, when God said,   450
Let th' Earth bring forth Soul living in her kind,
Cattle and Creeping things, and Beast of the Earth,
Each in their kind. The Earth obey'd, and straight

425. *loosely,* separately, alone.
Region: the upper air. Compare "the region cloud" of Shakespeare's
Sonnet xxxiii, and the note on I, 516.

427. *Intelligent,* conscious, comprehending.

429. *mutual;* perhaps the meaning is that the bird at the head of the
V is constantly relieved from behind.

432. *floats,* undulates, is fanned into waves.

439. *mantling:* compare the mantling wings of the seraphs in V, 279.

441. *The Dank,* the water.
tow'r, soar high in air.

450. The command of God is based on Genesis i, 24–25.

451. "Fowle," for "Soul," is the reading of the early editions.

Op'ning her fertile Womb teem'd at a Birth
Innumerous living Creatures, perfet forms,   455
Limb'd and full grown: out of the ground up rose
As from his Lair the wild Beast where he wons
In Forest wild, in Thicket, Brake, or Den;
Among the Trees in Pairs they rose, they walk'd:
The Cattle in the Fields and Meadows green: 460
Those rare and solitary, these in flocks
Pasturing at once, and in broad Herds upsprung.
The grassy Clods now Calv'd, now half appear'd
The Tawny Lion, pawing to get free
His hinder parts, then springs as broke from Bonds,   465
And Rampant shakes his Brinded mane; the Ounce,
The Libbard, and the Tiger, as the Mole
Rising, the crumbl'd Earth above them threw
In Hillocks; the swift Stag from under ground
Bore up his branching head: scarce from his mould   470
Behemoth biggest born of Earth upheav'd
His vastness: Fleec't the Flocks and bleating rose,
As Plants: ambiguous between Sea and Land
The River Horse and scaly Crocodile.
At once came forth whatever creeps the ground,   475
Insect or Worm; those wav'd thir limber fans

---

454. *teem'd*, bore, brought forth.

455. *Innumerous*, countless.

457. *wons*, lives, dwells.

461. *rare*, few, scattered. The word keeps its Latin meaning.

463. The calving clods and indeed the entire treatment of this passage suggest the doctrine of Lucretius that the earth, our *alma mater*, when fertilized by moisture in her prime, brought forth all manner of creatures. (*De rerum natura*, II, 991–8.)

466. *Brinded*, brindled.
Ounce, lynx or panther.

471. *Behemoth*: the Hebrew word, occurring in Job xl, 15, means a great beast—perhaps the elephant in Milton's mind.

473. *As Plants*, like plants, *i.e.*, growing out of the earth.
ambiguous, uncertain.

474. *River Horse* literally translates the Greek words which, transliterated, give "hippopotamus."

476. *Worm* includes the serpents. In IX, 1068 Adam calls Satan "that false worm."

For wings, and smallest Lineaments exact
In all the Liveries deckt of Summer's pride
With spots of Gold and Purple, azure and green:
These as a line thir long dimension drew,   480
Streaking the ground with sinuous trace; not all
Minims of Nature; some of Serpent kind
Wondrous in length and corpulence involv'd
Thir Snaky folds, and added wings.   First crept
The Parsimonious Emmet, provident   485
Of future, in small room large heart enclos'd,
Pattern of just equality perhaps
Hereafter, join'd in her popular Tribes
Of Commonalty: swarming next appear'd
The Female Bee that feeds her Husband Drone   490
Deliciously, and builds her waxen Cells
With Honey stor'd: the rest are numberless,
And thou thir Natures know'st, and gav'st them Names,
Needless to thee repeated; nor unknown
The Serpent subtl'st Beast of all the field,   495
Of huge extent sometimes, with brazen Eyes
And hairy Mane terrific, though to thee
Not noxious, but obedient at thy call.
Now Heav'n in all her Glory shone, and roll'd
Her motions, as the great first-Mover's hand   500

477. *Lineaments exact* refers to the delicate parts and colours of insects.

478. *Liveries,* costumes.

480. *as a line,* like a line (*i.e.,* drawn on paper). *dimension,* length.

482. *Minims,* tiny creatures.

483. *corpulence involv'd,* coiled or tangled body.

484. The addition of wings seems to indicate that, like Lucretius, Milton thought of the earth in the beginning as bringing forth monsters. (Compare *De rerum natura* V, 837–854.)

485. The *Emmet* evokes Horace's ant, which was not ignorant or heedless of the future. (*Satires* I, i, 35.)

490. Milton seems to have confused the queen bee with the drones.

493. Compare VIII, 352.

497. Milton imagined the serpent, before it was cursed for its part in Eve's temptation, as a different creature from its subsequent self. Here he embellishes it with a mane, like the sea-serpents which Virgil describes as devouring Laocoön and his sons. (*Aen.* II, 203–207.)

498. *noxious,* dangerous, hurtful.

First wheel'd thir course; Earth in her rich attire
Consummate lovely smil'd; Air, Water, Earth,
By Fowl, Fish, Beast, was flown, was swum, was walkt
Frequent; and of the Sixt day yet remain'd;
There wanted yet the Master work, the end   505
Of all yet done; a Creature who not prone
And Brute as other Creatures, but endu'd
With Sanctity of Reason, might erect
His Stature, and upright with Front serene
Govern the rest, self-knowing, and from thence   510
Magnanimous to correspond with Heav'n,
But grateful to acknowledge whence his good
Descends, thither with heart and voice and eyes
Directed in Devotion, to adore
And worship God Supreme who made him chief   515
Of all his works: therefore the Omnipotent
Eternal Father (For where is not hee
Present) thus to his Son audibly spake.
    Let us make now Man in our image, Man
In our similitude, and let them rule   520

---

503. Compare the impersonal, Latin construction with that in VI, 335.

504. *Frequent*, in throngs.

505. *the end*, the object. Compare the note on 79 above.

509. The belief that man's upright attitude is a symbol of a kind of
divinity was widespread. Cicero's book *On the Nature of the Gods* (II,
lvi) and Lactantius' *Divine Institutes* (II, i, § 15–18) stated it in historic
passages. G. C. Taylor compares Du Bartas' lnes:

> "Yet, *not his Face down to the earth-ward bending*,
>   Like Beasts that but regard their belly, . . .
>   . . . but towards the Azure Skyes.
>   Also thou plantedst the Intellectual Pow'r." (53 rc)

The belief goes back to Plato's *Timaeus* (90 A), but its most classical
statement was by Ovid. (*Met.*, I, 81–6.)

510. *from thence*, on that account.

511. *correspond*, communicate.

518. For this audible speech of the Father in the empyrean heaven
with the Son on earth Milton probably felt that he had a precedent in
the voice from heaven which spoke audibly at the baptism and transfiguration of Christ. Compare the note on VI, 728. Line 589 below
points out that by his omnipresence God was with his Son while he was
also in heaven.

519. The next five lines paraphrase Genesis i, 26.

Over the Fish and Fowl of Sea and Air,
Beast of the Field, and over all the Earth,
And every creeping thing that creeps the ground.
This said, he form'd thee, *Adam,* thee O Man
Dust of the ground, and in thy nostrils breath'd   525
The breath of Life; in his own Image hee
Created thee, in the Image of God
Express, and thou becam'st a living Soul.
Male he created thee, but thy consort
Female for Race; then bless'd Mankind, and said,   530
Be fruitful, multiply, and fill the Earth,
Subdue it, and throughout Dominion hold
Over Fish of the Sea, and Fowl of the Air,
And every living thing that moves on the Earth.
Wherever thus created, for no place   535
Is yet distinct by name, thence, as thou know'st
He brought thee into this delicious Grove,
This Garden, planted with the Trees of God,
Delectable both to behold and taste;
And freely all thir pleasant fruit for food   540
Gave thee, all sorts are here that all th' Earth yields,
Variety without end; but of the Tree
Which tasted works knowledge of Good and Evil,
Thou may'st not; in the day thou eat'st, thou di'st;
Death is the penalty impos'd, beware,   545
And govern well thy appetite, lest sin
Surprise thee, and her black attendant Death.
Here finish'd hee, and all that he had made
View'd, and behold all was entirely good;
So Ev'n and Morn accomplish'd the Sixt day: 550
Yet not till the Creator from his work,
Desisting, though unwearied, up return'd
Up to the Heav'n of Heav'ns his high abode,

---

524. Raphael goes on, speaking directly to Adam, to paraphrase Genesis
i, 27–31.

528. *Express* has its Latin force of "manifest," or perhaps "moulded."

531. The quoted lines are a paraphrase of Genesis i, 28.

537. Genesis ii, 15, says that God put Adam into the Garden and in
the Apochryphal book of II Esdras, iii, 6, Milton read, "And thou leddest
him into paradise, which thy right hand had planted."

548. The emphatic *hee* refers to God.

Thence to behold this new created World
Th' addition of his Empire, how it show'd   555
In prospect from his Throne, how good, how fair,
Answering his great Idea. Up he rode
Follow'd with acclamation and the sound
Symphonious of ten thousand Harps that tun'd
Angelic harmonies: the Earth, the Air   560
Resounded, (thou remember'st, for thou heard'st)
The Heav'ns and all the Constellations rung,
The Planets in thir stations list'ning stood,
While the bright Pomp ascended jubilant.
Open, ye everlasting Gates, they sung,   565
Open, ye Heav'ns, your living doors; let in
The great Creator from his work return'd
Magnificent, his Six days' work, a World;
Open, and henceforth oft; for God will deign
To visit oft the dwellings of just Men   570
Delighted, and with frequent intercourse
Thither will send his winged Messengers
On errands of supernal Grace. So sung
The glorious Train ascending: He through Heav'n,
That open'd wide her blazing Portals, led   575
To God's Eternal house direct the way,
A broad and ample road, whose dust is Gold
And pavement Stars, as Stars to thee appear,
Seen in the Galaxy, that Milky way
Which nightly as a circling Zone thou seest   580
Powder'd with Stars. And now on Earth the Seventh
Ev'ning arose in *Eden,* for the Sun
Was set, and twilight from the East came on,

---

557. The *great Idea* is the pattern on which Messiah, like a Platonic demiurge, has constructed the universe. The recollection of Plato seems definite, for his creator surveys his work and approves its correspondence to his pattern, as he does in the *Timaeus* (37 c).

564. *Pomp* has its Greek meaning of "a splendid procession."

565. The invocation translates Psalm xxiv, 7, which has been echoed in 206 above.

571. In *C.D.,* I, v, Milton pointed out that in the Old Testament "the name of God seems to be attributed to angels because as heavenly messengers they bear the appearance of the divine glory and person, and even speak in the very words of the Deity."

Forerunning Night; when at the holy mount
Of Heav'n's high-seated top, th' Imperial Throne   585
Of Godhead, fixt for ever firm and sure,
The Filial Power arriv'd, and sat him down
With his great Father, for he also went
Invisible, yet stay'd (such privilege
Hath Omnipresence) and the work ordain'd,   590
Author and end of all things, and from work
Now resting, bless'd and hallow'd the Sev'nth day,
As resting on that day from all his work,
But not in silence holy kept; the Harp
Had work and rested not, the solemn Pipe,   595
And Dulcimer, all Organs of sweet stop,
All sounds on Fret by String or Golden Wire
Temper'd soft Tunings, intermixt with Voice
Choral or Unison; of incense Clouds
Fuming from Golden Censers hid the Mount.   600
Creation and the Six days' acts they sung,
Great are thy works, *Jehovah,* infinite
Thy power; what thought can measure thee or tongue
Relate thee; greater now in thy return
Than from the Giant Angels; thee that day   605
Thy Thunders magnifi'd; but to create
Is greater than created to destroy.
Who can impair thee, mighty King, or bound
Thy Empire? easily the proud attempt

---

584. Compare the description of the holy mount in V, 643.

591. God is the end, or object of all things because they are created for his glory.

592. The blessing of the Sabbath is based on Genesis ii, 2–3.

597. *Fret,* the bar on the finger-board of a guitar to regulate the fingering.

599. *Unison* is said of voices sounding all in one pitch, as opposed to *Choral.*

600. Perhaps there is a reminiscence of the censer of the angel at God's altar after the opening of the seventh seal in Revelation viii, 3.

605. The *Giant Angels* are the demons. We have already found them compared with the Titans whom Hesiod says attacked the Olympian gods. Compare the note on VI, 644.

607. *created,* anything created.

608. *impair,* injure in any way.

Of Spirits apostate and thir Counsels vain   610
Thou hast repell'd, while impiously they thought
Thee to diminish, and from thee withdraw
The number of thy worshippers.   Who seeks
To lessen thee, against his purpose serves
To manifest the more thy might: his evil   615
Thou usest, and from thence creat'st more good.
Witness this new-made World, another Heav'n
From Heaven Gate not far, founded in view
On the clear *Hyaline,* the Glassy Sea;
Of amplitude almost immense, with Stars   620
Numerous, and every Star perhaps a World
Of destin'd habitation; but thou know'st
Thir seasons: among these the seat of men,
Earth with her nether Ocean circumfus'd,
Thir pleasant dwelling-place.   Thrice happy men,   625
And sons of men, whom God hath thus advanc't,
Created in his Image, there to dwell
And worship him, and in reward to rule
Over his Works, on Earth, in Sea, or Air,
And multiply a Race of Worshippers   630
Holy and just: thrice happy if they know

619. The *clear Hyaline,* the crystalline sphere.   Hyaline is an English equivalent of the Greek word meaning "glassy."   (Compare Rev., iv, 6.)

622. Compare the suggestion that the stars may be inhabited in VIII, 153–8. The idea goes back to Plato (*Timaeus,* 41).

624. *nether Ocean circumfus'd,* the lower ocean which ancient geography regarded as encircling the earth, as opposed to the waters above the firmament.   Compare the note on 261 above.

627. Even yet Milton believed that "there are some remnants of the divine image left in man, the union of which in one individual renders him more fit and disposed for the kingdom of God than another." (*C.D.,* I, iv.)

629. There is an echo of Psalm viii, 6: "Thou madest him to have dominion over the works of thy hands; thou hast put all things under his feet."

631. Milton betrays the depth of his own pleasure in Adam's idyllic happiness in Paradise by recalling the most famous line in Virgil's praise of the life of the Italian peasants in the *Georgics,* II, 458–9:

> "O, happy, if he knew his happy state,
>   The swain, who, free from bus'ness and debate,
> Receives his easy food from Nature's hand.
>   (Dryden's translation.)

Thir happiness, and persevere upright.
  So sung they, and the Empyrean rung,
With *Halleluiahs:* Thus was Sabbath kept.
And thy request think now fulfill'd, that ask'd   635
How first this World and face of things began,
And what before thy memory was done
From the beginning, that posterity
Inform'd by thee might know; if else thou seek'st
Aught, not surpassing human measure, say.   640

The End of the Seventh Book.

---

632. Compare the repeated warning to *persevere* when Raphael finally takes leave of Adam in VIII, 639.

636. *face of things,* outward or visible nature. For Milton's readers the transition from man's creation in the image of God in Book VII to his wonder at the marvels of nature in Book VIII was familiar. In a commentary on a parallel thought in Aristotle's *Politics,* I, i, Loys le Roy compared the passages from Plato and Lactantius which are mentioned in the note on l. 509 above, and then he added, "Man is begotten . . . after the image and similitude of God . . . to celebrate his honour . . . to the end he may view the order of the celestiall bodies, and keepe . . . the habitation of this middle terrestrial globe." (I. D.'s translation, London, 1598, p. 18.)

BOOK VIII

THE ARGUMENT

Adam *inquires concerning celestial Motions, is doubtfully answer'd, and exhorted to search rather things more worthy of knowledge:* Adam *assents, and still desirous to detain* Raphael, *relates to him what he remember'd since his own Creation, his placing in Paradise, his talk with God concerning solitude and fit society, his first meeting and Nuptials with* Eve, *his discourse with the Angel thereupon; who after admonitions repeated departs.*

THE Angel ended, and in *Adam's* Ear
So Charming left his voice, that he a while
Thought him still speaking, still stood fixt to hear;
Then as new wak't thus gratefully repli'd.
What thanks sufficient, or what recompense   5
Equal have I to render thee, Divine
Historian, who thus largely hast allay'd
The thirst I had of knowledge, and voutsaf't
This friendly condescension to relate
Things else by me unsearchable, now heard   10
With wonder, but delight, and, as is due,
With glory attribúted to the high
Creator; something yet of doubt remains,
Which only thy solution can resolve.
When I behold this goodly Frame, this World   15
Of Heav'n and Earth consisting, and compute,
Thir magnitudes, this Earth a spot, a grain,
An Atom, with the Firmament compar'd
And all her number'd Stars, that seem to roll

3. *stood fixt,* remained fascinated by the angel's words.

15. *Frame,* creation, universe.   Compare V, 154, and VII, 273.

19. Probably *number'd* means "numerous" (as in VII, 621), but Milton may have remembered Psalm cxlvii, 4: "He (God) telleth the number of the stars; he calleth them all by their names."   Adam's entire speech is coloured by Psalm viii.

Spaces incomprehensible (for such   20
Thir distance argues and thir swift return
Diurnal) merely to officiate light
Round this opacous Earth, this punctual spot,
One day and night; in all thir vast survey
Useless besides, reasoning I oft admire,   25
How Nature wise and frugal could commit
Such disproportions, with superfluous hand
So many nobler Bodies to create,
Greater so manifold to this one use,
For aught appears, and on thir Orbs impose   30
Such restless revolution day by day
Repeated, while the sedentary Earth,
That better might with far less compass move,
Serv'd by more noble than herself, attains
Her end without least motion, and receives,   35

---

22. *officiate*, furnish.

23. *opacous*, dark, shadowy.

punctual, point-like, tiny. Since the solar system itself, wrote Thomas
Digges, is "but a poynct in respect of the immensity of that immoveable
heaven, we may easily consider what little portion of God's frame, our
Elementare Corruptible World is," (*A Prognostication everlastinge.* N 4 r)

24. *one* is logically parallel with *merely* in 22 above, and with *one* in
29 below.

25. *admire,* wonder, question. In IV, 593–7, Milton is impartial between the Copernican and Ptolemaic theories. Here, although Adam
seems to accept the Ptolemaic view of the earth, Milton represents him
as puzzled, like Robert Burton, to understand "what fury is that, . . .
that shall drive the Heavens about with such incomprehensible celerity in
24 hours." (*Anatomy,* II, ii, 3.) Joseph Glanvill, who believed that
before the fall Adam's sight penetrated to the bounds of creation, wrote
that " 'twas as absurd in the judgement of his senses, that the Sun and
Stars should be so very much, less then this Globe, as the contrary seems
in ours; and 'tis not unlikely that he had as clear a perception of the
earth's motion, as we think we have of its quiescence." (*Vanity,* p. 5.)

30. *Orbs,* the concentric, hollow spheres which were supposed to revolve around the earth, every one moving one of the planets (or, in the
case of the outermost sphere, the whole body of fixed stars, which even
Copernicus regarded as being all equi-distant from the centre of our
universe).

32. *sedentary,* seated, established. Compare "the steadfast earth" in
II, 927.

33. *compass,* space, area covered. Compare the phrase, "fetch a compass," used for making any kind of circular tour.

As Tribute such a sumless journey brought
Of incorporeal speed, her warmth and light;
Speed, to describe whose swiftness Number fails.
  So spake our Sire, and by his count'nance seem'd
Ent'ring on studious thoughts abstruse, which *Eve*   40
Perceiving where she sat retir'd in sight,
With lowliness Majestic from her seat,
And Grace that won who saw to wish her stay,
Rose, and went forth among her Fruits and Flow'rs,
To visit how they prosper'd, bud and bloom,   45
Her Nursery; they at her coming sprung
And toucht by her fair tendance gladlier grew.
Yet went she not, as not with such discourse
Delighted, or not capable her ear
Of what was high: such pleasure she reserv'd,   50
Adam relating, she sole Auditress;
Her Husband the Relater she preferr'd
Before the Angel, and of him to ask
Chose rather: hee, she knew, would intermix
Grateful digressions, and solve high dispute   55
With conjugal Caresses, from his Lip
Not Words alone pleas'd her. O when meet now
Such pairs, in Love and mutual Honour join'd?
With Goddess-like demeanour forth she went;
Not unattended, for on her as Queen   60
A pomp of winning Graces waited still,
And from about her shot Darts of desire
Into all Eyes to wish her still in sight.
And *Raphael* now to *Adam's* doubt propos'd
Benevolent and facile thus repli'd.   65

---

36. *sumless,* immeasurable.

37. *incorporeal* is equivalent to *spiritual* as used in 110 below. The thought is that warmth and light are a tribute paid to earth at the price of incalculable travels made by the heavenly bodies at terrific speeds.

46. *Nursery* is used as it is by King Lear (I, i, 126) saying that he loved Cordelia and had "thought to set my rest on her kind nursery." It does not mean a "nursery garden," but—abstractly—the objects of Eve's care.

61. *pomp,* a procession. Compare VII, 564.

64. *doubt propos'd,* question raised. Compare 13 above.

65. *facile* still retained its Latin force of "easy of access," "gracious."

  To ask or search I blame thee not, for Heav'n
Is as the Book of God before thee set,
Wherein to read his wond'rous Works, and learn
His Seasons, Hours, or Days, or Months, or Years;
This to attain, whether Heav'n move or Earth,   70
Imports not, if thou reck'n right; the rest
From Man or Angel the great Architect
Did wisely to conceal, and not divulge
His secrets to be scann'd by them who ought
Rather admire; or if they list to try   75
Conjecture, he his Fabric of the Heav'ns
Hath left to thir disputes, perhaps to move
His laughter at thir quaint Opinions wide
Hereafter, when they come to model Heav'n
And calculate the Stars, how they will wield   80
The mighty frame, how build, unbuild, contrive
To save appearances, how gird the Sphere
With Centric and Eccentric scribbl'd o'er,
Cycle and Epicycle, Orb in Orb:

---

  67. "The Book of God" or "the book of the Creation" was a traditional metaphor among liberal theologians, who, like Richard Baxter,
condemned the sceptical philosophy which "most readeth the book of
Nature and least understandeth or feeleth the meaning of it." (*The
Reasons of the Christian Religion*, p. 108.)

  75. *admire*, to admire.

  78. *wide, i.e.*, of the truth. For God's *laughter* see II, 190–1. Burton
thought that "those monstrous orbs of *Eccentricks*, and *Eccentre Epicycles
deserentes;* which howsoever *Ptolemy, Alhasen, Vitellio, Purbachius, Magi-
nus, Clavius,* & many of their associates, stiffly maintain to be real orbs,
eccentrick, concentrick, circles aequant, &c. are absurd and ridiculous."
(*Anatomy*, II, ii, 3.)

  82. *To save appearances*, to account for everything apparent, *i.e.*, for
all the phenomena in the movements of the heavenly bodies.

  83. *Centric and Eccentric*, spheres whose centres were respectively fixed
or not fixed upon the earth as the centre of the universe. Burton mentions one astronomer whose hypothesis made "the Earth as before the
universal Center," but made the sun (although its sphere was conceived
as geocentric) the centre of the orbits of "the five upper planets," and
ascribed "diurnal motion" to the eighth sphere (that of the fixed stars),
and so, "as a tinker stops one hole and makes two," the astronomer
"reforms some [errors], and mars all." (*Anatomy*, II, ii, 3.)

  84. *Epicycle:* "A small circle, having its centre on the circumference
of a greater circle. In the Ptolemaic system . . . each of the 'seven

Already by thy reasoning this I guess,   85
Who art to lead thy offspring, and supposest
That bodies bright and greater should not serve
The less not bright, nor Heav'n such journeys run,
Earth sitting still, when she alone receives
The benefit: consider first, that Great   90
Or Bright infers not Excellence: the Earth
Though, in comparison of Heav'n, so small,
Nor glistering, may of solid good contain
More plenty than the Sun that barren shines,
Whose virtue on itself works no effect,   95
But in the fruitful Earth; there first receiv'd
His beams, unactive else, thir vigor find.
Yet not to Earth are those bright Luminaries
Officious, but to thee Earth's habitant.
And for the Heav'n's wide Circuit, let it speak   100
The Maker's high magnificence, who built
So spacious, and his Line stretcht out so far;
That Man may know he dwells not in his own;
An Edifice too large for him to fill,
Lodg'd in a small partition, and the rest   105
Ordain'd for uses to his Lord best known.
The swiftness of those Circles áttribute,
Though numberless, to his Omnipotence,
That to corporeal substances could add
Speed almost Spiritual; mee thou think'st not slow,   110
Who since the Morning hour set out from Heav'n
Where God resides, and ere mid-day arriv'd
In *Eden,* distance inexpressible
By Numbers that have name.   But this I urge,

---

planets' was supposed to revolve in an epicycle, the centre of which
moved along a greater circle called a deferent." *N. E. D.*

　　95. For the effect of the sun's virtue *in* the earth see III, 608–12.

　　99. *Officious, serviceable;* compare *officiate* in line 22 above.

　　102. Compare God's question to Job about the earth: "Who hath laid
the measures thereof, if thou knowest? or who hath stretched the line
upon it?"   (Job xxxviii, 5.)

　　105. *partition,* division, part.

　　108. *numberless,* incomputable.   Compare the use of *Numbers* in 114.

　　113. Raphael's *distance* has been made much more comprehensible in
V, 247–274.

Admitting Motion in the Heav'ns, to show   115
Invalid that which thee to doubt it mov'd;
Not that I so affirm, though so it seem
To thee who hast thy dwelling here on Earth.
God to remove his ways from human sense,
Plac'd Heav'n from Earth so far, that earthly sight,   120
If it presume, might err in things too high,
And no advantage gain. What if the Sun
Be Centre to the World, and other Stars
By his attractive virtue and their own
Incited, dance about him various rounds?   125
Thir wandring course now high, now low, then hid,
Progressive, retrograde, or standing still,
In six thou seest, and what if sev'nth to these
The Planet Earth, so steadfast though she seem,
Insensibly three different Motions move?   130
Which else to several Spheres thou must ascribe,
Mov'd contrary with thwart obliquities,
Or save the Sun his labour, and that swift
Nocturnal and Diurnal rhomb suppos'd,
Invisible else above all Stars, the Wheel   135
Of Day and Night; which needs not thy belief,
If Earth industrious of herself fetch Day
Travelling East, and with her part averse
From the Sun's beam meet Night, her other part

---

124. *attractive virtue,* power of attraction. Compare the picture of the planets turned by the sun's "magnetic beam" in III, 583.

126. *wand'ring* is an allusion to the original (Greek) meaning of the word "planet." The Copernican system makes the earth a "wanderer," and therefore the "seventh" planet; while the sun ceases to be a planet, as it is regarded in the Ptolemaic system.

130. *Insensibly,* imperceptibly. The *Motions* are (1) rotation, (2) orbital revolution and (3) the very slow revolution of the earth's pole around that of the ecliptic which causes the precession of the equinoxes. This last is the "trepidation" of III, 483.

132. The *thwart obliquities* are the various transverse movements which must be attributed to the heavenly bodies if the earth is regarded as stationary.

134. The *Nocturnal and Diurnal rhomb suppos'd* was the invisible sphere, the *primum mobile,* which the Ptolemaic theory invented to explain the apparent daily rotation of the spheres of the seven planets and also that of the fixed stars, all of which it was imagined as containing.

137. *industrious,* active, *i.e.,* moving as opposed to stationary.

Still luminous by his ray.   What if that light   140
Sent from her through the wide transpicuous air,
To the terrestrial Moon be as a Star
Enlight'ning her by Day, as she by Night
This Earth? reciprocal, if Land be there,
Fields and Inhabitants: Her spots thou seest   145
As Clouds, and Clouds may rain, and Rain produce
Fruits in her soft'n'd Soil, for some to eat
Allotted there; and other Suns perhaps
With thir attendant Moons thou wilt descry
Communicating Male and Female Light,   150
Which two great Sexes animate the World,
Stor'd in each Orb perhaps with some that live.
For such vast room in Nature unpossest
By living Soul, desert and desolate,
Only to shine, yet scarce to contribute   155
Each Orb a glimpse of Light, convey'd so far
Down to this habitable, which returns
Light back to them, is obvious to dispute.
But whether thus these things, or whether not,

---

142. The *terrestrial Moon* is the moon understood, as Milton is about to suggest, to be an inhabited orb like the earth.

145. "If the earth move," thought Burton (*Anatomy*, II, ii, 3), "it is a Planet, & shines to them in the *Moon*, & to the other Planetary Inhabitants, as the *Moon* and they to us upon the earth: but shine she doth, as *Galileo, Kepler*, and others prove, and then, *per consequens*, the rest of the Planets are inhabited, as well as the *Moon*."

149. *Moons* is equivalent to "planets," for Milton is reasoning here, like Burton, that "if our world be small in respect, why may we not suppose a plurality of worlds, those infinite stars visible in the Firmament to be so many Suns; . . . to have likewise their subordinate Planets, as the Sun hath his dancing still around him? . . . Though they seem close to us, they are infinitely distant, and so . . . there are infinite habitable worlds: what hinders?" (*Anatomy*, II, ii, 3.)

150. *Communicating Male and Female Light*, interchanging direct and reflected light.

155. *Only to shine*, merely for the sake of illumination, while each starry orb contributes only the smallest modicum of light to this habitable (*i.e.*, the inhabited earth).

158. *obvious*, open. In his Seventh Prolusion Milton asked his fellow students at Cambridge whether they could believe that "the vast spaces of boundless air are illuminated and adorned with everlasting lights . . . merely to serve as a lantern to base and slothful men."

Whether the Sun predominant in Heav'n   160
Rise on the Earth, or Earth rise on the Sun,
Hee from the East his flaming road begin,
Or Shee from West her silent course advance
With inoffensive pace that spinning sleeps
On her soft Axle, while she paces Ev'n,   165
And bears thee soft with the smooth Air along,
Solicit not thy thoughts with matters hid,
Leave them to God above, him serve and fear;
Of other Creatures, as him pleases best,
Wherever plac't, let him dispose: joy thou   170
In what he gives to thee, this Paradise
And thy fair *Eve:* Heav'n is for thee too high
To know what passes there; be lowly wise:
Think only what concerns thee and thy being;
Dream not of other Worlds, what Creatures there   175
Live, in what state, condition or degree,
Contented that thus far hath been reveal'd
Not of Earth only but of highest Heav'n.
    To whom thus *Adam* clear'd of doubt, repli'd.
How fully hast thou satisfi'd me, pure   180
Intelligence of Heav'n, Angel serene,
And freed from intricacies, taught to live
The easiest way, nor with perplexing thoughts
To interrupt the sweet of Life, from which
God hath bid dwell far off all anxious cares,   185
And not molest us, unless we ourselves
Seek them with wand'ring thoughts, and notions vain.
But apt the Mind or Fancy is to rove

---

173. So Du Bartas advised:

> "*Be sober wise:* so, bound thy frail desire:
> And what thou canst not comprehend, *admire*."
> (161 lc)

181. *Intelligence* was used regularly to mean an "angelic being." George Puttenham spoke of poets as the first students of "Celestial courses, by reason of the continuall motion of the heavens, searching after the first mover, and from thence by degrees comming to know and consider of the substances separate & abstract, which we call the divine intelligences or good Angels." (*The Arte of English Poesie*, I, iii.)

188. Milton is not attacking scientific curiosity but arguing in agreement with Glanvill that, "To say, *Reason* opposeth *Faith*, is to scandalize both:

Uncheckt, and of her roving is no end;
Till warn'd, or by experience taught, she learn   190
That not to know at large of things remote
From use, obscure and subtle, but to know
That which before us lies in daily life,
Is the prime Wisdom; what is more is fume,
Or emptiness, or fond impertinence,   195
And renders us in things that most concern
Unpractis'd, unprepar'd, and still to seek.
Therefore from this high pitch let us descend
A lower flight, and speak of things at hand
Useful, whence haply mention may arise   200
Of something not unseasonable to ask
By sufferance, and thy wonted favour deign'd.
Thee I have heard relating what was done
Ere my remembrance: now hear mee relate
My Story, which perhaps thou hast not heard;   205
And Day is yet not spent; till then thou seest
How subtly to detain thee I devise,
Inviting thee to hear while I relate,
Fond, were it not in hope of thy reply:
For while I sit with thee, I seem in Heav'n,   210
And sweeter thy discourse is to my ear
Than Fruits of Palm-tree pleasantest to thirst
And hunger both, from labour, at the hour
Of sweet repast; they satiate, and soon fill,
Though pleasant, but thy words with Grace Divine   215
Imbu'd, bring to thir sweetness no satiety.
  To whom thus *Raphael* answer'd heav'nly meek.
Nor are thy lips ungraceful, Sire of men,
Nor tongue ineloquent; for God on thee
Abundantly his gifts hath also pour'd   220

'Tis *Imagination* is the Rebel; *Reason* contradicts its impious suggestions."
(*Vanity*, p. 103.)

194. *fume*, vapour, vanity.

195. *fond impertinence*, foolish irrelevance, trifling. Compare *fond* in
209 below.

197. *still to seek*, always groping, always unprovided with a solution
of life's problems.

202. *By sufferance*, by thy condescension.

213. *from labour*, after labour.

Inward and outward both, his image fair:
Speaking or mute all comeliness and grace
Attends thee, and each word, each motion forms.
Nor less think wee in Heav'n of thee on Earth
Than of our fellow servant, and inquire   225
Gladly into the ways of God with Man:
For God we see hath honour'd thee, and set
On Man his Equal Love: say therefore on;
For I that Day was absent, as befell,
Bound on a voyage uncouth and obscure,   230
Far on excursion toward the Gates of Hell;
Squar'd in full Legion (such command we had)
To see that none thence issu'd forth a spy,
Or enemy, while God was in his work,
Lest hee incent at such eruption bold,   235
Destruction with Creation might have mixt.
Not that they durst without his leave attempt,
But us he sends upon his high behests
For state, as Sovran King, and to enure
Our prompt obedience. Fast we found, fast shut   240
The dismal Gates, and barricado'd strong;
But long ere our approaching heard within
Noise, other than the sound of Dance or Song,
Torment, and loud lament, and furious rage.
Glad we return'd up to the coasts of Light   245
Ere Sabbath Ev'ning: so we had in charge.
But thy relation now; for I attend,
Pleas'd with thy words no less than thou with mine.
    So spake the Godlike Power, and thus our Sire.
For Man to tell how human Life began   250
Is hard: for who himself beginning knew?
Desire with thee still longer to converse

---

221. Compare the stress upon Adam as God's image in VII, 519 and
627.

230. *uncouth,* unknown, unfamiliar.

232. *Squar'd:* compare the use of the word in I, 758.

239. *For state,* to preserve the dignity of God's state.
enure, discipline, habituate.

244. Compare the account of the rage of the demons in I, 666–9.

246. The *Sabbath Ev'ning* is described in VII, 592–601.

251. *beginning,* at his beginning.

Induc'd me. As new wak't from soundest sleep
Soft on the flow'ry herb I found me laid
In Balmy Sweat, which with his Beams the Sun   255
Soon dri'd, and on the reeking moisture fed.
Straight toward Heav'n my wond'ring Eyes I turn'd,
And gaz'd a while the ample Sky, till rais'd
By quick instinctive motion up I sprung,
As thitherward endeavouring, and upright   260
Stood on my feet; about me round I saw
Hill, Dale, and shady Woods, and sunny Plains,
And liquid Lapse of murmuring Streams; by these,
Creatures that liv'd, and mov'd, and walk'd, or flew,
Birds on the branches warbling; all things smil'd,   265
With fragrance and with joy my heart o'erflow'd.
Myself I then perus'd, and Limb by Limb
Survey'd, and sometimes went, and sometimes ran
With supple joints, as lively vigor led:
But who I was, or where, or from what cause,   270
Knew not; to speak I tri'd, and forthwith spake,
My Tongue obey'd and readily could name
Whate'er I saw. Thou Sun, said I, fair Light,
And thou enlight'n'd Earth, so fresh and gay,
Ye Hills and Dales, ye Rivers, Woods, and Plains   275
And ye that live and move, fair Creatures, tell,
Tell, if ye saw, how came I thus, how here?
Not of myself; by some great Maker then,
In goodness and in power preëminent;
Tell me, how may I know him, how adore,   280
From whom I have that thus I move and live,
And feel that I am happier than I know.
While thus I call'd, and stray'd I knew not whither,
From where I first drew Air, and first beheld
This happy Light, when answer none return'd,   285
On a green shady Bank profuse of Flow'rs

---

256. The feeding of the sun was not a mere figure of speech for
evaporation, as the note on V, 426, explains.

260. Milton reverts to the Platonic belief that man's upright stature
indicates his heavenly origin. Compare VII, 509, and note.

263. *Lapse,* flow, sliding movement.

268. *went,* walked.

Pensive I sat me down; there gentle sleep
First found me, and with soft oppression seiz'd
My drowsed sense, untroubl'd, though I thought
I then was passing to my former state   290
Insensible, and forthwith to dissolve:
When suddenly stood at my Head a dream,
Whose inward apparition gently mov'd
My fancy to believe I yet had being,
And liv'd: One came, methought, of shape Divine,   295
And said, thy Mansion wants thee, *Adam*, rise,
First Man, of Men innumerable ordain'd
First Father, call'd by thee I come thy Guide
To the Garden of bliss, thy seat prepar'd.
So saying, by the hand he took me rais'd,   300
And over Fields and Waters, as in Air
Smooth sliding without step, last led me up
A woody Mountain; whose high top was plain,
A Circuit wide, enclos'd, with goodliest Trees
Planted, with Walks, and Bowers, that what I saw   305
Of Earth before scarce pleasant seem'd.   Each Tree
Load'n with fairest Fruit, that hung to the Eye
Tempting, stirr'd in me sudden appetite
To pluck and eat; whereat I wak'd, and found
Before mine Eyes all real, as the dream   310
Had lively shadow'd: Here had new begun
My wand'ring, had not hee who was my Guide
Up hither, from among the Trees appear'd,
Presence Divine.   Rejoicing, but with awe,
In adoration at his feet I fell   315
Submiss: he rear'd me, and Whom thou sought'st I am,
Said mildly, Author of all this thou seest
Above, or round about thee or beneath.
This Paradise I give thee, count it thine

---

292. Compare Adam's discussion of dreams in V, 100–13.

296. The *Mansion* is the Earthly Paradise in Eden, outside of which
Adam was created.   Compare the note on VII, 537.

303. Compare the account of the mountain of Paradise in IV, 133–149.

311. *lively shadow'd,* made appear like the living reality.

316. *submiss* has its Latin force as a participle meaning "cast down."
"prostrate."

To Till and keep, and of the Fruit to eat: 320
Of every Tree that in the Garden grows
Eat freely with glad heart; fear here no dearth:
But of the Tree whose operation brings
Knowledge of good and ill, which I have set
The Pledge of thy Obedience and thy Faith,   325
Amid the Garden by the Tree of Life,
Remember what I warn thee, shun to taste,
And shun the bitter consequence: for know,
The day thou eat'st thereof, my sole command
Transgrest, inevitably thou shalt die;   330
From that day mortal, and this happy State
Shalt lose, expell'd from hence into a World
Of woe and sorrow.   Sternly he pronounc'd
The rigid interdiction, which resounds
Yet dreadful in mine ear, though in my choice   335
Not to incur; but soon his clear aspect
Return'd and gracious purpose thus renew'd.
Not only these fair bounds, but all the Earth
To thee and to thy Race I give; as Lords
Possess it, and all things that therein live,   340
Or live in Sea, or Air, Beast, Fish, and Fowl.
In sign whereof each Bird and Beast behold
After thir kinds; I bring them to receive

320. Compare Genesis ii, 15–17: "And the Lord God took the man, and
put him into the garden of Eden to dress it and to keep it.   And the
Lord God commanded the man, saying, Of every tree of the garden
thou mayest freely eat: But of the tree of the knowledge of good and
evil, thou shalt not eat of it: for in the day that thou eatest thereof thou
shalt surely die."

325. *Pledge,* symbol or test.

330. *die,* as the next line indicates, meant to the speaker "become
mortal."   Contrary to prevailing opinion, Milton seems to have thought
that there had always been a limit "set to the duration of human life"
and that even before the fall Adam was not immortal.   In V, 493–503,
Raphael suggests that Adam's destiny may ultimately be a change into
some such celestial kind of being as his own.   And in *C. D.,* I, viii,
Milton says that "it is evident that God, at least after the fall of man,
limited human life to a certain term."

335. *though in my choice,* though it is within my power of choice.

337. *purpose,* speech, discourse.
renew'd, recommenced.

340. Compare VII, 531, and note.

From thee thir Names, and pay thee fealty
With low subjection; understand the same   345
Of Fish within thir wat'ry residence,
Not hither summon'd, since they cannot change
Thir Element to draw the thinner Air.
As thus he spake, each Bird and Beast behold
Approaching two and two, These cow'ring low   350
With blandishment, each Bird stoop'd on his wing.
I nam'd them, as they pass'd, and understood
Thir Nature, with such knowledge God endu'd
My sudden apprehension: but in these
I found not what methought I wanted still;   355
And to the Heav'nly vision thus presum'd.
  O by what Name, for thou above all these,
Above mankind, or aught than mankind higher,
Surpassest far my naming, how may I
Adore thee, Author of this Universe,   360
And all this good to man, for whose well being
So amply, and with hands so liberal
Thou hast provided all things: but with mee
I see not who partakes.   In solitude
What happiness, who can enjoy alone,   365
Or all enjoying, what contentment find?
Thus I presumptuous; and the vision bright,
As with a smile more bright'n'd, thus repli'd.
  What call'st thou solitude, is not the Earth
With various living creatures, and the Air   370

---

352. For Milton and many of his contemporaries a convincing proof
that man was made in the image of God and therefore "endued with
natural wisdom" was the fact that "without extraordinary wisdom he
could not have given names to the whole animal creation with such
sudden intelligence." (*C. D.,* I, vii.)

354. *sudden apprehension,* prompt perception.

355. Behind this line is Genesis ii, 20: "And Adam gave names to all
cattle, and to the fowl of the air, and to every beast of the field: but for
Adam there was not found an help meet for him."   Rashi's commentary
on the verse, in the Buxtorf Bible, says that when God brought the animals to Adam to be named, he brought them before him in pairs, a
male and a female.   And Adam said, "For all of them there is a help
meet; but for me there is no help meet."   (Quoted by Fletcher, *Rabbinical Readings,* p. 172.)

356. *presum'd,* dared speak.

Replenisht, and all these at thy command
To come and play before thee, know'st thou not
Thir language and thir ways, they also know,
And reason not contemptibly; with these
Find pastime, and bear rule; thy Realm is large.   375
So spake the Universal Lord, and seem'd
So ordering.   I with leave of speech implor'd,
And humble deprecation thus repli'd.
    Let not my words offend thee, Heav'nly Power,
My Maker, be propitious while I speak.   380
Hast thou not made me here thy substitute,
And these inferior far beneath me set?
Among unequals what society
Can sort, what harmony or true delight?
Which must be mutual, in proportion due   385
Giv'n and receiv'd; but in disparity
The one intense, the other still remiss
Cannot well suit with either, but soon prove
Tedious alike: Of fellowship I speak
Such as I seek, fit to participate   390
All rational delight, wherein the brute
Cannot be human consort; they rejoice
Each with thir kind, Lion with Lioness;
So fitly them in pairs thou hast combin'd;
Much less can Bird with Beast, or Fish with Fowl   395
So well converse, nor with the Ox the Ape;
Worse then can Man with Beast, and least of all.
    Whereto th' Almighty answer'd, not displeas'd.
A nice and subtle happiness I see
Thou to thyself proposest, in the choice   400
Of thy Associates, *Adam,* and wilt taste
No pleasure, though in pleasure, solitary.

---

374. Before the fall it seems that the *reason* of the animals was superior, like that of man, to what it became afterwards. When Eve tasted the fruit the whole "Earth felt the wound" (IX, 782).

379. Compare Abraham's plea, "Oh let not the Lord be angry, and I will speak."   (Gen. xviii, 30.)

384. *sort,* be appropriate, be satisfying.

387. Man's nature is *intense, i. e.,* aspiring, while that of animals is *remiss, i. e.,* downcast, sordid.

399. *nice,* delicate.

What think'st thou then of mee, and this my State,
Seem I to thee sufficiently possest
Of happiness, or not? who am alone   405
From all Eternity, for none I know
Second to mee or like, equal much less.
How have I then with whom to hold converse
Save with the Creatures which I made, and those
To me inferior, infinite descents   410
Beneath what other Creatures are to thee?
   He ceas'd, I lowly answer'd. To attain
The highth and depth of thy Eternal ways
All human thoughts come short, Supreme of things;
Thou in thyself art perfet, and in thee   415
Is no deficience found; not so is Man,
But in degree, the cause of his desire
By conversation with his like to help,
Or solace his defects. No need that thou
Shouldst propagate, already infinite;   420
And through all numbers absolute, though One;
But Man by number is to manifest
His single imperfection, and beget
Like of his like, his Image multipli'd,
In unity defective, which requires   425
Collateral love, and dearest amity.
Thou in thy secrecy although alone,
Best with thyself accompanied, seek'st not
Social communication, yet so pleas'd,
Canst raise thy Creature to what highth thou wilt   430
Of Union or Communion, deifi'd;

---

407. The line seems to echo Horace's reference to the supreme deity,
"than whom no greater exists, and to whom there is none similar nor
second" (*Odes,* I, 12, 17–18), but the conception is Aristotelian. (*Eude-
mian Ethics,* VI, xii.)

420. Adam's speech repeats one of Milton's Arian arguments from
C. D., I, v: "For questionless, it was in God's power consistently with
the perfection of his own essence not to have begotten the Son, inasmuch as generation does not pertain to the nature of the Deity, who
stands in no need of propagation."

421. *numbers* is used in its Latin sense of "parts" or respects, but in
the line below it is used in its ordinary sense. God is perfect in all respects, because he is absolute; but man fulfils himself only in society.

425. *unity,* singleness, solitude.

I by conversing cannot these erect
From prone, nor in thir ways complacence find.
Thus I embold'n'd spake, and freedom us'd
Permissive, and acceptance found, which gain'd   435
This answer from the gracious voice Divine.

   Thus far to try thee, *Adam,* I was pleas'd,
And find thee knowing not of Beasts alone,
Which thou hast rightly nam'd, but of thyself,
Expressing well the spirit within thee free,   440
My Image, not imparted to the Brute,
Whose fellowship therefore unmeet for thee
Good reason was thou freely shouldst dislike,
And be so minded still; I, ere thou spak'st,
Knew it not good for Man to be alone,   445
And no such company as then thou saw'st
Intended thee, for trial only brought,
To see how thou couldst judge of fit and meet:
What next I bring shall please thee, be assur'd,
Thy likeness, thy fit help, thy other self,   450
Thy wish, exactly to thy heart's desire.

  Hee ended, or I heard no more, for now
My earthly by his Heav'nly overpower'd,
Which it had long stood under, strain'd to the highth
In that celestial Colloquy sublime,   455
As with an object that excels the sense,
Dazzl'd and spent, sunk down, and sought repair
Of sleep, which instantly fell on me, call'd
By Nature as in aid, and clos'd mine eyes.

---

432. *these,* the animals.

433. *prone,* proneness, the reverse of the uprightness which is man's nature. Compare 260 above.

450. Against the biblical term for a wife, "help meet" (*fit help*) Milton puts the classical term for an ideal friend, an *other self.* In *Doctrine and Discipline of Divorce,* interpreting "God's intention" in creating Eve, he wrote, "a meet and happy conversation is the chiefest and the noblest end of marriage." (I, ii.)

453. *My earthly, i.e.,* nature. Adam, exhausted by the strain of the unequal conversation, falls asleep. Milton is following Genesis, ii, 21-2: "And the Lord God caused a deep sleep to fall upon Adam, and he slept: and he took one of his ribs. . . . And the rib, which the Lord God had taken from man, made he a woman, and brought her unto the man."

Mine eyes he clos'd, but op'n left the Cell   460
Of Fancy my internal sight, by which
Abstract as in a trance methought I saw,
Though sleeping, where I lay, and saw the shape
Still glorious before whom awake I stood;
Who stooping op'n'd my left side, and took   465
From thence a Rib, with cordial spirits warm,
And Life-blood streaming fresh; wide was the wound,
But suddenly with flesh fill'd up and heal'd:
The Rib he form'd and fashion'd with his hands;
Under his forming hands a Creature grew,   470
Manlike, but different sex, so lovely fair,
That what seem'd fair in all the World, seem'd now
Mean, or in her summ'd up, in her contain'd
And in her looks, which from that time infus'd
Sweetness into my heart, unfelt before,   475
And into all things from her Air inspir'd
The spirit of love and amorous delight.
Shee disappear'd, and left me dark, I wak'd
To find her, or for ever to deplore
Her loss, and other pleasures all abjure: 480
When out of hope, behold her, not far off,
Such as I saw her in my dream, adorn'd
With what all Earth or Heaven could bestow
To make her amiable: On she came,
Led by her Heav'nly Maker, though unseen,   485
And guided by his voice, nor uninform'd
Of nuptial Sanctity and marriage Rites:
Grace was in all her steps, Heav'n in her Eye,
In every gesture dignity and love.
I overjoy'd could not forbear aloud.   490

---

461. Adam himself explains the part of *Fancy* in dreams in V, 102–9.

462. *Abstract,* abstracted, drawn into a trance.

466. *Cordial spirits* is a technical term meaning the "vital spirits" which
the heart was supposed to distribute to the body. Compare the note
on V, 484.

481. *When out of hope,* when I had given up hope.

482. This *dream* is movingly like the vision of his deceased wife which
Milton drew in Sonnet 14.

490. *could not forbear aloud,* could not forbear speaking aloud.

This turn hath made amends; thou hast fulfill'd
Thy words, Creator bounteous and benign,
Giver of all things fair, but fairest this
Of all thy gifts, nor enviest.   I now see
Bone of my Bone, Flesh of my Flesh, my Self   495
Before me; Woman is her Name, of Man
Extracted; for this cause he shall forgo
Father and Mother, and to his Wife adhere;
And they shall be one Flesh, one Heart, one Soul.

　　She heard me thus, and though divinely brought,   500
Yet Innocence and Virgin Modesty,
Her virtue and the conscience of her worth,
That would be woo'd, and not unsought be won,
Not obvious, not obtrusive, but retir'd,
The more desirable, or to say all,   505
Nature herself, though pure of sinful thought,
Wrought in her so, that seeing me, she turn'd;
I follow'd her, she what was Honour knew,
And with obsequious Majesty approv'd
My pleaded reason.   To the Nuptial Bow'r   510
I led her blushing like the Morn: all Heav'n,
And happy Constellations on that hour
Shed thir selectest influence; the Earth
Gave sign of gratulation, and each Hill;
Joyous the Birds; fresh Gales and gentle Airs   515
Whisper'd it to the Woods, and from thir wings
Flung Rose, flung Odours from the spicy Shrub,

---

494. *nor enviest,* nor dost thou grudge thy gifts.   Milton was thinking
of the Greek gods, who did envy men their happiness.

495. Repetition in Matthew xix, 4–6, and Mark x, 6–8, gave sanctity
to Genesis ii, 23–4: "And Adam said, This is now bone of my bones,
and flesh of my flesh: she shall be called Woman, because she was taken
out of Man.   Therefore shall a man leave his father and his mother,
and shall cleave unto his wife: and they shall be one flesh."

502. *conscience,* consciousness.

504. *obvious,* bold, forward.

508. *Honour* is perhaps an allusion to Hebrews xiii, 4: "Marriage is
honourable in all."

513. Compare the dance of the stars, "shedding sweet influence," as
a portent of the happiness of the whole universe, at the Creation.
(VII, 375.)

Disporting, till the amorous Bird of Night
Sung Spousal, and bid haste the Ev'ning Star
On his Hill top, to light the bridal Lamp.   520
Thus I have told thee all my State, and brought
My Story to the sum of earthly bliss
Which I enjoy, and must confess to find
In all things else delight indeed, but such
As us'd or not, works in the mind no change,   525
Nor vehement desire, these delicacies
I mean of Taste, Sight, Smell, Herbs, Fruits, and Flow'rs,
Walks, and the melody of Birds; but here
Far otherwise, transported I behold,
Transported touch; here passion first I felt,   530
Commotion strange, in all enjoyments else
Superior and unmov'd, here only weak
Against the charm of Beauty's powerful glance.
Or Nature fail'd in mee, and left some part
Not proof enough such Object to sustain,   535
Or from my side subducting, took perhaps
More than enough; at least on her bestow'd
Too much of Ornament, in outward show
Elaborate, of inward less exact.
For well I understand in the prime end   540
Of Nature her th' inferior, in the mind
And inward Faculties, which most excel,

---

518. The *amorous Bird of Night,* the nightingale.   Compare v, 39–41.

519. The evening star, Hesperus, is the planet Venus, and its appearance was the traditional signal for lighting nuptial torches from Catullus' epithalamium (lxii) to Spenser's:

> "Long though it be, at last I see it gloome
>   And the bright evening-star with golden creast
>   Appeare out of the east."
>   (*Epithalamion,* 285–7.)

532. *Superior and unmov'd, i. e.,* Adam finds himself superior to and unmoved by all other pleasures.

538. Compare *S. A.,* 1025–30; where the chorus asks about women:

> "Is it for that such outward ornament
>   Was lavish't on thir Sex, that inward gifts
>   Were left for haste unfinish'd, judgment scant,
>   Capacity not rais'd to apprehend
>   Or value what is best
>   In choice, but oftest to affect the wrong?"

In outward also her resembling less
His Image who made both, and less expressing
The character of that Dominion giv'n   545
O'er other Creatures; yet when I approach
Her loveliness, so absolute she seems
And in herself complete, so well to know
Her own, that what she wills to do or say,
Seems wisest, virtuousest, discreetest, best;   550
All higher knowledge in her presence falls
Degraded, Wisdom in discourse with her
Loses discount'nanc't, and like folly shows;
Authority and Reason on her wait,
As one intended first, not after made   555
Occasionally; and to consummate all,
Greatness of mind and nobleness thir seat
Build in her loveliest, and create an awe
About her, as a guard Angelic plac't.
To whom the Angel with contracted brow.   560
    Accuse not Nature, she hath done her part;
Do thou but thine, and be not diffident
Of Wisdom, she deserts thee not, if thou
Dismiss not her, when most thou need'st her nigh,
By attribúting overmuch to things   565
Less excellent, as thou thyself perceiv'st.
For what admir'st thou, what transports thee so,
An outside? fair no doubt, and worthy well
Thy cherishing, thy honouring, and thy love,
Not thy subjection: weigh with her thyself;   570
Then value: Oft-times nothing profits more
Than self-esteem, grounded on just and right
Well manag'd; of that skill the more thou know'st,

---

547. *absolute,* perfect.

556. *Occasionally,* for an occasion, or need, arising more or less accidentally.

561. Raphael's warning here is paralleled by God's rebuke to Adam after the fall (X, 145–56) and seemed necessary to Milton to prepare for Adam's surrender to Eve's charm after she has eaten the fruit. (IX, 952–999.)

569. Compare the marriage service in the *Book of Common Prayer:* "I take thee to my wedded wife . . . to love and to cherish."

573. *skill,* power or faculty—here self-esteem.

The more she will acknowledge thee her Head,
And to realities yield all her shows;   575
Made so adorn for thy delight the more,
So awful, that with honour thou may'st love
Thy mate, who sees when thou art seen least wise.
But if the sense of touch whereby mankind
Is propagated seem such dear delight   580
Beyond all other, think the same voutsaf't
To Cattle and each Beast; which would not be
To them made common and divulg'd, if aught
Therein enjoy'd were worthy to subdue
The Soul of Man, or passion in him move.   585
What higher in her society thou find'st
Attractive, human, rational, love still;
In loving thou dost well, in passion not,
Wherein true Love consists not; love refines
The thoughts, and heart enlarges, hath his seat   590
In Reason, and is judicious, is the scale
By which to heav'nly Love thou may'st ascend,
Not sunk in carnal pleasure, for which cause
Among the Beasts no Mate for thee was found.

---

574. Milton turned the verse in I Corinthians, xi, 3, which reads, "the head of the woman is the man."

576. *adorn,* adorned.

589. The distinction between sacred and profane love, the objects of both of which might be a woman, was a widespread theme in Renaissance painting and poetry. An example is Spenser's *Hymne in Honour of Love* (190–4):

> "Such is the powre of that sweet passion,
> That it all sordid basenesse doth expell,
> And the refyned mynd doth newly fashion
> Unto a fairer forme, which now doth dwell
> In his high thought, that would it selfe excell."

591. The *scale* is the *scale of Nature.* Compare V, 509–12 and IX, 112.

592. By *heav'nly Love* Milton meant the "divine love" of Plato's *Symposium* as it had been Christianized by poets from Dante to Spenser. In *An Hymne of Heavenly Love* (271–3) Spenser says that God's love so inflames the spirit

> "With burning zeale, through every part entire,
> That in no earthly thing thou shalt delight,
> But in his sweet and amiable sight."

To whom thus half abash't *Adam* repli'd.   595
Neither her out-side form'd so fair, nor aught
In procreation common to all kinds
(Though higher of the genial Bed by far,
And with mysterious reverence I deem)
So much delights me, as those graceful acts,   600
Those thousand decencies that daily flow
From all her words and actions, mixt with Love
And sweet compliance, which declare unfeign'd
Union of Mind, or in us both one Soul;
Harmony to behold in wedded pair   605
More grateful than harmonious sound to the ear.
Yet these subject not; I to thee disclose
What inward thence I feel, not therefore foil'd,
Who meet with various objects, from the sense
Variously representing; yet still free   610
Approve the best, and follow what I approve.
To love thou blam'st me not, for love thou say'st
Leads up to Heav'n, is both the way and guide;
Bear with me then, if lawful what I ask;
Love not the heav'nly Spirits, and how thir Love   615
Express they, by looks only, or do they mix
Irradiance, virtual or immediate touch?
   To whom the Angel with a smile that glow'd
Celestial rosy red, Love's proper hue,
Answer'd. Let it suffice thee that thou know'st   620
Us happy, and without Love no happiness.
Whatever pure thou in the body enjoy'st
(And pure thou wert created) we enjoy

---

598. *genial,* nuptial, procreative.

599. *mysterious* is used with the connotation that it is in IV, 743 and 750.

601. *decencies,* graces.

608. *not therefore foil'd,* not conquered by the objects of sense.

622. Milton must have sympathized with Henry More's notion of the angels singing, playing and dancing together, "reaping the lawful pleasures of the very animal life, in a far higher degree than we are capable of in this world. . . . Wherefore they cannot but enravish one another's souls, while they are mutual spectators of the perfect pulchritude of one another's person and comely carriage, of their graceful dancing, their melodious singing and playing." (*Immortality of the Soul,* p. 200.)

In eminence, and obstacle find none
Of membrane, joint, or limb, exclusive bars: 625
Easier than Air with Air, if Spirits embrace,
Total they mix, Union of Pure with Pure
Desiring; nor restrain'd conveyance need
As Flesh to mix with Flesh, or Soul with Soul.
But I can now no more; the parting Sun   630
Beyond the Earth's green Cape and verdant Isles
Hesperian sets, my Signal to depart.
Be strong, live happy, and love, but first of all
Him whom to love is to obey, and keep
His great command; take heed lest Passion sway   635
Thy Judgment to do aught, which else free Will
Would not admit; thine and of all thy Sons
The weal or woe in thee is plac't; beware.
I in thy persevering shall rejoice,
And all the Blest: stand fast; to stand or fall   640
Free in thine own Arbitrement it lies.
Perfet within, no outward aid require;
And all temptation to transgress repel.
    So saying, he arose; whom *Adam* thus
Follow'd with benediction. Since to part,   645
Go heavenly Guest, Ethereal Messenger,
Sent from whose sovran goodness I adore.
Gentle to me and affable hath been

---

624. *In eminence,* in the highest degree.

625. *exclusive,* excluding, obstructive.

627. Henry More's definition of spirit as "penetrable but indiscerptible body" made him regard the angels as capable of the closest possible union.

631. The *Earth's green Cape,* Cape Verde.
The *verdant Isles* are the Cape Verde Islands.

632. *Hesperian* may modify *Isles,* for the Cape Verde Islands were sometimes identified with the Gardens of the Hesperides; but it seems more likely to apply to the setting sun.

634. The line stems from I John v, 3: "For this is the love of God that we keep his commandments."

639. Compare the stress upon *persevering* in VII, 632.

640. The *Blest* are all the blessed spirits, or angels.

647. *from whose,* from him whose.

648. Compare the use of *affable* in VII, 41 with reference to Raphael.

Thy condescension, and shall be honour'd ever
With grateful Memory: thou to mankind   650
Be good and friendly still, and oft return.
    So parted they, the Angel up to Heav'n
From the thick shade, and *Adam* to his Bow'r.

The End of the Eighth Book.

BOOK IX

THE ARGUMENT

Satan *having compast the Earth, with meditated guile returns as a mist by Night into Paradise, enters into the Serpent sleeping.* Adam *and* Eve *in the Morning go forth to thir labours, which* Eve *proposes to divide in several places, each labouring apart:* Adam *consents not, alleging the danger, lest that Enemy, of whom they were forewarn'd, should attempt her found alone:* Eve *loath to be thought not circumspect or firm enough, urges her going apart, the rather desirous to make trial of her strength;* Adam *at last yields: The Serpent finds her alone; his subtle approach, first gazing, then speaking, with much flattery extolling* Eve *above all other Creatures.* Eve *wond'ring to hear the Serpent speak, asks how he attain'd to human speech and such understanding not till now; the Serpent answers, that by tasting of a certain Tree in the Garden he attain'd both to Speech and Reason, till then void of both:* Eve *requires him to bring her to that Tree, and finds it to be the Tree of Knowledge forbidden: The Serpent now grown bolder, with many wiles and arguments induces her at length to eat; she pleas'd with the taste deliberates awhile whether to impart thereof to* Adam *or not, at last brings him of the Fruit, relates what persuaded her to eat thereof:* Adam *at first amaz'd, but perceiving her lost, resolves through vehemence of love to perish with her; and extenuating the trespass, eats also of the Fruit: The effects thereof in them both; they seek to cover thir nakedness; then fall to variance and accusation of one another.*

No MORE of talk where God or Angel Guest
With Man, as with his Friend, familiar us'd
To sit indulgent, and with him partake
Rural repast, permitting him the while

---

1. *Angel Guest:* so Adam called Raphael—looking forward to the talk which has just ended—when he first appeared (V, 328). An episode in their talk has been Adam's account of his conversation with God (VIII, 311-499).

Venial discourse unblam'd: I now must change   5
Those Notes to Tragic; foul distrust, and breach
Disloyal on the part of Man, revolt,
And disobedience: On the part of Heav'n
Now alienated, distance and distaste,
Anger and just rebuke, and judgment giv'n,   10
That brought into this World a world of woe,
Sin and her shadow Death, and Misery
Death's Harbinger: Sad task, yet argument
Not less but more Heroic than the wrath
Of stern *Achilles* on his Foe pursu'd   15
Thrice Fugitive about *Troy* Wall; or rage
Of *Turnus* for *Lavinia* disespous'd,
Or *Neptune's* ire or *Juno's,* that so long
Perplex'd the *Greek* and *Cytherea's* Son;
If answerable style I can obtain   20
Of my Celestial Patroness, who deigns
Her nightly visitation unimplor'd,
And dictates to me slumb'ring, or inspires
Easy my unpremeditated Verse:
Since first this Subject for Heroic Song   25

---

6. *Tragic* is the keynote of the last four books of the poem. The word is used with more than a trace of its medieval meaning, for the falls of Lucifer and Adam were traditionally the greatest of tragedies, as Chaucer's Monk defined the term—a story

> "Of hym that stood in greet prosperitee,
> And is yfallen out of heigh degree."

Basically, however, Milton used the word in the moral sense which he immediately suggests. Although the remaining books are all streaked with pessimism, the tragic theme definitely yields, in Book X, to the theme of redemption.

11. Compare Milton's use of the same play on *world* in XI, 627.

15. As in the invocations to Books I and VII, Milton challenges comparison with the pagan epics. The *wrath of stern Achilles* alludes to the opening line of the *Iliad* so as to bring out the barbarity of his relentless pursuit and murder of Hector.

17. Milton contrasts his subject with that of the latter part of the *Aeneid,* the struggle of Aeneas and Turnus for the hand of Lavinia, and with the persecution of Ulysses by Neptune and Juno's injustice to Aeneas simply because she had quarrelled with his mother, Venus (Cytherea).

21. *Celestial Patroness,* Urania, who has been invoked in I, 6 and VII, 1.

Pleas'd me long choosing, and beginning late;
Not sedulous by Nature to indite
Wars, hitherto the only Argument
Heroic deem'd, chief maistry to dissect
With long and tedious havoc fabl'd Knights   30
In Battles feign'd; the better fortitude
Of Patience and Heroic Martyrdom
Unsung; or to describe Races and Games,
Or tilting Furniture, emblazon'd Shields,
Impreses quaint, Caparisons and Steeds;   35
Bases and tinsel Trappings, gorgeous Knights
At Joust and Tournament; then marshall'd Feast
Serv'd up in Hall with Sewers, and Seneschals;
The skill of Artifice or Office mean,
Not that which justly gives Heroic name   40
To Person or to Poem. Mee of these
Nor skill'd nor studious, higher Argument
Remains, sufficient of itself to raise
That name, unless an age too late, or cold

26. *long choosing and beginning late;* see the Introduction § 3.

29. *chief maistry to dissect:* the best skill of the authors of the medieval romances, Milton insinuates, was their talent for elaborate accounts of bloody fighting.

33. In II, 528–38, Milton mentions the sports of the waiting demons in hell and in IV, 551–2, he alludes to the "heroic games" of the angels guarding Paradise, but he has nothing like the athletic episodes in the *Iliad* (XXIII) and *Aeneid* (V).

34. *tilting Furniture,* equipment of the knight armed for tournament.

35. *Impreses quaint,* odd or ingenious devices or symbolic ornaments on the shields of knights.

36. *Bases,* housings for chargers. They were often made of silk, heavily embroidered.

38. *Sewers,* officers in charge of guests at a banquet. The word literally means "one who seats."

44. *an age too late:* the Proem to Book V of *The Faerie Queene* is the best literary statement of the "scientific" reasons for a prevailing opinion that the world was decaying. John Norden's *Vicissitudo Rerum* (1600) deplored the world-wide decline in human nature which it related to the proof that the progress of the sun differs

"farre from pristine gredience:
The *Solstices* and *Equinoxes* run,
As in pretended disobedience.
(*con.* p. 272.)

Climate, or Years damp my intended wing   45
Deprest, and much they may, if all be mine,
Not Hers who brings it nightly to my Ear.
  The Sun was sunk, and after him the Star
Of *Hesperus,* whose Office is to bring
Twilight upon the Earth, short Arbiter   50
Twixt Day and Night, and now from end to end
Night's Hemisphere had veil'd the Horizon round:
When *Satan* who late fled before the threats
Of *Gabriel* out of *Eden,* now improv'd
In meditated fraud and malice, bent   55
On man's destruction, maugre what might hap
Of heavier on himself, fearless return'd.
By Night he fled, and at Midnight return'd
From compassing the Earth, cautious of day,
Since *Uriel* Regent of the Sun descri'd   60
His entrance, and forewarn'd the Cherubim
That kept thir watch; thence full of anguish driv'n,
The space of seven continu'd Nights he rode
With darkness, thrice the Equinoctial Line
He circl'd, four times cross'd the Car of Night   65

----

44. (*con.*)
         The *Sunne* observed by *Artes* diligence,
             Is found in fourteene hundred yeeres to fall,
             Neere twelve *Degrees* towards the Center ball."
                 (Stanza 41.)
At Cambridge Milton wrote an exercise in lively Latin hexameters
on the topic that "Nature is not subject to old age," and here he finds
his will to write his epic in conflict with the pessimistic theory.

45. *Climate:* in the Preface to Book II of *Reason of Church Government* Milton mentioned adversity of "our climate, or the fate of this
age" as obstacles to the writing of his epic. In the *History of Britain* he
refers to southern lands as regions where "the sun ripens wits as well as
fruits," and, like most of his contemporaries, he accepted the belief inherited from Aristotle (*Politics,* VII, vi, 1) that the northern Europeans
lacked intelligence and skill.

46. *deprest:* Milton's intended poetic flight would be depressed if his
subject were not enough in itself to *raise* (43, above) it.

54. *improv'd:* taught by his experience (with Gabriel, IV, 873–1015)
how to refine his intended deceit.

56. *maugre,* in spite of. Compare III, 255.

60. *Uriel . . . descri'd:* in IV, 549–88.

From Pole to Pole, traversing each Colure;
On the eighth return'd, and on the Coast averse
From entrance or Cherubic Watch, by stealth
Found unsuspected way. There was a place,
Now not, though Sin, not Time, first wrought the change,   70
Where *Tigris* at the foot of Paradise
Into a Gulf shot under ground, till part
Rose up a Fountain by the Tree of Life;
In with the River sunk, and with it rose
Satan involv'd in rising Mist, then sought   75
Where to lie hid; Sea he had searcht and Land
From *Eden* over *Pontus,* and the Pool
Mæotis, up beyond the River *Ob;*
Downward as far Antarctic; and in length
West from *Orontes* to the Ocean barr'd   80
At *Darien,* thence to the Land where flows
Ganges and *Indus:* thus the Orb he roam'd
With narrow search; and with inspection deep
Consider'd every Creature, which of all
Most opportune might serve his Wiles, and found   85
The Serpent subtlest Beast of all the Field.

---

66. *traversing each Colure:* after avoiding the sun for three days by
flying around the earth at the equator opposite to it, Satan avoided it
by encircling the earth twice on the colure (or circle of longitude) drawn
around the globe through the poles and through the points on the
equator where it is cut by the ecliptic, and twice on the opposite, or
solstitial colure.

67. *the Coast averse,* the side opposite.

71. Milton had the authority of Josephus (*Antiquities,* I, i, 3) for
relating the Tigris to the river which "went out of Eden to water the
garden." (Gen. ii, 10.)

76. Satan had first flown north over *Pontus* (the Black Sea) and *the
Poll Maeotis* (the Sea of Azof) beyond the river Ob, or Obi, on the arctic
shore of Siberia. Milton's repeated references to the Ob in his *Brief
History of Moscovia* prove his interest.

80. *Orontes,* the chief river of Syria.

81. *Darien,* the isthmus of Panama.

82. *the Orb,* the globe of the world.

83. *narrow,* close, careful.

86. Genesis iii, 1, says that "the Serpent was more subtil than any
beast of the field which the Lord God had made"; and its character
not only allows Satan to use it to deceive Eve, but screens him from
suspicion until Adam suddenly surmises the truth in X, 1032–5.

Him after long debate, irresolute
Of thoughts revolv'd, his final sentence chose
Fit Vessel, fittest Imp of fraud, in whom
To enter, and his dark suggestions hide   90
From sharpest sight: for in the wily Snake,
Whatever sleights none would suspicious mark,
As from his wit and native subtlety
Proceeding, which in other Beasts observ'd
Doubt might beget of Diabolic pow'r   95
Active within beyond the sense of brute.
Thus he resolv'd, but first from inward grief
His bursting passion into plaints thus pour'd:·
   O Earth, how like to Heav'n, if not preferr'd
More justly, Seat worthier of Gods, as built   100
With second thoughts, reforming what was old!
For what God after better worse would build?
Terrestrial Heav'n, danc't round by other Heav'ns
That shine, yet bear thir bright officious Lamps,
Light above Light, for thee alone, as seems,   105
In thee concentring all thir precious beams
Of sacred influence: As God in Heav'n
Is Centre, yet extends to all, so thou
Centring receiv'st from all those Orbs; in thee,
Not in themselves, all thir known virtue appears   110
Productive in Herb, Plant, and nobler birth
Of Creatures animate with gradual life
Of Growth, Sense, Reason, all summ'd up in Man.
With what delight could I have walkt thee round,
If I could joy in aught, sweet interchange   115
Of Hill and Valley, Rivers, Woods and Plains,

---

88. *Of thoughts revolv'd,* among his endlessly circling thoughts. *sentence,* decision.

89. *Imp,* child (in a figurative sense).

95. *Doubt,* suspicion.

104. *officious:* compare VIII, 99, and note.

107. *sacred* because light is sacred, for "God is light" (III, i, and note).

112. In "the scale of Nature" (see V, 509) the lowest living order was the vegetables, capable only of growth; above them stood the animals, capable of both growth and sensation; and finally came man, adding *Reason.*

Now Land, now Sea, and Shores with Forest crown'd,
Rocks, Dens, and Caves; but I in none of these
Find place or refuge; and the more I see
Pleasures about me, so much more I feel   120
Torment within me, as from the hateful siege
Of contraries; all good to me becomes
Bane, and in Heav'n much worse would be my state.
But neither here seek I, no nor in Heav'n
To dwell, unless by maistring Heav'n's Supreme;   125
Nor hope to be myself less miserable
By what I seek, but others to make such
As I, though thereby worse to me redound:
For only in destroying I find ease
To my relentless thoughts; and him destroy'd,   130
Or won to what may work his utter loss,
For whom all this was made, all this will soon
Follow, as to him linkt in weal or woe,
In woe then; that destruction wide may range:
To mee shall be the glory sole among   135
The infernal Powers, in one day to have marr'd
What he *Almighty* styl'd, six Nights and Days
Continu'd making, and who knows how long
Before had been contriving, though perhaps
Not longer than since I in one Night freed   140
From servitude inglorious well nigh half
Th' Angelic Name, and thinner left the throng
Of his adorers: hee to be aveng'd,
And to repair his numbers thus impair'd,
Whether such virtue spent of old now fail'd   145

---

119. *place or refuge,* a home or even a retreat.

121. *siege,* seat or dwelling.

123. *Bane,* evil. For the thought, compare Satan's soliloquy in IV, 32–113.

133. *Follow:* when Eve tasted the fruit of the Tree of Knowledge all nature "gave signs of woe" (783 below). In X, 651–714, the reason becomes clear.

140. In this suggestion Satan deceives himself, for he knows that his journey to earth was resolved upon in hell only because the fame of a new world to be created had been rife in heaven before his revolt. (II, 345–51.)

More Angels to Create, if they at least
Are his Created, or to spite us more,
Determin'd to advance into our room
A Creature form'd of Earth, and him endow,
Exalted from so base original,   150
With Heav'nly spoils, our spoils; What he decreed
He effected; Man he made, and for him built
Magnificent this World, and Earth his seat,
Him Lord pronounc'd, and, O indignity!
Subjected to his service Angel wings,   155
And flaming Ministers to watch and tend
Thir earthy Charge: Of these the vigilance
I dread, and to elude, thus wrapt in mist
Of midnight vapour glide obscure, and pry
In every Bush and Brake, where hap may find   160
The Serpent sleeping, in whose mazy folds
To hide me, and the dark intent I bring.
O foul descent! that I who erst contended
With Gods to sit the highest, am now constrain'd
Into a Beast, and mixt with bestial slime,   165
This essence to incarnate and imbrute,
That to the highth of Deity aspir'd;
But what will not Ambition and Revenge
Descend to? who aspires must down as low
As high he soar'd, obnoxious first or last   170

---

146. *if they . . . are his created:* an example of wishful thinking which contrasts with Satan's acknowledgement that he is God's creature in his earlier soliloquy (IV, 43). Compare V, 853.

149. Tasso (and Vida in the *Christiad*) made Satan, when speaking to the demons in hell, appeal to their contempt of man on the ground that

"... in our Place, the Heavens possess he must,
      Vile Man, begot of Clay, and born of Dust."
      (*Jerusalem Delivered,* Fairfax's translation, IV, x.)

155. Satan makes a grievance of his discovery that God "gives his angels charge" (Ps. xci, 11) of mankind.

156. With the *flaming Ministers* compare the "flaming Cherubim" of VI, 102.

166. *This essence:* compare the note on I, 138 and see the Introduction, §15.

170. *obnoxious* keeps its Latin force of "liable to" or "exposed to."

To basest things. Revenge, at first though sweet,
Bitter ere long back on itself recoils;
Let it; I reck not, so it light well aim'd,
Since higher I fall short, on him who next
Provokes my envy, this new Favorite   175
Of Heav'n, this Man of Clay, Son of despite,
Whom us the more to spite his Maker rais'd
From dust: spite then with spite is best repaid.

So saying, through each Thicket Dank or Dry,
Like a black mist low creeping, he held on   180
His midnight search, where soonest he might find
The Serpent: him fast sleeping soon he found
In Labyrinth of many a round self-roll'd,
His head the midst, well stor'd with subtle wiles:
Not yet in horrid Shade or dismal Den,   185
Nor nocent yet, but on the grassy Herb
Fearless unfear'd he slept: in at his Mouth
The Devil enter'd, and his brutal sense,
In heart or head, possessing soon inspir'd

---

172. Compare IV, 15–18.

175. *envy* has been the motive secondary to pride with Satan; announced in I, 35, prompting his revolt against the Son of God in V, 662,
and confirming his purpose against mankind in IV, 503. In this Milton
followed a rabbinical and patristic tradition which he found exemplified
widely in literature. For Du Bartas Satan was replete with

>   "envious heart-break to see yet to shine
>   In Adam's face God's image, all divine."
>   (*The Imposture,* p. 186.)

In the Foreword to Vondel's *Lucifer* pride and envy are made the
mainsprings of Satan's nature and St. Augustine's definition of envy as
hatred of another's happiness is quoted. Compare *The City of God,*
XII, xi.

178. Compare the charge against Beëlzebub of doing "all to spite the
great Creator" in II, 384–5.

180. *Like a black mist:* a reminiscence, perhaps, of Thetis rising "like
a cloud" from the sea at Achilles' prayer (*Il.* I, 359), and an expression
of the current belief that,

>   "as in liquid clouds exhaled thickly,
>   Water and air, as moist, do mingle quickly,
>   The evil angels slide too easily
>   As subtile spirits into our phantasy."
>   (Du Bartas, p. 188.)

187. *Fearless unfear'd,* fearing nothing and not yet terrible to others.
The allusion is to the coming curse. (X, 181.)

With act intelligential; but his sleep   190
Disturb'd not, waiting close th' approach of Morn.
Now whenas sacred Light began to dawn
In *Eden* on the humid Flow'rs, that breath'd
Thir morning incense, when all things that breathe
From th' Earth's great Altar send up silent praise   195
To the Creator, and his Nostrils fill
With grateful Smell, forth came the human pair
And join'd thir vocal Worship to the Quire
Of Creatures wanting voice, that done, partake
The season, prime for sweetest Scents and Airs: 200
Then cómmune how that day they best may ply
Thir growing work: for much thir work outgrew
The hands' dispatch of two Gard'ning so wide.
And *Eve* first to her Husband thus began.
    Adam, well may we labour still to dress   205
This Garden, still to tend Plant, Herb and Flow'r.
Our pleasant task enjoin'd, but till more hands
Aid us, the work under our labour grows,
Luxurious by restraint; what we by day
Lop overgrown, or prune, or prop, or bind,   210
One night or two with wanton growth derides
Tending to wild. Thou therefore now advise
Or hear what to my mind first thoughts present,
Let us divide our labours, thou where choice
Leads thee, or where most needs, whether to wind   215
The Woodbine round this Arbour, or direct
The clasping Ivy where to climb, while I
In yonder Spring of Roses intermixt
With Myrtle, find what to redress till Noon:
For while so near each other thus all day   220

---

190. *act,* activity.

191. *close,* hidden.

192. *whenas,* when.

197. Milton remembered the passages when, as in Genesis viii, 21, "the Lord smelled a sweet savour" from altars of sacrifice.

199. *wanting,* lacking.

205. *still,* always, constantly.

212. *wild,* wildness.

218. *Spring* meant a grove or copse of young trees or shrubs.

Our task we choose, what wonder if so near
Looks intervene and smiles, or object new
Casual discourse draw on, which intermits
Our day's work brought to little, though begun
Early, and th' hour of Supper comes unearn'd.   225
    To whom mild answer *Adam* thus return'd.
Sole *Eve,* Associate sole, to me beyond
Compare above all living Creatures dear,
Well hast thou motion'd, well thy thoughts imploy'd
How we might best fulfil the work which here   230
God hath assign'd us, nor of me shalt pass
Unprais'd: for nothing lovelier can be found
In Woman, than to study household good,
And good works in her Husband to promote.
Yet not so strictly hath our Lord impos'd   235
Labour, as to debar us when we need
Refreshment, whether food, or talk between,
Food of the mind, or this sweet intercourse
Of looks and smiles, for smiles from Reason flow,
To brute deni'd, and are of Love the food,   240
Love not the lowest end of human life.
For not to irksome toil, but to delight
He made us, and delight to Reason join'd.
These paths and Bowers doubt not but our joint hands
Will keep from Wilderness with ease, as wide   245
As we need walk, till younger hands ere long
Assist us: But if much converse perhaps
Thee satiate, to short absence I could yield.
For solitude sometimes is best society,
And short retirement urges sweet return.   250
But other doubt possesses me, lest harm
Befall thee sever'd from me; for thou know'st

---

229. *Motioned,* suggested, "moved" in the parliamentary sense.

241. *end,* object.

245. *wilderness,* wildness.

249. *solitude:* the thought was a commonplace going back to Cicero's remark that Africanus was never so little alone as when he was by himself. (*De re publica,* I, xvii, 27.)

As in the case of "satiety" in VIII, 216, Milton seems to have weighted the two final syllables too lightly to feel them as an extra foot in the pentameter.

What hath been warn'd us, what malicious Foe
Envying our happiness, and of his own
Despairing, seeks to work us woe and shame   255
By sly assault; and somewhere nigh t hand
Watches, no doubt, with greedy hope to find
His wish and best advantage, us asunder,
Hopeless to circumvent us join'd, where each
To other speedy aid might lend at need;   260
Whether his first design be to withdraw
Our fealty from God, or to disturb
Conjugal Love, than which perhaps no bliss
Enjoy'd by us excites his envy more;
Or this, or worse, leave not the faithful side   265
That gave thee being, still shades thee and protects.
The Wife, where danger or dishonour lurks,
Safest and seemliest by her Husband stays,
Who guards her, or with her the worst endures.

   To whom the Virgin Majesty of *Eve,*   270
As one who loves, and some unkindness meets,
With sweet austere composure thus repli'd.

   Offspring of Heav'n and Earth, and all Earth's Lord,
That such an Enemy we have, who seeks
Our ruin, both by thee inform'd I learn,   275
And from the parting Angel over-heard
As in a shady nook I stood behind,
Just then return'd at shut of Ev'ning Flow'rs.
But that thou shouldst my firmness therefore doubt
To God or thee, because we have a foe   280
May tempt it, I expected not to hear.
His violence thou fear'st not, being such,
As wee, not capable of death or pain,

---

264. Rabbinical commentary on the statement that "the serpent was
more subtil than any beast of the field" (Gen. iii, 1) explained that the
serpent was envious of the wedded happiness of Adam and Eve.   And
Josephus says that "the serpent, which then lived together with Adam
and his wife, shewed an envious disposition, at his supposal of their
living happily; . . . and persuaded the woman out of a malicious intention to taste of the tree of knowledge." (*Antiquities,* I, i, 4.)   Compare
IV, 502–3.

265. *the . . . side That gave thee being:* compare the creation of
Eve in VIII, 465–71.

270. *Virgin,* virginal, innocent.

Can either not receive, or can repel.
His fraud is then thy fear, which plain infers   285
Thy equal fear that my firm Faith and Love
Can by his fraud be shak'n or seduc't;
Thoughts, which how found they harbour in thy breast,
Adam, misthought of her to thee so dear?
  To whom with healing words *Adam* repli'd.   290
Daughter of God and Man, immortal *Eve,*
For such thou art, from sin and blame entire:
Not diffident of thee do I dissuade
Thy absence from my sight, but to avoid
Th' attempt itself, intended by our Foe.   295
For hee who tempts, though in vain, at least asperses
The tempted with dishonour foul, suppos'd
Not incorruptible of Faith, not proof
Against temptation: thou thyself with scorn
And anger wouldst resent the offer'd wrong,   300
Though ineffectual found: misdeem not then,
If such affront I labour to avert
From thee alone, which on us both at once
The Enemy, though bold, will hardly dare,
Or daring, first on mee th' assault shall light.   305
Nor thou his malice and false guile contemn;
Subtle he needs must be, who could seduce
Angels, nor think superfluous others' aid.
I from the influence of thy looks receive
Access in every Virtue, in thy sight   310
More wise, more watchful, stronger, while shame, thou looking on,
Shame to be overcome or over-reacht
Would utmost vigor raise, and rais'd unite.

---

284. *can either not receive, etc.,* either are incapable of suffering or
can resist.

288. *Thoughts which how found,* how did such thoughts find?

289. *misthought,* misjudgement.

292. *entire* has its Latin force of "whole," "unimpaired" and therefore "innocent."

296. *asperses* means literally "sprinkles."

298. *Faith,* fidelity, loyalty.

310. *Access,* increase. Perhaps Milton thought of Plato's value for the
mutual emulation of friends as an incentive to virtue. (*Symposium,*
178-9.)

Why shouldst not thou like sense within thee feel   315
When I am present, and thy trial choose
With me, best witness of thy Virtue tri'd.
  So spake domestic *Adam* in his care
And Matrimonial Love, but *Eve,* who thought
Less attribúted to her Faith sincere,   320
Thus her reply with accent sweet renew'd.
  If this be our condition, thus to dwell
In narrow circuit strait'n'd by a Foe,
Subtle or violent, we not endu'd
Single with like defence, wherever met,   325
How are we happy, still in fear of harm?
But harm precedes not sin: only our Foe
Tempting affronts us with his foul esteem
Of our integrity: his foul esteem
Sticks no dishonour on our Front, but turns   330
Foul on himself; then wherefore shunn'd or fear'd
By us? who rather double honour gain
From his surmise prov'd false, find peace within,
Favour from Heav'n, our witness from th' event.
And what is Faith, Love, Virtue unassay'd   335
Alone, without exterior help sustain'd?
Let us not then suspect our happy State
Left so imperfet by the Maker wise,
As not secure to single or combin'd.
Frail is our happiness, if this be so,   340
And *Eden* were no *Eden* thus expos'd.
  To whom thus *Adam* fervently repli'd.
O Woman, best are all things as the will
Of God ordain'd them, his creating hand
Nothing imperfet or deficient left   345

---

315. *sense,* sensation, experience.

323. *strait'n'd,* confined, limited.

325. *wherever met: i. e.,* wherever the foe may be met by either Adam or Eve singly.

330. *Front,* brow. The word points back to *affronts* (328), playing on the unfavourable meaning of the latter word and the favourable connotation of the former. Compare the note on II, 302.

334. *event* has its literal Latin meaning of "outcome," "result."

339. *not secure, etc.,* not within our confident control, regardless whether we are alone or together.

Of all that he Created, much less Man,
Or aught that might his happy State secure,
Secure from outward force; within himself
The danger lies, yet lies within his power:
Against his will he can receive no harm.   350
But God left free the Will, for what obeys
Reason, is free, and Reason he made right,
But bid her well beware, and still erect,
Lest by some fair appearing good surpris'd
She dictate false, and misinform the Will   355
To do what God expressly hath forbid.
Not then mistrust, but tender love enjoins,
That I should mind thee oft, and mind thou me.
Firm we subsist, yet possible to swerve,
Since Reason not impossibly may meet   360
Some specious object by the Foe suborn'd,
And fall into deception unaware,
Not keeping strictest watch, as she was warn'd.
Seek not temptation then, which to avoid
Were better, and most likely if from mee   365
Thou sever not: Trial will come unsought.
Wouldst thou approve thy constancy, approve
First thy obedience; th' other who can know,
Not seeing thee attempted, who attest?
But if thou think, trial unsought may find   370
Us both securer than thus warn'd thou seem'st,
Go; for thy stay, not free, absents thee more;
Go in thy native innocence, rely
On what thou hast of virtue, summon all,

---

351. Before the Fall Milton is determined to make Adam fully conscious of the freedom of the will, so distinctly stated by God in III,
96–128, and by Raphael in V, 520–40, and to make Adam confess his
own favourite doctrine that "the gift of reason has been implanted in
all, by which they may of themselves resist bad desires." (*C. D.*, I, iv.)

353. *erect*, alert.

358. *mind*, remind.

361. *suborned*: compare Spenser (cited by *N. E. D.*): "Evill thinges
being decked and suborned with gay attyre of goodly wordes."

367. *approve*, vindicate, give proof of.

371. *securer* has its literal Latin sense of "less careful," "less on
guard."

For God towards thee hath done his part, do thine.   375
  So spake the Patriarch of Mankind, but *Eve*
Persisted, yet submiss, though last, repli'd.
  With thy permission then, and thus forewarn'd
Chiefly by what thy own last reasoning words
Touch'd only, that our trial, when least sought,   380
May find us both perhaps far less prepar'd,
The willinger I go, nor much expect
A Foe so proud will first the weaker seek;
So bent, the more shall shame him his repulse.
Thus saying, from her Husband's hand her hand   385
Soft she withdrew, and like a Wood-Nymph light,
Oread or *Dryad,* or of *Delia's* Train,
Betook her to the Groves, but *Delia's* self
In gait surpass'd and Goddess-like deport,
Though not as shee with Bow and Quiver arm'd,   390
But with such Gard'ning Tools as Art yet rude,
Guiltless of fire had form'd, or Angels brought.
To *Pales,* or *Pomona,* thus adorn'd,
Likest she seem'd, *Pomona* when she fled
Vertumnus, or to *Ceres* in her Prime,   395
Yet Virgin of *Proserpina* from *Jove.*
Her long with ardent look his Eye pursu'd
Delighted, but desiring more her stay.
Oft he to her his charge of quick return
Repeated, shee to him as oft engag'd   400

377. *submiss,* submitted (a participle). Virtually it means "submissively."

387. *Oread or Dryad,* mountain or wood nymph. Her birthplace, Delos, gave Diana (Artemis) the name *Delia.* Milton thought of Diana with the conventional bow and arrows, leading her train of nymphs in quest of game.

389. *deport,* bearing, manner.

393. *Pales* was a primitive Roman goddess of flocks and herds.

394. Milton remembered Ovid's picture of the goddess of fruit, Pomona, with her pruning hook (*Met.* XIV, 628), and his story of her long resistance to the wood-god, Vertumnus.

395. Renaissance painters were fond of the figure of the young Ceres, who Ovid says (*Met.* V, 341) was the first to use the plough. It would have been inappropriate to compare Eve to the older Ceres who suffered "all that pain" (IV, 271) in seeking her daughter Proserpina through the world.

To be return'd by Noon amid the Bow'r,
And all things in best order to invite
Noontide repast, or Afternoon's repose.
O much deceiv'd, much failing, hapless *Eve,*
Of thy presum'd return! event perverse!   405
Thou never from that hour in Paradise
Found'st either sweet repast, or sound repose;
Such ambush hid among sweet Flow'rs and Shades
Waited with hellish rancour imminent
To intercept thy way, or send thee back   410
Despoil'd of Innocence, of Faith, of Bliss.
For now, and since first break of dawn the Fiend,
Mere Serpent in appearance, forth was come,
And on his Quest, where likeliest he might find
The only two of Mankind, but in them   415
The whole included Race, his purpos'd prey.
In Bow'r and Field he sought, where any tuft
Of Grove or Garden-Plot more pleasant lay,
Thir tendance or Plantation for delight,
By Fountain or by shady Rivulet.   420
He sought them both, but wish'd his hap might find
Eve separate, he wish'd, but not with hope
Of what so seldom chanc'd, when to his wish,
Beyond his hope, *Eve* separate he spies,
Veil'd in a Cloud of Fragrance, where she stood,   425
Half spi'd, so thick the Roses bushing round
About her glow'd, oft stooping to support
Each Flow'r of slender stalk, whose head though gay
Carnation, Purple, Azure, or speckt with Gold,
Hung drooping unsustain'd, them she upstays   430
Gently with Myrtle band, mindless the while,

---

413. *Mere* meant "identically itself" rather than, more or less, "contemptible," as it does today. Milton may have meant that the serpent, whatever kind of creature it was before it was cursed, was certainly not the monster of rabbinical tradition. Andreini's *L'Adamo,* Act II, scene iii, improves upon the tradition to make the tempting fiend appear in the form of a serpent from the waist down and of a lovely maiden otherwise.

418. *more pleasant,* exceptionally pleasant.

419. *tendance,* object of care. Compare "nursery" in VIII, 46.

431. *mindless,* heedless, careless (of herself).

Herself, though fairest unsupported Flow'r,
From her best prop so far, and storm so nigh.
Nearer he drew, and many a walk travers'd
Of stateliest Covert, Cedar, Pine, or Palm,   435
Then voluble and bold, now hid, now seen
Among thick-wov'n Arborets and Flow'rs
Imborder'd on each Bank, the hand of *Eve:*
Spot more delicious than those Gardens feign'd
Or of reviv'd *Adonis,* or renown'd   440
Alcinoüs, host of old *Laertes'* Son,
Or that, not Mystic, where the Sapient King
Held dalliance with his fair *Egyptian* Spouse.
Much hee the Place admir'd, the Person more.
As one who long in populous City pent,   445
Where Houses thick and Sewers annoy the Air,
Forth issuing on a Summer's Morn to breathe
Among the pleasant Villages and Farms

436. *voluble* keeps its Latin force of "turning" or "rolling upon itself."

438. *imborder'd,* planted to form borders.
the hand of Eve, the handiwork of Eve.

440. Of the many references to the garden where Venus nursed Adonis after his mortal wound by the boar, Spenser's was the most elaborate in Elizabethan literature:

> "So faire a place as Nature can devize:
> Whether in Paphos, or Cytheron hill,
> Or it in Gnidus bee, I wote not well;
> But well I wote by triall, that this same
> All other pleasaunt places doth excell,
> And called is by her lost lovers name,
> The Gardin of Adonis, far renowmd by fame," *etc.*
> (*F.Q.* III, vi, 29.)

441. Compare the note on *Laertes'* Son, Ulysses' visit to *Alcinoüs'* garden in V, 341.

442. *not Mystic* has the force of "real" or "historical," for the garden of Adonis as Spenser and the mythographers treated it was an allegory in which Adonis represented the sun and its vivifying power. To this pagan mystery is opposed the garden where Solomon, the *Sapient King,* brought his bride when he "made affinity with Pharaoh king of Egypt, and took Pharaoh's daughter." (I Kings iii, 1.) Milton was thinking here of the many allusions to Solomon's garden in the Song of Solomon, which he may have understood, on the strength of the address to the "prince's daughter" in vii, 1, as an epithalamium written for the Egyptian princess.

446. *annoy,* make noxious or noisome.

Adjoin'd, from each thing met conceives delight,
The smell of Grain, or tedded Grass, or Kine,   450
Or Dairy, each rural sight, each rural sound;
If chance with Nymphlike step fair Virgin pass,
What pleasing seem'd, for her now pleases more,
She most, and in her look sums all Delight.
Such Pleasure took the Serpent to behold   455
This Flow'ry Plat, the sweet recess of *Eve*
Thus early, thus alone; her Heav'nly form
Angelic, but more soft, and Feminine,
Her graceful Innocence, her every Air
Of gesture or least action overaw'd   460
His Malice, and with rapine sweet bereav'd
His fierceness of the fierce intent it brought:
That space the Evil one abstracted stood
From his own evil, and for the time remain'd
Stupidly good, of enmity disarm'd,   465
Of guile, of hate, of envy, of revenge;
But the hot Hell that always in him burns,
Though in mid Heav'n, soon ended his delight,
And tortures him now more, the more he sees
Of pleasure not for him ordain'd: then soon   470
Fierce hate he recollects, and all his thoughts
Of mischief, gratulating, thus excites.
     Thoughts, whither have ye led me, with what sweet
Compulsion thus transported to forget
What hither brought us, hate, not love, nor hope   475
Of Paradise for Hell, hope here to taste
Of pleasure, but all pleasure to destroy,
Save what is in destroying, other joy
To me is lost.   Then let me not let pass
Occasion which now smiles, behold alone   480

450. *tedded,* spread, scattered (*i.e.,* to make hay).
Kine, cattle.
453. *for her,* on her account.
454. *sums,* represents and completes (all the beauty of the landscape).
456. *plat,* plot of ground.
461. *rapine,* robbery.
467. *Hell that always in him burns:* compare the note on IV, 20.
472. *gratulating,* rejoicing or gloating.

The Woman, opportune to all attempts,
Her Husband, for I view far round, not nigh,
Whose higher intellectual more I shun,
And strength, of courage haughty, and of limb
Heroic built, though of terrestrial mould,   485
Foe not informidable, exempt from wound,
I not; so much hath Hell debas'd, and pain
Infeebl'd me, to what I was in Heav'n.
Shee fair, divinely fair, fit Love for Gods,
Not terrible, though terror be in Love   490
And beauty, not approacht by stronger hate,
Hate stronger, under show of Love well feign'd,
The way which to her ruin now I tend.
  So spake the Enemy of Mankind, enclos'd
In Serpent, Inmate bad, and toward *Eve*   495
Address'd his way, not with indented wave,
Prone on the ground, as since, but on his rear,
Circular base of rising folds, that tow'r'd
Fold above fold a surging Maze, his Head
Crested aloft, and Carbuncle his Eyes;   500
With burnisht Neck of verdant Gold, erect
Amidst his circling Spires, that on the grass
Floated redundant: pleasing was his shape,
And lovely, never since of Serpent kind
Lovelier, not those that in *Illyria* chang'd   505
Hermione and *Cadmus,* or the God
In *Epidaurus;* nor to which transform'd

---

481. *opportune,* opportunely circumstanced.

485. *terrestrial mould,* earth. Compare *mould* in II, 139.

486. *exempt from wound:* compare 283 above and the note on VI, 327.

491. *not approacht,* unless approached.

492. *Hate stronger, etc.:* Hate is stronger when disguised as Love.

502. *Spires* keeps its Latin force of "loops" or "coils."

505. *chang'd, i.e.,* metamorphosed Cadmus and Hermione into them-
selves. The word itself is an allusion to Ovid's *Metamorphoses,* where
(IV, 563–603) Milton remembered the story of the transformation of
Cadmus and Harmonia (Hermione) into serpents.

506. *The God* is Aesculapius, the deity of healing, whom Ovid
described (*Met.* XV, 670–4) as manifesting himself like a serpent, with
flashing eyes and head held as high as a man's breast, in his temple in
Epidaurus, in Argolis.

Ammonian Jove, or *Capitoline* was seen,
Hee with *Olympias,* this with her who bore
Scipio the highth of *Rome.*   With tract oblique   510
At first, as one who sought access, but fear'd
To interrupt, side-long he works his way.
As when a Ship by skilful Steersman wrought
Nigh River's mouth or Foreland, where the Wind
Veers oft, as oft so steers, and shifts her Sail;   515
So varied hee, and of his tortuous Train
Curl'd many a wanton wreath in sight of *Eve,*
To lure her Eye; shee busied heard the sound
Of rustling Leaves, but minded not, as us'd
To such disport before her through the Field,   520
From every Beast, more duteous at her call,
Than at *Circean* call the Herd disguis'd.
Hee bolder now, uncall'd before her stood;
But as in gaze admiring: Oft he bow'd
His turret Crest, and sleek enamell'd Neck,   525
Fawning, and lick'd the ground whereon she trod.
His gentle dumb expression turn'd at length
The Eye of *Eve* to mark his play; he glad
Of her attention gain'd, with Serpent Tongue
Organic, or impulse of vocal Air,   530
His fraudulent temptation thus began.

---

508. Plutarch, in his life of Alexander the Great, doubtfully relates
a tradition that Alexander's mother, *Olympias,* revealed to him that he
was the son of Jupiter Ammon (compare IV, 277) and that her divine
lover had taken the form of a serpent.

509. *her who bore Scipio,* Sempronia, who was said to have borne
Scipio Africanus to Jupiter in secret.

522. One of the striking touches in Homer's story of the encounter
of Ulysses' men with the *Herd disguis'd,* the mob of wild animals outside the palace of the enchantress Circe, is the friendliness of the beasts,
"like dogs fawning on a returning master."   (*Od.,* X, 214–19.)

525. *turret,* tower-like.

530. *Organic:* either Satan directly moved the serpent's speech organs
or he made the air vocal with some more direct impulse. Du Bartas
raises the question whether Satan did "govern the dragon . . . and his
tongue direct" or moved it as one violin string induces a vibration in
another,

> "Or as a star which, though far distant, pours
> Upon our heads hapless or happy showers."
> (*The Imposture,* pp. 189–90.)

Wonder not, sovran Mistress, if perhaps
Thou canst, who art sole Wonder, much less arm
Thy looks, the Heav'n of mildness, with disdain,
Displeas'd that I approach thee thus, and gaze   535
Insatiate, I thus single, nor have fear'd
Thy awful brow, more awful thus retir'd.
Fairest resemblance of thy Maker fair,
Thee all things living gaze on, all things thine
By gift, and thy Celestial Beauty adore   540
With ravishment beheld, there best beheld
Where universally admir'd: but here
In this enclosure wild, these Beasts among,
Beholders rude, and shallow to discern
Half what in thee is fair, one man except,   545
Who sees thee? (and what is one?) who shouldst be seen
A Goddess among Gods, ador'd and serv'd
By Angels numberless, thy daily Train.
   So gloz'd the Tempter, and his Proem tun'd;
Into the Heart of *Eve* his words made way,   550
Though at the voice much marvelling; at length
Not unamaz'd she thus in answer spake.
What may this mean?   Language of Man pronounc't
By Tongue of Brute, and human sense exprest?
The first at least of these I thought deni'd   555
To Beasts, whom God on thir Creation-Day
Created mute to all articulate sound;
The latter I demur, for in thir looks

---

533. *sole Wonder* resembles Comus' salute to the Lady as "foreign
Wonder" (*Comus*, 265) and the serpent's speeches are pitched in the
key of Comus' appeal to the Lady.

549. *gloz'd* recalls Comus'

> "glozing courtesy,
> Baited with reasons not unplausible." (161–2.)

552. *Not unamaz'd:* Milton perhaps shared Sir Thomas Browne's surprise that Eve's amazement included no suspicion. She was deceived,
Browne says, by no "invisible insinuation," but by "an open and
discoverable apparition, that is, in the form of a Serpent; whereby although there were many occasions of suspicion, and such as could not
easily escape a weaker circumspection, yet did the unwary apprehension
of Eve take no advantage thereof." (*Pseudodoxia*, I, i.)

558. *demur,* entertain doubts of. God has said that the beasts in
Eden "know And reason not contemptibly." (VIII, 373–4.)

Much reason, and in thir actions oft appears.
Thee, Serpent, subtlest beast of all the field   560
I knew, but not with human voice endu'd;
Redouble then this miracle, and say,
How cam'st thou speakable of mute, and how
To me so friendly grown above the rest
Of brutal kind, that daily are in sight?   565
Say, for such wonder claims attention due.
    To whom the guileful Tempter thus repli'd.
Empress of this fair World, resplendent *Eve,*
Easy to mee it is to tell thee all
What thou command'st and right thou shouldst be obey'd: 570
I was at first as other Beasts that graze
The trodden Herb, of abject thoughts and low,
As was my food, nor aught but food discern'd
Or Sex, and apprehended nothing high:
Till on a day roving the field, I chanc'd   575
A goodly Tree far distant to behold
Loaden with fruit of fairest colours mixt,
Ruddy and Gold: I nearer drew to gaze;
When from the boughs a savoury odour blown,
Grateful to appetite, more pleas'd my sense   580
Than smell of sweetest Fennel, or the Teats
Of Ewe or Goat dropping with Milk at Ev'n,
Unsuckt of Lamb or Kid, that tend thir play.
To satisfy the sharp desire I had
Of tasting those fair Apples, I resolv'd   585
Not to defer; hunger and thirst at once,
Powerful persuaders, quick'n'd at the scent
Of that alluring fruit, urg'd me so keen.
About the Mossy Trunk I wound me soon,
For high from ground the branches would require   590
Thy utmost reach or *Adam's:* Round the Tree
All other Beasts that saw, with like desire
Longing and envying stood, but could not reach.
Amid the Tree now got, where plenty hung

---

563. *of mute,* from mute condition. Compare the note on IV, 153.

581. *Fennel* was supposed to be a favourite food of snakes. Compare Lyly (*Sappho and Phao,* II, iv): "Fancy is a worme, that feedeth first upon fenell." Another popular belief made them suck the teats of sheep.

Tempting so nigh, to pluck and eat my fill   595
I spar'd not, for such pleasure till that hour
At Feed or Fountain never had I found.
Sated at length, ere long I might perceive
Strange alteration in me, to degree
Of Reason in my inward Powers, and Speech   600
Wanted not long, though to this shape retain'd.
Thenceforth to Speculations high or deep
I turn'd my thoughts, and with capacious mind
Consider'd all things visible in Heav'n,
Or Earth, or Middle, all things fair and good;   605
But all that fair and good in thy Divine
Semblance, and in thy Beauty's heav'nly Ray
United I beheld; no Fair to thine
Equivalent or second, which compell'd
Mee thus, though importune perhaps, to come   610
And gaze, and worship thee of right declar'd
Sovran of Creatures, universal Dame.
  So talk'd the spirited sly Snake; and *Eve*
Yet more amaz'd unwary thus repli'd.
  Serpent, thy overpraising leaves in doubt   615
The virtue of that Fruit, in thee first prov'd:
But say, where grows the Tree, from hence how far?
For many are the Trees of God that grow
In Paradise, and various, yet unknown
To us, in such abundance lies our choice,   620
As leaves a greater store of Fruit untoucht,
Still hanging incorruptible, till men
Grow up to thir provision, and more hands
Help to disburden Nature of her Birth.

---

599. *to degree, etc.,* amounting to the gift of a degree of reason
in the mind, to which speech was soon added, although there was
no change of outward form.

605. *Middle,* the air. Compare the note on I, 516, where the word
is used in a related technical sense.

612. *Dame* keeps its original Latin force of "mistress."

613. *spirited,* spirit-possessed.

623. *to thir provision,* to numbers proportionate to what has been
provided.

624. *Birth* is spelled "bearth" in the original, a form which indicates
the meaning of "fruit" of every kind better than the modern spelling
of this word.

To whom the wily Adder, blithe and glad.   625
Empress, the way is ready, and not long,
Beyond a row of Myrtles, on a Flat,
Fast by a Fountain, one small Thicket past
Of blowing Myrrh and Balm; if thou accept
My conduct, I can bring thee thither soon.   630
    Lead then, said *Eve*. Hee leading swiftly roll'd
In tangles, and made intricate seem straight,
To mischief swift. Hope elevates, and joy
Bright'ns his Crest, as when a wand'ring Fire,
Compact of unctuous vapour, which the Night   635
Condenses, and the cold invirons round,
Kindl'd through agitation to a Flame,
Which oft, they say, some evil Spirit attends,
Hovering and blazing with delusive Light,
Misleads th' amaz'd Night-wanderer from his way   640
To Bogs and Mires, and oft through Pond or Pool,
There swallow'd up and lost, from succour far.
So glister'd the dire Snake, and into fraud
Led *Eve* our credulous Mother, to the Tree
Of prohibition, root of all our woe;   645
Which when she saw, thus to her guide she spake.
    Serpent, we might have spar'd our coming hither,
Fruitless to mee, though Fruit be here to excess,
The credit of whose virtue rest with thee,
Wondrous indeed, if cause of such effects.   650
But of this Tree we may not taste nor touch;
God so commanded, and left that Command

---

629. *blowing,* blooming.

634. *wand'ring Fire,* Will-o'-the-Wisp, Jack-o'-Lantern.

635. *compact,* composed.
unctuous, oily.

638. After the scientific explanation Milton turns to the popular superstition of "Fiery Spirits" which Burton says "are such as commonly work by blazing stars, firedrakes, or *ignes fatui.*" (*Anatomy*, I, ii, 1, 2.) Compare the allusion in *Comus* (433) to evil things walking by night
           "In fog, or fire, by lake, or moorish fen."

643. *fraud:* compare the use of the word in VII, 143.

644. *the Tree Of prohibition,* a Hebraism for "the forbidden tree."

648. *Fruitless . . . Fruit:* such dubious puns were admired (*e.g.,* in A. Fraunce's *Arcadian Rhetorike,* I, 24) as part of the "bravery" of good poetry.

Sole Daughter of his voice; the rest, we live
Law to ourselves, our Reason is our Law.
   To whom the Tempter guilefully repli'd.   655
Indeed? hath God then said that of the Fruit
Of all these Garden Trees ye shall not eat,
Yet Lords declar'd of all in Earth or Air?
   To whom thus *Eve* yet sinless. Of the Fruit
Of each Tree in the Garden we may eat,   660
But of the Fruit of this fair Tree amidst
The Garden, God hath said, Ye shall not eat
Thereof, nor shall ye touch it, lest ye die.
   She scarce had said, though brief, when now more bold
The Tempter, but with show of Zeal and Love   665
To Man, and indignation at his wrong,
New part puts on, and as to passion mov'd,
Fluctuates disturb'd, yet comely, and in act
Rais'd, as of some great matter to begin.
As when of old some Orator renown'd   670
In *Athens* or free *Rome,* where Eloquence
Flourish'd, since mute, to some great cause addrest,
Stood in himself collected, while each part,
Motion, each act won audience ere the tongue,
Sometimes in highth began, as no delay   675
Of Preface brooking through his Zeal of Right.

---

653. *Daughter of his voice,* a literal translation of a Hebrew phrase. *the rest,* with respect to the rest.

654. Milton applied St. Paul's remark about the virtuous Gentiles who, though outside the Hebrew law, were "a law unto themselves." (Romans ii, 14.)

667. *New part puts on,* assumes a new role or character in the drama, pretending to be moved to passionate indignation.

670. Milton's admiration for the part played by the orator in classic Greece and Rome appears in his quotation from Euripides, prefixed to *Areopagitica:*

    "This is true liberty, when free-born men,
      Having to advise the public, may speak free."

In Sonnet x he refers to Isocrates as the "old man eloquent" and in *P.R.* (IV, 269) to the Athenian orators who

    "Wielded at will that fierce Democracy."

673. *part, i.e.,* of the body.

674. *audience,* attention, hearing.

675. *highth, i.e.,* height of feeling.

So standing, moving, or to highth upgrown
The Tempter all impassion'd thus began.
  O Sacred, Wise, and Wisdom-giving Plant,
Mother of Science, Now I feel thy Power   680
Within me clear, not only to discern
Things in thir Causes, but to trace the ways
Of highest Agents, deem'd however wise.
Queen of this Universe, do not believe
Those rigid threats of Death; ye shall not Die: 685
How should ye? by the Fruit? it gives you Life
To Knowledge: By the Threat'ner? look on mee,
Mee who have touch'd and tasted, yet both live,
And life more perfet have attain'd than Fate
Meant mee, by vent'ring higher than my Lot.   690
Shall that be shut to Man, which to the Beast
Is open? or will God incense his ire
For such a petty Trespass, and not praise
Rather your dauntless virtue, whom the pain
Of Death denounc't, whatever thing Death be,   695
Deterr'd not from achieving what might lead
To happier life, knowledge of Good and Evil;
Of good, how just? of evil, if what is evil
Be real, why not known, since easier shunn'd?
God therefore cannot hurt ye, and be just;   700
Not just, not God; not fear'd then, nor obey'd:
Your fear itself of Death removes the fear.
Why then was this forbid?   Why but to awe,
Why but to keep ye low and ignorant,
His worshippers; he knows that in the day   705
Ye Eat thereof, your Eyes that seem so clear,
Yet are but dim, shall perfetly be then
Op'n'd and clear'd, and ye shall be as Gods,
Knowing both Good and Evil as they know.
That ye should be as Gods, since I as Man,   710

------

  680. *Science* has its Latin force of "knowledge."
  683. *highest Agents,* active beings of the highest ranks, men or even
angels, however wise they may be supposed.
  686. *Life to Knowledge,* life as well as knowledge.
  700. *ye,* as often happened in Elizabethan English, is used objectively.
  710. Compare Adam's discovery of the same argument in 933–6 below.

Internal Man, is but proportion meet,
I of brute human, yee of human Gods.
So ye shall die perhaps, by putting off
Human, to put on Gods, death to be wisht,
Though threat'n'd, which no worse than this can bring.   715
And what are Gods that Man may not become
As they, participating God-like food?
The Gods are first, and that advantage use
On our belief, that all from them proceeds;
I question it, for this fair Earth I see,   720
Warm'd by the Sun, producing every kind,
Them nothing: If they all things, who enclos'd
Knowledge of Good and Evil in this Tree,
That whoso eats thereof, forthwith attains
Wisdom without their leave? and wherein lies   725
Th' offence, that Man should thus attain to know?
What can your knowledge hurt him, or this Tree
Impart against his will if all be his?
Or is it envy, and can envy dwell
In heav'nly breasts? these, these and many more   730
Causes import your need of this fair Fruit.
Goddess humane, reach then, and freely taste.
    He ended, and his words replete with guile
Into her heart too easy entrance won:
Fixt on the Fruit she gaz'd, which to behold   735
Might tempt alone, and in her ears the sound
Yet rung of his persuasive words, impregn'd
With Reason, to her seeming, and with Truth;
Meanwhile the hour of Noon drew on, and wak'd
An eager appetite, rais'd by the smell   740
So savoury of that Fruit, which with desire,

    711. *Internal Man* corresponds to the serpent's reference to his "in-
ward Powers" (600 above) as having been raised to the human level,
though his form is unchanged.

    713. *putting off Human, etc.,* putting off humanity to put on divinity.

    722. *If they* (produced) *all things.*

    729. Compare the note on VI, 788.

    731. *import,* indicate, prove.

    732. *humane* probably means "kind" and not "human."

    737. *impregn'd,* pregnant, filled.

    741. Genesis iii, 6, says that Eve yielded when she saw that "the

Inclinable now grown to touch or taste,
Solicited her longing eye; yet first
Pausing a while, thus to herself she mus'd.
　Great are thy Virtues, doubtless, best of Fruits,   745
Though kept from Man, and worthy to be admir'd,
Whose taste, too long forborne, at first assay
Gave elocution to the mute, and taught
The Tongue not made for Speech to speak thy praise:
Thy praise hee also who forbids thy use,   750
Conceals not from us, naming thee the Tree
Of Knowledge, knowledge both of good and evil;
Forbids us then to taste, but his forbidding
Commends thee more, while it infers the good
By thee communicated, and our want: 755
For good unknown, sure is not had, or had
And yet unknown, is as not had at all.
In plain then, what forbids he but to know,
Forbids us good, forbids us to be wise?
Such prohibitions bind not. But if Death   760
Bind us with after-bands, what profits then
Our inward freedom? In the day we eat
Of this fair Fruit, our doom is, we shall die.
How dies the Serpent? hee hath eat'n and lives,
And knows, and speaks, and reasons, and discerns,   765
Irrational till then. For us alone
Was death invented? or to us deni'd
This intellectual food, for beasts reserv'd?
For Beasts it seems: yet that one Beast which first
Hath tasted, envies not, but brings with joy   770
The good befall'n him, Author unsuspect,
Friendly to man, far from deceit or guile.
What fear I then, rather what know to fear
Under this ignorance of Good and Evil,
Of God or Death, of Law or Penalty?   775

---

tree was good for food . . . and a tree to be desired to make one
wise."

　742. *Inclinable,* easily inclined (as she was at the moment).

　758. *In plain,* in clear language.

　771. *Author unsuspect,* authority (for the information), not to be
suspected.

Here grows the Cure of all, this Fruit Divine,
Fair to the Eye, inviting to the Taste,
Of virtue to make wise: what hinders then
To reach, and feed at once both Body and Mind?
  So saying, her rash hand in evil hour   780
Forth reaching to the Fruit, she pluck'd, she eat:
Earth felt the wound, and Nature from her seat
Sighing through all her Works gave signs of woe,
That all was lost. Back to the Thicket slunk
The guilty Serpent, and well might, for *Eve*   785
Intent now wholly on her taste, naught else
Regarded, such delight till then, as seem'd,
In Fruit she never tasted, whether true
Or fancied so, through expectation high
Of knowledge, nor was God-head from her thought.   790
Greedily she ingorg'd without restraint,
And knew not eating Death: Satiate at length,
And hight'n'd as with Wine, jocund and boon,
Thus to herself she pleasingly began.
  O Sovran, virtuous, precious of all Trees   795
In Paradise, of operation blest
To Sapience, hitherto obscur'd, infam'd,
And thy fair Fruit let hang, as to no end
Created; but henceforth my early care,
Not without Song, each Morning, and due praise   800
Shall tend thee, and the fertile burden ease
Of thy full branches offer'd free to all;
Till dieted by thee I grow mature
In knowledge, as the Gods who all things know;

---

783. The vague sense of disaster here anticipates what occurs in
X, 651–714.

792. *knew not eating Death,* knew not that she was eating death.

793. *boon,* jolly. Compare "boon-companion."

795. *Sovran, virtuous, precious,* followed by the genitive phrase,
mean "most sovereign, virtuous and precious." The construction, like
that in 792, is Greek or Latin.

796. *blest To Sapience,* gifted with power to confer wisdom.

797. *infam'd,* misreputed, made the subject of evil fame.

800. *Not without Song,* not omitting song. The construction is a
Latinism.

Though others envy what they cannot give;   805
For had the gift been theirs, it had not here
Thus grown.   Experience, next to thee I owe,
Best guide; not following thee, I had remain'd
In ignorance, thou op'n'st Wisdom's way,
And giv'st access, though secret she retire.   810
And I perhaps am secret; Heav'n is high,
High and remote to see from thence distinct
Each thing on Earth; and other care perhaps
May have diverted from continual watch
Our great Forbidder, safe with all his Spies   815
About him.   But to *Adam* in what sort
Shall I appear? shall I to him make known
As yet my change, and give him to partake
Full happiness with mee, or rather not,
But keep the odds of Knowledge in my power   820
Without Copartner? so to add what wants
In Female Sex, the more to draw his Love,
And render me more equal, and perhaps,
A thing not undesirable, sometime
Superior: for inferior who is free?   825
This may be well: but what if God have seen
And Death ensue? then I shall be no more,
And *Adam* wedded to another *Eve,*
Shall live with her enjoying, I extinct;
A death to think.   Confirm'd then I resolve,   830
Adam shall share with me in bliss or woe:

---

805. *others* refers to the gods. Eve is influenced by the serpent's
suggestion that the earth bears its fruit without the help of the creator
(720–2 above).

811. *secret,* hidden, unseen. The thought is modelled on Job xxii,
13–14: "How doth God know? can he judge through the dark cloud?
Thick clouds are a covering to him, that he seeth not."

815. *safe, i.e.,* from Eve's point of view God is not dangerous.
Compare "safe guide," XI, 371.

828. Eve's jealousy was a motive which Milton found in several
rabbinical sources, such, *e.g.,* as *Yosippon* or the Pseudo-Josephus,
where he read that she "said in her heart, 'Woe unto me that I have
eaten this death, for now I will die; and Adam, my husband, who has
not eaten of it, will live forever, and God will couple him with another woman.' "

So dear I love him, that with him all deaths
I could endure, without him live no life.
  So saying, from the Tree her step she turn'd,
But first low Reverence done, as to the power   835
That dwelt within, whose presence had infus'd
Into the plant sciential sap, deriv'd
From Nectar, drink of Gods. *Adam* the while
Waiting desirous her return, had wove
Of choicest Flow'rs a Garland to adorn   840
Her Tresses, and her rural labours crown,
As Reapers oft are wont thir Harvest Queen.
Great joy he promis'd to his thoughts, and new
Solace in her return, so long delay'd;
Yet oft his heart, divine of something ill,   845
Misgave him; hee the falt'ring measure felt;
And forth to meet her went, the way she took
That Morn when first they parted; by the Tree
Of Knowledge he must pass, there he her met,
Scarce from the Tree returning; in her hand   850
A bough of fairest fruit that downy smil'd,
New gather'd, and ambrosial smell diffus'd.
To him she hasted, in her face excuse
Came Prologue, and Apology to prompt,
Which with bland words at will she thus addrest.   855
  Hast thou not wonder'd, *Adam*, at my stay?
Thee I have misst, and thought it long, depriv'd
Thy presence, agony of love till now
Not felt, nor shall be twice, for never more
Mean I to try, what rash untri'd I sought,   860

832. Milton seems to have been consciously varying the terms of
Lydia's devotion in the closing lines of Horace's Ode (III, ix), familiar
in translations by Herrick and Ben Jonson.

837. *sciential,* endowed or endowing with knowledge.

839. *wove,* woven. The ending was often dropped in the perfect
participle. Compare *Coriolanus*, II, iii, 163: "Have you chose this man?"

845. *divine,* foreseeing. A Latinism. Compare the verb "divine."

846. *the falt'ring measure,* the irregular beat.

853. *excuse Came Prologue, etc.,* excuse came like the prologue to a
speech or play to *prompt* or lead on the following Apology, or formal
defence of her conduct.

860. *rash untri'd,* because I was rash and it was untried or unfamiliar.

The pain of absence from thy sight. But strange
Hath been the cause, and wonderful to hear:
This Tree is not as we are told, a Tree
Of danger tasted, nor to evil unknown
Op'ning the way, but of Divine effect   865
To open Eyes, and make them Gods who taste;
And hath been tasted such: the Serpent wise,
Or not restrain'd as wee, or not obeying,
Hath eat'n of the fruit, and is become,
Not dead, as we are threat'n'd, but thenceforth   870
Endu'd with human voice and human sense,
Reasoning to admiration, and with mee
Persuasively hath so prevail'd, that I
Have also tasted, and have also found
Th' effects to correspond, opener mine Eyes,   875
Dim erst, dilated Spirits, ampler Heart,
And growing up to Godhead; which for thee
Chiefly I sought, without thee can despise.
For bliss, as thou hast part, to me is bliss,
Tedious, unshar'd with thee, and odious soon.   880
Thou therefore also taste, that equal Lot
May join us, equal Joy, as equal Love;
Lest thou not tasting, different degree
Disjoin us, and I then too late renounce
Deity for thee, when Fate will not permit.   885
    Thus *Eve* with Count'nance blithe her story told;
But in her Cheek distemper flushing glow'd.
On th' other side, *Adam,* soon as he heard
The fatal Trespass done by *Eve,* amaz'd,
Astonied stood and Blank, while horror chill   890

---

864. *tasted,* if tasted.

867. *tasted,* proved by tasting.

872. *to admiration,* so as to seem marvellous.

884. *too late renounce, i.e.,* too late try to renounce.

890. *Astonied* suggests Job xvii, 8: "Upright men shall be astonied at this."

horror chill and *joints relax'd:* the phrases are Virgilian. So Aeneas confesses:

> "Mute and amaz'd, my hair with terror stood,
>   Fear shrunk my sinews, and congeal'd my blood."
>   (*Aen.* III, 29–30. Dryden's translation.)

Ran through his veins, and all his joints relax'd;
From his slack hand the Garland wreath'd for *Eve*
Down dropp'd, and all the faded Roses shed:
Speechless he stood and pale, till thus at length
First to himself he inward silence broke.   895
    O fairest of Creation, last and best
Of all God's Works, Creature in whom excell'd
Whatever can to sight or thought be form'd,
Holy, divine, good, amiable, or sweet!
How art thou lost, how on a sudden lost,   900
Defac't, deflow'r'd, and now to Death devote?
Rather how hast thou yielded to transgress
The strict forbiddance, how to violate
The sacred Fruit forbidd'n! some cursed fraud
Of Enemy hath beguil'd thee, yet unknown,   905
And mee with thee hath ruin'd, for with thee
Certain my resolution is to Die;
How can I live without thee, how forgo
Thy sweet Converse and Love so dearly join'd,
To live again in these wild Woods forlorn?   910
Should God create another *Eve,* and I
Another Rib afford, yet loss of thee
Would never from my heart; no no, I feel
The Link of Nature draw me: Flesh of Flesh,
Bone of my Bone thou art, and from thy State   915
Mine never shall be parted, bliss or woe.
    So having said, as one from sad dismay
Recomforted, and after thoughts disturb'd
Submitting to what seem'd remediless,
Thus in calm mood his Words to *Eve* he turn'd.   920
    Bold deed thou hast presum'd, advent'rous *Eve,*

---

901. *devote,* doomed. The Latinism resembles that in III, 208.

914. Compare VIII, 495, and its note.

916. Among the many possible sources for this traditional behaviour
of Adam Milton may have remembered St. Augustine's opinion that
"it is to be thought, that the first man did not yield to his wife in this
transgression of God's precept, as if he thought she spoke the truth;
but only being compelled to it by this social love to her, being but
one with one, and both of one nature and kind, for it is not in vain
that the apostle says: 'Adam was not deceived: but the woman was
deceived.'" (*The City of God,* XII, xi. John Healey's translation.)

And peril great provok't, who thus hast dar'd
Had it been only coveting to Eye
That sacred Fruit, sacred to abstinence,
Much more to taste it under ban to touch.   925
But past who can recall, or done undo?
Not God Omnipotent, nor Fate, yet so
Perhaps thou shalt not Die, perhaps the Fact
Is not so heinous now, foretasted Fruit,
Profan'd first by the Serpent, by him first   930
Made common and unhallow'd ere our taste;
Nor yet on him found deadly, he yet lives,
Lives, as thou said'st, and gains to live as Man
Higher degree of Life, inducement strong
To us, as likely tasting to attain   935
Proportional ascent, which cannot be
But to be Gods, or Angels Demi-gods.
Nor can I think that God, Creator wise,
Though threat'ning, will in earnest so destroy
Us his prime Creatures, dignifi'd so high,   940
Set over all his Works, which in our Fall,
For us created, needs with us must fail,
Dependent made; so God shall uncreate,
Be frustrate, do, undo, and labour lose,
Not well conceiv'd of God, who though his Power   945
Creation could repeat, yet would be loath
Us to abolish, lest the Adversary
Triumph and say; Fickle their State whom God
Most Favours, who can please him long?   Mee first
He ruin'd, now Mankind; whom will he next?   950
Matter of scorn, not to be given the Foe.
However I with thee have fixt my Lot,
Certain to undergo like doom, if Death

---

922. *hast:* the second edition reads *hath,* a possible reading, for it
generalizes the thought by shifting the subject to an indefinite third person. Originally a comma followed *dar'd,* making *to eye* depend upon
coveting.

932. Compare the serpent's argument, 710–12 above.

947. *Adversary:* compare the notes on I, 361, and VI, 282.

953. *Certain,* resolved. A Latinism, probably reminiscent of the
phrase used of Aeneas' resolve to depart and Dido's resolve to die in
Aeneid IV, 554 and 564.

Consort with thee, Death is to mee as Life;
So forcible within my heart I feel   955
The Bond of Nature draw me to my own,
My own in thee, for what thou art is mine;
Our State cannot be sever'd, we are one,
One Flesh; to lose thee were to lose myself.

    So *Adam,* and thus *Eve* to him repli'd.   960
O glorious trial of exceeding Love,
Illustrious evidence, example high!
Ingaging me to emulate, but short
Of thy perfection, how shall I attain,
Adam, from whose dear side I boast me sprung,   965
And gladly of our Union hear thee speak,
One Heart, one Soul in both; whereof good proof
This day affords, declaring thee resolv'd,
Rather than Death or aught than Death more dread
Shall separate us, linkt in Love so dear,   970
To undergo with mee one Guilt, one Crime,
If any be, of tasting this fair Fruit,
Whose virtue, for of good still good proceeds,
Direct, or by occasion hath presented
This happy trial of thy Love, which else   975
So eminently never had been known.
Were it I thought Death menac't would ensue
This my attempt, I would sustain alone
The worst, and not persuade thee, rather die
Deserted, than oblige thee with a fact   980
Pernicious to thy Peace, chiefly assur'd
Remarkably so late of thy so true,
So faithful Love unequall'd; but I feel
Far otherwise th' event, not Death, but Life
Augmented, op'n'd Eyes, new Hopes, new Joys,   985
Taste so Divine, that what of sweet before
Hath toucht my sense, flat seems to this, and harsh.
On my experience, *Adam,* freely taste,
And fear of Death deliver to the Winds.

    So saying, she embrac'd him, and for joy   990

---

967. Compare Adam's words to Raphael, VIII, 603–5.
980. *oblige* keeps its Latin force of "involve in guilt."
Fact, deed.

Tenderly wept, much won that he his Love
Had so ennobl'd, as of choice to incur
Divine displeasure for her sake, or Death.
In recompense (for such compliance bad
Such recompense best merits) from the bough   995
She gave him of that fair enticing Fruit
With liberal hand: he scrupl'd not to eat
Against his better knowledge, not deceiv'd,
But fondly overcome with Female charm.
Earth trembl'd from her entrails, as again   1000
In pangs, and Nature gave a second groan,
Sky low'r'd, and muttering Thunder, some sad drops
Wept at completing of the mortal Sin
Original; while *Adam* took no thought,
Eating his fill, nor *Eve* to iterate   1005
Her former trespass fear'd, the more to soothe
Him with her lov'd society, that now
As with new Wine intoxicated both
They swim in mirth, and fancy that they feel
Divinity within them breeding wings   1010
Wherewith to scorn the Earth: but that false Fruit
Far other operation first display'd,
Carnal desire inflaming, hee on *Eve*
Began to cast lascivious Eyes, she him
As wantonly repaid; in Lust they burn: 1015
Till *Adam* thus 'gan *Eve* to dalliance move.
  Eve, now I see thou art exact of taste,

---

999. *charm* seems to be used in the sense that it is in VIII, 533, *i.e.,*
of Eve's beauty, and not in the sense that it has in VIII, 2, where it
means the music of the voice of Raphael.

1000. Compare 783 above.

1003. *mortal Sin Original:* in *C.D.* I, xi, Milton accepted the orthodox
doctrine that "sin originated, first, in the instigation of the devil" and
that "undoubtedly all sinned in Adam." He recognized the "principle uniformly acted upon in the divine proceedings, and recognized
by all nations, . . . that the penalty incurred by the violation of things
sacred (and such was the tree of knowledge of good and evil) attaches
not only to the criminal himself, but to the whole of his posterity."

1017. *taste . . . savour:* Milton indulges in a play on the literal and
figurative meanings of "taste," remembering a remark of Cicero that
a man of a discerning heart is not always lacking a discerning palate.
(*De finibus,* II, viii.)

And elegant, of Sapience no small part,
Since to each meaning savour we apply,
And Palate call judicious; I the praise   1020
Yield thee, so well this day thou hast purvey'd.
Much pleasure we have lost, while we abstain'd
From this delightful Fruit, nor known till now
True relish, tasting; if such pleasure be
In things to us forbidden, it might be wish'd,   1025
For this one Tree had been forbidden ten.
But come, so well refresh't, now let us play,
As meet is, after such delicious Fare;
For never did thy Beauty since the day
I saw thee first and wedded thee, adorn'd   1030
With all perfections, so inflame my sense
With ardor to enjoy thee, fairer now
Than ever, bounty of this virtuous Tree.
   So said he, and forbore not glance or toy
Of amorous intent, well understood   1035
Of *Eve,* whose Eye darted contagious Fire.
Her hand he seiz'd, and to a shady bank,
Thick overhead with verdant roof imbowr'd
He led her nothing loath; Flow'rs were the Couch,
Pansies, and Violets, and Asphodel,   1040
And Hyacinth, Earth's freshest softest lap.
There they thir fill of Love and Love's disport
Took largely, of thir mutual guilt the Seal,
The solace of thir sin, till dewy sleep
Oppress'd them, wearied with thir amorous play.   1045
Soon as the force of that fallacious Fruit,
That with exhilarating vapour bland
About thir spirits had play'd, and inmost powers
Made err, was now exhal'd, and grosser sleep
Bred of unkindly fumes, with conscious dreams   1050

1026. *for,* instead of.

1042. Compare the words of the lewd woman in Proverbs vii, 18:
"Come, let us take our fill of love until the morning; let us solace
ourselves with loves." The scene is vaguely suggestive of that between
Zeus and Hera in *Iliad,* XIV, 292–353.

1049. The *grosser sleep* has been prepared for by the emphasis on
Adam's "Aery light" sleep in V, 4.

1050. *unkindly,* unnatural.

Encumber'd, now had left them, up they rose
As from unrest, and each the other viewing,
Soon found thir Eyes how op'n'd, and thir minds
How dark'n'd; innocence, that as a veil
Had shadow'd them from knowing ill, was gone,   1055
Just confidence, and native righteousness,
And honour from about them, naked left
To guilty shame: hee cover'd, but his Robe
Uncover'd more.   So rose the *Danite* strong
Herculean Samson from the Harlot-lap   1060
Of *Philistean Dalilah,* and wak'd
Shorn of his strength, They destitute and bare
Of all thir virtue: silent, and in face
Confounded long they sat, as struck'n mute,
Till *Adam,* though not less than *Eve* abasht,   1065
At length gave utterance to these words constrain'd.

   O *Eve,* in evil hour thou didst give ear
To that false Worm, of whomsoever taught
To counterfeit Man's voice, true in our Fall,
False in our promis'd Rising; since our Eyes   1070
Op'n'd we find indeed, and find we know
Both Good and Evil, Good lost, and Evil got,
Bad Fruit of Knowledge, if this be to know,
Which leaves us naked thus, of Honour void,
Of Innocence, of Faith, of Purity,   1075
Our wonted Ornaments now soil'd and stain'd,
And in our Faces evident the signs
Of foul concupiscence; whence evil store;
Even shame, the last of evils; of the first
Be sure then.   How shall I behold the face   1080

1058. *his Robe, i.e.,* shame.   The thought is a reminiscence of Psalm
cix, 29: "Let mine adversaries be clothed with shame."

1059. *the Danite,* Samson, who came of the tribe of Dan, and the
story of whose betrayal by his Philistine wife, Dalilah, as told in Judges
xvi, 4–20, Milton was to re-evoke in a famous episode in *S.A.,* 710–1073.

1064. *struck'n* is an instance of preservation of the participial ending
where modern usage has dropped it.   For the uncertainty about this
see the note on 839 above.

1068. *Worm,* serpent.

1079. *last,* extreme, worst.   The meaning is a Latinism.

· 80. Compare X, 722–5, and XI, 315–17.

Henceforth of God or Angel, erst with joy
And rapture so oft beheld? those heav'nly shapes
Will dazzle now this earthly, with thir blaze
Insufferably bright. O might I here
In solitude live savage, in some glade   1085
Obscur'd, where highest Woods impenetrable
To Star or Sun-light, spread thir umbrage broad,
And brown as Evening: Cover me ye Pines,
Ye Cedars, with innumerable boughs
Hide me, where I may never see them more.   1090
But let us now, as in bad plight, devise
What best may for the present serve to hide
The Parts of each from other, that seem most
To shame obnoxious, and unseemliest seen,
Some Tree whose broad smooth Leaves together sew'd,   1095
And girded on our loins, may cover round
Those middle parts, that this new comer, Shame,
There sit not, and reproach us as unclean.
    So counsell'd hee, and both together went
Into the thickest Wood, there soon they chose   1100
The Figtree, not that kind for Fruit renown'd,
But such as at this day to *Indians* known
In *Malabar* or *Decan* spreads her Arms

1086. *impenetrable To Star:* compare *Arcades,* 88–9:
                "Under the shady roof
                    Of branching Elm Star-proof."

1088. *brown,* shadowy, dark. Compare *Imbrown'd* in IV, 246.

1090. *them, i.e.,* the "heavenly shapes" of 1082.

1091. *as in, i.e.,* since we are in. A similar Latinism occurs in
X, 978.

1094. *obnoxious,* liable. Compare 170 above.

1101. *The Figtree* is the banyan, called "the arched Indian Fig-tree"
in Gerard's *Herball,* where Milton may have read: "The ends (of its
branches) hang downe, and touch the ground, where they take roote
and grow in such sort, that those twigs become great trees; and these,
being grown up unto the like greatnesse, do cast their branches or
twiggy tendrils unto the earth, where they likewise take hold and
roote; by meanes whereof it cometh to passe, that of one tree is made
a great wood or desart of trees, which the Indians do use for ccverture
against the extreme heate of the sun."

1103. *Malabar,* the southwestern coast of India. *Decan,* Deccan, the
whole peninsula of India, especially the hinterland east of Goa.

Branching so broad and long, that in the ground
The bended Twigs take root, and Daughters grow   1105
About the Mother Tree, a Pillar'd shade
High overarch't, and echoing Walks between;
There oft the *Indian* Herdsman shunning heat
Shelters in cool, and tends his pasturing Herds
At Loopholes cut through thickest shade: Those Leaves   1110
They gather'd, broad as *Amazonian* Targe,
And with what skill they had, together sew'd,
To gird thir waist, vain Covering if to hide
Thir guilt and dreaded shame; O how unlike
To that first naked Glory.   Such of late   1115
Columbus found th' *American* so girt
With feather'd Cincture, naked else and wild
Among the Trees on Isles and woody Shores.
Thus fenc't, and as they thought, thir shame in part
Cover'd, but not at rest or ease of Mind,   1120
They sat them down to weep, nor only Tears
Rain'd at thir Eyes, but high Winds worse within
Began to rise, high Passions, Anger, Hate,
Mistrust, Suspicion, Discord, and shook sore
Thir inward State of Mind, calm Region once   1125
And full of Peace, now toss't and turbulent:
For Understanding rul'd not, and the Will
Heard not her lore, both in subjection now
To sensual Appetite, who from beneath
Usurping over sovran Reason claim'd   1130
Superior sway: From thus distemper'd breast,
Adam, estrang'd in look and alter'd style,
Speech intermitted thus to *Eve* renew'd.
   Would thou hadst heark'n'd to my words, and stay'd
With me, as I besought thee, when that strange   1135
Desire of wand'ring this unhappy Morn,
I know not whence possess'd thee; we had then
Remain'd still happy, not as now, despoil'd
Of all our good, sham'd, naked, miserable.

1111. *Amazonian Targe,* the targets or light shields of the Amazons.

1132. *alter'd style,* changed manner (of conversation).   The phrase is
a Latinism.

Let none henceforth seek needless cause to approve   1140
The Faith they owe; when earnestly they seek
Such proof, conclude, they then begin to fail.

   To whom soon mov'd with touch of blame thus *Eve.*
What words have pass't thy Lips, *Adam* severe,
Imput'st thou that to my default, or will   1145
Of wand'ring, as thou call'st it, which who knows
But might as ill have happ'n'd thou being by,
Or to thyself perhaps: hadst thou been there,
Or here th' attempt, thou couldst not have discern'd
Fraud in the Serpent, speaking as he spake;   1150
No ground of enmity between us known,
Why hee should mean me ill, or seek to harm.
Was I to have never parted from thy side?
As good have grown there still a lifeless Rib.
Being as I am, why didst not thou the Head   1155
Command me absolutely not to go,
Going into such danger as thou said'st?
Too facile then thou didst not much gainsay,
Nay, didst permit, approve, and fair dismiss.
Hadst thou been firm and fixt in thy dissent,   1160
Neither had I transgress'd, nor thou with mee.

   To whom then first incenst *Adam* repli'd.
Is this the Love, is this the recompense
Of mine to thee, ingrateful *Eve,* exprest
Immutable when thou wert lost, not I,   1165
Who might have liv'd and joy'd immortal bliss,
Yet willingly chose rather Death with thee:
And am I now upbraided, as the cause
Of thy transgressing? not enough severe,
It seems, in thy restraint: what could I more?   1170
I warn'd thee, I admonish'd thee, foretold
The danger, and the lurking Enemy
That lay in wait; beyond this had been force,

   1140. Adam recalls Eve's words in 335–6 above.

   1144. *What words have passed thy Lips:* a reminiscence of Ulysses'
speech to Agamemnon in *Iliad* XIV, 83, or some recurrence of the same
warning phrase in Homer.

   1155. *the Head* recalls Eve's words in IV, 443.

   1164. *Of mine to thee . . . exprest Immutable,* of my love to thee,
which was shown to be immutable, *etc.*

And force upon free Will hath here no place.
But confidence then bore thee on, secure 1175
Either to meet no danger, or to find
Matter of glorious trial; and perhaps
I also err'd in overmuch admiring
What seem'd in thee so perfet, that I thought
No evil durst attempt thee, but I rue 1180
That error now, which is become my crime,
And thou th' accuser. Thus it shall befall
Him who to worth in Women overtrusting
Lets her Will rule; restraint she will not brook,
And left to herself, if evil thence ensue, 1185
Shee first his weak indulgence will accuse.
    Thus they in mutual accusation spent
The fruitless hours, but neither self-condemning,
And of thir vain contést appear'd no end.

The End of the Ninth Book

BOOK X

THE ARGUMENT

Man's *transgression known, the Guardian Angels forsake Paradise, and return up to Heaven to approve thir vigilance, and are approv'd, God declaring that the entrance of* Satan *could not be by them prevented. He sends his Son to judge the Transgressors, who descends and gives Sentence accordingly; then in pity clothes them both, and reascends.* Sin *and* Death *sitting till then at the Gates of Hell, by wondrous sympathy feeling the success of* Satan *in this new World, and the sin by Man there committed, resolve to sit no longer confin'd in Hell, but to follow* Satan *thir Sire up to the place of Man: To make the way easier from Hell to this World to and fro, they pave a broad Highway or Bridge over* Chaos, *according to the Track that* Satan *first made; then preparing for Earth, they meet him proud of his success returning to Hell; thir mutual gratulation.* Satan *arrives at* Pandemonium, *in full assembly relates with boasting his success against Man; instead of applause is entertained with a general hiss by all his audience, transform'd with himself also suddenly into Serpents, according to his doom giv'n in Paradise; then deluded with a show of the forbidden Tree springing up before them, they greedily reaching to take of the Fruit, chew dust and bitter ashes. The proceedings of* Sin *and* Death; *God foretells the final Victory of his Son over them, and the renewing of all things; but for the present commands his Angels to make several alterations in the Heavens and Elements.* Adam *more and more perceiving his fall'n condition heavily bewails, rejects the condolement of* Eve; *she persists and at length appeases him: then to evade the Curse likely to fall on thir Offspring, proposes to* Adam *violent ways, which he approves not, but conceiving better hope, puts her in mind of the late Promise made them, that her Seed should be reveng'd on the Serpent, and exhorts her with him to seek Peace of the offended Deity, by repentance and supplication.*

MEANWHILE the heinous and despiteful act
Of *Satan* done in Paradise, and how
Hee in the Serpent had perverted *Eve,*
Her Husband shee, to taste the fatal fruit,
Was known in Heav'n; for what can scape the Eye   5
Of God All-seeing, or deceive his Heart
Omniscient, who in all things wise and just,
Hinder'd not *Satan* to attempt the mind
Of Man, with strength entire, and free will arm'd,
Complete to have discover'd and repulst   10
Whatever wiles of Foe or seeming Friend.
For still they knew, and ought to have still remember'd
The high Injunction not to taste that Fruit,
Whoever tempted; which they not obeying,
Incurr'd, what could they less, the penalty,   15
And manifold in sin, deserv'd to fall.
Up into Heav'n from Paradise in haste
Th' Angelic Guards ascended, mute and sad
For Man, for of his state by this they knew,
Much wond'ring how the subtle Fiend had stol'n   20
Entrance unseen. Soon as th' unwelcome news

1. *despiteful:* compare the notes on IX, 175 and 178.

6. *God All-seeing:* compare the note on IX, 811.

7. *wise and just:* the thought focusses the chapter "Of the Divine
Decrees" (*C.D.* I, iii), where Milton urges that God "suffered both men
and angels to stand or fall at their own uncontrolled choice, . . . not
necessitating the evil consequences which ensued, but leaving them
contingent; hence the covenant was of this kind— . . . if thou eat not
the forbidden fruit, thou shalt live; if thou eat, thou shalt die."

9. Compare the note on IX, 351.

10. *Complete to,* fully endowed with power to. The comma at the
end of 9 indicates that *Complete* modifies *mind* in 8.

16. *manifold in sin;* in *C.D.* I, xi, Milton wrote that the sin of Adam
and Eve "comprehended at once distrust in the divine veracity; . . .
unbelief; ingratitude; disobedience; gluttony; in the man excessive
uxoriousness, in the woman a want of proper regard for her husband,
in both an insensibility to the welfare of their offspring; . . . parricide,
theft, invasion of the rights of others, sacrilege, deceit, persumption in
aspiring to divine attributes, fraud, . . . pride, and arrogance." Compare III, 96 and 211.

18. *Th' Angelic Guards:* Gabriel, Ithuriel, Zephon and their troop.
Compare IX, 61 and IV, 561–1015, *passim.*

19. *by this,* by this time.

From Earth arriv'd at Heaven Gate, displeas'd
All were who heard, dim sadness did not spare
That time Celestial visages, yet mixt
With pity, violated not thir bliss.   25
About the new-arriv'd, in multitudes
Th' ethereal People ran, to hear and know
How all befell: they towards the Throne Supreme
Accountable made haste to make appear
With righteous plea, thir utmost vigilance,   30
And easily approv'd; when the most High
Eternal Father from his secret Cloud,
Amidst in Thunder utter'd thus his voice.

  Assembl'd Angels, and ye Powers return'd
From unsuccessful charge, be not dismay'd,   35
Nor troubl'd at these tidings from the Earth,
Which your sincerest care could not prevent,
Foretold so lately what would come to pass,
When first this Tempter cross'd the Gulf from Hell.
I told ye then he should prevail and speed   40
On his bad Errand, Man should be seduc't
And flatter'd out of all, believing lies
Against his Maker; no Decree of mine
Concurring to necessitate his Fall,
Or touch with lightest moment of impulse   45
His free Will, to her own inclining left
In even scale. But fall'n he is, and now
What rests, but that the mortal Sentence pass

---

29. *Accountable* modifies *vigilance* and its meaning here is "justifiable."
Compare "unaccountable."

31. *approv'd,* vindicated.

32. *his secret Cloud;* compare II, 264, and its note.

33. *in Thunder:* Milton's whole conception is coloured by the chapter
on the throne of God in the Apocalypse, and there he read that "out
of the throne proceeded lightnings and thunderings and voices." (Rev.
iv, 5.)

35. *charge,* commission, duty.

40. *I told ye then:* compare III, 92–7.
speed, succeed.

45. *moment* is used again in the sense of a weight sufficient to turn
the scales. Compare VI, 239.

48. *rests,* remains, is left to do.

On his transgression, Death denounc't that day,
Which he presumes already vain and void,   50
Because not yet inflicted, as he fear'd,
By some immediate stroke; but soon shall find
Forbearance no acquittance ere day end.
Justice shall not return as bounty scorn'd.
But whom send I to judge them? whom but thee   55
Vicegerent Son, to thee I have transferr'd
All Judgment, whether in Heav'n, or Earth, or Hell.
Easy it might be seen that I intend
Mercy colleague with Justice, sending thee
Man's Friend, his Mediator, his design'd   60
Both Ransom and Redeemer voluntary,
And destin'd Man himself to judge Man fall'n.
    So spake the Father, and unfolding bright
Toward the right hand his Glory, on the Son

50. *he presumes . . . vain:* compare IX, 927–37.

52. *some immediate stroke:* "This death," Milton wrote in *C.D.* xii, "consists, first, in the loss, or at least in the obscuration to a great extent of that right reason which enabled man to discern the chief good. . . . It consists, secondly, in . . . deprivation of righteousness and liberty to do good. . . . Lastly, sin is its own punishment, and produces . . . the death of the spiritual life."

53. *acquittance,* acquittal, exoneration.

56. *to thee I have transferr'd All Judgment:* "The Son," Milton remarks in *C.D.* I, v, "was entitled to the name of God . . . in the capacity . . . of a judge." Milton's faith in "his future judicial advent" was a part of his broader theological acceptance of the scripture: "For the Father judgeth no man, but hath committed all judgment unto the son." (John v, 22.)

59. Compare the *Nativity Ode,* 141–6:
            "Yea, Truth and Justice then
            Will down return to men,
    Th' enamell'd *Arras* of the Rain-bow wearing,
            And Mercy set between,
            Thron'd in Celestial sheen,
    With radiant feet the tissued clouds down steering."

60. *"The mediatorial office of Christ is that whereby . . . he voluntarily performed, and continues to perform, on behalf of man, whatever is requisite for obtaining reconciliation with God, and eternal salvation."* (*C.D.* I, xv.)

64. Compare the allusions to the Son's participation in the glory of God in III, 139, and VI, 679–83. Behind all these passages is Hebrews i, 3: "Who being the brightness of his glory, and the express image of his person, . . . sat down on the right hand of the Majesty on high."

Blaz'd forth unclouded Deity; he full   65
Resplendent all his Father manifest
Express'd, and thus divinely answer'd mild.
　Father Eternal, thine is to decree,
Mine both in Heav'n and Earth to do thy will
Supreme, that thou in mee thy Son belov'd   70
May'st ever rest well pleas'd. I go to judge
On Earth these thy transgressors, but thou know'st,
Whoever judg'd, the worst on mee must light,
When time shall be, for so I undertook
Before thee; and not repenting, this obtain   75
Of right, that I may mitigate thir doom
On me deriv'd, yet I shall temper so
Justice with Mercy, as may illustrate most
Them fully satisfied, and thee appease.
Attendance none shall need, nor Train, where none   80
Are to behold the Judgment, but the judg'd,
Those two; the third best absent is condemn'd,
Convict by flight, and Rebel to all Law:
Conviction to the Serpent none belongs.
　Thus saying, from his radiant Seat he rose   85
Of high collateral glory: him Thrones and Powers,
Princedoms, and Dominations ministrant
Accompanied to Heaven Gate, from whence
Eden and all the Coast in prospect lay.
Down he descended straight; the speed of Gods   90
Time counts not, though with swiftest minutes wing'd.
Now was the Sun in Western cadence low

---

　70. With *Son belov'd* compare III, 168–70.

　74. *When time shall be:* compare the same words in III, 284. In both
passages the allusion is to Galatians iv, 4: "But when the fullness of the
time was come, God sent forth his Son, made of a woman."
　so I undertook: i.e., in III, 227–65.

　77. *deriv'd* keeps its Latin force of "diverted."

　78. *illustrate* keeps the Latin meaning of "shed light upon" or
"glorify."

　80. *none shall need,* there shall be no need of.

　83. *Convict,* convicted.

　84. *Conviction,* formal proof of guilt.

　89. *Coast,* region round about.

　92. *cadence* keeps its Latin force of "falling" or "descent."

From Noon, and gentle Airs due at thir hour
To fan the Earth now wak'd, and usher in
The Ev'ning cool when he from wrath more cool   95
Came the mild Judge and Intercessor both
To sentence Man: the voice of God they heard
Now walking in the Garden, by soft winds
Brought to thir Ears, while day declin'd, they heard,
And from his presence hid themselves among   100
The thickest Trees, both Man and Wife, till God
Approaching, thus to *Adam* call'd aloud.
    Where art thou *Adam,* wont with joy to meet
My coming seen far off?   I miss thee here,
Not pleas'd, thus entertain'd with solitude,   105
Where obvious duty erewhile appear'd unsought:
Or come I less conspicuous, or what change
Absents thee, or what chance detains?   Come forth.
He came, and with him *Eve,* more loath, though first
To offend, discount'nanc't both, and discompos'd;   110
Love was not in thir looks, either to God
Or to each other, but apparent guilt,
And shame, and perturbation, and despair,
Anger, and obstinacy, and hate, and guile.
Whence *Adam* falt'ring long, thus answer'd brief.   115
    I heard thee in the Garden, and of thy voice
Afraid, being naked, hid myself.   To whom
The gracious Judge without revile repli'd.
    My voice thou oft hast heard, and hast not fear'd,

---

93. *Noon,* noon-height, the meridian.

95. *cool . . . cool,* another of Milton's plays on words.   Compare the note on I, 642.

97. Compare Genesis iii, 8: "And they heard the voice of the Lord God walking in the garden in the cool of the day: and Adam and his wife hid themselves from the presence of the Lord God amongst the trees of the garden."
The following thirteen verses are closely followed in 103–223.

101. For Milton's reason for calling the Son *God* so definitely here see the note on 56 above.

106. *obvious* has its Latin force of "standing in the way" or "confronting."   Here the meaning is "welcoming."

112. *apparent* has its Latin meaning, "evident."

118. *revile,* revilement, reproach.

But still rejoic't, how is it now become   120
So dreadful to thee? that thou art naked, who
Hath told thee? hast thou eaten of the Tree
Whereof I gave thee charge thou shouldst not eat?
    To whom thus *Adam* sore beset repli'd.
O Heav'n! in evil strait this day I stand   125
Before my Judge, either to undergo
Myself the total Crime, or to accuse
My other self, the partner of my life;
Whose failing, while her Faith to me remains,
I should conceal, and not expose to blame   130
By my complaint; but strict necessity
Subdues me, and calamitous constraint,
Lest on my head both sin and punishment,
However insupportable, be all
Devolv'd; though should I hold my peace, yet thou   135
Wouldst easily detect what I conceal.
This Woman whom thou mad'st to be my help,
And gav'st me as thy perfet gift, so good,
So fit, so acceptable, so Divine,
That from her hand I could suspect no ill,   140
And what she did, whatever in itself,
Her doing seem'd to justify the deed;
Shee gave me of the Tree, and I did eat.
    To whom the sovran Presence thus repli'd.
Was shee thy God, that her thou didst obey   145
Before his voice, or was shee made thy guide,
Superior, or but equal, that to her
Thou didst resign thy Manhood, and the Place
Wherein God set thee above her made of thee,
And for thee, whose perfection far excell'd   150
Hers in all real dignity: Adorn'd
She was indeed, and lovely to attract
Thy Love, not thy Subjection, and her Gifts
Were such as under Government well seem'd,
Unseemly to bear rule, which was thy part   155

---

    120. *still,* always.
    128. *My other self:* compare the note on VIII, 450.
    141. *whatever in itself,* whatever its character in itself, apart from
the doer.

And person, hadst thou known thyself aright.
    So having said, he thus to *Eve* in few:
Say Woman, what is this which thou hast done?
    To whom sad *Eve* with shame nigh overwhelm'd,
Confessing soon, yet not before her Judge   160
Bold or loquacious, thus abasht repli'd.
    The Serpent me beguil'd and I did eat.
    Which when the Lord God heard, without delay
To Judgment he proceeded on th' accus'd
Serpent though brute, unable to transfer   165
The Guilt on him who made him instrument
Of mischief, and polluted from the end
Of his Creation; justly then accurst,
As vitiated in Nature: more to know
Concern'd not Man (since he no further knew)   170
Nor alter'd his offence; yet God at last
To Satan first in sin his doom appli'd,
Though in mysterious terms, judg'd as then best:
And on the Serpent thus his curse let fall.
    Because thou hast done this, thou art accurst   175
Above all Cattle, each Beast of the Field;
Upon thy Belly groveling thou shalt go,
And dust shalt eat all the days of thy Life.
Between Thee and the Woman I will put
Enmity, and between thine and her Seed;   180
Her Seed shall bruise thy head, thou bruise his heel.
    So spake this Oracle, then verifi'd
When *Jesus* son of *Mary* second *Eve*,
Saw Satan fall like Lightning down from Heav'n,

---

156. *person* has its Latin meaning of a "character" or rôle in a drama.

165. *unable* applies to the *Serpent*. Milton is trying to reconcile the
literal account of Eve's temptation by the serpent in Genesis with the
rabbinical and patristic theory that Satan spoke through the serpent.
Like the rabbinical commentators, Adam is slow to "conjecture" (1133
below) the devil's part in the imposture.   Some responsibility seemed
to Milton to attach to the serpent for allowing itself to be polluted
from the *end* (object) of its creation.

174. The curse follows Genesis iii, 14–15.

183. *Mary second Eve:* compare V, 386–7.

184. In Christ's statement to his disciples that he "beheld Satan as
lightning fall from heaven" (Luke x, 18) Milton recognized the ful-

Prince of the Air; then rising from his Grave   185
Spoil'd Principalities and Powers, triumpht
In open show, and with ascension bright
Captivity led captive through the Air,
The Realm itself of Satan long usurpt,
Whom he shall tread at last under our feet;   190
Ev'n hee who now foretold his fatal bruise,
And to the Woman thus his Sentence turn'd.
   Thy sorrow I will greatly multiply
By thy Conception; Children thou shalt bring
In sorrow forth, and to thy Husband's will   195
Thine shall submit, hee over thee shall rule.
   On *Adam* last thus judgment he pronounc'd.
Because thou hast heark'n'd to the voice of thy Wife,
And eaten of the Tree concerning which
I charg'd thee, saying: Thou shalt not eat thereof,   200
Curs'd is the ground for thy sake, thou in sorrow
Shalt eat thereof all the days of thy Life;
Thorns also and Thistles it shall bring thee forth
Unbid, and thou shalt eat th' Herb of th' Field,
In the sweat of thy Face shalt thou eat Bread,   205
Till thou return unto the ground, for thou
Out of the ground wast taken, know thy Birth,
For dust thou art, and shalt to dust return.
   So judg'd he Man, both Judge and Saviour sent,
And th' instant stroke of Death denounc't that day   210
Remov'd far off; then pitying how they stood
Before him naked to the air, that now
Must suffer change, disdain'd not to begin
Thenceforth the form of servant to assume,

filment of the prophecy that the seed of the woman should "bruise the
serpent's head." (Gen. iii, 15.)

185. Milton thought of the air as traditionally the haunt of demons
(compare the note on I, 516) and of Satan's title of "the prince of the
power of the air." (Eph. ii, 2.)

186. Psalm lxviii, 18: "Thou hast ascended on high, thou hast led
captivity captive," seemed to Milton a prophecy of Christ's triumph
and he interpreted Christ's resurrection, like St. Paul, as the spoiling of
"principalities and powers" (*i.e.,* of evil in both spirit and human manifestation). (Col. ii, 15.)

193. *Thy sorrow, etc.,* follows Genesis iii, 16–19.

214. Genesis iii, 21, says simply that "the Lord God made coats of

As when he wash'd his servants' feet, so now   215
As Father of his Family he clad
Thir nakedness with Skins of Beasts, or slain,
Or as the Snake with youthful Coat repaid;
And thought not much to clothe his Enemies:
Nor hee thir outward only with the Skins   220
Of Beasts, but inward nakedness, much more
Opprobrious, with his Robe of righteousness,
Arraying cover'd from his Father's sight.
To him with swift ascent he up return'd,
Into his blissful bosom reassum'd   225
In glory as of old, to him appeas'd
All, though all-knowing, what had past with Man
Recounted, mixing intercession sweet.
Meanwhile ere thus was sinn'd and judg'd on Earth,
Within the Gates of Hell sat Sin and Death,   230
In counterview within the Gates, that now
Stood open wide, belching outrageous flame
Far into *Chaos,* since the Fiend pass'd through,
Sin opening, who thus now to Death began.
  O Son, why sit we here each other viewing   235
Idly, while Satan our great Author thrives

---

skins and clothed them," but Milton interpreted the passage in the
light of Christ's washing the feet of his disciples (John xiii, 5) and
taking "upon him the form of a servant" (Phil. ii, 7).

217. *or slain Or, etc.*: Milton hesitates whether to think that the beasts
were slain to provide skins or that the cast sloughs of serpents or other
animals were used.

218. *repaid,* recompensed for the cast slough by a new skin.

219. *thought not much,* did not grudge.
  With *his Enemies* compare Spenser's praise of the mercy which sends
the angels of God

      "To serve to wicked man, to serve his wicked foe."
                        (*F.Q.* II, viii, 1.)

222. *Robe of righteousness* is a phrase from Isaiah lxi, 10.

229. *was sinn'd and judg'd* is a Latin construction paralleled in
VI, 335.

230. *Sin and Death:* compare the notes on II, 650 and 660.

231. *counterview,* opposition face to face on each side of hell gate
(II, 649).

235. *O Son:* compare Sin's introduction of Death as her and Satan's
son in II, 727–814.

In other Worlds, and happier Seat provides
For us his offspring dear? It cannot be
But that success attends him; if mishap,
Ere this he had return'd, with fury driv'n   240
By his Avengers, since no place like this
Can fit his punishment, or their revenge.
Methinks I feel new strength within me rise,
Wings growing, and Dominion giv'n me large
Beyond this Deep; whatever draws me on,   245
Or sympathy, or some connatural force
Powerful at greatest distance to unite
With secret amity things of like kind
By secretest conveyance. Thou my Shade
Inseparable must with mee along: 250
For Death from Sin no power can separate.
But lest the difficulty of passing back
Stay his return perhaps over this Gulf
Impassable, Impervious, let us try
Advent'rous work, yet to thy power and mine   255
Not unagreeable, to found a path
Over this Main from Hell to that new World
Where Satan now prevails, a Monument
Of merit high to all th' infernal Host,
Easing thir passage hence, for intercourse,   260
Or transmigration, as thir lot shall lead.
Nor can I miss the way, so strongly drawn
By this new felt attraction and instinct.
    Whom thus the meagre Shadow answer'd soon.
Go whither Fate and inclination strong   265
Leads thee, I shall not lag behind, nor err
The way, thou leading, such a scent I draw
Of carnage, prey innumerable, and taste
The savour of Death from all things there that live:

---

246. For Milton's contemporaries *sympathy* meant the mysterious common response of remote things to the influences of the stars or of other powers.

256. *found* has its literal Latin meaning of "lay a foundation."

257. *main*, the "sea" of Chaos across which Satan made his "voyage" (II, 919).

260. *intercourse*, coming and going.

261. *transmigration*, emigration, permanent removal.

Nor shall I to the work thou enterprisest   270
Be wanting, but afford thee equal aid.
  So saying, with delight he snuff'd the smell
Of mortal change on Earth. As when a flock
Of ravenous Fowl, though many a League remote,
Against the day of Battle, to a Field,   275
Where Armies lie encampt, come flying, lur'd
With scent of living Carcasses design'd
For death, the following day, in bloody fight.
So scented the grim Feature, and upturn'd
His Nostril wide into the murky Air,   280
Sagacious of his Quarry from so far.
Then Both from out Hell Gates into the waste
Wide Anarchy of *Chaos* damp and dark
Flew diverse, and with Power (thir Power was great)
Hovering upon the Waters; what they met   285
Solid or slimy, as in raging Sea
Tost up and down, together crowded drove
From each side shoaling towards the mouth of Hell.
As when two Polar Winds blowing adverse
Upon the *Cronian* Sea, together drive   290
Mountains of Ice, that stop th' imagin'd way
Beyond *Petsora* Eastward, to the rich
Cathaian Coast. The aggregated Soil

---

274. The *ravenous Fowl* are probably reminiscent of Lucan's description of the vultures that scented the battle of Pharsalia. (Newton cites *Pharsalia*, VII, 831–7.) Todd quotes Beaumont and Fletcher's *Beggar's Bush:*

> " 'Tis said of vultures
> They scent a field fought; and do smell the carcases
> By many hundred miles."

279. *Feature* is used vaguely in its Latin or Italian sense of "something made," "creature" or "form."

288. *shoaling,* solidifying into a shoal.

290. The *Cronian Sea,* the Arctic Ocean.

291. *th' imagined way,* the northeast passage for which Hudson sought.

292. "The river Pechora," Milton wrote in *Moscovia,* "holding his course through Siberia, how far the Russians thereabouts know not, runneth into the sea at seventy-two mouths, full of ice."

293. Milton seems to have distinguished Cathay from China proper, and thought of it as a great empire, the "destined" seat of Chingiz

Death with his Mace petrific, cold and dry,
As with a Trident smote, and fix't as firm   295
As *Delos* floating once; the rest his look
Bound with *Gorgonian* rigour not to move,
And with *Asphaltic* slime; broad as the Gate,
Deep to the Roots of Hell the gather'd beach
They fasten'd, and the Mole immense wrought on   300
Over the foaming deep high Archt, a Bridge
Of length prodigious joining to the Wall
Immoveable of this now fenceless world
Forfeit to Death; from hence a passage broad,
Smooth, easy, inoffensive down to Hell.   305
So, if great things to small may be compar'd,
Xerxes, the Liberty of *Greece* to yoke,
From *Susa* his *Memnonian* Palace high
Came to the Sea, and over *Hellespont*
Bridging his way, *Europe* with *Asia* join'd,   310
And scourg'd with many a stroke th' indignant waves.

Kaan (XI, 386–8), in northeastern Asia, as the Mercator maps represented it.

296. Out of the warring elements in chaos—"hot, cold, moist and
dry" (II, 898)—Death separates the cold and dry atoms for the masonry
of his bridge and petrifies them with a touch of his mace, as Neptune
was supposed to have moulded the island of Delos out of the sea with
his trident. Later Zeus was supposed to have anchored the island at
the centre of the Cyclades.

297. Milton images Death as able, like the Gorgon, Medusa, in the
myth of Perseus, to turn everything at which he looks into stone, and
yet as working like a practical mason with asphaltic slime made of hot
and moist atoms to consolidate his bridge.

299. With *beach* compare the idea of *shoaling* in 288.

302. The *Wall* is the shell of the created universe.

303. *fenceless,* undefended, defenceless.

305. *inoffensive* has its Latin force of "free of stumbling-blocks,"
"passable."

307. In his account of Xerxes' expedition against Greece Herodotus
(VII, 33–6) lays stress upon the insult to the gods which was involved
in the famous scourging of the waves of the Hellespont for their
resistance to the building of the pontoon bridge from the Asiatic to the
European shore.

308. The citadel of Susa (the biblical Shushan, the winter capital of
the Persian kings) was supposed to have been founded by Tithonus, the
mythical lover of Aurora, by whom he had a son, Memnon.

Now had they brought the work by wondrous Art
Pontifical, a ridge of pendent Rock
Over the vext Abyss, following the track
Of *Satan,* to the selfsame place where hee   315
First lighted from his Wing, and landed safe
From. out of *Chaos* to the outside bare
Of this round World: with Pins of Adamant
And Chains they made all fast, too fast they made
And durable; and now in little space   320
The confines met of Empyrean Heav'n
And of this World, and on the left hand Hell
With long reach interpos'd; three sev'ral ways
In sight, to each of these three places led.
And now thir way to Earth they had descri'd,   325
To Paradise first tending, when behold
Satan in likeness of an Angel bright
Betwixt the *Centaur* and the *Scorpion* steering
His *Zenith,* while the Sun in *Aries* rose:
Disguis'd he came, but those his Children dear   330
Thir Parent soon discern'd, though in disguise.
Hee, after *Eve* seduc't, unminded slunk
Into the Wood fast by, and changing shape
To observe the sequel, saw his guileful act

313. The literal meaning of the word "pontifex" is a bridge-builder; hence *pontifical.*

314. *vext,* harried by storms, as Milton describes it in II, 894–967, and VII, 211–15.

316. Satan's lighting on the "opacous globe" of the universe is described in III, 418–30.

321. The meeting *Confines* are the lower end of the stair which binds the empyrean heaven to the shell of the universe (III, 510), the passage thence down to the Earth, and the new and sinister causeway which Sin and Death have built from Hell to the junction of the other two ways, interposing Hell, though by a "long reach," between Heaven and Earth. Milton was following a rabbinical tradition (found in *Midrash Tehillim,* xc) when he represented Hell as lying to the left, *i.e.,* to God's left as he sits in Heaven and looks down.

328. Satan flies toward the constellation of the *Centaur* and the *Scorpion* when the sun is opposite to them in *Aries* so as to avoid being seen by Uriel. (Compare IX, 58–69.)

329. Satan is obliged to fly straight up to the zenith because the opening in the shell of the universe is imagined as there.

332. *after Eve seduc't,* after the seduction of Eve.

By *Eve,* though all unweeting, seconded   335
Upon her Husband, saw thir shame that sought
Vain covertures; but when he saw descend
The Son of God to judge them, terrifi'd
Hee fled, not hoping to escape, but shun
The present, fearing guilty what his wrath   340
Might suddenly inflict; that past, return'd
By Night, and list'ning where the hapless Pair
Sat in thir sad discourse, and various plaint,
Thence gather'd his own doom, which understood
Not instant, but of future time. With joy   345
And tidings fraught, to Hell he now return'd,
And at the brink of *Chaos,* near the foot
Of this new wondrous Pontifice, unhop't
Met who to meet him came, his Offspring dear.
Great joy was at thir meeting, and at sight   350
Of that stupendious Bridge his joy increas'd.
Long hee admiring stood, till Sin, his fair
Enchanting Daughter, thus the silence broke.

   O Parent, these are thy magnific deeds,
Thy Trophies, which thou view'st as not thine own,   355
Thou art thir Author and prime Architect:
For I no sooner in my Heart divin'd,
My Heart, which by a secret harmony
Still moves with thine, join'd in connexion sweet,
That thou on Earth hadst prosper'd, which thy looks   360
Now also evidence, but straight I felt
Though distant from thee Worlds between, yet felt

---

   335. *unweeting,* unaware, unsuspecting.

   337. *Vain covertures,* the leaves with which Adam and Eve first
covered themselves (IX, 1110–14).

   344. With the full stop after *time,* as in the first and second edition,
was must be read into the line before *understood,* or else *which* must
be taken as its object and an unexpressed *he* be felt as its subject.

   345. *joy And tidings* seems to be intended as an hendiadys, a figure
of speech which coördinates two words one of which logically modifies
the other. So the meaning is "joyful tidings."

   347. *foot,* end or bridge-"head."

   348. *Pontifice,* bridge structure. Compare the note on 313 above.

   351. *stupendious* was the prevailing form of the word.

   358. The *secret harmony* is the sympathy of 246 above.

That I must after thee with this thy Son;
Such fatal consequence unites us three:
Hell could no longer hold us in her bounds,   365
Nor this unvoyageable Gulf obscure
Detain from following thy illustrious track.
Thou hast achiev'd our liberty, confin'd
Within Hell Gates till now, thou us impow'r'd
To fortify thus far, and overlay   370
With this portentous Bridge the dark Abyss.
Thine now is all this World, thy virtue hath won
What thy hands builded not, thy Wisdom gain'd
With odds what War hath lost, and fully aveng'd
Our foil in Heav'n; here thou shalt Monarch reign,   375
There didst not; there let him still Victor sway,
As Battle hath adjudg'd, from this new World
Retiring, by his own doom alienated,
And henceforth Monarchy with thee divide
Of all things, parted by th' Empyreal bounds,   380
His Quadrature, from thy Orbicular World,
Or try thee now more dang'rous to his Throne.
   Whom thus the Prince of Darkness answer'd glad.
Fair Daughter, and thou Son and Grandchild both,
High proof ye now have giv'n to be the Race   385
Of *Satan* (for I glory in the name,
Antagonist of Heav'n's Almighty King)
Amply have merited of me, of all
Th' Infernal Empire, that so near Heav'n's door

----

364. *consequence,* dependence.

370. *fortify,* construct (what amounts to a military road).

372. *virtue* keeps its Latin force of "manliness" or "courage."

374. *odds,* overplus.

375. *foil,* defeat.

378. *doom,* judgement.

381. Milton thought of the empyrean heaven as the city lying "four-square," described in Revelation xxi, 16, but of the created universe as a hollow orb.

382. *try,* prove, find by trial.

386. Satan is first introduced (in I, 81–2) with stress upon the meaning of his name as the "Arch-Enemy."

389. *Th' Infernal Empire,* the denizens of Hell.

Triumphal with triumphal act have met,   390
Mine with this glorious Work, and made one Realm
Hell and this World, one Realm, one Continent
Of easy thorough-fare. Therefore while I
Descend through Darkness, on your Road with ease
To my associate Powers, them to acquaint   395
With these successes, and with them rejoice,
You two this way, among these numerous Orbs
All yours, right down to Paradise descend;
There dwell and Reign in bliss, thence on the Earth
Dominion exercise and in the Air,   400
Chiefly on Man, sole Lord of all declar'd,
Him first make sure your thrall, and lastly kill.
My Substitutes I send ye, and Create
Plenipotent on Earth, of matchless might
Issuing from mee: on your joint vigor now   405
My hold of this new Kingdom all depends,
Through Sin to Death expos'd by my exploit.
If your joint power prevail, th' affairs of Hell
No detriment need fear, go and be strong.
    So saying he dismiss'd them, they with speed   410
Thir course through thickest Constellations held
Spreading thir bane; the blasted Stars lookt wan,
And Planets, Planet-strook, real Eclipse
Then suffer'd. Th' other way *Satan* went down
The Causey to Hell Gate; on either side   415
Disparted *Chaos* over-built exclaim'd,
And with rebounding surge the bars assail'd,
That scorn'd his indignation: through the Gate,
Wide open and unguarded, *Satan* pass'd,
And all about found desolate; for those   420

----

390. *Triumphal with triumphal, i.e.,* my triumphal act with your triumphal work, the bridge.

397. So Satan had dropped from the shell of the universe to earth "amongst innumerable stars" (III, 565) and Raphael descended, sailing "between worlds and worlds" (V, 268).

413. *Planet-strook* and "moon-struck" were familiar astrological terms applied to persons supposed to have suffered the unfavourable influence of a planet. Milton says that the planets themselves suffered a similar effect from Sin and Death.

415. *Causey,* causeway.

Appointed to sit there, had left thir charge,
Flown to the upper World; the rest were all
Far to the inland retir'd, about the walls
Of *Pandæmonium,* City and proud seat
Of *Lucifer,* so by allusion call'd,   425
Of that bright Star to *Satan* paragon'd.
There kept thir Watch the Legions, while the Grand
In Council sat, solicitous what chance
Might intercept thir Emperor sent, so hee
Departing gave command, and they observ'd.   430
As when the *Tartar* from his *Russian* Foe
By *Astracan* over the Snowy Plains
Retires, or *Bactrian* Sophi from the horns
Of *Turkish* Crescent, leaves all waste beyond
The Realm of *Aladule,* in his retreat   435
To *Tauris* or *Casbeen.* So these the late
Heav'n-banisht Host, left desert utmost Hell
Many a dark League, reduc't in careful Watch
Round thir Metropolis, and now expecting
Each hour their great adventurer from the search   440

---

424. For the founding of *Pandæmonium* see I, 670–757.

426. The *bright star* whose association with Satan gave him his name of *Lucifer,* or the "light-bringer," was the planet Venus. Compare the notes on I, 361, and VII, 132.

427. The *Grand* are the grandees, the "great consulting Peers" of 456 below.

429. *so,* i. e., that they should continue to sit in council.

430. *observ'd* complied with the command.

432. Milton repeatedly mentions Astracan in his *History of Moscovia.* It was a city on the Volga, not far from the Caspian, a great frontier post in the extension of Russian control over the Tartars.

433. Gilbert points to Anthony Jenkinson's account of the flight of the *Bactrian* (*i.e.,* Persian) Sophi in Hakluyt (I, 351) as Milton's source: "This Sophie that now raigneth is nothing valiant . . . and through his pusillanimitie the Turke hath much invaded his countreys, even nigh unto the Citie of Teveris, wherein he was wont to keepe his chiefe court. And now having forsaken the same, is chiefly resiant at Casbin. . . . "

435. Purchas (*Pilgrimage,* 75) describes the realm of the Persian king Aladule or Aladeules, which was wasted by Sultan Zelim.

436. Tauris, or Tebriz, was a famous Persian city and former capital.

438. *Reduc't* keeps its Latin force as a military term meaning "led back," as applied to a retreating army.

Of Foreign Worlds: he through the midst unmarkt,
In show Plebeian Angel militant
Of lowest order, pass't; and from the door
Of that *Plutonian* Hall, invisible
Ascended his high Throne, which under state   445
Of richest texture spread, at th' upper end
Was plac't in regal lustre. Down a while
He sat, and round about him saw unseen:
At last as from a Cloud his fulgent head
And shape Star-bright appear'd, or brighter, clad   450
With what permissive glory since his fall
Was left him, or false glitter: All amaz'd
At that so sudden blaze the *Stygian* throng
Bent thir aspect, and whom they wish'd beheld,
Thir mighty Chief return'd: loud was th' acclaim: 455
Forth rush'd in haste the great consulting Peers,
Rais'd from thir dark *Divan,* and with like joy
Congratulant approach'd him, who with hand
Silence, and with these words attention won.

    Thrones, Dominations, Princedoms, Virtues, Powers,   460
For in possession such, not only of right,
I call ye and declare ye now, return'd
Successful beyond hope, to lead ye forth
Triumphant out of this infernal Pit
Abominable, accurst, the house of woe,   465
And Dungeon of our Tyrant: Now possess,
As Lords, a spacious World, to our native Heaven
Little inferior, by my adventure hard
With peril great achiev'd. Long were to tell
What I have done, what suffer'd, with what pain   470
Voyag'd th' unreal, vast, unbounded deep
Of horrible confusion, over which

---

    445. *state,* the canopy over a chair of state such as Satan's throne
in II, 1–4.

    451. *permissive,* permitted (*i. e.,* by God).

    454. *aspect,* look. The word has its Latin meaning of "a look at."

    461. *Possession* of the newly conquered universe, as well as their claim
to their lost heavenly ranks, justifies the titles by which Satan salutes the
demons.

    471. Chaos is *unreal* because its elements are formless. Compare the
note on VII, 103.

By Sin and Death a broad way now is pav'd
To expedite your glorious march; but I
Toil'd out my úncouth passage, forc't to ride   475
Th' untractable Abyss, plung'd in the womb
Of unoriginal *Night* and *Chaos* wild,
That jealous of thir secrets fiercely oppos'd
My journey strange, with clamorous uproar
Protesting Fate supreme; thence how I found   480
The new created World, which fame in Heav'n
Long had foretold, a Fabric wonderful
Of absolute perfection, therein Man
Plac't in a Paradise, by our exile
Made happy: Him by fraud I have seduc'd   485
From his Creator, and the more to increase
Your wonder, with an Apple; he thereat
Offended, worth your laughter, hath giv'n up
Both his beloved Man and all his World,
To Sin and Death a prey, and so to us,   490
Without our hazard, labour, or alarm,
To range in, and to dwell, and over Man
To rule, as over all he should have rul'd.
True is, mee also he hath judg'd, or rather
Mee not, but the brute Serpent in whose shape   495
Man I deceiv'd: that which to mee belongs,
Is enmity, which he will put between
Mee and Mankind; I am to bruise his heel;
His Seed, when is not set, shall bruise my head:
A World who would not purchase with a bruise,   500
Or much more grievous pain? Ye have th' account
Of my performance: What remains, ye Gods,
But up and enter now into full bliss.
    So having said, a while he stood, expecting
Thir universal shout and high applause   505
To fill his ear, when contrary he hears
On all sides, from innumerable tongues
A dismal universal hiss, the sound

---

475. *uncouth,* unknown. Compare II, 407 and 827.

477. "Night, eldest of things," (II, 962) is unoriginal because nothing
came before it to originate it.

491. *alarm* has its military meaning of "a call to arms."

Of public scorn; he wonder'd, but not long
Had leisure, wond'ring at himself now more;   510
His Visage drawn he felt to sharp and spare,
His Arms clung to his Ribs, his Legs entwining
Each other, till supplanted down he fell
A monstrous Serpent on his Belly prone,
Reluctant, but in vain, a greater power   515
Now rul'd him, punisht in the shape he sinn'd,
According to his doom: he would have spoke,
But hiss for hiss return'd with forked tongue
To forked tongue, for now were all transform'd
Alike, to Serpents all as accessories   520
To his bold Riot: dreadful was the din
Of hissing through the Hall, thick swarming now
With complicated monsters, head and tail,
Scorpion and Asp, and *Amphisbæna* dire,
Cerastes horn'd, *Hydrus,* and *Ellops* drear,   525
And *Dipsas* (not so thick swarm'd once the Soil
Bedropt with blood of *Gorgon,* or the Isle

---

513. *supplanted* has its literal Latin meaning of "tripped by the heels."

514. Milton is giving imaginative form to a belief which found expression in Jacob Boehme's statement that, after their revolt, the devils "lost their beauteous feature and image and became like serpents, dragons, worms and evil beasts." (*Three Principles,* IV, 64.) Suggestions for the details of Satan's transformation may have come from Dante's vision of the four robbers whose spirits turned into serpents. (*Inferno,* XXV, 49–151.) By his own confession (in IX, 505), Milton, like Dante, was interested in Ovid's account (*Met.* IV, 576–89) of the gradual metamorphosis of Cadmus into a serpent.

521. *Riot,* revolt.

523. *complicated* has its Latin meaning of "intertwined."

524. The *Amphisbaena* was a fabulous snake with a head at both ends. Dante mentions it in his list of the dragons in the seventh circle of hell (*Inferno,* XXIV, 82–90).

525. Milton's epithet for *Cerastes* translates its Greek name. The *Hydrus* was a fabulous watersnake.
Ellops seems originally to have been a name given by the Greeks to swordfish. The primitive meaning may be "gliding."

526. The *Dipsas* was a serpent supposed to produce raging thirst by its bite.

527. In the *Pharsalia* (IX, 700–33) Lucan mentions the varieties of serpents which were supposed to have sprung from the drops of blood

Ophiusa) but still greatest hee the midst,
Now Dragon grown, larger than whom the Sun
Ingender'd in the *Pythian* Vale on slime,   530
Huge *Python,* and his Power no less he seem'd
Above the rest still to retain; they all
Him follow'd issuing forth to th' open Field,
Where all yet left of that revolted Rout
Heav'n-fall'n, in station stood or just array,   535
Sublime with expectation when to see
In Triumph issuing forth thir glorious Chief;
They saw, but other sight instead, a crowd
Of ugly Serpents; horror on them fell,
And horrid sympathy; for what they saw,   540
They felt themselves now changing; down thir arms,
Down fell both Spear and Shield, down they as fast,
And the dire hiss renew'd, and the dire form
Catcht by Contagion, like in punishment,
As in thir crime. Thus was th' applause they meant,   545
Turn'd to exploding hiss, triumph to shame
Cast on themselves from thir own mouths. There stood
A Grove hard by, sprung up with this thir change,
His will who reigns above, to aggravate
Thir penance, laden with fair Fruit, like that   550
Which grew in Paradise, the bait of *Eve*
Us'd by the Tempter: on that prospect strange
Thir earnest eyes they fix'd, imagining
For one forbidden Tree a multitude
Now ris'n, to work them furder woe or shame;   555

---

that fell from the Gorgon's head as Perseus carried it across Libya.
Compare the allusion in 297 above.

528. *Ophiusa,* the "snaky" or "snake-filled," was a name given by
the Greeks to several of the islands in the Balearic archipelago.

531. Milton alludes to Ovid's story of the earth's unwilling engender-
ing of the serpent Python, of mountainous size, from the mud left
after Deucalion's flood. (*Met.* I, 438–440.)

535. *station . . . array:* both terms have military connotation.

536. *sublime* has its literal Latin meaning of "uplifted."

541. *changing,* becoming.

551. The trees, loaded with the *bait of Eve,* suggest the scion of the
Tree of Knowledge below which Dante found a host of famished spirits
in Purgatory (XXIV, 103–17).

Yet parcht with scalding thirst and hunger fierce,
Though to delude them sent, could not abstain,
But on they roll'd in heaps, and up the Trees
Climbing, sat thicker than the snaky locks
That curl'd *Megæra*: greedily they pluck'd   560
The Fruitage fair to sight, like that which grew
Near that bituminous Lake where *Sodom* flam'd;
This more delusive, not the touch, but taste
Deceiv'd; they fondly thinking to allay
Thir appetite with gust, instead of Fruit   565
Chew'd bitter Ashes, which th' offended taste
With spattering noise rejected: oft they assay'd,
Hunger and thirst constraining, drugg'd as oft,
With hatefullest disrelish writh'd thir jaws
With soot and cinders fill'd; so oft they fell   570
Into the same illusion, not as Man
Whom they triumph'd, once lapst.   Thus were they plagu'd
And worn with Famine long, and ceaseless hiss,
Till thir lost shape, permitted, they resum'd,
Yearly enjoin'd, some say, to undergo   575
This annual humbling certain number'd days,

560. *Megæra,* one of the Furies or Eumenides, the avengers of crime, goddesses with serpents in their hair.

562. Milton thought of Josephus' account of *that bituminous Lake* (the Dead Sea) and of the apples of Sodom, the city which, "for the impiety of its inhabitants, was burnt by lightning; . . . and the traces . . . are still to be seen, as well as the ashes growing in their fruits, which fruits have a colour as if they were fit to be eaten; but if you pluck them with your hands, they dissolve into smoke and ashes." (*Wars,* IV, viii.)

565. *gust,* keen relish, gusto.

568. *drugg'd,* nauseated.

572. *triumph'd* is used transitively to mean "triumphed over." *lapst,* fell.

573. *Famine* is set off from *long* by a comma in the original editions, where no comma follows *long.*

576. Newton found a distant analogue to this *annual humbling* in the confession of Ariosto's fairy Manto that she and all her kind, since she is a descendant of Cadmus (compare the note on 514 above), are obliged to assume the form of a serpent every seventh day. (*Orlando Furioso,* XLIII, 98.) Milton goes on to find another bond between Greek mythology and Christian tradition in the legend of *Ophion,* whose name seems to mean "a serpent" and who, since he was one

To dash thir pride, and joy for Man seduc't.
However some tradition they dispers'd
Among the Heathen of thir purchase got,
And Fabl'd how the Serpent, whom they call'd   580
Ophion with *Eurynome,* the wide-
Encroaching *Eve* perhaps, had first the rule
Of high *Olympus,* thence by *Saturn* driv'n
And *Ops,* ere yet *Dictæan Jove* was born.
Meanwhile in Paradise the hellish pair   585
Too soon arriv'd, *Sin* there in power before,
Once actual, now in body, and to dwell
Habitual habitant; behind her *Death*
Close following pace for pace, not mounted yet
On his pale Horse: to whom *Sin* thus began.   590
   Second of *Satan* sprung, all conquering *Death,*
What think'st thou of our Empire now, though earn'd
With travail difficult, not better far
Than still at Hell's dark threshold to have sat watch,
Unnam'd, undreaded, and thyself half starv'd?   595
   Whom thus the Sin-born Monster answer'd soon.
To mee, who with eternal Famine pine,
Alike is Hell, or Paradise, or Heaven,
There best, where most with ravin I may meet;
Which here, though plenteous, all too little seems   600
To stuff this Maw, this vast unhide-bound Corpse.

---

of the Titans who were enemies of the gods, was readily identified
with Satan.   His wife, *Eurynome,* was supposed to have shared the rule
of Olympus with him.   The form of the myth as Milton recalls it here
is seemingly derived from Apollonius Rhodius' *Argonautica,* I, 503–509.

581. *wide-Encroaching* is intended as an epithet analogous to the
literal meaning of the name *Eurynome,* "wide-ruling."   Milton perhaps
found an added reason for identifying Eurynome with Eve in the fact
that the titaness was supposed to be the mother of the Graces.

584. *Ops* and her husband, *Saturn,* were the parents of Jove, whom
Milton calls *Dictaean* because he had a famous shrine on Mount Dicte,
in Crete.

586. Before reaching Eden in person Sin was there *in power,* when
Eve and Adam "fell."

590. The *pale Horse* is a reminiscence of Revelation VI, 8: "And I
looked, and behold a pale horse; and his name that sat on him was
Death."

601. *unhide-bound,* loose-skinned and therefore empty-bellied.

To whom th' incestuous Mother thus repli'd.
Thou therefore on these Herbs, and Fruits, and Flow'rs
Feed first, on each Beast next, and Fish, and Fowl,
No homely morsels, and whatever thing   605
The Scythe of Time mows down, devour unspar'd,
Till I in Man residing through the Race,
His thoughts, his looks, words, actions all infect,
And season him thy last and sweetest prey.
   This said, they both betook them several ways,   610
Both to destroy, or unimmortal make
All kinds, and for destruction to mature
Sooner or later; which th' Almighty seeing
From his transcendent Seat the Saints among,
To those bright Orders utter'd thus his voice.   615
   See with what heat these Dogs of Hell advance
To waste and havoc yonder World, which I
So fair and good created, and had still
Kept in that state, had not the folly of Man
Let in these wasteful Furies, who impute   620
Folly to mee, so doth the Prince of Hell
And his Adherents, that with so much ease
I suffer them to enter and possess
A place so heav'nly, and conniving seem
To gratify my scornful Enemies,   625
That laugh, as if transported with some fit
Of Passion, I to them had quitted all,
At random yielded up to their misrule;
And know not that I call'd and drew them thither
My Hell-hounds, to lick up the draff and filth   630
Which man's polluting Sin with taint hath shed
On what was pure, till cramm'd and gorg'd, nigh burst
With suckt and glutted offal, at one sling
Of thy victorious Arm, well-pleasing Son,

---

617. *havoc,* which was used regularly as a transitive verb, was originally
a battle cry raised when troops were ready to begin plundering.

620. The "cry of Hell-hounds" (II, 654) about Sin's middle makes
her no less monstrous than the Furies, one of whom Milton mentioned
in 560 above.

624. *conniving* is used with a recollection of its Latin significance
of "shutting the eyes," *i. e.,* deliberately ignoring.

Both *Sin,* and *Death,* and yawning *Grave* at last   635
Through *Chaos* hurl'd, obstruct the mouth of Hell
For ever, and seal up his ravenous Jaws.
Then Heav'n and Earth renew'd shall be made pure
To sanctity that shall receive no stain:
Till then the Curse pronounc't on both precedes.   640
    He ended, and the heav'nly Audience loud
Sung *Halleluia,* as the sound of Seas,
Through multitude that sung: Just are thy ways,
Righteous are thy Decrees on all thy Works;
Who can extenuate thee?   Next, to the Son,   645
Destin'd restorer of Mankind, by whom
New Heav'n and Earth shall to the Ages rise,
Or down from Heav'n descend.   Such was thir song,
While the Creator calling forth by name
His mighty Angels gave them several charge,   650
As sorted best with present things.   The Sun
Had first his precept so to move, so shine,
As might affect the Earth with cold and heat
Scarce tolerable, and from the North to call
Decrepit Winter, from the South to bring   655
Solstitial summer's heat.   To the blanc Moon
Her office they prescrib'd, to th' other five
Thir planetary motions and aspécts

---

635. In the background are St. Paul's words: "Death is swallowed
up in victory," *etc.* (I Cor. xv, 54–6.)

638. The inspiration of *Heav'n and Earth renew'd* (compare 647–8
below) is in St. John's vision of "a new heaven and a new earth
. . . new Jerusalem, coming down from God out of heaven." (Rev.
xxi, 1–2.)   Milton expressed his faith in "the destruction of the present
unclean and polluted world." (*C.D.* I, xxxiii.)

642. Compare Revelation xix, 6: "And I heard as it were the voice
of a great multitude, and as the voice of many waters, . . . saying,
Alleluia!"

651. *sorted,* corresponded. Milton has prepared carefully (*e. g.,* in
IX, 782 and 1000–4) for the following treatment of the idea that after
the Fall the whole order of nature was altered and "became subject to
mortality and a curse on account of man.   Even the beasts are not exempt.   Gen. iii, 14; vi, 7." (*C.D.* I, xiii.)

656. *blanc* is spelled thus regularly when Milton intends it to mean
"pale" or "light-coloured."

657. *th' other five* (*i.e.,* planets).

In *Sextile, Square,* and *Trine,* and *Opposite,*
Of noxious efficacy, and when to join   660
In Synod unbenign, and taught the fixt
Thir influence malignant when to show'r,
Which of them rising with the Sun, or falling,
Should prove tempestuous: To the Winds they set
Thir corners, when with bluster to confound   665
Sea, Air, and Shore, the Thunder when to roll
With terror through the dark Aereal Hall.
Some say he bid his Angels turn askance
The Poles of Earth twice ten degrees and more
From the Sun's Axle; they with labour push'd   670
Oblique the Centric Globe: Some say the Sun
Was bid turn Reins from th' Equinoctial Road
Like distant breadth to *Taurus* with the Sev'n
Atlantic Sisters, and the *Spartan* Twins
Up to the *Tropic* Crab; thence down amain   675
By *Leo* and the *Virgin* and the *Scales,*

---

659. A *Sextile* aspect of the planets is one of 60° and a *Trine* one of 120°, or one-third of the Zodiac, of separation.

661. *Synod* is Milton's equivalent for the astrological term "conjunction," *i. e.,* the position of two planets when they appear to be in the same part of the heavens as seen from the earth. Conjunction was one of the "indifferent" aspects of Astrology.

662. Compare the "selectest influence" (VIII, 513) of the constellations shed upon Adam's nuptial hour.

665. The *corners* of the winds are the quarters of the sky from which they blow.

668. Milton imagines the angels turning the axis of the earth *askance* so as to alter the sun's apparent annual course from the equator, thereby doing away with the perpetual spring that reigned before the Fall.

672. Alternatively, he imagines the sun leaving *th' Equinoctial Road* to follow the ecliptic.

673. Leaving the equator as it rises higher and higher over the northern hemisphere in the spring, the sun finds itself in the constellation of Taurus, in whose neck are the *Seven Atlantic Sisters,* the Pleiades.

674. The *Spartan Twins,* Gemini, are the next sign in the Zodiac.

675. When the Sun enters the *Crab, Cancer,* it is ready for the summer solstice, and thence it seems to descend again toward the equator through the constellations of *Leo,* or the Lion, the Virgin and the Scales.

As deep as *Capricorn,* to bring in change
Of Seasons to each Clime; else had the Spring
Perpetual smil'd on Earth with vernant Flow'rs,
Equal in Days and Nights, except to those   680
Beyond the Polar Circles; to them Day
Had unbenighted shone, while the low Sun
To recompense his distance, in thir sight
Had rounded still th' *Horizon,* and not known
Or East or West, which had forbid the Snow   685
From cold *Estotiland,* and South as far
Beneath *Magellan.*   At that tasted Fruit
The Sun, as from *Thyéstean* Banquet, turn'd
His course intended; else how had the World
Inhabited, though sinless, more than now,   690
Avoided pinching cold and scorching heat?
These changes in the Heav'ns, though slow, produc'd
Like change on Sea and Land, sideral blast,
Vapour, and Mist, and Exhalation hot,
Corrupt and Pestilent: Now from the North   695
Of *Norumbega,* and the *Samoed* shore
Bursting thir brazen Dungeon, arm'd with ice
And snow and hail and stormy gust and flaw,
Boreas and *Cæcias* and *Argestes* loud

677. Below the equator the sun describes a similar course as far
south as the tropic of *Capricorn.*

684. The sun, when its course was the celestial equator, could not
have *known Or East or West, i. e.,* could never have seemed to rise
or set at the poles.

686. There were fabulous tales of Estotiland, a vague region which
Mercator located as the northeastern coast of Labrador.

687. *Magellan* means the Straits of Magellan.

688. The sun is said to have averted its face from the banquet consisting of his own sons which Thyestes ate at the table of his brother,
Atreus, the father of Agamemnon.

693. *sideral* (*i. e.,* sidereal) *blast,* a blasting influence from the stars.

696. *Norumbega* was a name vaguely applied to northern New
England, where says Burton (*Anatomy* II, ii, 3) "in 45 lat. all the sea
is frozen Ice."

In the *History of Moscovia,* 8, Milton cites the account of the Samoeds,
or inhabitants of the arctic shore of northeastern Russia, in Purchas'
Pilgrimes 3, 522, 546 and 555.

699. *Boreas* is the north wind.
Argestes, the northwest   *Cæcias,* the northeast.

And *Thrascias* rend the Woods and Seas upturn;   700
With adverse blast up-turns them from the South
Notus and *Afer* black with thundrous Clouds
From *Serraliona;* thwart of these as fierce
Forth rush the *Levant* and the *Ponent* Winds
Eurus and *Zephir* with thir lateral noise,   705
Sirocco, and *Libecchio.* Thus began
Outrage from lifeless things; but Discord first
Daughter of Sin, among th' irrational,
Death introduc'd through fierce antipathy:
Beast now with Beast gan war, and Fowl with Fowl,   710
And Fish with Fish; to graze the Herb all leaving,
Devour'd each other; nor stood much in awe
Of Man, but fled him, or with count'nance grim
Glar'd on him passing: these were from without
The growing miseries, which *Adam* saw   715
Already in part, though hid in gloomiest shade,
To sorrow abandon'd, but worse felt within,
And in a troubl'd Sea of passion tost,
Thus to disburd'n sought with sad complaint.
O miserable of happy! is this the end   720

---

700. *Thrascias,* probably because it blew from Thrace, was the name given by the Greeks to the north-northwest wind.

702. *Notus* was the south wind.
Afer, meaning literally "African," was the southwest wind. It is the only name in the list which is purely Latin and which names a wind from any except the Greek point of view.

703. *Serraliona,* the modern Sierra Leone on the west African coast.

704. *Levant,* which was used like "Orient" to mean the east, is opposed to *Ponent,* which refers, like "Occident," to the setting sun and means the west.

705. *Eurus,* the southeast wind of the Greeks, and Zephyr, the west wind, are thought of as blowing *laterally, i. e.,* at right angles to the north and south winds.

706. *Sirocco* is the Italian name for the strong southeast wind and *Libecchio,* or *Libeccio,* for the southwest wind.

707. With *Discord* compare "Nature's Concord" in VI, 311. Discord was traditionally one of the great powers of hell, as Milton, following Boccaccio, has represented her in II, 967.

718. Milton found biblical support for his essentially Greek conception of wickedness as uncontrolled passion in Isaiah lvii, 20: "The wicked are like the troubled sea, when it cannot rest."

Of this new glorious World, and mee so late
The Glory of that Glory, who now become
Accurst of blessed, hide me from the face
Of God, whom to behold was then my highth
Of happiness: yet well, if here would end   725
The misery, I deserv'd it, and would bear
My own deservings; but this will not serve;
All that I eat or drink, or shall beget,
Is propagated curse. O voice once heard
Delightfully, *Increase and multiply,*   730
Now death to hear! for what can I increase
Or multiply, but curses on my head?
Who of all Ages to succeed, but feeling
The evil on him brought by me, will curse
My Head?   Ill fare our Ancestor impure,   735
For this we may thank *Adam;* but his thanks
Shall be the execration; so besides
Mine own that bide upon me, all from mee
Shall with a fierce reflux on mee redound,
On mee as on thir natural centre light   740
Heavy, though in thir place. O fleeting joys
Of Paradise, dear bought with lasting woes!
Did I request thee, Maker, from my Clay
To mould me Man, did I solicit thee
From darkness to promote me, or here place   745
In this delicious Garden? as my Will
Concurr'd not to my being, it were but right
And equal to reduce me to my dust,
Desirous to resign, and render back
All I receiv'd, unable to perform   750
Thy terms too hard, by which I was to hold
The good I sought not. To the loss of that,

---

730. *Increase and multiply* was a part of God's blessing in Genesis
i, 28.

738. *Mine own* refers to *curses* in 732.

739. *redound* keeps its Latin force of "flow back," *i. e.,* like a returning wave.

743. Milton remembered the curse in Isaiah xlv, 9: "Woe unto him
that striveth with his maker! . . . Shall the clay say to him that
fashioneth it, What makest thou?"

748. *equal,* just, fair.

Sufficient penalty, why hast thou added
The sense of endless woes? inexplicable
Thy Justice seems; yet to say truth, too late,   755
I thus contest; then should have been refus'd
Those terms whatever, when they were propos'd:
Thou didst accept them; wilt thou enjoy the good,
Then cavil the conditions? and though God
Made thee without thy leave, what if thy Son   760
Prove disobedient, and reprov'd, retort,
Wherefore didst thou beget me? I sought it not:
Wouldst thou admit for his contempt of thee
That proud excuse? yet him not thy election,
But Natural necessity begot.   765
God made thee of choice his own, and of his own
To serve him, thy reward was of his grace,
Thy punishment then justly is at his Will.
Be it so, for I submit, his doom is fair,
That dust I am, and shall to dust return: 770
O welcome hour whenever! why delays
His hand to execute what his Decree
Fix'd on this day? why do I overlive,
Why am I mockt with death, and length'n'd out
To deathless pain? how gladly would I meet   775
Mortality my sentence, and be Earth
Insensible, how glad would lay me down
As in my Mother's lap? there I should rest
And sleep secure; his dreadful voice no more
Would Thunder in my ears, no fear of worse   780
To mee and to my offspring would torment me
With cruel expectation. Yet one doubt
Pursues me still, lest all I cannot die,

---

758. *Thou* refers to Adam himself.

762. Milton reverted to the following verse in Isaiah xlv, 10: "Woe
unto him that saith unto his father, What begettest thou?"

764. *election,* choice. Milton drew a sharp distinction between human
and divine begetting to prove that the Son of God is inferior to the
Father, for, "if God generate by a physical necessity, he can generate
nothing but a co-equal Deity." (*C.D.* I, v.)

778. So Michael refers to the earth as Adam's "mother's lap" in
XI, 536.

Lest that pure breath of Life, the Spirit of Man
Which God inspir'd, cannot together perish   785
With this corporeal Clod; then in the Grave,
Or in some other dismal place, who knows
But I shall die a living Death?   O thought
Horrid, if true! yet why? it was but breath
Of Life that sinn'd; what dies but what had life   790
And sin? the Body properly hath neither.
All of me then shall die: let this appease
The doubt, since human reach no further knows.
For though the Lord of all be infinite,
Is his wrath also? be it, man is not so,   795
But mortal doom'd. How can he exercise
Wrath without end on Man whom Death must end?
Can he make deathless Death? that were to make
Strange contradiction, which to God himself
Impossible is held, as Argument   800
Of weakness, not of Power. Will he draw out,
For anger's sake, finite to infinite
In punisht man, to satisfy his rigour
Satisfi'd never; that were to extend
His Sentence beyond dust and Nature's Law,   805
By which all Causes else according still
To the reception of thir matter act,
Not to th' extent of thir own Sphere. But say

---

784. Adam wrestles with the problem which Milton settled to his
own satisfaction when he wrote of the creation story in Genesis i, 26,
that "it was not the body alone that was then made, but the soul of
man also (in which our likeness to God principally consists); which
precludes us from attributing pre-existence to the soul which was then
formed." (*C.D.* I, vii.)   "What could be more absurd," he asked, "than
that the mind, which is the part principally offending, should escape the
threatened death; and that the body alone, to which immortality was
equally allotted, . . . should pay the penalty of sin by undergoing death,
though not implicated in the transgression?" (*Ibid.,* I, xiii.)

785. *inspir'd* has its Latin meaning of "inbreathed."

799. Writing about the divine omnipotence Milton said that, "It
must be remembered that the power of God is not exerted in things
which imply a contradiction." (*C.D.* I, ii.)

807. To explain the term *reception* Newton quotes the axiom: *Omne
efficiens agit secundum vires recipientis, non suas*—"every efficient (*i. e.,*
everything which acts on others) acts according to the powers of whatever receives its action, not according to its own powers."

That Death be not one stroke, as I suppos'd,
Bereaving sense, but endless misery   810
From this day onward, which I feel begun
Both in me, and without me, and so last
To perpetuity; Ay me, that fear
Comes thund'ring back with dreadful revolution
On my defenseless head; both Death and I   815
Am found Eternal, and incorporate both,
Nor I on my part single, in mee all
Posterity stands curst: Fair Patrimony
That I must leave ye, Sons; O were I able
To waste it all myself, and leave ye none!   820
So disinherited how would ye bless
Me now your Curse! Ah, why should all mankind
For one man's fault thus guiltless be condemn'd,
If guiltless?   But from mee what can proceed,
But all corrupt, both Mind and Will deprav'd,   825
Not to do only, but to will the same
With me? how can they then acquitted stand
In sight of God?   Him after all Disputes
Forc't I absolve: all my evasions vain
And reasonings, though through Mazes, lead me still   830
But to my own conviction: first and last
On mee, mee only, as the source and spring
Of all corruption, all the blame lights due;
So might the wrath.   Fond wish! couldst thou support
That burden heavier than the Earth to bear,   835
Than all the World much heavier, though divided
With that bad Woman?   Thus what thou desir'st,
And what thou fear'st, alike destroys all hope
Of refuge, and concludes thee miserable

---

810. *Bereaving sense,* depriving of all power of sensation. The haunting dread throughout this soliloquy is like Hamlet's fear of consciousness
       "When we have shuffled off this mortal coil."
                        (III, i, 67.)

816. *Am;* the verb agrees with the nearer subject.
incorporate, united in one body.

823. Adam's answer to his own question corresponds with Milton's
reasoning to prove that the posterity of Adam and Eve "are judged and
condemned in them, so that without doubt they also sinned in them."
(*C.D.* I, xi.)

Beyond all past example and futúre,   840
To *Satan* only like both crime and doom.
O Conscience, into what Abyss of fears
And horrors hast thou driv'n me; out of which
I find no way, from deep to deeper plung'd!
    Thus *Adam* to himself lamented loud   845
Through the still Night, not now, as ere man fell,
Wholesome and cool, and mild, but with black Air
Accompanied, with damps and dreadful gloom,
Which to his evil Conscience represented
All things with double terror: On the ground   850
Outstretcht he lay, on the cold ground, and oft
Curs'd his Creation, Death as oft accus'd
Of tardy execution, since denounc't
The day of his offence. Why comes not Death,
Said hee, with one thrice ácceptable stroke   855
To end me?   Shall Truth fail to keep her word,
Justice Divine not hast'n to be just?
But Death comes not at call, Justice Divine
Mends not her slowest pace for prayers or cries.
O Woods, O Fountains, Hillocks, Dales and Bow'rs,   860
With other echo late I taught your Shades
To answer, and resound far other Song.
Whom thus afflicted when sad *Eve* beheld,
Desolate where she sat, approaching nigh,
Soft words to his fierce passion she assay'd: 865
But her with stern regard he thus repell'd.
    Out of my sight, thou Serpent, that name best
Befits thee with him leagu'd, thyself as false
And hateful; nothing wants, but that thy shape,
Like his, and colour Serpentine may show   870
Thy inward fraud, to warn all Creatures from thee

---

840. *past example* must be that of Satan.

842. Compare the personification of Conscience in IV, 23.

858. *Justice divine, etc.*: Newton pointed out that the thought is an inversion of the commonplace with which Horace ended a famous Ode (III, ii): "Rarely has Punishment abandoned the fleeing criminal, though her pace be halting." Tibullus has the same thought (I, ix, 4); and many other sources for it—ranging back to the Greek conception of "tardy-footed Nemesis"—were familiar to Milton.

Henceforth; lest that too heav'nly form, pretended
To hellish falsehood, snare them. But for thee
I had persisted happy, had not thy pride
And wand'ring vanity, when least was safe,   875
Rejected my forewarning, and disdain'd
Not to be trusted, longing to be seen
Though by the Devil himself, him overweening
To over-reach, but with the Serpent meeting
Fool'd and beguil'd, by him thou, I by thee,   880
To trust thee from my side, imagin'd wise,
Constant, mature, proof against all assaults,
And understood not all was but a show
Rather than solid virtue, all but a Rib
Crooked by nature, bent, as now appears,   885
More to the part siníster from me drawn,
Well if thrown out, as supernumerary
To my just number found. O why did God,
Creator wise, that peopl'd highest Heav'n
With Spirits Masculine, create at last   890
This novelty on Earth, this fair defect
Of Nature, and not fill the World at once
With Men as Angels without Feminine,
Or find some other way to generate
Mankind? this mischief had not then befall'n,   895
And more that shall befall, innumerable
Disturbances on Earth through Female snares,
And strait conjunction with this Sex: for either
He never shall find out fit Mate, but such

872. *pretended* has its literal meaning of "held out," *i. e.*, as a screen
or disguise.

886. *sinister:* the tradition that the rib taken from Adam to make
Eve came from his left side is made a part of his account of her
creation in VIII, 465. Milton plays on the literal meaning of *sinister,
i. e.*, "left" and on its derived meaning of "ill-omened."

887. *supernumerary* may refer to an old belief that Adam was created
with an extra rib made for the creation of Eve.

888. The thought echoes a famous invective against women in Euripides' *Hippolytus,* 616–18. Compare *S. A.*, 1053–60.

899. *Mate* is perhaps an equivalent for the Hebrew word which is
rendered *help meet* in Genesis ii, 18. The thought here recalls Rabbi
Rashi's commentary: *"help meet* (literally, *help as-over-against-him*).
This means if he is lucky, a help; if unlucky, an antagonist with whom

As some misfortune brings him, or mistake,   900
Or whom he wishes most shall seldom gain
Through her perverseness, but shall see her gain'd
By a far worse, or if she love, withheld
By Parents, or his happiest choice too late
Shall meet, already linkt and Wedlock-bound   905
To a fell Adversary, his hate or shame:
Which infinite calamity shall cause
To Human life, and household peace confound.

    He added not, and from her turn'd, but *Eve*
Not so repulst, with Tears that ceas'd not flowing,   910
And tresses all disorder'd, at his feet
Fell humble, and imbracing them, besought
His peace, and thus proceeded in her plaint.

    Forsake me not thus, *Adam,* witness Heav'n
What love sincere, and reverence in my heart   915
I bear thee, and unweeting have offended,
Unhappily deceiv'd; thy suppliant
I beg, and clasp thy knees; bereave me not,
Whereon I live, thy gentle looks, thy aid,
Thy counsel in this uttermost distress,   920
My only strength and stay: forlorn of thee,
Whither shall I betake me, where subsist?
While yet we live, scarce one short hour perhaps,
Between us two let there be peace, both joining,
As join'd in injuries, one enmity   925
Against a Foe by doom express assign'd us,
That cruel Serpent: On me exercise not
Thy hatred for this misery befall'n,
On me already lost, mee than thyself
More miserable; both have sinn'd, but thou   930
Against God only, I against God and thee,
And to the place of judgment will return,
There with my cries importune Heaven, that all
The sentence from thy head remov'd may light
On me, sole cause to thee of all this woe,   935
Mee mee only just object of his ire.

    She ended weeping, and her lowly plight,

---

to fight." Fletcher (*Rabbinical Readings,* p. 174) indicates the interest
of the commentary to Milton when he wrote the divorce tracts.

Immovable till peace obtain'd from fault
Acknowledg'd and deplor'd, in *Adam* wrought
Commiseration; soon his heart relented　　　　　　　940
Towards her, his life so late and sole delight,
Now at his feet submissive in distress,
Creature so fair his reconcilement seeking,
His counsel whom she had displeas'd, his aid;
As one disarm'd, his anger all he lost,　　　　　　945
And thus with peaceful words uprais'd her soon.

　　Unwary, and too desirous, as before,
So now of what thou know'st not, who desir'st
The punishment all on thyself; alas,
Bear thine own first, ill able to sustain　　　　　950
His full wrath whose thou feel'st as yet least part,
And my displeasure bear'st so ill. If Prayers
Could alter high Decrees, I to that place
Would speed before thee, and be louder heard,
That on my head all might be visited,　　　　　　955
Thy frailty and infirmer Sex forgiv'n,
To me committed and by me expos'd.
But rise, let us no more contend, nor blame
Each other, blam'd enough elsewhere, but strive
In offices of Love, how we may light'n　　　　　960
Each other's burden in our share of woe;
Since this day's Death denounc't, if aught I see,
Will prove no sudden, but a slow-pac't evil,
A long day's dying to augment our pain,
And to our Seed (O hapless Seed!) deriv'd.　　　　965

　　To whom thus *Eve*, recovering heart, repli'd.
Adam, by sad experiment I know
How little weight my words with thee can find,
Found so erroneous, thence by just event

---

　　938. *Immovable* seems to qualify Adam, who is inflexible until Eve's
confession of her fault brings peace between them. The thought recurs
in *Samson Agonistes,* 1003–7:

> "Yet beauty, though injurious, hath strange power,
> After offence returning, to regain
> Love once possest, nor can be easily
> Repuls't, without much inward passion felt
> And secret sting of amorous remorse."

　　959. *elsewhere, i. e.,* at "the place of judgment" (932 above).

Found so unfortunate; nevertheless,   970
Restor'd by thee, vile as I am, to place
Of new acceptance, hopeful to regain
Thy Love, the sole contentment of my heart,
Living or dying, from thee I will not hide
What thoughts in my unquiet breast are ris'n,   975
Tending to some relief of our extremes,
Or end, though sharp and sad, yet tolerable,
As in our evils, and of easier choice.
If care of our descent perplex us most,
Which must be born to certain woe, devour'd   980
By Death at last, and miserable it is
To be to others cause of misery,
Our own begotten, and of our Loins to bring
Into this cursed World a woeful Race,
That after wretched Life must be at last   985
Food for so foul a Monster, in thy power
It lies, yet ere Conception to prevent
The Race unblest, to being yet unbegot.
Childless thou art, Childless remain: So Death
Shall be deceiv'd his glut, and with us two   990
Be forc'd to satisfy his Rav'nous Maw.
But if thou judge it hard and difficult,
Conversing, looking, loving, to abstain
From Love's due Rites, Nuptial embraces sweet,
And with desire to languish without hope,   995
Before the present object languishing
With like desire, which would be misery
And torment less than none of what we dread,
Then both ourselves and Seed at once to free
From what we fear for both, let us make short,   1000
Let us seek Death, or he not found, supply
With our own hands his Office on ourselves;
Why stand we longer shivering under fears,
That show no end but Death, and have the power,

---

978. *As in our evils,* in such evils as ours; a Latinism.

979. *descent,* descendants.

987. *prevent,* forestall, cut off in advance.

996. By *the present object* Eve means herself as being in **Adam's** presence.

Of many ways to die the shortest choosing,   1005
Destruction with destruction to destroy.
  She ended here, or vehement despair
Broke off the rest; so much of Death her thoughts
Had entertain'd, as dy'd her Cheeks with pale.
But *Adam* with such counsel nothing sway'd,   1010
To better hopes his more attentive mind
Labouring had rais'd, and thus to *Eve* replied.
  Eve, thy contempt of life and pleasure seems
To argue in thee something more sublime
And excellent than what thy mind contemns;   1015
But self-destruction therefore sought, refutes
That excellence thought in thee, and implies,
Not thy contempt, but anguish and regret
For loss of life and pleasure overlov'd.
Or if thou covet death, as utmost end   1020
Of misery, so thinking to evade
The penalty pronounc't, doubt not but God
Hath wiselier arm'd his vengeful ire than so
To be forestall'd; much more I fear lest Death
So snatcht will not exempt us from the pain   1025
We are by doom to pay; rather such acts
Of contumacy will provoke the highest
To make death in us live: Then let us seek
Some safer resolution, which methinks
I have in view, calling to mind with heed   1030
Part of our Sentence, that thy Seed shall bruise
The Serpent's head; piteous amends, unless
Be meant, whom I conjecture, our grand Foe
Satan, who in the Serpent hath contriv'd
Against us this deceit: to crush his head   1035
Would be revenge indeed; which will be lost
By death brought on ourselves, or childless days
Resolv'd, as thou proposest; so our Foe
Shall 'scape his punishment ordain'd, and wee
Instead shall double ours upon our heads.   1040
No more be mention'd then of violence
Against ourselves, and wilful barrenness,
That cuts us off from hope, and savours only

―――――――

1033. On Adam's *conjecture* compare the note at 165 above.

Rancour and pride, impatience and despite,
Reluctance against God and his just yoke   1045
Laid on our Necks. Remember with what mild
And gracious temper he both heard and judg'd
Without wrath or reviling; wee expected
Immediate dissolution, which we thought
Was meant by Death that day, when lo, to thee   1050
Pains only in Child-bearing were foretold,
And bringing forth, soon recompens't with joy,
Fruit of thy Womb: On mee the Curse aslope
Glanc'd on the ground, with labour I must earn
My bread; what harm? Idleness had been worse;   1055
My labour will sustain me; and lest Cold
Or Heat should injure us, his timely care
Hath unbesought provided, and his hands
Cloth'd us unworthy, pitying while he judg'd;
How much more, if we pray him, will his ear   1060
Be open, and his heart to pity incline,
And teach us further by what means to shun
Th' inclement Seasons, Rain, Ice, Hail and Snow,
Which now the Sky with various Face begins
To show us in this Mountain, while the Winds   1065
Blow moist and keen, shattering the graceful locks
Of these fair spreading Trees; which bids us seek
Some better shroud, some better warmth to cherish
Our Limbs benumb'd, ere this diurnal Star
Leave cold the Night, how we his gather'd beams   1070
Reflected, may with matter sere foment,

1045. *Reluctance,* resistance, recalcitrance.

1050. *that day* is actually the preceding day.

1053. *the Curse aslope Glanc'd on the ground:* Adam means that the curse which might have affected him directly glanced off (like an arrow grazing its mark) and fell upon the ground. Compare 201 above.

1065. Compare the representation of Paradise as a *mountain* or plateau in IV, 132–72.

1066. *locks:* compare Spenser's line:

"The faded lockes fall from the loftie oke."
(*The Shepheardes Calendar, November,* 125.)

1069. *this diurnal Star,* the sun.

1070. *how,* following *seek* in 1067, means "to find out how."

1071. *foment,* warm, heat.

Or by collision of two bodies grind
The Air attrite to Fire, as late the Clouds
Justling or pusht with Winds rude in thir shock
Tine the slant Lightning, whose thwart flame driv'n down
Kindles the gummy bark of Fir or Pine,   1076
And sends a comfortable heat from far,
Which might supply the Sun: such Fire to use,
And what may else be remedy or cure
To evils which our own misdeeds have wrought,   1080
Hee will instruct us praying, and of Grace
Beseeching him, so as we need not fear
To pass commodiously this life, sustain'd
By him with many comforts, till we end
In dust, our final rest and native home.   1085
What better can we do, than to the place
Repairing where he judg'd us, prostrate fall
Before him reverent, and there confess
Humbly our faults, and pardon beg, with tears
Watering the ground, and with our sighs the Air   1090
Frequenting, sent from hearts contrite, in sign
Of sorrow unfeign'd, and humiliation meek.
Undoubtedly he will relent and turn
From his displeasure; in whose look serene,
When angry most he seem'd and most severe,   1095
What else but favour, grace, and mercy shone?
    So spake our Father penitent, nor *Eve*
Felt less remorse: they forthwith to the place
Repairing where he judg'd them prostrate fell
Before him reverent, and both confess'd   1100

1073. *attrite* is felt as having both its Latin form as a perfect passive participle and meaning, "rubbed," "worked by friction."

1075. *Tine,* kindle.
thwart, transverse, slanting.

1076. The theory that primitive men secured fire from the kindling of the forest trees by lightning is paralleled in Lucretius' *De rerum natura,* V, 1091–5, and the context of the passage corresponds with Milton's context here. Compare the Lucretian influence suggested in the note on VII, 463.

1081. *praying, i. e.,* if we pray.

1091. *Frequenting* has its Latin meaning of "crowding" or "filling full."

Humbly thir faults, and pardon begg'd, with tears
Watering the ground, and with thir sighs the Air
Frequenting, sent from hearts contrite, in sign
Of sorrow unfeign'd, and humiliation meek.

The End of the Tenth Book.

BOOK XI

THE ARGUMENT

The Son of God presents to his Father the Prayers of our first Parents now repenting, and intercedes for them: God accepts them, but declares that they must no longer abide in Paradise; sends Michael *with a Band of Cherubim to dispossess them; but first to reveal to* Adam *future things:* Michael's *coming down.* Adam *shows to* Eve *certain ominous signs; he discerns* Michael's *approach, goes out to meet him: the Angel denounces thir departure.* Eve's *Lamentation.* Adam *pleads, but submits: The Angel leads him up to a high Hill, sets before him in vision what shall happ'n till the Flood.*

Thus they in lowliest plight repentant stood
Praying, for from the Mercy-seat above
Prevenient Grace descending had remov'd
The stony from thir hearts, and made new flesh
Regenerate grow instead, that sighs now breath'd   5

---

1. In what seems glaring inconsistency with "prostrate" in X, 1099, Milton wrote *stood*, probably because he preferred to think of Adam as standing to pray (as in IV, 720), and because he liked to think that "no particular posture of the body in prayer was injoined, even under the law." (*C.D.* II, iv.)

2. Milton's image is that of the mercy-seat in Aaron's tabernacle with its "two cherubim of gold, of beaten work, . . . in the two ends" (Exod., xxv, 18), for tradition made it a type of the intercession of angels, or of Christ, in heaven.

3. *Prevenient Grace* is used in its full theological sense of grace which anticipates repentance.

4. *stony* is an adjective used as an abstract noun, with an allusion to Ezekiel xi, 19: "I will take the stony heart out of their flesh, and will give them an heart of flesh."

5. *sighs . . . Unutterable* recall St. Paul's assurance that "the Spirit itself maketh intercession for us with groanings which cannot be uttered." (Rom. viii, 26.)

354

Unutterable, which the Spirit of prayer
Inspir'd, and wing'd for Heav'n with speedier flight
Than loudest Oratory: yet thir port
Not of mean suitors, nor important less
Seem'd thir Petition, than when th' ancient Pair   10
In Fables old, less ancient yet than these,
Deucalion and chaste *Pyrrha* to restore
The Race of Mankind drown'd, before the Shrine
Of *Themis* stood devout. To Heav'n thir prayers
Flew up, nor miss'd the way, by envious winds   15
Blown vagabond or frustrate: in they pass'd
Dimensionless through Heav'nly doors: then clad
With incense, where the Golden Altar fum'd,
By thir great Intercessor, came in sight
Before the Father's Throne: Them the glad Son   20
Presenting, thus to intercede began.

  See Father, what first fruits on Earth are sprung
From thy implanted Grace in Man, these Sighs
And Prayers, which in this Golden Censer, mixt
With Incense, I thy Priest before thee bring,   25
Fruits of more pleasing savour from thy seed
Sown with contrition in his heart, than those
Which his own hand manuring all the Trees
Of Paradise could have produc't, ere fall'n
From innocence. Now therefore bend thin ear   30
To supplication, hear his sighs though mute;
Unskilful with what words to pray, let mee

---

12. Milton thought of one of the most familiar scenes in Ovid's
Metamorphoses (I, 321–80), the prayer of the survivors of "Deucalion's
flood" to "fate-revealing Themis," the goddess of justice.

15. Milton is contrasting these *prayers* with the "fruits
     Of painful superstition and blind zeal" (III, 451–2)
which "a violent cross wind . . blows . . transverse," in the limbo of
vanity.

17. *dimensionless* implies the immateriality of the prayers, for exten-
sionlessness and incorporeality were the terms by which Descartes defined
spiritual things.
  clad With incense, etc.: compare the angel of Revelation, viii, 3, who
"stood at the altar, having a golden censer; and there was given unto
him much incense, that he should offer it with the prayers of all
saints upon the golden altar which was before the throne."

28. *manuring,* dressing, cultivating. Compare IV, 628.

Interpret for him, mee his Advocate
And propitiation, all his works on mee
Good or not good ingraft, my Merit those   35
Shall perfet, and for these my Death shall pay.
Accept me, and in mee from these receive
The smell of peace toward Mankind, let him live
Before thee reconcil'd, at least his days
Number'd, though sad, till Death, his doom (which I   40
To mitigate thus plead, not to reverse)
To better life shall yield him, where with mee
All my redeem'd may dwell in joy and bliss,
Made one with me as I with thee am one.

   To whom the Father, without Cloud, serene.   45
All thy request for Man, accepted Son,
Obtain, all thy request was my Decree:
But longer in that Paradise to dwell,
The Law I gave to Nature him forbids:
Those pure immortal Elements that know   50
No gross, no unharmonious mixture foul,
Eject him tainted now, and purge him off
As a distemper, gross to air as gross,
And mortal food, as may dispose him best
For dissolution wrought by Sin, that first   55
Distemper'd all things, and of incorrupt
Corrupted. I at first with two fair gifts
Created him endow'd, with Happiness
And Immortality: that fondly lost,
This other serv'd but to eternize woe;   60
Till I provided Death; so Death becomes
His final remedy, and after Life
Tri'd in sharp tribulation, and refin'd

33. Compare "we have an advocate with the Father, Jesus Christ the
righteous: And he is the propitiation for our sins." I John ii, 1–2.

43. The prayer for the *redeem'd* echoes Christ's prayer: "Holy Father,
keep through thine own name those whom thou hast given me, that
they may be one, as we are." (John xvii, 11.)

50. The *pure Elements* of Eden are regarded as expelling fallen man
as Belial says that the "ethereal mould" of heaven, "incapable of stain,"
would automatically "purge off the baser fire" of the rebel angels, if
they were to invade heaven from hell. (II, 134–42.)

56. *of incorrupt,* from a state of incorruption. Compare the note
on IV, 153.

By Faith and faithful works, to second Life,
Wak't in the renovation of the just,   65
Resigns him up with Heav'n and Earth renew'd.
But let us call to Synod all the Blest
Through Heav'n's wide bounds; from them I will not hide
My judgments, how with Mankind I proceed,
As how with peccant Angels late they saw;   70
And in thir state, though firm, stood more confirm'd.

    He ended, and the Son gave signal high
To the bright Minister that watch'd, hee blew
His Trumpet, heard in *Oreb* since perhaps
When God descended, and perhaps once more   75
To sound at general Doom. Th' Angelic blast
Fill'd all the Regions: from thir blissful Bow'rs
Of *Amarantin* Shade, Fountain or Spring,
By the waters of Life, where'er they sat
In fellowships of joy: the Sons of Light   80
Hasted, resorting to the Summons high,
And took thir Seats; till from his Throne supreme
Th' Almighty thus pronounc'd his sovran Will.

    O Sons, like one of us Man is become
To know both Good and Evil, since his taste   85
Of that defended Fruit; but let him boast

----

64. Here and in the "faith not void of works" of XII, 427, Milton
stresses his very much qualified assent to the Lutheran doctrine of
justification by faith.

74. The *Trumpet,* which summoned the angelic armies in VI, 60,
Milton says *may* have been heard on earth when God gave the ten
commandments to Moses on Mount Sinai, or Horeb, and *may* be heard
again when God "shall send his angels with a great sound of the
trumpet" (Matt. xxiv, 31) for the last judgement. In *Nativity Ode,*
157–8, Milton compared "the wakeful trump of doom" to

                "such a horrid clang
            As on Mount Sinai rang."

78. Compare the note on *Amarant* in III, 352.

79. With *the waters of Life* compare the "River of Bliss" in III, 358,
and its note.

84. "And the Lord God said, Behold, the man is become as one of
us, to know good and evil: and now, lest he put forth his hand, and
take also of the tree of life, and eat, and live for ever: Therefore the
Lord God sent him forth from the garden of Eden, to till the ground
from whence he was taken." (Gen. iii, 22–3.)

86. *defended,* prohibited.

His knowledge of Good lost, and Evil got,
Happier, had it suffic'd him to have known
Good by itself, and Evil not at all.
He sorrows now, repents, and prays contrite,   90
My motions in him; longer than they move,
His heart I know, how variable and vain
Self-left.   Lest therefore his now bolder hand
Reach also of the Tree of Life, and eat,
And live for ever, dream at least to live   95
For ever, to remove him I decree,
And send him from the Garden forth to Till
The Ground whence he was taken, fitter soil.
      Michael, this my behest have thou in charge,
Take to thee from among the Cherubim   100
Thy choice of flaming Warriors, lest the Fiend
Or in behalf of Man, or to invade
Vacant possession some new trouble raise:
Haste thee, and from the Paradise of God
Without remorse drive out the sinful Pair,   105
From hallow'd ground th' unholy, and denounce
To them and to thir Progeny from thence
Perpetual banishment.   Yet lest they faint
At the sad Sentence rigorously urg'd,
For I behold them soft'nd and with tears   110
Bewailing thir excess, all terror hide.
If patiently thy bidding they obey,
Dismiss them not disconsolate; reveal
To *Adam* what shall come in future days,
As I shall thee enlighten, intermix   115
My Cov'nant in the woman's seed renew'd;
So send them forth, though sorrowing, yet in peace:
And on the East side of the Garden place,

----

91. *My motions,* my influence, *i. e.,* the "prevenient grace" of 3 above.

93. *Self-left,* when left to itself.

99. Compare the note on *Michael* at VI, 44.

105. *remorse,* sorrow or pity.   Compare V, 566.

106. *denounce,* proclaim (something unwelcome).

118. "So he drove out the man; and he placed at the east of the garden of Eden cherubim, and a flaming sword which turned every way, to keep the way of the tree of life." (Gen. iii, 24.)

Where entrance up from *Eden* easiest climbs,
Cherubic watch, and of a Sword the flame   120
Wide waving, all approach far off to fright,
And guard all passage to the Tree of Life:
Lest Paradise a receptácle prove
To Spirits foul, and all my Trees thir prey,
With whose stol'n Fruit Man once more to delude.   125
     He ceas'd; and th' Archangelic Power prepar'd
For swift descent, with him the Cohort bright
Of watchful Cherubim; four faces each
Had, like a double *Janus,* all thir shape
Spangl'd with eyes more numerous than those   130
Of *Argus,* and more wakeful than to drowse,
Charm'd with *Arcadian* Pipe, the Pastoral Reed
Of *Hermes,* or his opiate Rod.   Meanwhile
To resalute the World with sacred Light
Leucóthea wak'd, and with fresh dews imbalm'd   135
The Earth, when *Adam* and first Matron *Eve*
Had ended now thir Orisons, and found
Strength added from above, new hope to spring
Out of despair, joy, but with fear yet linkt;
Which thus to *Eve* his welcome words renew'd.   140
     Eve, easily may Faith admit, that all
The good which we enjoy, from Heav'n descends;
But that from us aught should ascend to Heav'n
So prevalent as to concern the mind
Of God high-blest, or to incline his will,   145
Hard to belief may seem; yet this will Prayer,

---

129. The cherubs are compared to the Roman god of gates, Janus, because his double-faced images suggested Ezekiel's description of them as having four faces. For an earlier use of Ezekiel's symbolism see VI, 750, and its note.

130. Ezekiel (i, 18) describes the cherubs as involved in rings that were "full of eyes."

131. Ovid relates that Juno put *Argus,* whose "head was set about with a hundred eyes, which took their rest in sleep two at a time in turn" (*Met.* I, 625–6) to watch her rival, Io; and that Mercury (Hermes) lulled all the eyes to sleep with his Arcadian pipes and medicated rod (716).

135. *Leucothea,* whose Greek name means "the shining goddess," is a symbol of dawn, since Ovid (*Fasti,* VI, 479 and 545) identified her with the Roman goddess of the dawn, Matuta.

Or one short sigh of human breath, up-borne
Ev'n to the Seat of God.   For since I sought
By Prayer th' offended Deity to appease,
Kneel'd and before him humbl'd all my heart,   150
Methought I saw him placable and mild,
Bending his ear; persuasion in me grew
That I was heard with favour; peace return'd
Home to my Breast, and to my memory
His promise, that thy Seed shall bruise our Foe;   155
Which then not minded in dismay, yet now
Assures me that the bitterness of death
Is past, and we shall live.   Whence Hail to thee
Eve rightly call'd, Mother of all Mankind,
Mother of all things living, since by thee   160
Man is to live, and all things live for Man.
    To whom thus *Eve* with sad demeanour meek.
Ill worthy I such title should belong
To me transgressor, who for thee ordain'd
A help, became thy snare; to mee reproach   165
Rather belongs, distrust and all dispraise:
But infinite in pardon was my Judge,
That I who first brought Death on all, am grac't
The source of life; next favourable thou,
Who highly thus to entitle me voutsaf'st,   170
Far other name deserving.   But the Field
To labour calls us now with sweat impos'd,
Though after sleepless Night; for see the Morn,
All unconcern'd with our unrest, begins
Her rosy progress smiling; let us forth,   175
I never from thy side henceforth to stray,
Where'er our day's work lies, though now enjoin'd
Laborious, till day droop; while here we dwell,

---

155. For the *promise* see X, 174–81, and compare XII, 148–51 and
233–35.

157. *bitterness of death:* a Hebraism for "bitter death." Compare
I Samuel xv, 32: "And Agag said, Surely the bitterness of death is
past."

159. "And Adam called his wife's name Eve; because she was the
mother of all living." (Gen. iii, 20.)

162. *sad,* serious, grave.

165. *help:* compare the note on "Mate" in X, 899.

What can be toilsome in these pleasant Walks?
Here let us live, though in fall'n state, content.   180
    So spake, so wish'd much humbl'd *Eve,* but Fate
Subscrib'd not; Nature first gave Signs, imprest
On Bird, Beast, Air, Air suddenly eclips'd
After short blush of Morn; nigh in her sight
The Bird of *Jove,* stoopt from his aery tow'r,   185
Two Birds of gayest plume before him drove:
Down from a Hill the Beast that reigns in Woods,
First hunter then, pursu'd a gentle brace,
Goodliest of all the Forest, Hart and Hind;
Direct to th' Eastern Gate was bent thir flight.   190
Adam observ'd, and with his Eye the chase
Pursuing, not unmov'd to *Eve* thus spake.
    O *Eve,* some furder change awaits us nigh,
Which Heav'n by these mute signs in Nature shows
Forerunners of his purpose, or to warn   195
Us haply too secure of our discharge
From penalty, because from death releast
Some days; how long, and what till then our life,
Who knows, or more than this, that we are dust,
And thither must return and be no more.   200
Why else this double object in our sight
Of flight pursu'd in th' Air and o'er the ground
One way the self-same hour? why in the East
Darkness ere Day's mid-course, and Morning light

182. *subscrib'd,* consented.

183. *eclips'd,* darkened, but Milton probably meant that an eclipse
of the sun was the cause. He is on the point of narrating the blight
which fell upon all life in Eden as a consequence of the "influence
malignant" (X, 662) that the heavenly bodies had begun to pour upon
the earth. In the *History of Britain* (*P.W.,* V, 287) he mentions a
year when there "was seen an eclipse of the sun in May, followed by
a sore pestilence."

185. *The Bird of Jove,* the eagle, and the lion, both feel their first
hunting impulse and drive their prey toward the eastern gate of Eden,
by which they and Adam and Eve also are soon to pass into banishment.
Compare XII, 638-9.
    Stooping was a technical term in falconry for the swoop of a hawk
from its tower (lofty flight) to strike its prey.

196. *secure,* confident.

204. The *light* is the glory of Michael's angels descending in "a Sky
of Jasper."

More orient in yon Western Cloud that draws   205
O'er the blue Firmament a radiant white,
And slow descends, with something heav'nly fraught.
　　He err'd not, for by this the heav'nly Bands
Down from a Sky of Jasper lighted now
In Paradise, and on a Hill made alt,   210
A glorious Apparition, had not doubt
And carnal fear that day dimm'd *Adam's* eye.
Not that more glorious, when the Angels met
Jacob in *Mahanaim,* where he saw
The field Pavilion'd with his Guardians bright;   215
Nor that which on the flaming Mount appear'd
In *Dothan,* cover'd with a Camp of Fire,
Against the *Syrian* King, who to surprise
One man, Assassin-like had levied War,
War unproclaim'd. The Princely Hierarch   220
In thir bright stand, there left his Powers to seize
Possession of the Garden; hee alone,
To find where *Adam* shelter'd, took his way,
Not unperceiv'd of *Adam,* who to *Eve,*
While the great Visitant approach'd, thus spake.   225
　　Eve, now expect great tidings, which perhaps
Of us will soon determine, or impose
New Laws to be observ'd; for I descry
From yonder blazing Cloud that veils the Hill
One of the heav'nly Host, and by his Gait   230
None of the meanest, some great Potentate
Or of the Thrones above, such Majesty
Invests him coming; yet not terrible,
That I should fear, nor sociably mild,
As *Raphaël,* that I should much confide,   235

---

210. *alt,* halt.

214. *Mahanaim* (*i. e.,* two hosts) was the name given by Jacob to a
place where "the angels of God met him." (Gen. xxxii, 1–2.) Compare the use made of Jacob's more famous vision of angels in III, 510–28.

217. After warning the King of Israel of a treacherous raid of the
King of Syria the prophet Elisha was surrounded by the Syrians in
Dothan, and would have been kidnapped, if the mountain had not been
"full of horses and chariots of fire round about Elisha." (II Kings vi, 17.)

227. *determine,* put an end to, make an end of.

235. Compare the allusions to Raphael, "the sociable Spirit," in V, 221.

But solemn and sublime, whom not to offend,
With reverence I must meet, and thou retire.
He ended; and th' Arch-Angel soon drew nigh,
Not in his shape Celestial, but as Man
Clad to meet Man; over his lucid Arms   240
A military Vest of purple flow'd
Livelier than *Melibæan,* or the grain
Of *Sarra,* worn by Kings and Heroes old
In time of Truce; *Iris* had dipt the woof;
His starry Helm unbuckl'd show'd him prime   245
In Manhood where Youth ended; by his side
As in a glistering *Zodiac* hung the Sword,
Satan's dire dread, and in his hand the Spear.
Adam bow'd low, hee Kingly from his State
Inclin'd not, but his coming thus declar'd.   250
　　Adam, Heav'n's high behest no Preface needs:
Sufficient that thy Prayers are heard, and Death,
Then due by sentence when thou didst transgress,
Defeated of his seizure many days
Giv'n thee of Grace, wherein thou mayst repent,   255
And one bad act with many deeds well done
May'st cover: well may then thy Lord appeas'd
Redeem thee quite from Death's rapacious claim;

---

242. *Melibœa* was a town at the foot of Mount Ossa in Thessaly, famous in ancient times for its purple, as Virgil suggests in the *Aeneid,* V, 251.

grain, dye.

243. *Sarra* was a name given in early times to Tyre; Milton recollected Virgil's use of the name (*e. g.,* in *Georg.* II, 506) as synonymous for the most splendid colour.

244. It is in "Iris woof", *i. e.,* in all the colours of the rainbow, of which Iris was the goddess, that the Attendant Spirit in *Comus* (83) is dressed.

247. *Zodiac* is used in its Greek sense to mean "a belt," but it carries a suggestion of the splendour of the celestial Zodiac and its constellations.

248. Compare the dread of the demons for Michael's sword in II, 293–5.

249. *State,* stateliness.

254. *Defeated, etc.,* frustrated in his arrest of you for many days. The language is legal. Michael's entire speech should be compared with God's utterances in 96–8 and 48–9 above.

But longer in this Paradise to dwell
Permits not; to remove thee I am come,   260
And send thee from the Garden forth to till
The ground whence thou wast tak'n, fitter Soil.
      He added not, for *Adam* at the news
Heart-strook with chilling gripe of sorrow stood,
That all his senses bound; *Eve,* who unseen   265
Yet all had heard, with audible lament
Discover'd soon the place of her retire.
      O unexpected stroke, worse than of Death!
Must I thus leave thee Paradise? thus leave
Thee Native Soil, these happy Walks and Shades,   270
Fit haunt of Gods? where I had hope to spend,
Quiet though sad, the respite of that day
That must be mortal to us both. O flow'rs,
That never will in other Climate grow,
My early visitation, and my last   275
At Ev'n, which I bred up with tender hand
From the first op'ning bud, and gave ye Names,
Who now shall rear ye to the Sun, or rank
Your Tribes, and water from th' ambrosial Fount?
Thee lastly nuptial Bower, by mee adorn'd   280
With what to sight or smell was sweet; from thee
How shall I part, and whither wander down
Into a lower World, to this obscure
And wild, how shall we breathe in other Air
Less pure, accustom'd to immortal Fruits?   285
      Whom thus the Angel interrupted mild.
Lament not *Eve,* but patiently resign
What justly thou hast lost; nor set thy heart,
Thus over-fond, on that which is not thine;
Thy going is not lonely, with thee goes   290
Thy Husband, him to follow thou art bound;

---

264. *gripe,* seizure. Compare "griping pain."

267. *Discover'd,* betrayed, exposed.
retire, retirement.

272. *respite,* the remainder of time granted by God's reprieve of the
sentence of death, which must ultimately be carried out.

275. *visitation,* objects of visit. Compare VIII, 46, note.

285. *Less pure;* compare the note on 50 above.

Where he abides, think there thy native soil.
   Adam by this from the cold sudden damp
Recovering, and his scatter'd spirits return'd,
To *Michael* thus his humble words address'd.   295
   Celestial, whether among the Thrones, or nam'd
Of them the Highest, for such of shape may seem
Prince above Princes, gently hast thou told
Thy message, which might else in telling wound,
And in performing end us; what besides   300
Of sorrow and dejection and despair
Our frailty can sustain, thy tidings bring
Departure from this happy place, our sweet
Recess, and only consolation left
Familiar to our eyes, all places else   305
Inhospitable appear and desolate,
Nor knowing us nor known: and if by prayer
Incessant I could hope to change the will
Of him who all things can, I would not cease
To weary him with my assiduous cries: 310
But prayer against his absolute Decree
No more avails than breath against the wind,
Blown stifling back on him that breathes it forth:
Therefore to his great bidding I submit.
This most afflicts me, that departing hence,   315
As from his face I shall be hid, depriv'd
His blessed count'nance; here I could frequent,
With worship, place by place where he voutsaf'd
Presence Divine, and to my Sons relate;
On this Mount he appear'd, under this Tree   320

---

292. The thought is a variant of the Roman maxim (attributed to Pacuvius) that wherever a man's true good is, there is his *native soil.*

294. Fear was supposed to scatter the vital and animal spirits from their respective seats in heart and head through the whole body.

309. *can* was often used transitively, as in Lovelace's *Poems:* "Yet can I musick too." (N.E.D.)

310. *weary,* importune. Milton is implicitly contrasting God with the unjust judge of Luke xviii, 5–7, who could be made to yield only to importunity.

316. Adam's words are an echo of Cain's after his curse for the murder of Abel: "Behold, thou hast driven me out this day from the face of the earth; and from thy face shall I be hid." (Gen. iv, 14.)

Stood visible, among these Pines his voice
I heard, here with him at this Fountain talk'd:
So many grateful Altars I would rear
Of grassy Turf, and pile up every Stone
Of lustre from the brook, in memory,   325
Or monument to Ages, and thereon
Offer sweet smelling Gums and Fruits and Flow'rs:
In yonder nether World where shall I seek
His bright appearances, or footstep trace?
For though I fled him angry, yet recall'd   330
To life prolong'd and promis'd Race, I now
Gladly behold though but his utmost skirts
Of glory, and far off his steps adore.
   To whom thus *Michael* with regard benign.
Adam, thou know'st Heav'n his, and all the Earth,   335
Not this Rock only; his Omnipresence fills
Land, Sea, and Air, and every kind that lives,
Fomented by his virtual power and warm'd:
All th' Earth he gave thee to possess and rule,
No despicable gift; surmise not then   340
His presence to these narrow bounds confin'd
Of Paradise or *Eden:* this had been
Perhaps thy Capital Seat, from whence had spread
All generations, and had hither come
From all the ends of th' Earth, to celebrate   345
And reverence thee thir great Progenitor.
But this preëminence thou hast lost, brought down
To dwell on even ground now with thy Sons:
Yet doubt not but in Valley and in Plain

328. *nether,* lower. The word alludes to the fact that Eden towers
above the surrounding world, into which Eve dreads to "wander
down." (282 above. Compare 347–50 below.)

335. The thought is a fusion of many biblical passages; notably of
Christ's warning to the woman of Samaria against worshipping God
only "in this mountain" (John iv, 21) and Jeremiah's question: "Can
any hide himself in secret places that I shall not see him? saith the
Lord: do not I fill heaven and earth? saith the Lord." (xxiii, 24.)
Compare VII, 168–9.

338. *Fomented,* filled with life-giving heat. Compare IV, 669.
virtual, filled with virtue, in the sense that the stars are said to
possess virtue in IV, 671.

349. *Valley and . . Plain:* compare the note on 328 above.

God is as here, and will be found alike   350
Present, and of his presence many a sign
Still following thee, still compassing thee round
With goodness and paternal Love, his Face
Express, and of his steps the track Divine.
Which that thou may'st believe, and be confirm'd,   355
Ere thou from hence depart, know I am sent
To show thee what shall come in future days
To thee and to thy Offspring; good with bad
Expect to hear, supernal Grace contending
With sinfulness of Men; thereby to learn   360
True patience, and to temper joy with fear
And pious sorrow, equally inur'd
By moderation either state to bear,
Prosperous or adverse: so shalt thou lead
Safest thy life, and best prepar'd endure   365
Thy mortal passage when it comes.   Ascend
This Hill; let *Eve* (for I have drencht her eyes)
Here sleep below while thou to foresight wak'st,
As once thou slep'st, while Shee to life was form'd.

   To whom thus *Adam* gratefully repli'd.   370
Ascend, I follow thee, safe Guide, the path
Thou lead'st me, and to the hand of Heav'n submit,
However chast'ning, to the evil turn
My obvious breast, arming to overcome

---

   357. The circumstances of Adam's vision of the future of mankind
suggest Daniel's vision (in which "Michael, the great prince," is involved) of the destiny of Israel in "the latter days." (Dan. x, 14.)
The device may owe something to the Apocalypse of Moses and certainly owes something to the great series of visions of the future by
Adam in *The Divine Weekes* of Du Bartas from *The Handicrafts* to
The Decay. Milton's chief classical example for the revelation of the
world's destiny which is to fill the remainder of Book XI and most of
XII was Aeneas' vision in the Elysian Fields of the heroes of Rome's
future, his destined descendants.

   363. *moderation either state to bear* suggests the title of Petrarch's
treatise "On the Remedies of both kinds of Fortune" (*i.e.*, of good and
bad), and indicates his perfect fusion of the Greek with the Christian
ideal of moderation.

   366. *mortal passage,* death.

   369. *while Shee to life was form'd:* compare VIII, 460–77.

   374. *obvious,* deliberately exposed. The literal meaning of the word
in Latin is "in the path," *i.e.,* situated so as inevitably to be met.

By suffering, and earn rest from labour won,   375
If so I may attain.   So both ascend
In the Visions of God: It was a Hill
Of Paradise the highest, from whose top
The Hemisphere of Earth in clearest Ken
Stretcht out to the amplest reach of prospect lay.   380
Not higher that Hill nor wider looking round,
Whereon for different cause the Tempter set
Our second *Adam* in the Wilderness,
To show him all Earth's Kingdoms and thir Glory.
His Eye might there command wherever stood   385
City of old or modern Fame, the Seat
Of mightiest Empire, from the destin'd Walls
Of *Cambalu,* seat of *Cathaian Can,*
And *Samarchand* by *Oxus, Temir's* Throne,
To *Paquin* of *Sinæan* Kings, and thence   390
To *Agra* and *Lahor* of great *Mogul*
Down to the golden *Chersonese,* or where

377. Compare Ezekiel x, 2: "In the visions of God brought he me
into the land of Israel, and set me upon a very high mountain."

383. To realize the comparison which Milton intended with the
hill where *our second Adam,* Christ, was tempted we should read his
treatment of the temptation in *P.R.* III, 251–440.   The basis of Milton's
panorama there is the statement that "the devil taketh him up into an
exceeding high mountain, and showeth him all the kingdoms of the
world, and the glory of them." (Matt. iv, 8.)

388. In the *History of Moscovia* Milton approvingly reproduced an
enthusiastic account brought back by some Russian travellers from
Camabalu (or Cambaluc), the "City of the Khan."   He mistakenly distinguished it from Pekin, for, like most of his contemporaries, he
thought of Cathay as a land distinct from and lying to the north of
China.

389. *Samarchand,* near the river Oxus in central Asia, was famous
mainly as the capital of *Temir* or Timur, the Tartar conqueror, as
Marlowe makes him prophesy that it will be in *Tamburlaine,* Part II,
4109.

390. *Paquin,* Pekin.
Sinaean, Chinese.

391. *Agra* in northeastern India and *Lahor* in the Punjab were both
capitals of the Moguls and both were the subjects of glowing accounts
in Purchas' *Pilgrimes.*

392. Purchas (*Pilgrimage,*) suggests (p. 557) that Siam, and that
(p. 697) Molucca or Sumatra, was the Golden Chersonese of Ptolemy
or the Ophir whence King Solomon brought his gold. (I Kings ix, 28.)

The *Persian* in *Ecbatan* sat, or since
In *Hispahan*, or where the *Russian Ksar*
In *Mosco*, or the Sultan in *Bizance*,   395
Turchestan-born; nor could his eye not ken
Th' Empire of *Negus* to his utmost Port
Ercoco and the less Marítime Kings
Mombaza, and *Quiloa*, and *Melind*,
And *Sofala* thought *Ophir*, to the Realm   400
Of *Congo*, and *Angola* fardest South;
Or thence from *Niger* Flood to *Atlas* Mount
The Kingdoms of *Almansor*, *Fez* and *Sus*,
Marocco and *Algiers*, and *Tremisen;*
On *Europe* thence, and where *Rome* was to sway   405
The World: in Spirit perhaps he also saw
Rich *Mexico* the seat of *Motezume*,

---

393. *Ecbatana* was one of the capitals of the ancient Persian kings.

394. *Ispahan* (*Hispahan* seems like a printer's error, for Milton more usually avoided aspirates) was famous as the greatest city in Persia and as having become the capital under Shah Abbás the Great about the year 1600.

395. *Bizance,* Byzantium, the modern Constantinople.

396. Milton calls the Turkish sultan *Turchestan-born* because the Turks had migrated from Turchestan in central Asia in the thirteenth century.

397. The Abyssinian name for the king of the country is *Negus.*

398. *Ercoco,* modern Arkiko, belonged to Abyssinia in Milton's time and was its only port on the Red Sea.

399. *Mombaza,* now the principal town in British East Africa, *Melind,* on the East African Coast, and *Quiloa,* or Kilwa-Kisiwani, an island seaport off the coast of Tanganyika Territory, are mentioned together by Purchas (*Pilgrimes,* 2, 1024) as cities of secondary maritime importance.

400. *Sofala,* in Portuguese East Africa, was a seaport famous for its traffic in gold. The name was given to the surrounding country also, where there were mines so rich that some writers identified it with Ophir. (But compare the note on *Chersonese* in 392.)

401. *Angola* is mentioned by Purchas (*Pilgrimes,* 2, 995) as governed by a king who was "but a Governour or Deputie under the king of Congo."

403. *The Kingdoms of Almansor* (or Mansur, 938–1002 A.D.) included Fez (a part of modern Morocco), *Sus* (in southwestern Morocco), and the whole north African territory from Algiers to the Atlantic, and extended into Spain.

404. *Tremisen* is the modern Tlemcen in western Algeria.

407. Montezuma was the Aztec emperor overthrown by Cortez.

And *Cusco* in *Peru*, the richer seat
Of *Atabalipa*, and yet unspoil'd
Guiana, whose great City *Geryon's* Sons   410
Call *El Dorado:* but to nobler sights
Michael from *Adam's* eyes the Film remov'd
Which that false Fruit that promis'd clearer sight
Had bred; then purg'd with Euphrasy and Rue
The visual Nerve, for he had much to see;   415
And from the Well of Life three drops instill'd.
So deep the power of these Ingredients pierc'd,
Ev'n to the inmost seat of mental sight,
That *Adam* now enforc't to close his eyes,
Sunk down and all his Spirits became intranst: 420
But him the gentle Angel by the hand
Soon rais'd, and his attention thus recall'd.

Adam, now ope thine eyes, and first behold
Th' effects which thy original crime hath wrought
In some to spring from thee, who never touch'd   425
Th' excepted Tree, nor with the Snake conspir'd,
Nor sinn'd thy sin, yet from that sin derive
Corruption to bring forth more violent deeds.

His eyes he op'n'd, and beheld a field,
Part arable and tilth, whereon were Sheaves   430

---

408. *Cusco,* or Cuzco, was the capital of the Peruvian emperor, Atabalipa, or Atahuallpa, whom Pizarro overthrew in 1533.

410. The *great City* in *yet unspoiled Guiana* was perhaps the fabulous
Manoa, ruled over by El Dorado, "the Gilded King," and supposed to
be somewhere in the region lying about the upper course of the
Orinoco.

Geryon's Sons, the Spaniards. Geryon, in Greek myth, was a three-
headed Spanish giant whom Hercules killed.

414. *Euphrasy* is the plant popularly called "eye-bright." Keightley
quotes from Gerard's *Herball* the statement that rue, "if boiled and
kept in pickle, . . when eaten, 'quickeneth the sight,' and also that
'applied with honey and the juice of fennell, it is a remedy against
dim eyes.'"

416. The *Well of Life* is an allusion to Psalm xxxvi, 9: "For with
thee is the fountain of life: in thy light shall we see light."

420. Compare the trance into which Adam sinks in VIII, 453. So
Daniel sinks into trance in the vision to which Milton has alluded in
357 above. (Dan. x, 8.)

430. *tilth,* land under cultivation. Milton is setting the scene for the
story of Cain's murder of Abel in Genesis iv, 1–16.

New reapt, the other part sheep-walks and folds;
I' th' midst an Altar as the Land-mark stood
Rustic, of grassy sord; thither anon
A sweaty Reaper from his Tillage brought
First Fruits, the green Ear, and the yellow Sheaf,   435
Uncull'd, as came to hand; a Shepherd next
More meek came with the Firstlings of his Flock
Choicest and best; then sacrificing, laid
The Inwards and thir Fat, with Incense strew'd,
On the cleft Wood, and all due Rites perform'd.   440
His Off'ring soon propitious Fire from Heav'n
Consum'd with nimble glance, and grateful steam;
The other's not, for his was not sincere;
Whereat hee inly rag'd, and as they talk'd,
Smote him into the Midriff with a stone   445
That beat out life; he fell, and deadly pale
Groan'd out his Soul with gushing blood effus'd.
Much at that sight was *Adam* in his heart
Dismay'd, and thus in haste to th' Angel cri'd.
    O Teacher, some great mischief hath befall'n   450
To that meek man, who well had sacrific'd;
Is Piety thus and pure Devotion paid?
    T' whom *Michael* thus, hee also mov'd, repli'd.
These two are Brethren, *Adam,* and to come
Out of thy loins; th' unjust the just hath slain,   455
For envy that his Brother's Offering found
From Heav'n acceptance; but the bloody Fact
Will be aveng'd, and th' other's Faith approv'd
Lose no reward, though here thou see him die,
Rolling in dust and gore. To which our Sire.   460
    Alas, both for the deed and for the cause!
But have I now seen Death? Is this the way
I must return to native dust? O sight

---

433. *sord,* meaning "sward," "green turf," did not become a dia-
lectal form until the nineteenth century.

436. *Uncull'd,* unselected. The word is contrasted with *Choicest* in
438.

441. Milton imported the *propitious Fire* into the story from the
many instances in the O.T. when fire from heaven consumes a sacrifice;
e.g., Leviticus ix, 24, Judges vi, 21, *etc.*

457. *Fact,* deed.

Of terror, foul and ugly to behold,
Horrid to think, how horrible to feel!   465
   To whom thus *Michaël*. Death thou hast seen
In his first shape on man; but many shapes
Of Death, and many are the ways that lead
To his grim Cave, all dismal; yet to sense
More terrible at th' entrance than within.   470
Some, as thou saw'st, by violent stroke shall die,
By Fire, Flood, Famine, by Intemperance more
In Meats and Drinks, which on the Earth shall bring
Diseases dire, of which a monstrous crew
Before thee shall appear; that thou may'st know   475
What misery th' inabstinence of *Eve*
Shall bring on men. Immediately a place
Before his eyes appear'd, sad, noisome, dark,
A Lazar-house it seem'd, wherein were laid
Numbers of all diseas'd, all maladies   480
Of ghastly Spasm, or racking torture, qualms
Of heart-sick Agony, all feverous kinds,
Convulsions, Epilepsies, fierce Catarrhs,
Intestine Stone and Ulcer, Colic pangs,
Dæmoniac Phrenzy, moping Melancholy   485
And Moon-struck madness, pining Atrophy,

469. The *Cave* vaguely suggests an underworld such as the Sheol
of the Hebrews and the Tartarus of the Greeks. Milton believed in
the death of both body and spirit, lasting until the general resurrection
when "the spirits of the elect (will) be as easily gathered together as
the smallest particles of their bodies" (*C.D.* I, xiii).

479. *Lazar* is derived from the name of the beggar, Lazarus, in Christ's
parable (Luke xvi, 20); it was a term applied generally to any victim
of the many skin diseases which were classed as "leprosy."
   Godwin, in his *Life of Chaucer* (II, p. 412), suggested that Milton
got "the first hint of his description of a lazar-house from *Piers Plowman,*
Passus XX"; but the spirit of Milton's scene is rather like that of Du
Bartas in the account of human misery which opens *The Furies*. The
scene was a part of Milton's original plan, for the fourth draft of a drama
in the Cambridge manuscript contained "a mask of all the evils of this
world."

485. Lines 485-7 were added by Milton in the second edition.
   The now obsolescent spelling *phrenzy* prevailed in the seventeenth
century in consequence of a mistaken Greek etymology.

486. *Moon-struck madness* is an allusion to the belief that insanity
(lunacy: The word is derived from Latin *luna,* the moon) might be
caused by the influence of the moon.

Marasmus, and wide-wasting Pestilence,
Dropsies, and Asthmas, and Joint-racking Rheums.
Dire was the tossing, deep the groans, despair
Tended the sick busiest from Couch to Couch;   490
And over them triumphant Death his Dart
Shook, but delay'd to strike, though oft invok't
With vows, as thir chief good, and final hope.
Sight so deform what heart of Rock could long
Dry-ey'd behold?   *Adam* could not, but wept,   495
Though not of Woman born; compassion quell'd
His best of Man, and gave him up to tears
A space, till firmer thoughts restrain'd excess,
And scarce recovering words his plaint renew'd.
    O miserable Mankind, to what fall   500
Degraded, to what wretched state reserv'd!
Better end here unborn.   Why is life giv'n
To be thus wrested from us? rather why
Obtruded on us thus? who if we knew
What we receive, would either not accept   505
Life offer'd, or soon beg to lay it down,
Glad to be so dismist in peace.   Can thus
Th' Image of God in man created once

---

487. *Marasmus,* any wasting away or "consumption" of the body.

492. *oft invok't* is a vague allusion to many passages in the classics
(*e.g.,* Sophocles' *Oedipus Colonneus,* 1220, and *Philoctetes,* 797–8) which
Milton may have remembered as echoed in Spenser's lines:

> ". . . death is an equall doome
> To good and bad, the commen in of rest."
>   (*F.Q.* II, i, 59.)

496. Here the reminiscence of *Macbeth* (V, viii, 37–9) must have been
conscious:

> "Though Byrnane wood be come to Dunsinane,
> And thou oppos'd, being of no woman borne,
> Yet I will try the last."

497. Again here the reminiscence is of *Macbeth* (V, viii, 23–4):

> "Accursed be that tongue that tels mee so;
> For it hath Cow'd my better part of man."

504. In making Adam guilty of what Sir Thomas Browne called the
"underweening of this life" Milton was probably thinking, like Browne,
of the saying of "the Stoic (*i.e.,* Seneca) that life would not be accepted
if it were offered unto such as knew it." (*Christian Morals,* III, xxv.)

508. Adam has heard from Raphael (VII, 519) that God made man

So goodly and erect, though faulty since,
To such unsightly sufferings be debas't 510
Under inhuman pains?   Why should not Man,
Retaining still Divine similitude
In part, from such deformities be free,
And for his Maker's Image sake exempt?

Thir Maker's Image, answer'd *Michael,* then 515
Forsook them, when themselves they vilifi'd
To serve ungovern'd appetite, and took
His Image whom they served, a brutish vice,
Inductive mainly to the sin of *Eve.*
Therefore so abject is thir punishment, 520
Disfiguring not God's likeness, but thir own,
Or if his likeness, by themselves defac't
While they pervert pure Nature's healthful rules
To loathsome sickness, worthily, since they
God's Image did not reverence in themselves. 525

I yield it just, said *Adam,* and submit.
But is there yet no other way, besides
These painful passages, how we may come
To Death, and mix with our connatural dust?

There is, said *Michael,* if thou well observe 530
The rule of not too much, by temperance taught,
In what thou eat'st and drink'st, seeking from thence
Due nourishment, not gluttonous delight,
Till many years over thy head return:
So may'st thou live, till like ripe Fruit thou drop 535
Into thy Mother's lap, or be with ease
Gather'd, not harshly pluckt, for death mature:
This is old age; but then thou must outlive
Thy youth, thy strength, thy beauty, which will change

in his own image and Milton represents him as adding the Platonic
argument for human nobility from man's upright posture. Compare
the note on VII, 509.

518. *His Image, i. e.,* appetite's.

529. *Connatural,* of like nature. Compare 463 and 199–200 above.

531. The maxim of nothing too much goes back in Latin literature
to Terence's *Andria* (I, i, 34) and in Greek it is much older.

535. The simile of *ripe Fruit* may be a reminiscence of Cicero's *Of
Old Age* (xix), but the commonplace of being "made ripe for death by
eld" need be sought no further afield than *The Faerie Queene,* II, x, 32.

To wither'd weak and gray; thy Senses then   540
Obtuse, all taste of pleasure must forgo,
To what thou hast, and for the Air of youth
Hopeful and cheerful, in thy blood will reign
A melancholy damp of cold and dry
To weigh thy Spirits down, and last consume   545
The Balm of Life.   To whom our Ancestor.
    Henceforth I fly not Death, nor would prolong
Life much, bent rather how I may be quit
Fairest and easiest of this cumbrous charge,
Which I must keep till my appointed day   550
Of rend'ring up, and patiently attend
My dissolution.   Michaël repli'd.
    Nor love thy Life, nor hate; but what thou liv'st
Live well, how long or short permit to Heav'n:
And now prepare thee for another sight.   555
    He look'd and saw a spacious Plain, whereon
Were Tents of various hue; by some were herds
Of Cattle grazing: others, whence the sound

---

544. Compare Burton's discussion of old age as the first and most
universal cause of melancholy, since old age is "cold and dry, and
of the same quality as Melancholy is, (and) must needs cause it, by
diminution of spirits and substance." (*Anatomy*, I, ii, 1, 5.)

551. *and patiently attend My dissolution:* Milton's insertion in the
second edition. The original phrasing seemed rhetorically complete to
Milton because his eye was on Job xiv, 14: "All the days of my appointed time will I wait, till my change come."

553. Martial's tenth *Epigram,* "Neither dread nor desire thy last
hour," probably made its impress here, and so did the similar advice
in Horace's famous "Soracte" *Ode* (I, ix, 9).

556. Milton's biblical basis for the scenes in the *spacious Plain* is the
account in Genesis iv, 20–2, of the sons of Lamech: Jabal, "the father
of such as dwell in tents," Jubal, "the father of all such as handle the
harp and organ," and Tubal-Cain, "an instructor of every artificer in
brass and iron." His embroidery of the subject owes much to Du
Bartas' picture of the metal workers over whom

"sweating Tubal stands,
Hastning the hot work in their sounding hands,
No time lost Jubal: th'un-full Harmony
Of uneven Hammers, beating diversly,
Wakens the tunes that his sweet numbery soule
Yer birth (some think) learn'd of the warbling Pole."
                                        (*Divine Weekes,* 107 lt.)

Of Instruments that made melodious chime
Was heard, of Harp and Organ; and who mov'd   560
Thir stops and chords was seen: his volant touch
Instinct through all proportions low and high
Fled and pursu'd transverse the resonant fugue.
In other part stood one who at the Forge
Labouring, two massy clods of Iron and Brass   565
Had melted (whether found where casual fire
.Had wasted woods on Mountain or in Vale,
Down to the veins of Earth, thence gliding hot
To some Cave's mouth, or whether washt by stream
From underground); the liquid Ore he drain'd   570
Into fit moulds prepar'd; from which he form'd
First his own Tools; then, what might else be wrought
Fusile or grav'n in metal. After these,
But on the hither side a different sort
From the high neighbouring Hills, which was thir Seat, 575
Down to the Plain descended: by thir guise
Just men they seem'd, and all thir study bent
To worship God aright, and know his works
Not hid, nor those things last which might preserve
Freedom and Peace to men: they on the Plain   580
Long had not walkt, when from the Tents behold
A Bevy of fair Women, richly gay
In Gems and wanton dress; to the Harp they sung
Soft amorous Ditties, and in dance came on:
The Men though grave, ey'd them, and let thir eyes   585

---

562. *Instinct,* by instinct or native talent. An allusion, perhaps, to
Du Bartas' idea that Jubal learned his musical art before birth from
the music of the "Pole," *i. e.,* the spheres.

573. *Fusile,* formed by casting or melting.

574. The scene shifts from the east of Eden to *the hither side* from
the English point of view, *i. e.,* the west, where tradition placed the
descendants of Seth. Josephus' account of the Sethites as living "without dissentions and in happy condition," and as "the inventors of that
peculiar sort of wisdom which is concerned with the heavenly bodies"
(*Antiquities* I, ii, 3) guided Milton here, and so did the Augustinian
theory that the Sethites were the same as the mysterious "sons of God"
(Gen. vi, 2) who "saw the daughters of men that they were fair, and
. . . took them wives of all which they chose." In V, 446–8 and in
P.R. II, 173–91, Milton interpreted the "sons of God" as the fallen
angels.

Rove without rein, till in the amorous Net
Fast caught, they lik'd, and each his liking chose;
And now of love they treat till th' Ev'ning Star
Love's Harbinger appear'd; then all in heat
They light the Nuptial Torch, and bid invoke   590
Hymen, then first to marriage Rites invok't;
With Feast and Music all the Tents resound.
Such happy interview and fair event
Of love and youth not lost, Songs, Garlands, Flow'rs,
And charming Symphonies attach'd the heart   595
Of *Adam,* soon inclin'd to admit delight,
The bent of Nature; which he thus express'd.

    True opener of mine eyes, prime Angel blest,
Much better seems this Vision, and more hope
Of peaceful days portends, than those two past;   600
Those were of hate and death, or pain much worse,
Here Nature seems fulfill'd in all her ends.

    To whom thus *Michael.* Judge not what is best
By pleasure, though to Nature seeming meet,
Created, as thou art, to nobler end   605
Holy and pure, conformity divine.
Those Tents thou saw'st so pleasant, were the Tents
Of wickedness, wherein shall dwell his Race
Who slew his Brother; studious they appear
Of Arts that polish Life, Inventors rare,   610
Unmindful of thir Maker, though his Spirit
Taught them, but they his gifts acknowledg'd none.
Yet they a beauteous offspring shall beget;
For that fair female Troop thou saw'st, that seem'd
Of Goddesses, so blithe, so smooth, so gay,   615
Yet empty of all good wherein consists

---

586. Compare Belial's recommendation of women
        "Skill'd to retire, and in retiring, draw
        Hearts after them tangl'd in Amorous Nets."
                                    (*P.R.* II, 161–2.)

588. The *Ev'ning Star* is Venus.

591. Milton thought of the classical precedents for such invocations
of the god of marriage, Hymen, as Spenser's in the *Epithalamion,* 140:
        " 'Hymen, Iö Hymen, Hymen,' they do shout."

607. *Tents Of wickedness:* compare Psalms lxxxiv, 10: "I had rather
be a doorkeeper in the house of my God, than to dwell in the tents
of wickedness,"

Woman's domestic honour and chief praise;
Bred only and completed to the taste
Of lustful appetence, to sing, to dance,
To dress, and troll the Tongue, and roll the Eye.   620
To these that sober Race of Men, whose lives
Religious titl'd them the Sons of God,
Shall yield up all thir virtue, all thir fame
Ignobly, to the trains and to the smiles
Of these fair Atheists, and now swim in joy,   625
(Erelong to swim at large) and laugh; for which
The world erelong a world of tears must weep.
    To whom thus *Adam* of short joy bereft.
O pity and shame, that they who to live well
Enter'd so fair, should turn aside to tread   630
Paths indirect, or in the mid way faint!
But still I see the tenor of Man's woe
Holds on the same, from Woman to begin.
    From Man's effeminate slackness it begins,
Said th' Angel, who should better hold his place   635
By wisdom, and superior gifts receiv'd.
But now prepare thee for another Scene.
    He look'd and saw wide Territory spread
Before him, Towns, and rural works between,
Cities of Men with lofty Gates and Tow'rs,   640
Concourse in Arms, fierce Faces threat'ning War,
Giants of mighty Bone, and bold emprise;
Part wield thir Arms, part curb the foaming Steed,

620. *troll,* wag.

622. *Sons of God:* compare the note on 574 above.

624. *trains,* tricks, deceits.

626. The play on *swim* is made in anticipation of the flood to be
described in 818–874 below.

631. *indirect,* crooked.

633. Todd was probably right in suggesting that *Woman,* following
Man's woe, was a deliberate allusion to a jocose etymology of the word
which was current in the seventeenth century.

635. Compare the note on IV, 296.

638. The panorama which opens here has many details in common
with the description of the shield of Achilles in the *Iliad* XVIII, 478–616.

643. *curb the foaming Steed:* Milton has used the epic phrase in another passage where he was consciously imitating the classics—II, 531.

Single or in Array of Battle rang'd
Both Horse and Foot, nor idly must'ring stood;   645
One way a Band select from forage drives
A herd of Beeves, fair Oxen and fair Kine
From a fat Meadow ground; or fleecy Flock,
Ewes and thir bleating Lambs over the Plain,
Thir Booty; scarce with Life the Shepherds fly,   650
But call in aid, which makes a bloody Fray;
With cruel Tournament the Squadrons join;
Where Cattle pastur'd late, now scatter'd lies
With Carcasses and Arms th' ensanguin'd Field
Deserted: Others to a City strong   655
Lay Siege, encampt; by Battery, Scale, and Mine,
Assaulting; others from the wall defend
With Dart and Jav'lin, Stones and sulphurous Fire;
On each hand slaughter and gigantic deeds.
In other part the scepter'd Heralds call   660
To Council in the City Gates: anon
Grey-headed men and grave, with Warriors mixt,
Assemble, and Harangues are heard, but soon
In factious opposition, till at last
Of middle Age one rising, eminent   665
In wise deport, spake much of Right and Wrong,
Of Justice, of Religion, Truth and Peace,
And Judgment from above: him old and young
Exploded, and had seiz'd with violent hands,
Had not a Cloud descending snatch'd him thence   670
Unseen amid the throng: so violence
Proceeded, and Oppression, and Sword-Law
Through all the Plain, and refuge none was found.
Adam was all in tears, and to his guide
Lamenting turn'd full sad; O what are these,   675
Death's Ministers, not Men, who thus deal Death
Inhumanly to men, and multiply

---

646. *Band select,* a band of picked men.

660. The council of elders called together by heralds while a city
is besieged is very close to *Iliad* XVIII, 503-510.

665. *Of middle Age one rising* is Enoch, who "walked with God"
and was translated to heaven at the "middle age" (in comparison with
that of most of the patriarchs) of 365 years. (Gen. v, 21-4.)

669. *Exploded,* hooted.

Ten thousandfold the sin of him who slew
His Brother; for of whom such massacre
Make they but of thir Brethren, men of men?   680
But who was that Just Man, whom had not Heav'n
Rescu'd, had in his Righteousness been lost?
  To whom thus *Michael;* These are the product
Of those ill-mated Marriages thou saw'st;
Where good with bad were matcht, who of themselves   685
Abhor to join; and by imprudence mixt,
Produce prodigious Births of body or mind.
Such were these Giants, men of high renown;
For in those days Might only shall be admir'd,
And Valour and Heroic Virtue call'd;   690
To overcome in Battle, and subdue
Nations, and bring home spoils with infinite
Man-slaughter, shall be held the highest pitch
Of human Glory; and for Glory done,
Of triumph, to be styl'd great Conquerors,   695
Patrons of Mankind, Gods, and Sons of Gods,
Destroyers rightlier call'd and Plagues of men.
Thus Fame shall be achiev'd, renown on Earth,
And what most merits fame in silence hid.
But hee the seventh from thee, whom thou beheld'st   700

685. The *Giants* which Genesis vi, 4 says "were in the earth in those
days" seem to have been the offspring of the sons of God and the
daughters of men. (Compare 574 above.) So Du Bartas regarded them:

> "From these profane, foul, cursed kisses sprung
> A cruell brood, feeding on bloud and wrong;
> Fell Gyants strange, of haughty hand and minde,
> Plagues of the World, and scourges of Mankinde."
>   (*Divine Weekes,* 109.)

690. In Torquato Tasso's *Discourse of Heroic Virtue and of Charity*
and in many other sources Milton found *Heroic Virtue* defined in
ethical and religious terms. He thought of it as including all the
virtues; *e. g.,* chastity in *Doctrine of Divorce,* I, v, and the justice, as the
foundation of royal dignity, in *Of Reformation in England,* II.

694. *for Glory done* is a difficult phrase, but the meaning seems to be
that the highest pitch of triumph given to men who have done glorious
deeds shall be the title of Conquerors.

698. Compare *Lycidas,* 78:

> "Fame is no plant that grows on mortal soil," *etc.*

700. *Hee the seventh from thee* is Enoch (compare 665 above) who
is mentioned thus in Jude I, 14.

The only righteous in a World perverse,
And therefore hated, therefore so beset
With Foes for daring single to be just,
And utter odious Truth, that God would come
To judge them with his Saints: Him the most High   705
Rapt in a balmy Cloud with winged Steeds
Did, as thou saw'st, receive, to walk with God
High in Salvation and the Climes of bliss,
Exempt from Death; to show thee what reward
Awaits the good, the rest what punishment;   710
Which now direct thine eyes and soon behold.
     He look'd, and saw the face of things quite chang'd;
The brazen Throat of War had ceast to roar,
All now was turn'd to jollity and game,
To luxury and riot, feast and dance,   715
Marrying or prostituting, as befell,
Rape or Adultery, where passing fair
Allur'd them; thence from Cups to civil Broils.
At length a Reverend Sire among them came,
And of thir doings great dislike declar'd,   720
And testifi'd against thir ways; hee oft
Frequented thir Assemblies, whereso met,
Triumphs or Festivals, and to them preach'd
Conversion and Repentance, as to Souls
In Prison under Judgments imminent: 725
But all in vain: which when he saw, he ceas'd
Contending, and remov'd his Tents far off;

---

705. Enoch's translation to heaven resembles that of the prophet
Elijah, which Milton has already mentioned in III, 520-2.

715. *luxury,* lust, sensuality.

717. *fair,* beauty, *i. e.,* beautiful women.

719. The *Reverend Sire* is Noah, who "was six hundred years old
when the flood of waters was upon the earth." (Gen. vii, 6.)

720. Milton was struck by Josephus' picture of Noah pleading with
the giants to "change their dispositions" when he saw that they "were
slaves to their wicked pleasures." (*Antiquities* I, iii, 1.) In the main
the account of the flood follows Genesis vi, 9-ix, 17.

722. *whereso,* wherever.

723. *Triumphs,* processions or public ceremonies.

724. "Spirits in prison" was a phrase in I Peter iii, 19, referring to
the "slaves to their wicked pleasures" to whom Noah preached.

Then from the Mountain hewing Timber tall,
Began to build a Vessel of huge bulk,
Measur'd by Cubit, length, and breadth, and highth,   730
Smear'd round with Pitch, and in the side a door
Contriv'd, and of provisions laid in large
For Man and Beast: when lo a wonder strange!
Of every Beast, and Bird, and Insect small
Came sevens, and pairs, and enter'd in, as taught   735
Thir order; last the Sire, and his three Sons
With thir four Wives; and God made fast the door.
Meanwhile the Southwind rose, and with black wings
Wide hovering, all the Clouds together drove
From under Heav'n; the Hills to their supply   740
Vapour, and Exhalation dusk and moist,
Sent up amain; and now the thick'n'd Sky
Like a dark Ceiling stood; down rush'd the Rain
Impetuous, and continu'd till the Earth
No more was seen; the floating Vessel swum   745
Uplifted; and secure with beaked prow
Rode tilting o'er the Waves, all dwellings else
Flood overwhelm'd, and them with all thir pomp
Deep under water roll'd; Sea cover'd Sea,
Sea without shore; and in thir Palaces   750
Where luxury late reign'd, Sea-monsters whelp'd

---

737. With the detail that *God made fast the door* (which is from Gen. vii, 16) Milton paused in his draft on the biblical account of the flood to turn to Ovid's story of Deucalion's flood (compare the note on 12 above), which he knew directly and also indirectly through its extensive influence on Du Bartas' description of Noah's flood in *The Divine Weekes*.

738. After recording Zeus's resolve to destroy men for their wickedness Ovid begins his account of the flood with the shutting up of the north wind and the release of the rainy south wind (*Met.* I, 262-9); and in his opening Du Bartas followed suit with the loosing of "Auster, and his lowring race."

750. The shoreless sea is a striking touch in Ovid's flood (*Met.* I, 292), which appears in Du Bartas' picture of "stormy waters" where

"Rivers and Seas have all one common shore,
(To wit) a Sable, water-loaden Sky,
Ready to rain new Oceans instantly."
                    (*Divine Weekes*, 109 rb.)

751. Here again the strangeness of Ovid's picture of the sea-monsters

And stabl'd; of Mankind, so numerous late,
All left, in one small bottom swum imbark't.
How didst thou grieve then, *Adam,* to behold
The end of all thy Offspring, end so sad,   755
Depopulation; thee another Flood,
Of tears and sorrow a Flood thee also drown'd,
And sunk thee as thy Sons; till gently rear'd
By th' Angel, on thy feet thou stood'st at last,
Though comfortless, as when a Father mourns   760
His Children, all in view destroy'd at once;
And scarce to th' Angel utter'd'st thus thy plaint.

    O Visions ill foreseen! better had I
Liv'd ignorant of future, so had borne
My part of evil only, each day's lot   765
Anough to bear; those now, that were dispens't
The burd'n of many Ages, on me light
At once, by my foreknowledge gaining Birth
Abortive, to torment me ere thir being,
With thought that they must be. Let no man seek   770
Henceforth to be foretold what shall befall
Him or his Children, evil he may be sure,
Which neither his foreknowing can prevent,
And hee the future evil shall no less
In apprehension than in substance feel   775
Grievous to bear: but that care now is past,
Man is not whom to warn: those few escap't
Famine and anguish will at last consume

---

haunting the cities and houses of men (*Met.* I, 299–303) reaches Milton
tinged with the quaintness of Du Bartas:

      "The Sturgeon, coasting over Castles, muses
      (Under the Sea) to see so many houses.
      The Endian Manat, and the Mullet float
      O'r Mountain tops, where erst the bearded Goat
      Did bound and brouz."
                     (*Divine Weekes,* 19 lb.)

    752. *stabl'd,* made their lairs.

    765. Compare Matthew vi, 34: "Sufficient unto the day is the evil
thereof."

    773. *neither . . . and:* the two conjunctions are parallel, the first
anticipating the second, as in "both . . . and." The construction is
a Latinism.

Wand'ring that wat'ry Desert: I had hope
When violence was ceas't, and War on Earth,   780
All would have then gone well, peace would have crown'd
With length of happy days the race of man;
But I was far deceiv'd; for now I see
Peace to corrupt no less than War to waste.
How comes it thus? unfold, Celestial Guide,   785
And whether here the Race of man will end.
To whom thus *Michael*.   Those whom last thou saw'st
In triumph and luxurious wealth, are they
First seen in acts of prowess eminent
And great exploits, but of true virtue void;   790
Who having spilt much blood, and done much waste
Subduing Nations, and achiev'd thereby
Fame in the World, high titles, and rich prey,
Shall change thir course to pleasure, ease, and sloth,
Surfeit, and lust, till wantonness and pride   795
Raise out of friendship hostile deeds in Peace.
The conquer'd also, and enslav'd by War
Shall with thir freedom lost all virtue lose
And fear of God, from whom thir piety feign'd
In sharp contést of Battle found no aid   800
Against invaders; therefore cool'd in zeal
Thenceforth shall practice how to live secure,
Worldly or dissolute, on what thir Lords
Shall leave them to enjoy; for th' Earth shall bear
More than anough, that temperance may be tri'd: 805
So all shall turn degenerate, all deprav'd,
Justice and Temperance, Truth and Faith forgot;
One Man except, the only Son of light
In a dark Age, against example good,
Against allurement, custom, and a World   810

---

779. *Wand'ring* is transitive.

807. This climax to a passage which is filled with Milton's passionate
political and ethical faith can be read as an attack upon the time-servers
in his own party and upon the dissolute members of the court and of
society. Perhaps the best light in which to regard it is as the record
of complete disillusion from the mood in which he painted England in
Areopagitica: "a noble and puissant nation," "entering the glorious ways
of truth and prosperous virtue, destined to become great and honorable
in these latter ages."

Offended; fearless of reproach and scorn,
Or violence, hee of thir wicked ways
Shall them admonish, and before them set
The paths of righteousness, how much more safe,
And full of peace, denouncing wrath to come   815
On thir impenitence; and shall return
Of them derided, but of God observ'd
The one just Man alive; by his command
Shall build a wondrous Ark, as thou beheld'st,
To save himself and household from amidst   820
A World devote to universal rack.
No sooner hee with them of Man and Beast
Select for life shall in the Ark be lodg'd,
And shelter'd round, but all the Cataracts
Of Heav'n set open on the Earth shall pour   825
Rain day and night, all fountains of the Deep
Broke up, shall heave the Ocean to usurp
Beyond all bounds, till inundation rise
Above the highest Hills: then shall this Mount
Of Paradise by might of Waves be mov'd   830
Out of his place, push'd by the horned flood,
With all his verdure spoil'd, and Trees adrift
Down the great River to the op'ning Gulf,
And there take root an Island salt and bare,
The haunt of Seals and Orcs, and Sea-mews' clang.   835
To teach thee that God áttributes to place

821. *devote,* dedicated to destruction. Compare the note on III, 208.
823. *Select,* chosen.
831. *horned,* branching into arms or horns as rivers do when they divide their streams. Milton was perhaps thinking of the Latin equivalent of the word in Virgil's allusion to the Po:

> ". . . Po first issues from his dark abodes,
> And, awful in his cradle, rules the floods:
> Two golden horns on his large front he wears,
> And his grim face a bull's resemblance bears."
> (*Georg.* IV, 370–2. Dryden's translation.)

833. The *great River* is either the Tigris or Euphrates; the *Gulf* is the Persian Gulf.
835. *Orcs,* a kind of whale. The word was used vaguely of any kind of sea monster by medieval writers.
clang is used of the noise of birds in VII, 422.

No sanctity, if none be thither brought
By Men who there frequent, or therein dwell.
And now what further shall ensue, behold.

    He look'd, and saw the Ark hull on the flood,   840
Which now abated, for the Clouds were fled,
Driv'n by a keen North-wind, that blowing dry
Wrinkl'd the face of Deluge, as decay'd;
And the clear Sun on his wide wat'ry Glass
Gaz'd hot, and of the fresh Wave largely drew,   845
As after thirst, which made thir flowing shrink
From standing lake to tripping ebb, that stole
With soft foot towards the deep, who now had stopt
His Sluices, as the Heav'n his windows shut.
The Ark no more now floats, but seems on ground   850
Fast on the top of some high mountain fixt.
And now the tops of Hills as Rocks appear;
With clamor thence the rapid Currents drive
Towards the retreating Sea thir furious tide.
Forthwith from out the Ark a Raven flies,   855
And after him, the surer messenger,
A Dove sent forth once and again to spy
Green Tree or ground whereon his foot may light;
The second time returning, in his Bill
An Olive leaf he brings, pacific sign: 860
Anon dry ground appears, and from his Ark
The ancient Sire descends with all his Train;
Then with uplifted hands, and eyes devout,
Grateful to Heav'n, over his head beholds
A dewy Cloud, and in the Cloud a Bow   865

---

    840. *hull,* drift like a ship without sails.

    842. Compare Genesis viii, 1: "And God made a wind to pass over the earth, and the waters asswaged." Ovid makes the north wind drive away the clouds after Deucalion's flood. (*Met.* I, 328.)

    845. Compare the conception of the sun supping with the ocean in V, 426.

    846. *thir* refers to *Wave,* which may have been dictated as a plural.

    849. The shutting of the windows of Heaven (compare Gen. viii, 2) is in accordance with the biblical conception and harmonized with Milton's cosmology. Compare the note on VII, 261. In the following account of the end of the flood Milton relied mainly on Genesis viii.

Conspicuous with three listed colours gay,
Betok'ning peace from God, and Cov'nant new.
Whereat the heart of *Adam* erst so sad
Greatly rejoic'd, and thus his joy broke forth.

O thou who future things canst represent   870
As present, Heav'nly instructor, I revive
At this last sight, assur'd that Man shall live
With all the Creatures, and thir seed preserve.
Far less I now lament for one whole World
Of wicked Sons destroy'd, than I rejoice   875
For one Man found so perfet and so just,
That God voutsafes to raise another World
From him, and all his anger to forget.
But say, what mean those colour'd streaks in Heav'n,
Distended as the Brow of God appeas'd,   880
Or serve they as a flow'ry verge to bind
The fluid skirts of that same wat'ry Cloud,
Lest it again dissolve and show'r the Earth?

To whom th' Archangel. Dext'rously thou aim'st;
So willingly doth God remit his Ire,   885
Though late repenting him of Man deprav'd,
Griev'd at his heart, when looking down he saw
The whole Earth fill'd with violence, and all flesh
Corrupting each thir way; yet those remov'd,
Such grace shall one just Man find in his sight,   890
That he relents, not to blot out mankind,
And makes a Covenant never to destroy
The Earth again by flood, nor let the Sea
Surpass his bounds, nor Rain to drown the World
With Man therein or Beast; but when he brings   895
Over the Earth a Cloud, will therein set
His triple-colour'd Bow, whereon to look

---

866. *three:* the number mentioned by Du Bartas also.
listed, striped.

867. The *Cov'nant* is the promise of God, of which the rainbow
was the pledge, never again to destroy the earth by water. (Gen. ix,
11–17.)

880. Compare the allusion in *Il Penseroso* (57–8) to the nightingale,
        "In her saddest sweetest plight,
            Soothing the rugged brow of Night."

889. *each thir way,* each in its own way.

And call to mind his Cov'nant: Day and Night,
Seed-time and Harvest, Heat and hoary Frost
Shall hold thir course, till fire purge all things new,   900
Both Heav'n and Earth, wherein the just shall dwell.

The End of the Eleventh Book.

---

898. Milton's account of the flood ends like that in Genesis viii, 22, to which he adds the promise of a "new heaven and a new earth," after the melting of elements "with fervent heat" in II Peter iii, 12–13. As a theme for poetry the final conflagration of the world had found striking expression in Vida's *Hymn to the Son of God,* and as a scientific dogma it held its place until after the publication in 1696 of William Whiston's *A New Theory of the Earth, From its Original, to the Consummation of all Things, . . . the General Conflagration.*

BOOK XII

THE ARGUMENT

The Angel Michael *continues from the Flood to relate what shall succeed; then, in the mention of* Abraham, *comes by degrees to explain, who that Seed of the Woman shall be, which was promised* Adam *and* Eve *in the Fall; his Incarnation, Death, Resurrection, and Ascension; the state of the Church till his second Coming.* Adam *greatly satisfied and recomforted by these Relations and Promises descends the Hill with* Michael; *wakens* Eve, *who all this while had slept, but with gentle dreams compos'd to quietness of mind and submission.* Michael *in either hand leads them out of Paradise, the fiery Sword waving behind them, and the Cherubim taking their Stations to guard the Place.*

As ONE who in his journey bates at Noon,
Though bent on speed, so here the Archangel paus'd
Betwixt the world destroy'd and world restor'd,
If *Adam* aught perhaps might interpose;
Then with transition sweet new Speech resumes.   5
  Thus thou hast seen one World begin and end;
And Man as from a second stock proceed.
Much thou hast yet to see, but I perceive
Thy mortal sight to fail; objects divine
Must needs impair and weary human sense: 10
Henceforth what is to come I will relate,
Thou therefore give due audience, and attend.
This second source of Men, while yet but few,
And while the dread of judgment past remains
Fresh in thir minds, fearing the Deity,   15
With some regard to what is just and right
Shall lead thir lives, and multiply apace,

---

1. *bates,* abates (*i. e.,* speed).

5. *transition* has its classical meaning of "a summary of what has been said and of what remains to say."

Labouring the soil, and reaping plenteous crop,
Corn, wine and oil; and from the herd or flock,
Oft sacrificing Bullock, Lamb, or Kid,   20
With large Wine-offerings pour'd, and sacred Feast,
Shall spend thir day's in joy unblam'd, and dwell
Long time in peace by Families and Tribes
Under paternal rule; till one shall rise
Of proud ambitious heart, who not content   25
With fair equality, fraternal state,
Will arrogate Dominion undeserv'd
Over his brethren, and quite dispossess
Concord and law of Nature from the Earth;
Hunting (and Men not Beasts shall be his game)   30
With War and hostile snare such as refuse
Subjection to his Empire tyrannous:
A mighty Hunter thence he shall be styl'd
Before the Lord, as in despite of Heav'n,
Or from Heav'n claiming second Sovranty;   35
And from Rebellion shall derive his name,
Though of Rebellion others he accuse.
Hee with a crew, whom like Ambition joins

18. *Labouring* is transitive.

24. *One, i. e.,* Nimrod (the "upstart"?), described in Genesis x, 9, as
"a mighty hunter before the Lord." From Josephus (*Antiquities,* I, iv, 2)
came the belief which prevailed in the seventeenth century that "the
secret design of *Nimrod* was to settle unto himself a place of dominion,
and . . . the beginning of his kingdom was *Babel.*" (Sir Thomas Browne,
Vulgar Errors, VII, vi.) Milton was acquainted with the discourse on
tyranny with which Du Bartas introduces his account of Nimrod in
Babalon, and in Du Bartas' applications to French politics he had an
example for his suggestion in *Eikonoklastes,* xi, that the bishops might
have told King Charles "that Nimrod, the first that hunted after faction,
is reputed by ancient tradition the first that founded monarchy."

30. Milton's epigram is an echo of Du Bartas' statement that Nimrod
"Leaves hunting Beasts, and hunteth Men."
(*The Divine Weekes,* 120.)

34. Milton suggests that the biblical phrase "before the Lord" may
mean that Nimrod was a rebel against God or that he falsely claimed
to be God's vicegerent on earth.

38. Milton follows the biblical account of the building of Babel
(Gen. xi, 2–9), except that he associates Nimrod with the enterprise.
For that tradition he had patristic authority as well as that of Josephus,
and the example of Dante's vision of Nimrod at the foot of his tower
(*Purgatorio,* XII, 34; compare *Inferno,* XXXI, 77).

With him or under him to tyrannize,
Marching from *Eden* towards the West, shall find   40
The Plain, wherein a black bituminous gurge
Boils out from under ground, the mouth of Hell;
Of Brick, and of that stuff they cast to build
A City and Tow'r, whose top may reach to Heav'n;
And get themselves a name, lest far disperst   45
In foreign Lands thir memory be lost,
Regardless whether good or evil fame.
But God who oft descends to visit men
Unseen, and through thir habitations walks
To mark thir doings, them beholding soon,   50
Comes down to see thir City, ere the Tower
Obstruct Heav'n Tow'rs, and in derision sets
Upon thir Tongues a various Spirit to rase
Quite out thir Native Language, and instead
To sow a jangling noise of words unknown: 55
Forthwith a hideous gabble rises loud
Among the Builders; each to other calls
Not understood, till hoarse, and all in rage,
As mockt they storm; great laughter was in Heav'n
And looking down, to see the hubbub strange   60
And hear the din; thus was the building left
Ridiculous, and the work Confusion nam'd.
     Whereto thus *Adam* fatherly displeas'd.
O execrable Son so to aspire
Above his Brethren, to himself assuming   65

---

41. From Josephus comes the idea that the brick in the Tower of
Babel was "cemented together with mortar, made of bitumen." (*Antiquities*, I, iv, 3.)

42. Milton may have known of some bituminous pool in the Babylonian region which was called a mouth of hell.

53. A *various Spirit*, a spirit of variance or contradiction.

55. *jangling noise* seems unquestionably to be a reminiscence of Sylvester's phrase in his translation of Du Bartas' *Babalon*. (*The Divine Weekes*, 121.)

59. Compare the notes on II, 191, and VIII, 78.

62. The name "Babel" seems to have been of Assyrian origin and
to have meant "Gate of the gods" or "of God." Milton followed the
Jewish tradition that "the tower is now called Babylon, because of
the confusion of that language which they readily understood before, for
the Hebrews mean by the word *Babel*, Confusion." (*Antiquities*, I, iv, 3.)

Authority usurpt, from God not giv'n:
He gave us only over Beast, Fish, Fowl
Dominion absolute; that right we hold
By his donation; but Man over men
He made not Lord; such title to himself   70
Reserving, human left from human free.
But this Usurper his encroachment proud
Stays not on Man; to God his Tower intends
Siege and defiance: Wretched man! what food
Will he convey up thither to sustain   75
Himself and his rash Army, where thin Air
Above the Clouds will pine his entrails gross,
And famish him of Breath, if not of Bread?
    To whom thus *Michael.* Justly thou abhorr'st
That Son, who on the quiet state of men   80
Such trouble brought, affecting to subdue
Rational Liberty; yet know withal,
Since thy original lapse, true Liberty
Is lost, which always with right Reason dwells
Twinn'd, and from her hath no dividual being: 85
Reason in man obscur'd, or not obey'd,
Immediately inordinate desires
And upstart Passions catch the Government
From Reason, and to servitude reduce
Man till then free. Therefore since hee permits   90
Within himself unworthy Powers to reign
Over free Reason, God in Judgment just
Subjects him from without to violent Lords;
Who oft as undeservedly enthral
His outward freedom: Tyranny must be,   95
Though to the Tyrant thereby no excuse.
Yet sometimes Nations will decline so low
From virtue, which is reason, that no wrong,
But Justice, and some fatal curse annext
Deprives them of thir outward liberty,   100

---

    82. In lines 82–101 Milton epitomizes his conviction that reason must
control the passions and, like Plato in the *Republic* (IV, VIII, and IX),
correlates political freedom with that principle.

    84. Compare the note on "right reason" in VI, 42. The twinning of
liberty with reason pervades Milton's prose works as well as *P.L.*
Compare the notes on III, 108, and IX, 351.

Thir inward lost: Witness th' irreverent Son
Of him who built the Ark, who for the shame
Done to his Father, heard this heavy curse,
Servant of Servants, on his vicious Race.
Thus will this latter, as the former World,   105
Still tend from bad to worse, till God at last
Wearied with their iniquities, withdraw
His presence from among them, and avert
His holy Eyes; resolving from thenceforth
To leave them to thir own polluted ways;   110
And one peculiar Nation to select
From all the rest, of whom to be invok'd,
A Nation from one faithful man to spring:
Him on this side *Euphrates* yet residing,
Bred up in Idol-worship; O that men   115
(Canst thou believe?) should be so stupid grown,
While yet the Patriarch liv'd, who scap'd the Flood,
As to forsake the living God, and fall
To worship thir own work in Wood and Stone
For Gods! yet him God the most High voutsafes   120
To call by Vision from his Father's house,
His kindred and false Gods, into a Land
Which he will show him, and from him will raise
A mighty Nation, and upon him show'r
His benediction so, that in his Seed   125
All Nations shall be blest; he straight obeys,

---

101. The *irreverent Son* of Noah was Ham, the father of Canaan.
"And Noah said, Cursed be Canaan; a servant of servants shall he be
unto his brethren." (Gen. ix, 25.)

105. The resemblance to Horace's *Ode,* III, vi, 46–8, which editors
find in the latter world tending from bad to worse is vague at best; but
Milton was undoubtedly influenced by the classic tradition of the world's
degeneration from a golden to an iron age as well as by the Bible in
his pessimistic view of history.

111. *one peculiar Nation,* Israel. Compare *C.D.* I, iv, where Milton
dissents from the Calvinistic conception of individual election, or choice,
by God, but recognizes "that general or national election, by which
God chose the whole nation of Israel for his own people."

113. *one faithful man,* Abraham, whom Milton says that God called
"from his father's house," although he "was even an idolator at the
time." (*C.D.* I, xvii.) Compare Joshua xxiv, 2.

121. Compare Genesis xii, 7: "And the Lord appeared unto Abram,
and said: Unto thy seed will I give this land."

Not knowing to what Land, yet firm believes:
I see him, but thou canst not, with what Faith
He leaves his Gods, his Friends, and native Soil
Ur of *Chaldæa,* passing now the Ford   130
To *Haran,* after him a cumbrous Train
Of Herds and Flocks, and numerous servitude;
Not wand'ring poor, but trusting all his wealth
With God, who call'd him, in a land unknown.
Canaan he now attains, I see his Tents   135
Pitcht about *Sechem,* and the neighbouring Plain
Of *Moreh;* there by promise he receives
Gift to his Progeny of all that Land;
From *Hamath* Northward to the Desert South
(Things by thir names I call, though yet unnam'd)   140
From *Hermon* East to the great Western Sea,
Mount *Hermon,* yonder Sea, each place behold
In prospect, as I point them; on the shore
Mount *Carmel;* here the double-founted stream
Jordan, true limit Eastward; but his Sons   145

---

128. "By faith Abraham, when he was called to go out into a place which he should after receive for an inheritance, obeyed." (Hebrews xi, 8.)

130. *Ur* was—probably correctly—understood to have been on the west bank of the Euphrates not far south of Babylon, while *Haran* lay on the east side of the river, as Michael has implied in 114 above.

132. *servitude,* servants. The story of the migration follows Genesis xii, 5–6.

136. *Sechem* (Shechem), where Abraham first camped in Canaan, is the modern town of Nablus, lying between Mounts Ebal and Gerizim.

139. *Hamath* is mentioned as the northern frontier of Canaan in Numbers xxxiv, 8. The town lies on the Orontes in Upper Syria.

141. *Hermon* is the highest mountain in Palestine, really a ridge of mountains to the northeast of the Sea of Galilee. Milton may have thought of God's promise to "drive out from before the children of Israel" all the inhabitants of the region "under Mount Hermon unto the entering into Hamath." (Joshua xiii, 5–6.) The *Western Sea* is the Mediterranean.

143. *on the shore Mount Carmel* is a reminiscence of "Carmel by the sea" in Jeremiah xlvi, 18. The promontory juts out into the Mediterranean near the southeast corner of Palestine.

145. The current notion that the Jordan was formed by the confluence of two non-existent streams, the Dan and the Jor, seems ultimately to have been due to St. Jerome's commentary on Genesis xiv,

Shall dwell to *Senir*, that long ridge of Hills.
This ponder, that all Nations of the Earth
Shall in his Seed be blessed; by that Seed
Is meant thy great deliverer, who shall bruise
The Serpent's head; whereof to thee anon   150
Plainlier shall be reveal'd. This Patriarch blest,
Whom *faithful Abraham* due time shall call,
A Son, and of his Son a Grandchild leaves,
Like him in faith, in wisdom, and renown;
The Grandchild with twelve Sons increast, departs   155
From *Canaan,* to a Land hereafter call'd
Egypt, divided by the River *Nile;*
See where it flows, disgorging at seven mouths
Into the Sea: to sojourn in that Land
He comes invited by a younger Son   160
In time of dearth, a Son whose worthy deeds
Raise him to be the second in that Realm
Of *Pharaoh:* there he dies, and leaves his Race
Growing into a Nation, and now grown
Suspected to a sequent King, who seeks   165
To stop thir overgrowth, as inmate guests
Too numerous; whence of guests he makes them slaves
Inhospitably, and kills thir infant Males:
Till by two brethren (those two brethren call
Moses and *Aaron*) sent from God to claim   170
His people from enthralment, they return
With glory and spoil back to thir promis'd Land.
But first the lawless Tyrant, who denies
To know thir God, or message to regard,
Must be compell'd by Signs and Judgments dire;   175
To blood unshed the Rivers must be turn'd,

---

14. The river is the eastern limit of Palestine. (Compare Numbers
xxxiv, 12.)

146. *Senir* is a name given to one of the peaks of Hermon in
I Chronicles v, 23.

153. *A Son,* Isaac. From this point Milton summarizes the Bible
record.

172. Milton refers to the rather dubious trick by which the Israelites
"spoiled the Egyptians" (Exod. xii, 36) when they left the country.
The summary of the ten plagues is based on Exodus vii, 19–xii.

173. *denies,* refuses.

Frogs, Lice and Flies must all his Palace fill
With loath'd intrusion, and fill all the land;
His Cattle must of Rot and Murrain die,
Botches and blains must all his flesh imboss,   180
And all his people; Thunder mixt with Hail,
Hail mixt with fire must rend th' *Egyptian* Sky
And wheel on th' Earth, devouring where it rolls;
What it devours not, Herb, or Fruit, or Grain,
A darksome Cloud of Locusts swarming down   185
Must eat, and on the ground leave nothing green:
Darkness must overshadow all his bounds,
Palpable darkness, and blot out three days;
Last with one midnight stroke all the first-born
Of *Egypt* must lie dead.   Thus with ten wounds   190
The River-dragon tam'd at length submits
To let his sojourners depart, and oft
Humbles his stubborn heart, but still as Ice
More hard'n'd after thaw, till in his rage
Pursuing whom he late dismiss'd, the Sea   195
Swallows him with his Host, but them lets pass
As on dry land between two crystal walls,
Aw'd by the rod of *Moses* so to stand
Divided, till his rescu'd gain thir shore:
Such wondrous power God to his Saint will lend,   200
Though present in his Angel, who shall go
Before them in a Cloud, and Pillar of Fire,

180. *imboss,* cover with bosses or swellings.

188. Compare the note on II, 406.

191. Milton thought of Ezekiel xxix, 3: "Behold, I am against thee, Pharaoh king of Egypt, the great dragon that lieth in the midst of his rivers."

197. The *crystal walls* are a reminiscence of Du Bartas' description of the same scene:

> "And on each side is flanked all along
>   With Wals of Crystall, beautiful and strong.
>
> .   .   .   .
>
> Two Wals of Glasse, built with a word alone."
>   (*The Divine Weekes,* 171, lc.)

The phrase from Sylvester's translation crept into Milton's boyish paraphrase of Psalm cxxxvi (line 49).

200. Compare the use of the word *Saint* in V, 247.

202. In Exodus xiii, 21, God is said to go before the Israelites in

By day a Cloud, by night a Pillar of Fire,
To guide them in thir journey, and remove
Behind them, while th' obdúrate King pursues: 205
All night he will pursue, but his approach
Darkness defends between till morning Watch;
Then through the Fiery Pillar and the Cloud
God looking forth will trouble all his Host
And craze thir Chariot wheels: when by command   210
Moses once more his potent Rod extends
Over the Sea; the Sea his Rod obeys;
On thir imbattl'd ranks the Waves return,
And overwhelm thir War: the Race elect
Safe towards *Canaan* from the shore advance   215
Through the wild Desert, not the readiest way,
Lest ent'ring on the *Canaanite* alarm'd
War terrify them inexpert, and fear
Return them back to *Egypt,* choosing rather
Inglorious life with servitude; for life   220
To noble and ignoble is more sweet
Untrain'd in Arms, where rashness leads not on.
This also shall they gain by thir delay
In the wide Wilderness, there they shall found
Thir government, and thir great Senate choose   225
Through the twelve Tribes, to rule by Laws ordain'd:

the form of a cloud by day and a pillar of fire by night, but Milton
in *C.D.* I, v, makes a point of the fact that God here lent his name to
an angel.

207. *defends,* prevents, forbids, *i. e.,* by coming between Pharaoh and
the Israelites.

210. *craze,* shatter.

The overthrow of the Egyptian chariots in the Red Sea is recorded
in Exodus xiv.

214. *War,* army.

217. Milton found the explanation for the indirect march into
Canaan in Exodus xiii, 17–18.

218. *inexpert* keeps its Latin meaning, "inexperienced."

225. Milton's rather tenuous basis for the Senate is found in the
seventy elders who are made the official witnesses of some of the acts
of Moses. (Exod. xxiv, 1–9; and Numbers xi, 16–30.) He agreed with
Harrington in *Oceana* that "Ancient prudence" (by which Harrington
meant government by law rather than by royal prerogative) was "first
discovered to mankind by God himself, in the fabrick of the *Commonwealth of Israel.*"

God from the Mount of *Sinai,* whose gray top
Shall tremble, he descending, will himself
In Thunder, Lightning and loud Trumpet's sound
Ordain them Laws; part such as appertain   230
To civil Justice, part religious Rites
Of sacrifice, informing them, by types
And shadows, of that destin'd Seed to bruise
The Serpent, by what means he shall achieve
Mankind's deliverance.   But the voice of God   235
To mortal ear is dreadful; they beseech
That *Moses* might report to them his will,
And terror cease; he grants what they besought,
Instructed that to God is no access
Without Mediator, whose high Office now   240
Moses in figure bears, to introduce
One greater, of whose day he shall foretell,
And all the Prophets in thir Age the times
Of great *Messiah* shall sing.   Thus Laws and Rites
Establisht, such delight hath God in Men   245
Obedient to his will, that he voutsafes
Among them to set up his Tabernacle,
The holy One with mortal Men to dwell:
By his prescript a Sanctuary is fram'd
Of Cedar, overlaid with Gold, therein   250
An Ark, and in the Ark his Testimony,
The Records of his Cov'nant, over these
A Mercy-seat of Gold between the wings
Of two bright Cherubim, before him burn

---

227. The scene on Mount Sinai when Moses received the Ten
Commandments amid thunders and lightnings (Exod. xix, 16–20) is
interestingly anticipated in XI, 73–6.

236. In Exodus xx, 19, the Israelites say "unto Moses, Speak thou
with us, and we will hear: but let not God speak with us, lest we die."

240. Moses was regarded as the first of the types of Christ as
Mediator (compare X, 60), mainly on the strength of the quotation of
Deuteronomy xviii, 15, in Acts iii, 22: "For Moses truly said unto the
fathers, A Prophet shall the Lord your God raise up unto you of your
brethren, like unto me."

247. The details of the *Tabernacle* are drawn, not altogether ac-
curately, from Exodus, xxv.

253. Compare the note on the *Mercy-seat* in XI, 2.

Seven Lamps as in a Zodiac representing   255
The Heav'nly fires; over the Tent a Cloud
Shall rest by Day, a fiery gleam by Night,
Save when they journey, and at length they come,
Conducted by his Angel to the Land
Promis'd to *Abraham* and his Seed: the rest   260
Were long to tell, how many Battles fought,
How many Kings destroy'd, and Kingdoms won,
Or how the Sun shall in mid Heav'n stand still
A day entire, and Night's due course adjourn,
Man's voice commanding, Sun in *Gibeon* stand,   265
And thou Moon in the vale of *Aialon,*
Till *Israel* overcome; so call the third
From *Abraham,* Son of *Isaac,* and from him
His whole descent, who thus shall *Canaan* win.

    Here *Adam* interpos'd. O sent from Heav'n,   270
Enlight'ner of my darkness, gracious things
Thou hast reveal'd, those chiefly which concern
Just *Abraham* and his Seed: now first I find
Mine eyes true op'ning, and my heart much eas'd,
Erewhile perplext with thoughts what would become   275
Of mee and all Mankind; but now I see
His day, in whom all Nations shall be blest,
Favour unmerited by me, who sought
Forbidd'n knowledge by forbidd'n means.
This yet I apprehend not, why to those   280
Among whom God will deign to dwell on Earth
So many and so various Laws are giv'n;
So many Laws argue so many sins
Among them; how can God with such reside?

---

    255. So Josephus describes the golden candle-stick as carrying "seven lamps, one by one, in imitation of the number of planets." (*Antiquities* III, vi, 7.)

    259. Compare the note on 202 above.

    263. The story of the sun standing still in Gibeah while the Israelites smote the armies of five kings (Joshua x, 12–13) was one of the subjects mentioned in the Cambridge MS. as a possible subject for Milton's future epic.

    267. *Israel,* meaning literally "he that striveth with God," was given to Jacob at Peniel (Gen. xxxii, 28) and afterward came to mean all "the children of Israel."

    277. The allusion is to God's promise to Abraham in Genesis xxii, 18.

To whom thus *Michael.* Doubt not but that sin   285
Will reign among them, as of thee begot;
And therefore was Law given them to evince
Thir natural pravity, by stirring up
Sin against Law to fight; that when they see
Law can discover sin, but not remove,   290
Save by those shadowy expiations weak,
The blood of Bulls and Goats, they may conclude
Some blood more precious must be paid for Man,
Just for unjust, that in such righteousness
To them by Faith imputed, they may find   295
Justification towards God, and peace
Of Conscience, which the Law by Ceremonies
Cannot appease, nor Man the moral part
Perform, and not performing cannot live.
So Law appears imperfet, and but giv'n   300
With purpose to resign them in full time
Up to a better Cov'nant, disciplin'd
From shadowy Types to Truth, from Flesh to Spirit,
From imposition of strict Laws, to free
Acceptance of large Grace, from servile fear   305
To filial, works of Law to works of Faith.
And therefore shall not *Moses,* though of God
Highly belov'd, being but the Minister
Of Law, his people into *Canaan* lead;
But *Joshua* whom the Gentiles *Jesus* call,   310

290. The thought is a fusion of many Pauline passages which teach
that "what things soever the law saith, it saith to them who are under
the law; that every mouth may be stopped, and all the world may
become guilty before God." (Rom. iii, 19.)

291. By *shadowy* Milton means that the sacrifices were shadows or
types of Christ's expiation of sin. Compare Hebrews x, 1: "For the law
having a shadow of good things to come, . . . can never with those
sacrifices which they offered year by year continually make the comers
thereunto perfect."

298. Milton's meaning is that no man can perform all of the moral
part in Moses' law and that only "the man which doeth those things
shall live by them." (Rom. x, 5.)

307. Compare *C.D.* I, xxvi: "The imperfection of the law was mani-
fested in the person of Moses himself; for Moses, who was a type of
the law, could not bring the children of Israel into the land of Canaan,
that is, into eternal rest; but an entrance was given to them under
Joshua, or Jesus." Jesus and Joshua both mean "a saviour."

His Name and Office bearing, who shall quell
The adversary Serpent, and bring back
Through the world's wilderness long wander'd man
Safe to eternal Paradise of rest.
Meanwhile they in thir earthly *Canaan* plac't   315
Long time shall dwell and prosper, but when sins
National interrupt thir public peace,
Provoking God to raise them enemies:
From whom as oft he saves them penitent
By Judges first, then under Kings; of whom   320
The second, both for piety renown'd
And puissant deeds, a promise shall receive
Irrevocable, that his Regal Throne
For ever shall endure; the like shall sing
All Prophecy, That of the Royal Stock   325
Of *David* (so I name this King) shall rise
A Son, the Woman's Seed to thee foretold,
Foretold to *Abraham,* as in whom shall trust
All Nations, and to Kings foretold, of Kings
The last, for of his Reign shall be no end.   330
But first a long succession must ensue,
And his next Son for Wealth and Wisdom fam'd,
The clouded Ark of God till then in Tents
Wand'ring, shall in a glorious Temple enshrine.
Such follow him, as shall be register'd   335
Part good, part bad, of bad the longer scroll,
Whose foul Idolatries, and other faults
Heapt to the popular sum, will so incense
God, as to leave them, and expose thir Land,
Thir City, his Temple, and his holy Ark   340
With all his sacred things, a scorn and prey
To that proud City, whose high Walls thou saw'st
Left in confusion, *Babylon* thence call'd.
There in captivity he lets them dwell
The space of seventy years, then brings them back,   345
Rememb'ring mercy, and his Cov'nant sworn

321. *The second,* David, to whom the prophet Nathan promised that
his throne should "be established for ever." (II Samuel vii, 16.)

332. The *next Son,* Solomon, whose building of the temple in Jerusalem
is elaborately described in I Kings vi–vii and II Chronicles iii–iv.

337. Compare the allusion to Solomon's idolatries in I, 399–403.

To *David,* stablisht as the days of Heav'n.
Return'd from *Babylon* by leave of Kings
Thir Lords, whom God dispos'd, the house of God
They first re-edify, and for a while   350
In mean estate live moderate, till grown
In wealth and multitude, factious they grow;
But first among the Priests dissension springs,
Men who attend the Altar, and should most
Endeavour Peace: thir strife pollution brings   355
Upon the Temple itself: at last they seize
The Sceptre, and regard not *David's* Sons,
Then lose it to a stranger, that the true
Anointed King *Messiah* might be born
Barr'd of his right; yet at his Birth a Star   360
Unseen before in Heav'n proclaims him come,
And guides the Eastern Sages, who enquire
His place, to offer Incense, Myrrh, and Gold;
His place of birth a solemn Angel tells
To simple Shepherds, keeping watch by night;   365

---

347. Milton followed prophetic tradition in making the exile of the
Hebrews in Babylon (from 606 to 536 B. C.) end as a fulfilment of
God's covenant with David to make "his throne as the days of heaven."
(Psalm lxxxix, 29.)

348. The *Kings* are Cyrus the Great, Darius and Artaxerxes, under
the first and last of whom especially the Hebrews undertook the
reëdification of Jerusalem which is recorded in the book of Ezra.

353. The story of the struggle for the high priesthood between Onias
and Jason, and later between Jason and Menelaus, in the second century B.C., is told in the Apocryphal book of II Maccabees iii–iv, and in
Josephus' *Antiquities* XII, iv–v.

356. *they,* the Asmonean family, which retained the high-priesthood
from 153 B.C. to 35 B.C.

357. Zerubbabel, who led the returning Hebrews from Babylon under
Cyrus, was the last direct descendant of David to govern in Palestine.

358. *a stranger:* perhaps Antiochus the Great, who made good his
claim to Palestine against Judas Maccabeus, and his successors generally
until the birth of Christ.

360. As the descendant of David, Christ was born king of the Jews,
although *barr'd* of his right to the throne. Contrast Milton's treatment
of the story of the Nativity in Matthew ii and Luke ii with his handling
of it in the *Nativity Ode* and in *P.R.* I, 242–54.

364. Milton seldom used *solemn* without a clear trace of its Latin
signification of something belonging to religious festival or ceremonial.

They gladly thither haste, and by a Quire
Of squadron'd Angels hear his Carol sung.
A Virgin is his Mother, but his Sire
The Power of the most High; he shall ascend
The Throne hereditary, and bound his Reign   370
With earth's wide bounds, his glory with the Heav'ns.
    He ceas'd, discerning *Adam* with such joy
Surcharg'd, as had like grief been dew'd in tears,
Without the vent of words, which these he breath'd.
    O Prophet of glad tidings, finisher   375
Of utmost hope! now clear I understand
What oft my steadiest thoughts have searcht in vain,
Why our great expectation should be call'd
The seed of Woman: Virgin Mother, Hail,
High in the love of Heav'n, yet from my Loins   380
Thou shalt proceed, and from thy Womb the Son
Of God most High; So God with man unites.
Needs must the Serpent now his capital bruise
Expect with mortal pain: say where and when
Thir fight, what stroke shall bruise the Victor's heel. 385
    To whom thus *Michael*. Dream not of thir fight,
As of a Duel, or the local wounds
Of head or heel: not therefore joins the Son
Manhood to Godhead, with more strength to foil
Thy enemy; nor so is overcome   390
Satan, whose fall from Heav'n, a deadlier bruise,
Disabl'd not to give thee thy death's wound:
Which hee, who comes thy Saviour, shall recure,
Not by destroying *Satan,* but his works
In thee and in thy Seed: nor can this be,   395

---

366. *thither, i. e.,* to Christ's birthplace.

371. The language seems intended to blend the promise in Psalm ii,
8 (which was supposed to refer to Christ): "Ask of me, and I shall
give thee . . . the uttermost parts of the earth for thy possession,"
with Virgil's prophecy that the fame of Caesar should be bounded by
the stars (*Aen.* I, 287).

374. *which* (i. e., of which) *he breath'd, etc.*

383. *capital* is a play on the literal Latin meaning of the word, "per-
taining to the head,"—where the serpent is to be "bruised"—and the
derived meaning, "fatal."

393. *recure,* restore, heal.

But by fulfilling that which thou didst want,
Obedience to the Law of God, impos'd
On penalty of death, and suffering death,
The penalty to thy transgression due,
And due to theirs which out of thine will grow: 400
So only can high Justice rest appaid.
The Law of God exact he shall fulfil
Both by obedience and by love, though love
Alone fulfil the Law; thy punishment
He shall endure by coming in the Flesh   405
To a reproachful life and cursed death,
Proclaiming Life to all who shall believe
In his redemption, and that his obedience
Imputed becomes theirs by Faith, his merits
To save them, not thir own, though legal works.   410
For this he shall live hated, be blasphem'd,
Seiz'd on by force, judg'd, and to death condemn'd
A shameful and accurst, nail'd to the Cross
By his own Nation, slain for bringing Life;
But to the Cross he nails thy Enemies,   415
The Law that is against thee, and the sins
Of all mankind, with him there crucifi'd,
Never to hurt them more who rightly trust
In this his satisfaction; so he dies,
But soon revives, Death over him no power   420
Shall long usurp; ere the third dawning light
Return, the Stars of Morn shall see him rise
Out of his grave, fresh as the dawning light,
Thy ransom paid, which Man from death redeems,
His death for Man, as many as offer'd Life   425
Neglect not, and the benefit embrace

---

401. *appaid,* contented, satisfied.

402. The thought reverts to the idea that life is possible only by
fulfilling the law of Moses (compare 298 above and its note) and
combines with it the idea that "love is the fulfilling of the law" (Rom.
xiii, 10).

409. *his merits* may be regarded as a direct object of *believe* in 407;
i.e., believe his merits, not their own works, however adequately fulfilling the law, to save them.

424. *Thy* refers not only to Adam but also to all humanity, whose
representative he is,

By Faith not void of works: this God-like act
Annuls thy doom, the death thou shouldst have di'd,
In sin for ever lost from life; this act
Shall bruise the head of *Satan,* crush his strength   430
Defeating Sin and Death, his two main arms,
And fix far deeper in his head thir stings
Than temporal death shall bruise the Victor's heel,
Or theirs whom he redeems, a death like sleep,
A gentle wafting to immortal Life.   435
Nor after resurrection shall he stay
Longer on Earth than certain times to appear
To his Disciples, Men who in his Life
Still follow'd him; to them shall leave in charge
To teach all nations what of him they learn'd   440
And his Salvation, them who shall believe
Baptizing in the profluent stream, the sign
Of washing them from guilt of sin to Life
Pure, and in mind prepar'd, if so befall,
For death, like that which the redeemer di'd.   445
All Nations they shall teach; for from that day
Not only to the Sons of *Abraham's* Loins
Salvation shall be Preacht, but to the Sons
Of *Abraham's* Faith wherever through the world;
So in his seed all Nations shall be blest.   450
Then to the Heav'n of Heav'ns he shall ascend
With victory, triúmphing through the air
Over his foes and thine; there shall surprise
The Serpent, Prince of air, and drag in Chains
Through all his Realm, and there confounded leave;   455
Then enter into glory, and resume

427. Compare the note on XI, 64.

433. For Milton's conception of man's death as "temporal" see the
note on XI, 469.

442. *profluent* is the English equivalent of the Latin word used by
Milton in his discussion of baptism as ideally being performed in running
water. (*C.D.* I, xxviii.)

447. Compare Galatians iii, 8: "And the scripture, foreseeing that
God would justify the heathen through faith, preached before the gospel
unto Abraham, saying, In thee shall all nations be blessed." In the
following eighty lines Milton fuses together countless reminiscences from
the New Testament, the Psalms and the Prophets.

454. Compare the note on Satan's title, Prince of the Air, in X, 185.

His Seat at God's right hand, exalted high
Above all names in Heav'n; and thence shall come,
When this world's dissolution shall be ripe,
With glory and power to judge both quick and dead,   460
To judge th' unfaithful dead, but to reward
His faithful, and receive them into bliss,
Whether in Heav'n or Earth, for then the Earth
Shall all be Paradise, far happier place
Than this of *Eden,* and far happier days.   465
    So spake th' Archangel *Michaël,* then paus'd,
As at the World's great period; and our Sire
Replete with joy and wonder thus repli'd.
    O goodness infinite, goodness immense!
That all this good of evil shall produce,   470
And evil turn to good; more wonderful
Than that which by creation first brought forth
Light out of darkness! full of doubt I stand,
Whether I should repent me now of sin
By mee done and occasion'd, or rejoice   475
Much more, that much more good thereof shall spring,
To God more glory, more good will to Men
From God, and over wrath grace shall abound.
But say, if our deliverer up to Heav'n
Must reascend, what will betide the few   480
His faithful, left among th' unfaithful herd,
The enemies of truth; who then shall guide
His people, who defend? will they not deal
Worse with his followers than with him they dealt?

---

457. Compare the note on III, 63, where the Son is seated *at God's right hand*.

460. *quick and dead,* living and dead. The phrase is from the Apostles' Creed, with Christ's words that "all that are in the graves shall hear his voice" (John v, 28) in the background.

473. Adam's idea, which is the pivot of Milton's "justification" of the ways of God to men, is stated no less distinctly by Du Bartas in words addressed to Adam:

> "Upon the Cross, Sin, Satan, Death and Hell;
> Making thee blessed more since thine offence
> Than in thy primer happy innocence."
>   (*The Divine Weekes,* 93 rc.)

478. Compare Romans v, 20: "But where sin abounded, grace did much more abound."

Be sure they will, said th' Angel; but from Heav'n   485
Hee to his own a Comforter will send,
The promise of the Father, who shall dwell
His Spirit within them, and the Law of Faith
Working through love, upon thir hearts shall write,
To guide them in all truth, and also arm   490
With spiritual Armor, able to resist
Satan's assaults, and quench his fiery darts,
What Man can do against them, not afraid,
Though to the death, against such cruelties
With inward consolations recompens't,   ·   495
And oft supported so as shall amaze
Thir proudest persecutors: for the Spirit
Pour'd first on his Apostles, whom he sends
To evangelize the Nations, then on all
Baptiz'd, shall them with wondrous gifts endue   500
To speak all Tongues, and do all Miracles,
As did thir Lord before them.   Thus they win
Great numbers of each Nation to receive
With joy the tidings brought from Heav'n: at length
Thir Ministry perform'd, and race well run,   505
Thir doctrine and thir story written left,
They die; but in thir room, as they forewarn,
Wolves shall succeed for teachers, grievous Wolves,
Who all the sacred mysteries of Heav'n
To thir own vile advantages shall turn   510
Of lucre and ambition, and the truth
With superstitions and traditions taint,
Left only in those written Records pure,
Though not but by the Spirit understood.
Then shall they seek to avail themselves of names,   515
Places and titles, and with these to join

486. In the promise of the *Comforter,* the Holy Spirit, Milton follows
John xv, 26.

489. The idea of God's love and laws written upon the heart is
found in Jeremiah xxxi, 33 and echoed in Hebrews viii, 10.

491. The source for the allegory of *spiritual Armour* is Ephesians
vi, 11–17.

508. *grievous Wolves* is St. Paul's term (Acts xx, 29), but Milton
first made it his own in the "grim wolf" of his attack on the venal
clergy in *Lycidas,* 128, and again in the "hireling wolves, whose gospell
is their maw" of the *Sonnet* to Cromwell.

Secular power, though feigning still to act
By spiritual, to themselves appropriating
The Spirit of God, promis'd alike and giv'n
To all Believers; and from that pretense,   520
Spiritual Laws by carnal power shall force
On every conscience; Laws which none shall find
Left them inroll'd, or what the Spirit within
Shall on the heart engrave. What will they then
But force the Spirit of Grace itself, and bind   525
His consort Liberty; what, but unbuild
His living Temples, built by Faith to stand,
Thir own Faith not another's: for on Earth
Who against Faith and Conscience can be heard
Infallible? yet many will presume: 530
Whence heavy persecution shall arise
On all who in the worship persevere
Of Spirit and Truth; the rest, far greater part,
Will deem in outward Rites and specious forms
Religion satisfi'd; Truth shall retire   535
Bestuck with sland'rous darts, and works of Faith
Rarely be found: so shall the World go on,
To good malignant, to bad men benign,
Under her own weight groaning, till the day
Appear of respiration to the just,   540
And vengeance to the wicked, at return
Of him so lately promis'd to thy aid,
The Woman's seed, obscurely then foretold,
Now amplier known thy Saviour and thy Lord,
Last in the Clouds from Heav'n to be reveal'd   545
In glory of the Father, to dissolve
Satan with his perverted World, then raise
From the conflagrant mass, purg'd and refin'd,

---

525. Compare II Corinthians iii, 17: "Now the Lord is that Spirit: and where the Spirit of the Lord is, there is liberty."

527. St. Paul called the body "the temple of the Holy Ghost." (I Cor. vi, 19.)

533. ". . . the true worshippers shall worship the Father in spirit and in truth." (John iv, 23.)

540. *respiration* is a more literal rendering of the Greek original than is "refreshing" in Acts iii, 19, and corresponds to the feeling with which Milton read the verse, which he was paraphrasing here.

New Heav'ns, new Earth, Ages of endless date
Founded in righteousness and peace and love,   550
To bring forth fruits Joy and eternal Bliss.
    He ended; and thus *Adam* last repli'd.
How soon hath thy prediction, Seer blest,
Measur'd this transient World, the Race of time,
Till time stand fixt: beyond is all abyss,   555
Eternity, whose end no eye can reach.
Greatly instructed I shall hence depart,
Greatly in peace of thought, and have my fill
Of knowledge, what this Vessel can contain;
Beyond which was my folly to aspire.   560
Henceforth I learn, that to obey is best,
And love with fear the only God, to walk
As in his presence, ever to observe
His providence, and on him sole depend,
Merciful over all his works, with good   565
Still overcoming evil, and by small
Accomplishing great things, by things deem'd weak
Subverting worldly strong, and worldly wise
By simply meek; that suffering for Truth's sake
Is fortitude to highest victory,   570
And to the faithful Death the Gate of Life;
Taught this by his example whom I now
Acknowledge my Redeemer ever blest.
    To whom thus also th' Angel last repli'd:
This having learnt, thou hast attain'd the sum   575
Of wisdom; hope no higher, though all the Stars
Thou knew'st by name, and all th' ethereal Powers,
All secrets of the deep, all Nature's works,
Or works of God in Heav'n, Air, Earth, or Sea,
And all the riches of this World enjoy'dst,   580
And all the rule, one Empire; only add
Deeds to thy knowledge answerable, add Faith,

---

549. Compare the promise of *New Heav'ns, new Earth,* after the destruction of the present universe by fire, with which Book XI ends.

559. *this vessel,* Adam's body. Compare I Thessalonians iv, 4.

565. *with good Still overcoming evil* transposes St. Paul's words in Romans xii, 21.

566. *and by small, etc.,* paraphrases a famous verse in I Corinthians i, 27.

Add Virtue, Patience, Temperance, add Love,
By name to come call'd Charity, the soul
Of all the rest: then wilt thou not be loath   585
To leave this Paradise, but shalt possess
A paradise within thee, happier far.
Let us descend now therefore from this top
Of Speculation; for the hour precise
Exacts our parting hence; and see the Guards,   590
By mee encampt on yonder Hill, expect
Thir motion, at whose Front a flaming Sword,
In signal of remove, waves fiercely round;
We may no longer stay: go, waken *Eve;*
Her also I with gentle Dreams have calm'd   595
Portending good, and all her spirits compos'd
To meek submission: thou at season fit
Let her with thee partake what thou hast heard,
Chiefly what may concern her Faith to know,
The great deliverance by her Seed to come   600
(For by the Woman's Seed) on all Mankind.
That ye may live, which will be many days,
Both in one Faith unanimous though sad,
With cause for evils past, yet much more cheer'd
With meditation on the happy end.   605
   He ended, and they both descend the Hill;
Descended, *Adam* to the Bow'r where *Eve*
Lay sleeping ran before, but found her wak't;
And thus with words not sad she him receiv'd.
   Whence thou return'st, and whither went'st, I know;   610
For God is also in sleep, and Dreams advise,

----

584. The lesson of charity as fulfilling all the Christian virtues, in accordance with St. Paul's familiar doctrine (I Cor. xiii, 1–8) is the last step in teaching Adam the heroic virtue which he must have to leave Paradise willingly. Compare the note on XI, 690.

587. Compare the hell within Satan, IV, 20.

589. *Speculation* has its Latin meaning of "looking out." Compare the "specular Mount" of *P.R.* IV, 236.

602. *many days* alludes to the statement that "the days that Adam lived were nine hundred and thirty years; and he died." (Gen. v, 5.)

611. Perhaps there is a trace of Achilles' words to Agamemnon: "A dream is of Zeus." (*Il.* I, 63.) There is certainly a reminiscence of the distinction which Bacon (*Essays*, XLII) said a certain rabbi drew between

Which he hath sent propitious, some great good
Presaging, since with sorrow and heart's distress
Wearied I fell asleep: but now lead on;
In mee is no delay; with thee to go,   615
Is to stay here; without thee here to stay,
Is to go hence unwilling; thou to mee
Art all things under Heav'n, all places thou,
Who for my wilful crime art banisht hence.
This further consolation yet secure   620
I carry hence; though all by mee is lost,
Such favour I unworthy am voutsaf't,
By mee the Promis'd Seed shall all restore.
    So spake our Mother *Eve,* and *Adam* heard
Well pleas'd, but answer'd not; for now too nigh   625
Th' Archangel stood, and from the other Hill
To thir fixt Station, all in bright array
The Cherubim descended; on the ground
Gliding meteorous, as Ev'ning Mist
Ris'n from a River o'er the marish glides,   630
And gathers ground fast at the Labourer's heel
Homeward returning. High in Front advanc't,
The brandisht Sword of God before them blaz'd
Fierce as a Comet; which with torrid heat,
And vapour as the *Libyan* Air adust,   635
Began to parch that temperate Clime; whereat
In either hand the hast'ning Angel caught
Our ling'ring Parents, and to th' Eastern Gate
Led them direct, and down the Cliff as fast
To the subjected Plain; then disappear'd.   640
They looking back, all th' Eastern side beheld
Of Paradise, so late thir happy seat,

---

a vision and a dream on the ground that the former is the clearer
revelation of God.

630. *marish,* marsh.

632. *advanc't,* held aloft.

635. *adust,* burnt. Milton thought of the flaming sword as scorching
Paradise like a blast of heated air blowing from the Libyan (*i. e.,* Sahara)
desert.

638. Compare the description of the *Eastern Gate* in IV, 542–8.

640. *subjected* has its literal Latin meaning of "lying beneath."

Wav'd over by that flaming Brand, the Gate
With dreadful Faces throng'd and fiery Arms:
Some natural tears they dropp'd, but wip'd them soon;   645
The World was all before them, where to choose
Thir place of rest, and Providence thir guide:
They hand in hand with wand'ring steps and slow,
Through *Eden* took thir solitary way.

The End

---

643. *Brand* may have been Milton's choice of word here because its meaning of "sword" seemed to have been derived from its basic meaning of "a torch" or "something burning." Compare Arthur's "sword, that flames like burning brond" in *The Faerie Queene*, II, iii, 18.

648. Since Michael was instructed in heaven to dismiss Adam and Eve "not disconsolate" (XI, 113), everything has prepared for the mood in which they quit the

> "blissful Paradise
> Of God . . . by him in the East
> Of *Eden* planted;"
>   (IV, 208–210.)

INDEX

INDEX OF BOOKS AND OF HISTORICAL
PERSONS

(Cited in the Introduction and Notes)

415